Responses to Language Varieties

IMPACT: Studies in Language and Society

ISSN 1385-7908

IMPACT publishes monographs, collective volumes, and text books on topics in sociolinguistics. The scope of the series is broad, with special emphasis on areas such as language planning and language policies; language conflict and language death; language standards and language change; dialectology; diglossia; discourse studies; language and social identity (gender, ethnicity, class, ideology); and history and methods of sociolinguistics.

For an overview of all books published in this series, please see
http://benjamins.com/catalog/impact

General Editor

Volume 39

Responses to Language Varieties. Variability, processes and outcomes
Edited by Alexei Prikhodkine and Dennis R. Preston

Responses to Language Varieties

Variability, processes and outcomes

Edited by

Alexei Prikhodkine
University of Geneva

Dennis R. Preston
Oklahoma State University

John Benjamins Publishing Company
Amsterdam / Philadelphia

DOI 10.1075/impact.39

Cataloging-in-Publication Data available from Library of Congress:
LCCN 2015029382 (PRINT) / 2015033604 (E-BOOK)

ISBN 978 90 272 5830 4 (HB)
ISBN 978 90 272 6793 1 (E-BOOK)

John Benjamins Publishing Co. · https://benjamins.com

Table of contents

Introduction   VII
    Alexei Prikhodkine & Dennis R. Preston

PART I **Theoretical Backgrounds**   1

Does language regard vary?   3
    Dennis R. Preston

REACT – A constructivist theoretic framework for attitudes   37
    Christoph Purschke

Mixing methods in the study of language attitudes: Theory and application   55
    Barbara Soukup

PART II **Implicit and/or explicit? When are attitudes "authentic"?**   85

The primary relevance of subconsciously offered attitudes: Focusing the
language ideological aspect of sociolinguistic change   87
    Tore Kristiansen

Applying the Implicit Association Test to language attitudes research   117
    Andrew J. Pantos

Implicit attitudes and the perception of sociolinguistic variation   137
    Brandon C. Loudermilk

PART III **What factors awaken attitudes?**   157

Got class? Community-shared conceptualizations of social class in
evaluative reactions to sociolinguistic variables   159
    Laura Staum Casasanto, Stefan Grondelaers & Roeland van Hout

Perceived foreign accent as a predicator of face-voice match   175
    Kathryn Campbell-Kibler and Elizabeth A. McCullough

Is Moroccan-flavoured Standard Dutch standard or not? On the use of
perceptual criteria to determine the limits of standard languages   191
    Stefan Grondelaers, Paul van Gent & Roeland van Hout

Attitudes and language detail: Effects of specifying linguistic stimuli   219
  Alexei Prikhodkine

Topic index   243

Name Index   247

Introduction*

Alexei Prikhodkine & Dennis R. Preston

This is a book about the responses people have to language varieties, about the variability of those responses, about the shape and content of the responses themselves, and about the variable cognitive and neural repositories and pathways they use in the development of those responses.

---

* The themes and issues of this book were explored at a symposium at the University of Lausanne entitled "Variation of Language Attitudes: Mechanisms and Stakes" on April 20, 2012. The presentations made there included

The cognitive foundations of Language Regard, *Dennis R. Preston (Oklahoma State University, USA)*

Listener judgment theory, *Christoph Purschke (Philipps-Universität Marburg, Germany)*

Which standard in French-speaking Switzerland? Form of the stimuli as a factor of language attitude variation, *Alexei Prikhodkine (University of Lausanne, Switzerland)*

Where is Dutch really heading? On the use of attitude measurements to determine the limits of standard languages, *Stefan Grondelaers (Radboud University Nijmegen, Holland)*

Attitudes and awareness we're unaware of, *Nancy Niedzielski (Rice University, USA)*

Construction of valid attitudinal data in investigations of linguistic variation and change, *Tore Kristiansen (University of Copenhagen, Denmark)*

Implicit Social Cognition and language attitudes research, *Andrew J. Pantos (Metropolitan State University of Denver, USA)*

I trust you implicitly… but not explicitly! How to get language attitudes without asking, *Laura Staum Casasanto (Stony Brook University, USA)*

Social information and speech perception: Scope and limits of proper names, *David Correia Saavedra & Alexei Prikhodkine (University of Lausanne, Switzerland).*

At that symposium, the participants decided to revise these presentations for publication and invite others for a section ("Sociocognitive Aspects of Language Attitude Variation") at the International Congress of Linguists in Geneva, July 23, 2013. The program there included the following:

The cycle of attitude and language change, *Dennis R. Preston (Oklahoma State University, USA)*

The cultural grounding of language attitudes, *Christoph Purschke (Philipps-Universität Marburg, Germany)*

What Houstonians don't know they know about language and race, *Nancy Niedzielski (Rice University, USA)*

DOI 10.1075/impact.39.001int
© 2015 John Benjamins Publishing Company

It is about variability in several senses. First, and surely best known, different linguistic stimuli elicit different responses. Second, people from different areas, of different ages, sexes, ethnicities, and social statuses, and from different communities of practice have different responses to the same language performances. Third, and less well studied perhaps, is the variability *within* the individual, one that rests on the fact that the beliefs about the speaker varieties that underlie responses are not simple, certainly not monolithic. Varying, even contradictory beliefs about such matters are a part of every person's makeup, and different settings, tasks, and even respondent moods may trigger first one then another response to the same stimulus.

The chapters in this volume explore the access to, the processing of, and the outcomes of that complexity, namely how responses to language are triggered, processed, and surface. This volume also looks at the internal detail of the responses themselves because they are a key to the complex variability of the beliefs that lie behind them. But it is also important to examine the specific content of such responses for their *own* value. How may a variety of responses be grouped together, for example, so that one may come to a better understanding of the dominating ideologies within speech communities while still taking into consideration individual variability?

This book investigates as well responses to language that are not necessarily attitudinal in the strict sense (i.e., "evaluative," e.g., Eagly & Chaiken 2005), and a great deal of attention is paid to the beliefs and cognitive structures that underlie responses (e.g., Bassili and Brown 2005) as well as to their organization

---

Attitudes, variation, and language detail: Effects of specifying linguistic stimuli, *Alexei Prikhodkine (University of Lausanne, Switzerland)*

Construction of valid attitudinal data in investigations of linguistic variation and change, *Tore Kristiansen (University of Copenhagen, Denmark)*

Where is Dutch really heading? On the use of attitude measurements to determine the limits of standard languages, *Roeland van Hout (Radboud University Nijmegen, Holland)*

Perception of speaker dialect and the Implicit Association Test: An ERP study, *Brandon C. Loudermilk (University of California at Davis, USA)*

Applying the Implicit Association Test to language attitudes research, *Andrew J. Pantos (Metropolitan State College of Denver, USA)*

Speaker evaluation as a speech event: A social constructionist recast of experimental research on 'language attitudes' and its implications, *Barbara Soukup (University of Vienna, Austria)*

Informal discussions among the participants in Lausanne and round table discussions in Geneva enhanced these presentations and eventually led to this collection.

into ideological systems.[1] More than a few traditions are represented here: from social psychology come classic, traditional experimental methods (e.g., matched guise, Lambert et al. 1960) as well as more current discourse-based analyses (e.g., Potter & Wetherell 1987); anthropological studies have introduced considerations of indexicality (Silverstein 2003), iconization, recursivity, and erasure (Irvine 2001), enregisterment (Agha 2003), and the construction of culturally based ideologies (Schieffelin et al. 1998); sociolinguists often focus on the specific rather than global elements of a variety that trigger responses (e.g., Graff et al. 1986) as well as on connected attitudinal and belief systems similar to the anthropological notion of ideology, as expressed in Eckert's notion of the "indexical field" (2008).

The chapters in this volume address a variety of questions concerning attitude, belief, and ideology in responses to language variety, in some cases singly, in others with a more general focus, including attempts to relate one style of research to another. In doing so they reflect the scholarly variability outlined above. If we accept the fact that even individuals house great variability in the underlying structures that inform responses, it follows that no single way of eliciting and studying those responses will do. These chapters provide a tour of the tools that have been productive in such investigations.

The first three chapters look at general problems and propose various solutions. In Chapter 1 Preston focuses on the variation that lies in wait in the underlying structures (the "attitudinal cognitorium") of the individual and on how such structures are activated and processed. This chapter pays particular attention to the variation that arises from the triggering of conscious versus nonconscious processing of stimuli, a theme further touched on in Chapters 4 (Kristiansen), 5 (Pantos), and 6 (Loudermilk) of this volume, although the problem of variation in the individual based on other factors is explored here as well. Also addressed in Chapter 1 is the role of all "language regard" factors, (i.e., beliefs, attitudes, and ideologies) in more general considerations of language variation and change.

Purschke's approach to the awakening and development of responses to language variety in Chapter 2 is grounded in the philosophically-oriented social psychological outline "REACT" (*Relevance, Evaluation, Activation, Construction,* and *Targeting*), and many of the themes treated are similar to those dealt with

---

1.   The classic definition of attitudes is extended here. *Affect* or "feelings" (Berkowitz 2000) are not limited to those that have an evaluative dimension nor are the *beliefs* (Fishbein & Ajzen 1975) that lie behind the triggering and expression of a response. Behaviors are not limited to "overt actions," particularly in light of recent experimental work that measures implicit responses.

in Chapter 1, but from a different perspective. Within this framework, Purschke provides the details of the characteristics involved in attitude attraction, formation, persistence, availability, and cultural continuity under the labels *routinization, sedimentation, synchronization, fixation, tradition*, and *hierarchization*. The chapter carefully differentiates between the strategies involved in *salience* ("…the perception of conspicuous phenomena…") as opposed to *pertinence* ("…the evaluation of the subjective life-world relevance of such phenomena….." It concludes with practical advice about how attention to the details of this social constructivist critique of the traditional approach to attitude study may be made use of through the employment of real-world settings.

The social constructionist view of attitudes is most directly addressed in Chapter 3, where Soukup discusses mixed methods research (MMR). Finding that such MMR has been hampered by an epistemological stand-off, Soukup proposes an account of language regard that aims to put qualitative and quantitative research epistemologically on an equal footing. The basis for this is the conceptualization of reponses to language variety as 'human epistemological constructs', within the logic of 'critical realism' (Scollon 2003). Soukup then puts this proposal into practice regarding standard and dialectal Austrian German. Her study backs up the findings from a qualitative (interactional sociolinguistic) analysis of conversational data from a TV discussion with findings from a quantitative speaker evaluation experiment that uses the 'open guise' technique to elicit responses. Thus, the chapter both theorizes and illustrates what an integrated social constructionist approach may look like, and how it does justice to the variability of research outcomes.

The next several chapters look in greater detail at the importance of using or distinguishing between data that are acquired through means that elicit conscious or nonconscious responses. Kristiansen examines in Chapter 4 the importance of conscious versus nonconscious elicitation in a study in Denmark that is now being replicated widely in a pan-European research program known as SLICE (Standard Languages in Continental Europe). The Danish findings showed that when asked to characterize their preference for a Danish speech style, the respondents from all regions identified their local variety as preferable; when given a matched-guise sample, however, they preferred the modern Copenhagen variety, the variety that has been shown to be the most influential in the entire country. Kristiansen argues, therefore, that the results from nonconscious modes of enquiry are those that are essential to the study of language variation and change, since, at least in the Danish work, those responses were the ones that corresponded to the proven direction of linguistic change. He goes on in this chapter to illustrate this distinction from studies in other areas.

In Chapter 5 Pantos introduces a detailed example of the implicit attitude test (IAT) research model in one of the first studies within linguistics to be conducted in that format. As Soukup pointed out in Chapter 3, even the matched-guise format runs the risk of respondents' being aware of the socially-charged nature of their linguistic evaluations and may not, therefore, be as "nonconscious" as one might hope. Pantos follows the social psychological model meticulously in a test designed to evaluate Korean-accented and non-foreign accented American English and compares, as Kristiansen does in the previous chapter, the results from that more *nonconscious* elicitation method with results from the same respondents who were given time to make a fully *conscious* response. The explicit or conscious findings showed a preference for the accented speaker but the IAT showed a clear preference for the unaccented samples. The chapter also shows correlation findings for the two studies and suggests that a sort of social hypercorrection may be influencing the explicit results.

In Chapter 6 Loudermilk looks into the underlying neurology of responses by means of the ERP (Event Related Potential) effects of a language variety stimulus. ERP data are derived from EEG studies of brain activity, which show that certain areas of the brain respond directly to specific linguistic domains (phonological, syntactic, etc…). The N400 signal has been shown to be an indicator of the ease or difficulty of semantic processing, and Loudermilk's study attempts to determine if standard and nonstandard versions of the -ing morpheme (-ING and IN') influence this pattern. He further sophisticates the study by presenting the same sort of variable -ing data to his respondents in an IAT study of the sort described in detail in Chapter 5. He then divides the respondents into high- and low-sensitivity responders and investigates the correlation between the type of IAT respondent and the ERP findings, demonstrating an interesting combination of neural patterning and implicit responses with regard to a well-studied sociolinguistic variable.

In Chapter 7, the focus changes from implicit and neurosociolinguistic studies of attitudes and attitude variability to demographic and linguistic features, although the value of implicit and explicit data elicitation is by no means ignored. Staum Casasanto et al. look at the role of social status or "class" in responses with reference to four phonetic variables in Dutch (two vocalic and two consonantal), and they carry out their research by using a detailed operationalization of the notion of status. They hope to awaken responses to status without focusing awareness on it, much as the matched guise technique intended to focus on the influence of linguistic variety while masking other factors of speaker identity. Their status variable was invoked by means of visual priming (automobiles, clothing, workplace surroundings, given names, and occupation) and were made part of a IAT-like experiment. The results show a complex pattern of ratings and interactions, some of which suggest new evaluations of traditionally lower-prestige variants.

Chapter 8 continues the use of visual primes in Campbell-Kibler and McCullough's study of the match between perceived foreign accentedness in

English and characteristic faces. Fifteen male faces reflecting European-American, East Asian, and Southeast Asian types were selected from those rated in a prestudy along continua for three dimensions: educatedness, accentedness, and masculinity. In a second prestudy English words pronounced by a variety of speakers were then rated for their degree of accentedness, and the highest and lowest scores for these were selected for the final experiment in which the respondents rated the quality of the match between face and voice when presented with a variety of the above matching possibilities (native speaker vs. foreign accented combined with the three face types). The results show not only the interrelationship of degree of accentedness and face type but also a role for type of accent (i.e., the perceived first language of the samples). Some data also suggest that radical mismatches between visual face priming and the data sample might need to be taken into consideration in further studies of this style of research.

In Chapter 9 another approach is taken to foreign accentedness. Grondelaers et al. ask if Moroccan-influenced Dutch might be considered one of the newer socially and regionally distinct varieties of the language that are gaining prestige, a movement in standard language definitions in Europe that has attracted considerable research effort (viz the reference to SLICE in the introduction to Chapter 4 above). Standard Dutch and Moroccan-influenced samples were played for respondents who rated them along twelve dimensions that fit into five previously determined effective general categories for Dutch language evaluation, namely *Status, Dynamism, Personal Integrity, Solidarity* and *Accent Norm*. In addition, each respondent was asked how "beautiful" each sample was. Their answer to the main question is overwhelmingly no – indicating that status and regional varieties of native speaker Dutch may participate in the broadening of boundaries for what may be considered standard, but foreign accented varieties, at least Moroccan Dutch, cannot. This chapter also includes some surprising statistical results in the factor analytic study of the differential pairs and a thorough review of the emergence of the newer, standardizing Dutch varieties.

In the last chapter (10), Prikhodkine goes where few studies of responses to language variety have gone before – to the lexicon, but his work focuses more generally on different levels of language detail in the presentation of stimuli (global or specific) and the variability in the expression of responses that arise from such different stimuli. In gathering his lexical data (from the French-speaking area in Western Switzerland) he employs several different strategies: he asked his respondents to (1) qualify the global category name "words for local French," (2) assess local words for their local typicality, (3) respond to a dictionary definition with a lexical item, (4) evaluate local items (and their counterparts from the French of France) on scales of correctness and friendliness, and (5) discuss with respondents their preferences for and ratings of local and other items. Results show that global category names tend to elicit attitudes for stigmatized *patois* features, while such general labels do not trigger attitudinal responses for Swiss prestigious features. This chapter also employs an interesting correlation variable for the findings, namely the origin of the lexical items themselves: local dialectal, German, archaic French, or local innovative French.

These chapters, taken together and singly, illustrate current turns in studies of responses to language variety – ranging from the strictly experimental to the discoursal. Most, however, illustrate the variability of individual as well as group responses, although the latter are amply measured and discussed. They show how that variability may be generated by different approaches to data elicitation, how it is stored and processed, and what different values the various response types may have for our general interests as well as for its role in the study of language variation and change.

Not all themes of this general enterprise could be explored in one setting – applied study (e.g., unemployability of accented speakers or attempts to change negative stereotypes), the acquisition of beliefs in the youngest members of a speech community, and numerous other topics remain to be addressed. We hope, however, that these areas and research in other areas of interest will be enhanced by the theoretical and methodological considerations outlined and exemplified here. Most importantly, we hope that the variety of approaches taken here will encourage multiple and new ways to elicit and analyze data, since no one of them will reveal the "true" response preference of a speech community to a specific variety. Such responses are but one aspect of the total ethnographic picture of a speech community, and we believe along with Hymes that "[i]f the community's own theory of linguistic repertoire and speech is considered (as it must be in any serious ethnographic account), matters become all the more complex and interesting" (1972: 39). The complexity of responses to and beliefs about language varieties is surely a part of any community's theory.

References

Agha, Asif. 2003. The social life of cultural value. *Language and Communication* 23: 231–73.
DOI: 10.1016/S0271-5309(03)00012-0

Albarracín, Dolores, Johnson, Blair T. & Zanna, Mark P. (eds). 2005. *The Handbook of Attitudes*. Mahwah NJ: Lawrence Erlbaum Associates.

Bassili, John N. & Brown, Rick D. 2005. Implicit and explicit attitudes: Research, challenges, and theory. In Albarracín et al. (eds), 543–74.

Berkowitz, Leonard. 2000. *Causes and Consequences of Feelings*. Cambridge: CUP.
DOI: 10.1017/CBO9780511606106

Eagly, Alice H. & Chaiken, Shelly. 2005. Attitude research in the 21st Century. In Albarracín et al. (eds), 743–67.

Eckert, Penelope. 2008. Variation and the indexical field. *Journal of Sociolinguistics* 12(4): 453–476. DOI: 10.1111/j.1467-9841.2008.00374.x

Fishbein, Martin & Ajzen, Icek. 1975. *Belief, Attitude, Intention, and Behavior: An Introduction to Theory and Research*. Reading MA: Addison-Wesley.

Graff, Davis, Labov, William & Harris, Wendell A. 1986. Testing listeners' reactions to phonological markers of ethnic identity: A new method for sociolinguistic research. In *Diversity and Diachrony* [Current Issues in Linguistic Theory 53], David Sankoff (ed.), 45–58. Amsterdam: John Benjamins. DOI: 10.1075/cilt.53.07gra

Hymes, Dell. 1972. Models of the interaction of language and social life. In *Directions in Sociolinguistics: The Ethnography of Communication*, John J. Gumperz & Dell Hymes (eds), 35–71. New York NY: Holt, Rinehart, and Winston.

Irvine, Judith. 2001. 'Style' as distinctiveness: The culture and ideology of linguistic differentiation. In *Style and Sociolinguistic Variation*, Penelope Eckert & John R. Rickford (eds), 21–43. Cambridge: CUP.

Lambert, Wallace E., Hodgson, Richard C., Gardner, Robert C. & Fillenbaum, Samuel. 1960. Evaluational reactions to spoken languages. *Journal of Abnormal and Social Psychology* 60: 44–51. DOI: 10.1037/h0044430

Potter, Jonathan & Wetherell, Margaret. 1987. *Discourse and Social Psychology*. London: Sage.

Schieffelin, Bambi, Wollard, Kathryn A. & Kroskrity, Paul (eds). 1998. *Language Ideologies: Practice and Theory*. Oxford: OUP.

Scollon, Ron. 2003. The dialogist in a positivist world: Theory in the social sciences and the humanities at the end of the twentieth century. *Social Semiotics* 13(1): 71–88. DOI: 10.1080/1035033032000133517

Silverstein, Michael. 2003. Indexical order and the dialectics of sociolinguistic life. *Language & Communication* 23: 193–229. DOI: 10.1016/S0271-5309(03)00013-2

PART I

Theoretical Backgrounds

Does language regard vary?

Dennis R. Preston

Oklahoma State University & Michigan State University (Emeritus)

This paper outlines a cognitive map for variation in language attitudes, metalinguistic beliefs about language, and language ideological frameworks – grouped together as "language regard." After establishing input, processing, and response models, it goes on to examine experimental findings that show variability in regard that are consistent with this map and to outline the importance of that variability to more general concerns of sociolinguistics, touching in particular on its explanatory position in studies of variation and change.

1. Introduction

Sociolinguistics is built on the foundation that social groups and individuals *produce* variable forms that indicate social identity and respond to social and linguistic environments. Some models suggest further that variability is an integral part of the process of language change, making that process available to scholarly enquiry (Weinreich, Labov & Herzog 1968: 99), something previously thought to be impossible (e.g., Hockett 1958: Chapter 52 ["The Nature of Sound Change"]).

Weinreich, Labov and Herzog explicitly refer to social factors in all five of what they call the problems of language variation and change: *constraints, transition, embedding, evaluation,* and *actuation* (101–102); I will be principally concerned here with evaluation:

> The theory of language change must establish empirically the subjective correlates of the several layers and variables in a heterogeneous structure. Such subjective correlates of evaluations cannot be deduced from the place of the variables within linguistic structure. Furthermore, the level of social awareness[1] is a major property of linguistic change which must be determined directly.

---

1. The phrase "level of social awareness" suggests the distinction between overt (conscious) and covert (unconscious) features highlighted in Labov's later characterization of *indicators, markers,* and *stereotypes* (e.g., 1972: 314).

DOI 10.1075/impact.39.01pre

> Subjective correlates of change are more categorical in nature than the changing
> pattern of behavior: their investigation deepens our understanding of the ways
> in which discrete categorization is imposed on the continuous process of
> change.   (186)

This passage directly relates "subjective correlates" to variation and change and
calls for their independent investigation, i.e., a study of such factors outside the
instances of their production distribution. It suggests, however, a uniformity of
these subjective correlates, one unlike the diversity found in production. Labov is
even more explicit about this in his later identification of the defining character of
a speech community:

> [Evaluation of /r/] is typical of many other empirical findings which confirm
> the view of New York City as a single speech community, *united by a uniform
> evaluation of linguistic features*, yet diversified by … stratification in …
> performance.   (Labov 1972: 117, italics mine)[2]

This uniformity might refer only to directionality – i.e., all New Yorkers agree
that nonprevocalic /r/ presence is more formal, but another interpretation is that
evaluation lacks variety, resulting in a search for "the" rather than "a" subjective
correlate. In this chapter I will argue that there are variable subjective responses,
both to one's own and other varieties, and that this variation is as important as
the variation found in production, although its patterns may not be the same.

One feature of these subjective correlates is that they are embedded in and
require an investigation of cognitive factors. Although it is difficult to conceive
of any area of linguistics that does not take cognitive facts into consideration, if
any subfields have overtly expressed such interest, it is those of language attitudes,
folk beliefs about language, and ideological frameworks, areas of investigation
grouped together here as *language regard* (Preston 2010a). I propose this label
because there are folk concerns about language that are not necessarily evaluative
and therefore not attitudinal – since many social psychologists take attitudes to
be an *evaluative* subset of beliefs (e.g., Kruglanski & Stroebe 2005: 327). I will also
not use *language beliefs* as the more inclusive term, for *beliefs* are "…estimates of

---

2. This notion of a uniformity of norms as the defining characteristic of a speech community is shared by Hymes:

> Tentatively, a *speech community* [italics in the original] is defined as a community
> sharing rules for the conduct and interpretation of speech, and rules for the
> interpretation of at least one linguistic variety. … The sharing of grammatical
> (variety) rules is not sufficient.   (1972: 54)

the likelihood that the knowledge one has acquired about a referent is correct …"
(Wyer & Albarracín 2005: 273), but some aspects of language regard are the result
of many such beliefs and other less well-specified conceptual bits. I also prefer
regard to *ideology*, a term that refers to the positioning of languages, varieties, and
their units in the belief structure of groups. As Irvine (1989) defines it, language
ideology is "…the cultural system of ideas about social and linguistic relationships…." I do not want to exclude any of these areas and therefore choose *regard*
as a more inclusive label. Like Weinreich et al., I consider the study of language
regard to be essential to sociolinguistics, especially for the explanatory characteristics it uncovers.

I begin anecdotally. Some time ago I became annoyed with the practice of
folklorists' respellings of some of the words of their respondents (Preston 1982).
It appeared to me that only lower-status, minority, and other negatively stereotyped respondents were so respelled. Although many were attempts to capture
what struck folklorists as local, colorful, or nonstandard, many were examples
of *eye-dialect*. Such respellings as *duz* for *does*, for example, captures nothing
of a local, colorful, or nonstandard pronunciation, since the most common US
English pronunciation is [dʌz] (or [dəz] under weak stress), and that pronunciation is surely reflected in *duz*. By studying a decade of articles from the *Journal
of American Folklore*,[3] I confirmed that respellings were more often applied to
caricatured groups or individuals perceived as ethnic, regional, or nonstandard
speakers, but my point here is the difference in regard that is triggered by a
spelling as opposed to a pronunciation. When one hears [dʌz], the speaker is
"normal," "like us," but when one sees *duz*, the speaker is downgraded, caricatured, or at best romanticized. (See Preston 1985b for experimental support.)
If spelling versus pronunciation (when no actual difference exists) can redirect
our regard, what other triggers for variability might there be and what underlies
such variable responses?

---

3.   I have space here only to refer the reader to the denial by folklorists of any attempt to
caricature minority, isolated, or culturally different groups. Although they pride themselves
on cultural relativism, they were oddly blind to their own "linguicism," claiming that their
quaint (and largely inaccurate) respellings were attempts to capture what they called either
the authentic or beautiful voices (or both) of their respondents. (See Fine 1983, and Preston
1983 for an exchange and Preston 2000 for a position that addresses respondent reclaiming
of personal voices.)

2. The cognitive backgrounds of language regard

2.1 Perception

Figure 1 outlines *Perception*[4] as beginning with sensation (*Sensing*), made complex by conscious versus nonconscious interpretations of *noticing* (see below), then processed by *Discrimination* and *Classification*, all making up the strategies that lead to *Comprehension*. There is a connection between *Production* and *Comprehension*, but few believe nowadays that comprehension is just a production mechanism run backwards.[5]

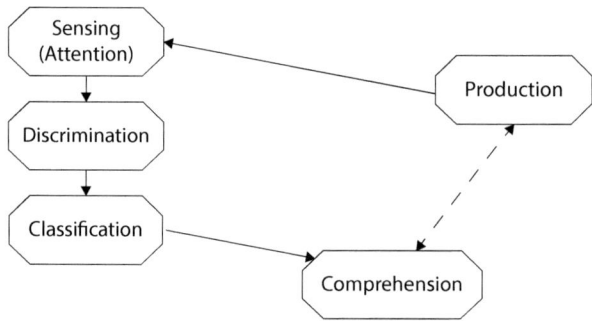

Figure 1. The required elements of language comprehension

2.2 The cycle of production, perception, and regard

Figure 2 adds language regard and indicates that it may result from nonconscious processes or deliberative ones, which may themselves be interconnected if one believes that the two mechanisms interact. It shows as well that language regard can influence all other components. Tracing these influences and showing how they contribute to variability in regard and its importance to the study of variation and change is the goal of this chapter.

First, however, I want to examine the components that trigger and shape language regard itself. The points of the triangle in Figure 3 are *a*: language (broadly conceived), *b*: conscious responses, and *c*: nonconscious responses.

---

4. This rough outline should be compatible with a variety of modern theories of speech perception, perhaps even ones that contradict one another.

5. The "few" and "just" of this sentence allow for the reasonable assumption that speech perception relies on or is at least guided by some production strategies (e.g., Liberman et al. 1967; Fowler 1986; Stevens 2002).

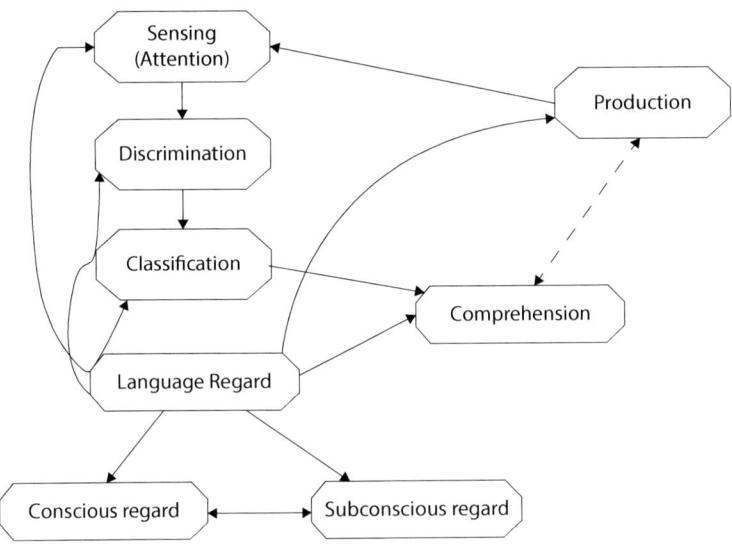

Figure 2. Regard and its influence on all elements of production and comprehension

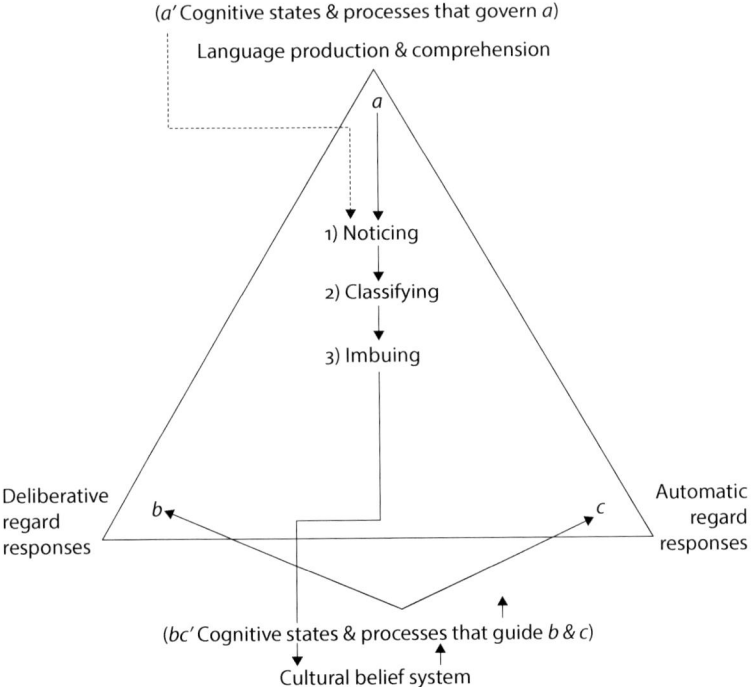

Figure 3. The relationships between language and language regard and their underlying components (modified from Niedzielski & Preston 2003: xi)

In this framework, which is similar to the one proposed by Purschke (this volume), one may trace the path of a language regard event. I begin with the assumption that there is nothing *inherent* in language itself (the *a* material of this triangle) that triggers language regard (but see, for example, van Bezooijen 2002) and suggest that, after *noticing*[6] (Step 1 of Figure 3), regard details are formed by an association between the noticed language feature (from any linguistic level) and beliefs about speakers and groups. Here is a detailed example:

> A speaker of American English produces an [aː] in the word "guide" (i.e., monophthongizes the vowel), an instance of production at *a*.
> Step 1: A hearer *notices a* (perhaps because their own pronunciation is diphthongal [aɪ]).
> Step 2: The hearer *classifies* this as "American Southern."
> Step 3: The hearer retrieves caricatures of "American Southerners" from their cultural belief system and imbues fact *a* with them.
> Through *b'*, a hearer has a regard response (at *b* or *c*).

This process must be slightly modified in some cases, for similar responses may arise even though the classificatory step is different. That is, there is the possibility of an *a* having been imbued so often by cultural belief material that it may carry characteristics with it directly, without any appeal to the group that provided the characteristic in the first place, a process Irvine calls iconization (2001: 33). For example,

> A speaker of American English produces an [aː] in "guide."
> Step 1: A hearer notices it.
> Step 2: The hearer classifies this as "ignorant," having imbued it with this identity so often that beliefs about Southerners are no longer necessary.
> Step 3: The hearer accesses beliefs about "ignorant language" from their cultural belief system and imbues fact *a* with them.
> Through *b'*, a hearer has a regard response (at *b* or *c*).

---

6. I believe that *noticing*, contra Schmidt 1995, can occur consciously or unconsciously, an interpretation consistent with modern social psychological thinking, particularly perhaps in the literature that focuses on the search for *implicit* responses (e.g., Devine 1989; Fazio et al. 1995; Dovidio et al. 1997). What I mean by *noticing* is simply this: the uptake of an event such that it can be processed. That the noticing of some language events is more likely than others is a given and is the subject of considerable work on *salience* (e.g., Preston 1996a, to appear; Sibata [1971] 1999; Silverstein 1981; Trudgill 1986: 10–21, as well as Labov's tripartite distinction referenced in Note 1). Since I am as much concerned here with nonconscious as conscious regard, I will not dwell on what it is in a language signal that triggers the sort of overt or conscious regard typical of folk linguistic research. I will assume here that all language production is noticed and given some regard status, even when there is nothing in the production to attract the attention of the hearer to any part of the signal as different or stereotypical. Those interested in the conditions that trigger overt knowledge of language variety should consult Sibata [1971] 1999; Silverstein 1981; Preston 1996a; and Preston to appear.

To flesh this out further, I borrow from social psychology in the representation in Figure 4. Objects to be regarded are presented within specific "eliciting conditions," which, as I will show below, is one of the explanations for the variability to be found in regard. Bassili and Brown (2005:553) account for how a perceiver begins to process the *attitude object* in terms of

A. the *elicitation conditions* it has been presented in (please note "Associated Representations"),
B. the perceiver's procedural capacities,
C. the perceiver's pre-existing knowledge, and
D. the perceiver's underlying conceptual structure, shown in Figure 4 as a "connectionist model" (e.g., McClelland & Rumelhart 1986).

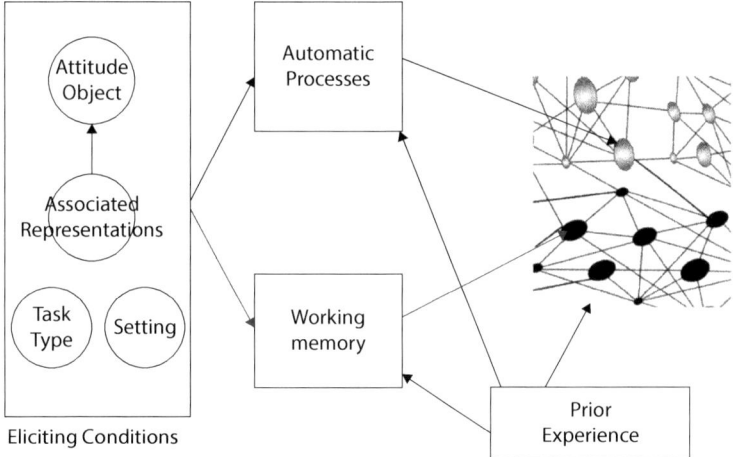

Figure 4. Outline of an attitudinal setting, procedural pathway, and activation of regard features (adapted from Bassili & Brown 2005:554)

Evaluation takes place within an attitudinal cognitorium (Rosenberg 1968), which has all the features of a neural network. Figure 5 enlarges the cognitorium and shows that some items are strong (1) and some weak (2); some connections are strong (3) and some weak (4); some items are not connected at all (5), and the connections between others are inhibited (6). All these connections and weights are formed by experience, a broad term meant to cover not just the fact of prior occurrences but also of their frequency, recency, intensity, and so on with regard to their importance in establishing both the strength and connectedness of items in the cognitorium.

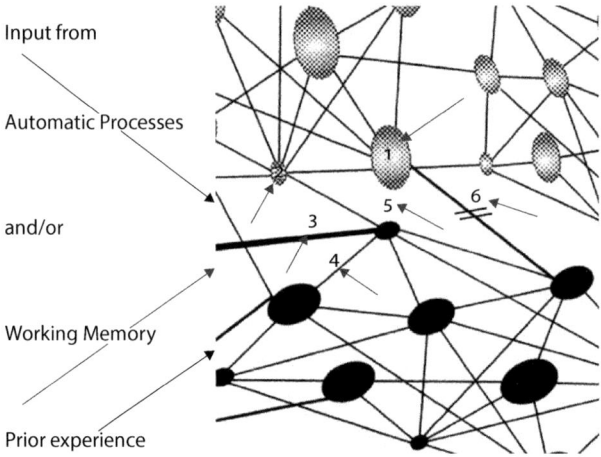

Input from

Automatic Processes

and/or

Working Memory

Prior experience

Figure 5. The internal shape of a regard cognitorium, i.e., the nodes and pathways in a connectionist network (modified from Bassili & Brown 2005: 554), showing (1) a strong node, (2) a weak node, (3) a strong connection, (4) a weak connection, (5) no connection, and (6) an inhibited connection

Once regard factors are triggered in the cognitorium, a response emerges, either an implicit one (Figure 6) or an explicit one (Figure 7).

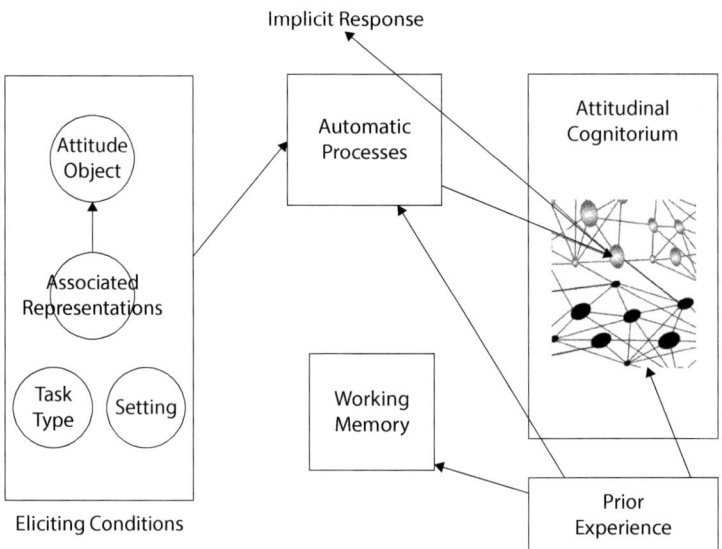

Figure 6. The emergence of an implicit regard response (modified from Bassili & Brown 2005: 554)

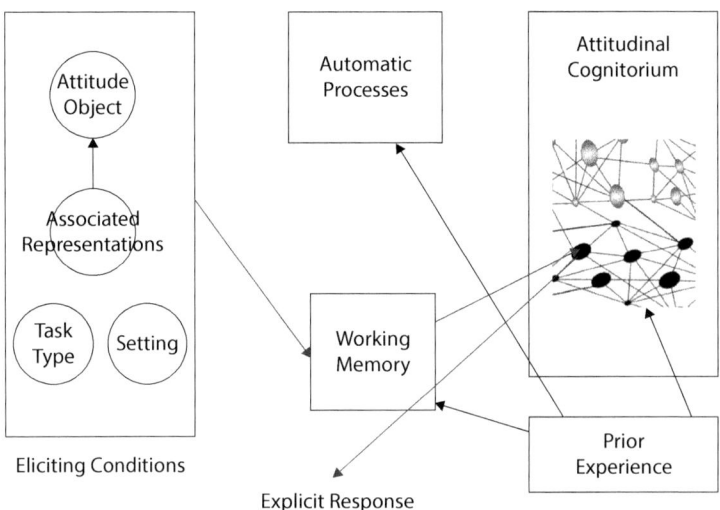

Figure 7. The emergence of an explicit regard response (modified from Bassili and Brown 2005:554

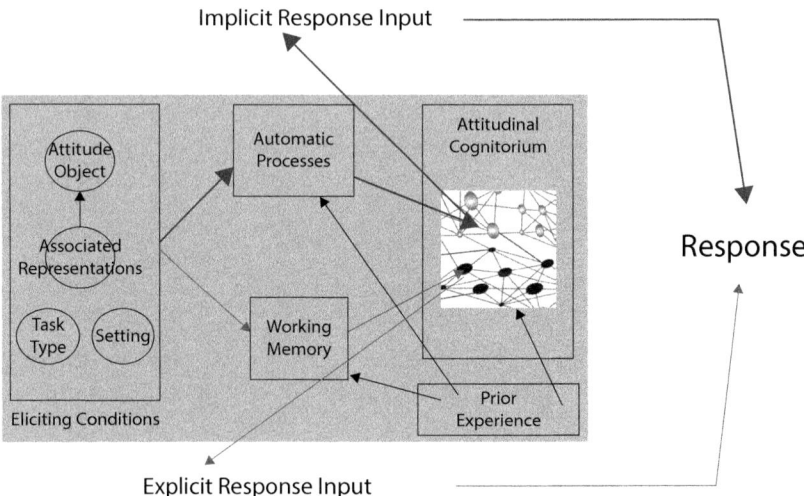

Figure 8. Weighted inputs in the emergence of a mostly implicit response (modified from Bassili & Brown 2005:554)

Even distinguishing between implicit and explicit responses, however, is an oversimplification; it implies that the response is the unique result of one or the other process. The cognitorium is usually activated by inputs from both automatic processes and working memory, however, and each type is weighted. In Figure 8

the automatic processes are strongest (thicker lines), suggesting major unconscious input, but the arrows could have been of opposite (or perhaps even of equal)
thicknesses. Note, however, that the "Response" is a result of the inputs from both
processes.

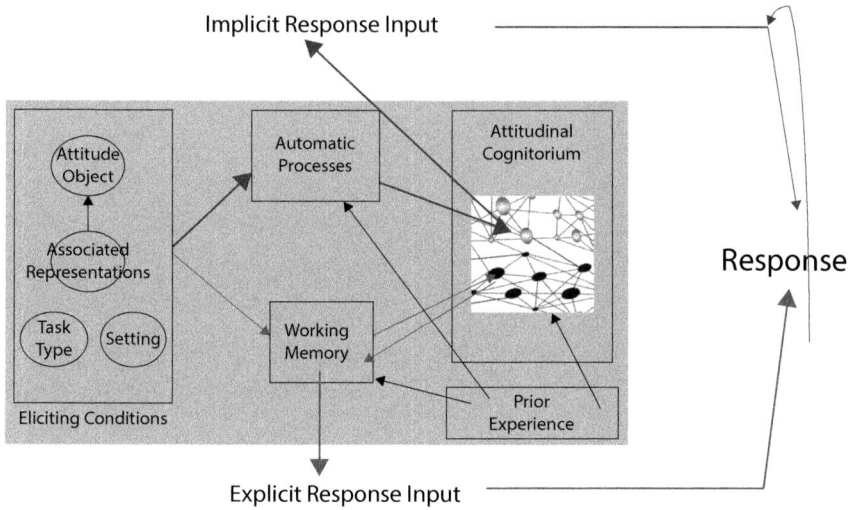

Figure 9. A "weight change" in the emergence of a response (modified from Bassili & Brown
2005:554)

Even greater complexity is shown in Figure 9 where "Working Memory" has
provided a corrective to the first dominant input from automatic processes due to
the fact that the implicitly triggered response might be criticized, for being rude,
racist, impolite, etc.... A "heavy" explicit pathway emerges from working memory
and reformulates the input, giving greater weight in the response to conscious
activity.

In what follows I give evidence for the variety and contradictions that can
arise if this characterization of the storage and retrieval of regard facts is a plausible explanation. I depend largely on data collected over two decades in southeastern Michigan (US).

3.   Evidence

In perceptual (folk) dialectology, one simple way of determining regional language
regard asks respondents to identify areas on the basis of a regard category. The

earliest of these (Preston 1985a) asked respondents to rate the US states for their use of "correct" and "pleasant" varieties of English.

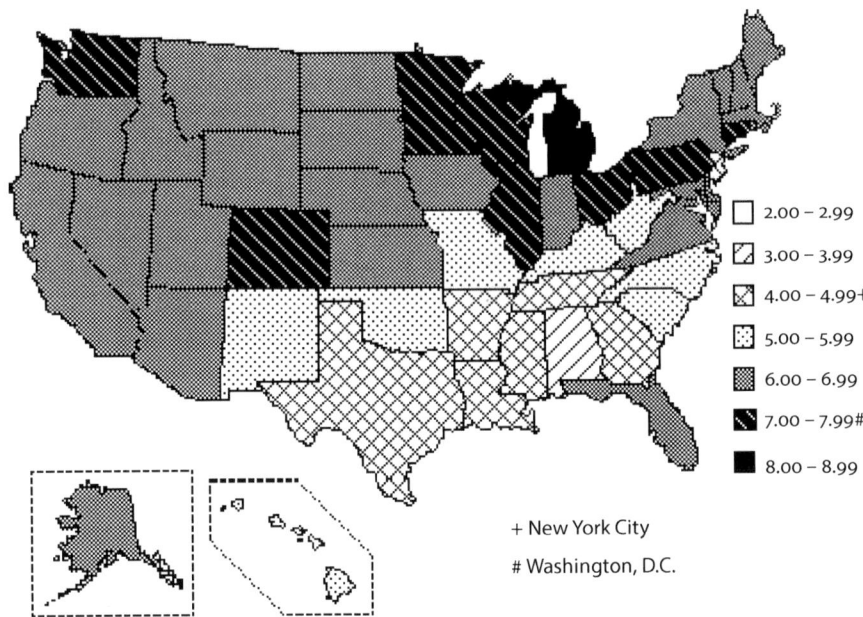

Figure 10. Southeastern Michigan ratings for the 50 US states, New York City, and Washington DC for correctness (1=least correct, 10=most correct) (Preston 1996b: 312)

As Figure 10 shows, only Michigan scores in the 8.00–8.99 range; its residents clearly believe their English to be the most correct in the country. Contrast the question of regional correctness of US English when presented to southern US speakers (Alabama).

Figure 11 shows that for Alabamians, there is still some bad English in the US South (Mississippi, Louisiana, and Texas), but they are all to the west of Alabama, which reckons itself a notch higher. But it does not fare so well either; Alabamians give themselves and most of the country fair-to-middling 5.00–5.99 scores, a far cry from the unique 8.00–8.99 Michiganders assigned themselves. Like Michiganders, however, they don't care much for New Jersey and New York City.

There is surely no need here to present further evidence of variation across regional and many other demographic divides. I will also not pursue at any great length the differences that arise from seeking patently different regard characteristics. Figure 12 shows what the same southeastern Michiganders whose results for "correctness" were shown in Figure 10 believe regarding "pleasantness."

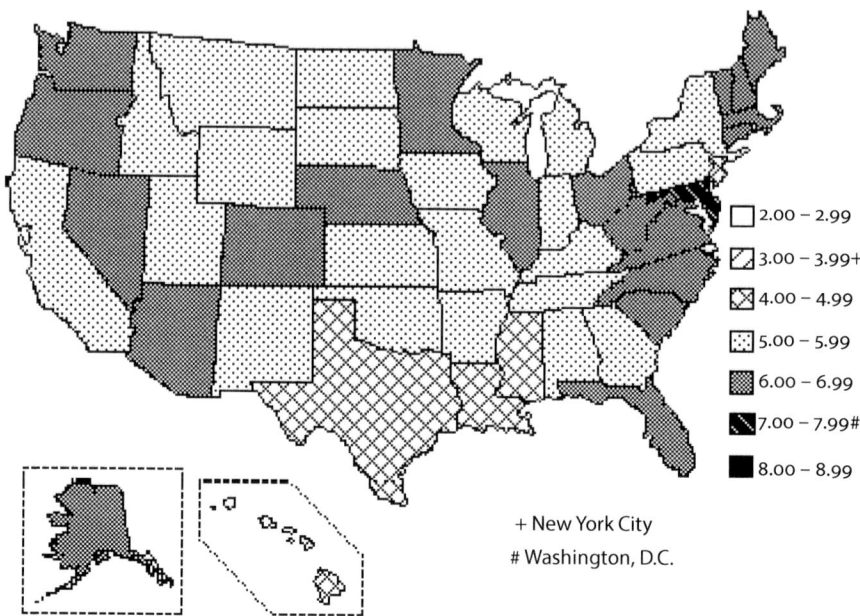

Figure 11. Alabama ratings for the 50 US states, New York City, and Washington DC for correctness (1=least correct, 10 =most correct) (Preston 1996b: 312)

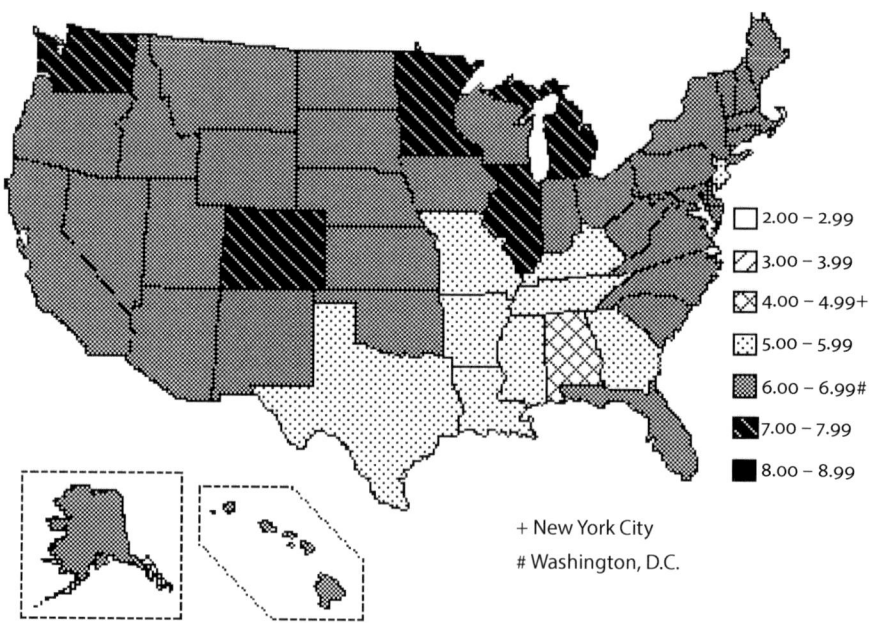

Figure 12. Southeastern Michigan ratings for the 50 US states, New York City, and Washington DC for pleasantness (1=least pleasant, 10=most pleasant) (Preston 1996b: 312)

These Michiganders, who are so focused on correctness, do not treat pleasantness so distinctively. Michigan is no longer unique; four other states (nearby Minnesota and Illinois, as well as Colorado and Washington) are equally pleasant; every southern state has come up one notch, and the overall pleasantness range is reduced from the correctness range of 3.00–3.99 to 8.00–8.99 to one of only 4.00–4.99 to 7.00–7.99.

Pleasantness is not at all like this for the Alabamians, as Figure 13 shows. Their focus is on pleasantness, and they find themselves as strongly and uniquely pleasant as the Michiganders did for their own correctness; their overall range is the strongest 2.00–2.99 (New Jersey pleasantness) to 8.00–8.99 (local pleasantness).

These contrasts confirm what did not really need confirmation – that there is variety in regard as one changes respondent demographics, but it also does away with one common sense prediction about such studies – that locals will always regard their speech as best, clearly not the case for Alabama correctness and only weakly so for Michigan pleasantness.

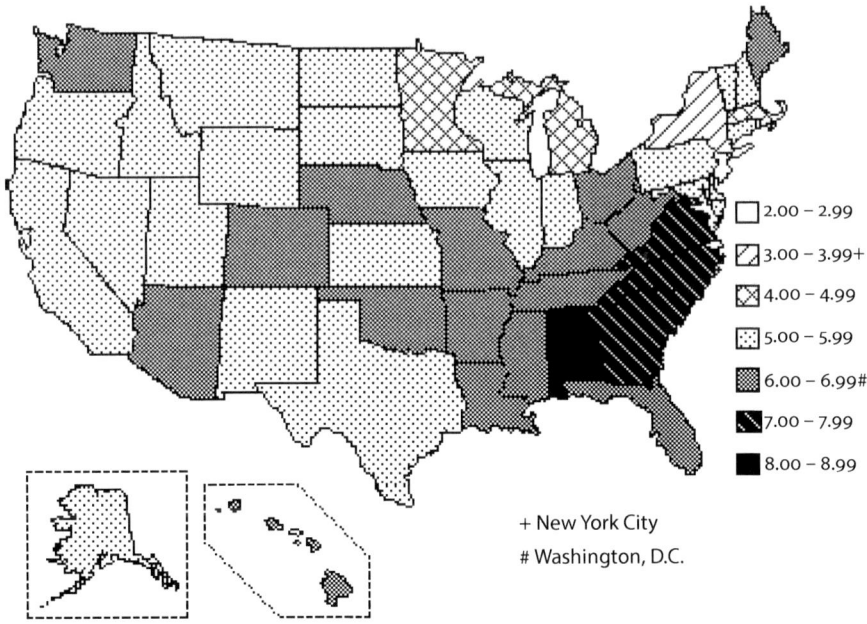

Figure 13. Alabama ratings for the 50 US states, New York City, and Washington DC for pleasantness (1=least pleasant, 10=most pleasant) (Preston 1996b: 312)

The oldest tradition in perceptual dialectology, however, does not ask respondents to rank sites for such characteristics as correctness and pleasantness but asks instead to what extent other regions are similar or different (e.g.,

Daan 1970; Grootaers 1959; Rensink 1955; Sibata 1959; and Weijnen 1946). When the same Michiganders whose correctness and pleasantness scores are shown in Figures 10 and 12 were asked to determine the degree of difference between local speech and the other 49 states, the results were as shown in Figure 14. But do different tasks tease out different regard responses from the same respondents?

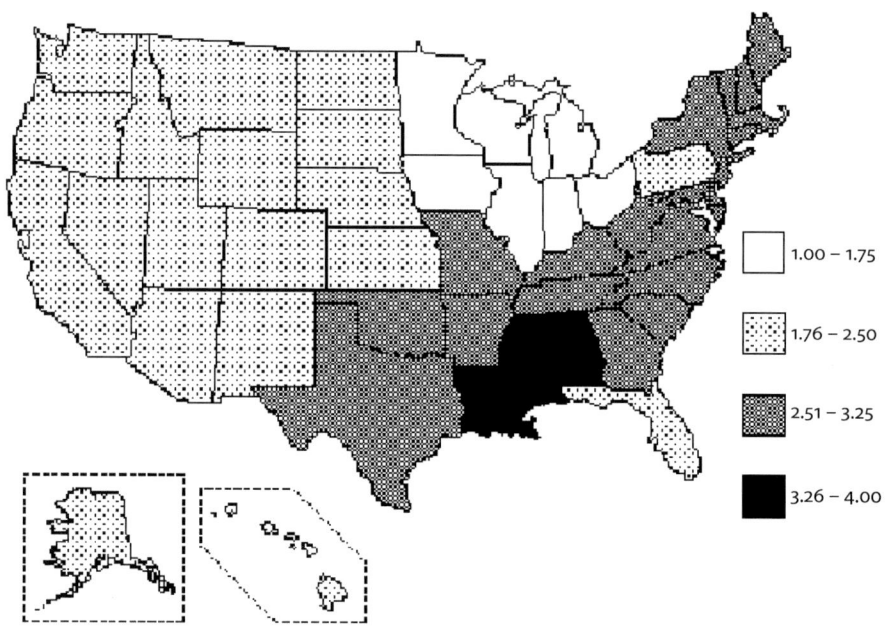

Figure 14. Southeastern Michigan mean score ranges for ratings for the 50 US states for degree of difference (1=not different, 2=slightly different, 3=very different, 4=unintelligibly different) (Preston 1996b: 312)

The Michigan respondents' differences in the ratings of correctness and pleasantness of varieties in the US was expected, but why do both differ from the task of ranking other areas for degree-of-difference (along the four-point scale shown in Figure 14)? Correctness (prestige, standardness) and pleasantness (solidarity) are well-established in the social psychological literature as the major constructs in language regard (e.g., Ryan et al. 1982). If Michigan is uniquely different for correctness (Figure 10) and equally pleasant as two nearby and two western states (Washington and Colorado, Figure 12), why isn't one or the other of those attributes (or a combination of the two) expressed or at least clearly influential in the degree of difference task results shown in Figure 14?

Perhaps the difference in scale (1–4 versus 1–10) masks the similarity between difference on the one hand and correctness or pleasantness on the other. A closer look at the maps will show that that is not the case. In Figure 14 both the northeast (all of New England as well as New York, New Jersey, Maryland, and Delaware) and nearly all of the South (except for Louisiana, Mississippi, and Alabama) are "very different" from Michigan, But in neither the correctness task (Figure 10) nor the pleasantness task (Figure 12) are the Northeast and South ranked similarly.

If there is such a mismatch between not just correctness and pleasantness (as expected) but also between those two and degree of difference, perhaps one should just note that *difference* is a new regard category. Perhaps.

Another technique in perceptual dialectology asks respondents to outline (and label) on a blank or minimally detailed map the areas of a region where people speak differently. This task should yield results very similar to the degree-of-difference ones shown in Figure 14. A generalized map of the same southeastern Michigan respondents was derived from individual maps such as those shown in Figures 15 and 16.

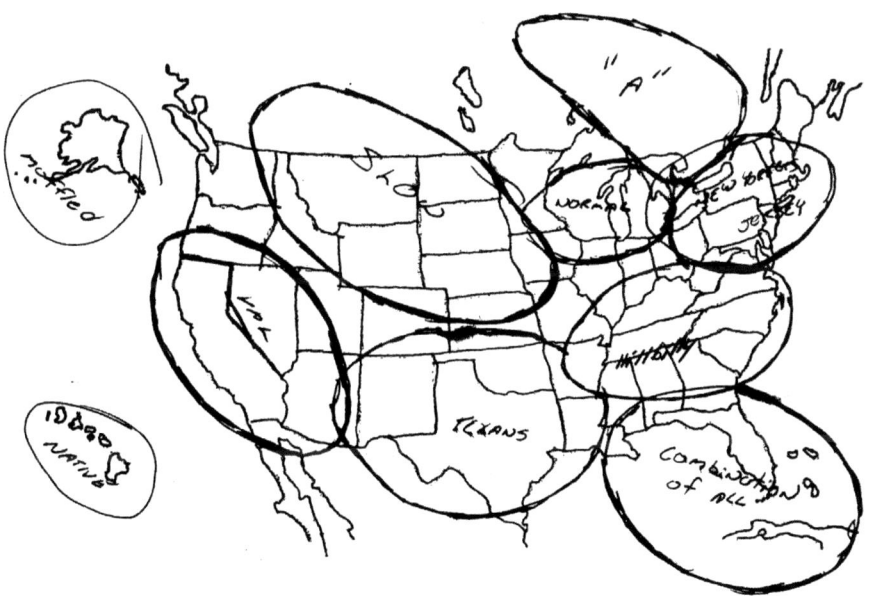

Figure 15. A hand-drawn map of US speech regions by a southeastern Michigan respondent

These individual maps, interesting as they are for ethnographic interpretation, do not reveal the general tendencies of local respondents. Figure 17 shows a

Figure 16. A hand-drawn map of US speech regions by a southeastern Michigan respondent

generalized map of US speech regions derived from 147 individual maps drawn by southeastern Michigan respondents.[7]

This task also results in areas that do not correspond to those given in Figures 10 (correctness), 12 (pleasantness), and 14 (degree of difference) for the same respondents. Here, for example, many respondents agree that Texas and California are separate speech regions, but neither is ever identified uniquely in the previous tasks. The core South is also considerably larger than the three states identified in Figure 14 and extends much farther east.

Again, one may argue that a task that asks for outlines of speech areas is different from one that asks for degrees of difference from the home area (or of such regard attributes as pleasantness and correctness). Indeed it is, but I argue here that just such minor task differences allow respondents to retrieve slightly different cultural meanings from their cognitoria.

---

7. Figure 17 is based on a procedure developed by Preston and Howe (1987); it is now superseded by GIS mapping software; for an outline of GIS procedures in the framework of perceptual dialectology see Montgomery & Stoeckle 2013.

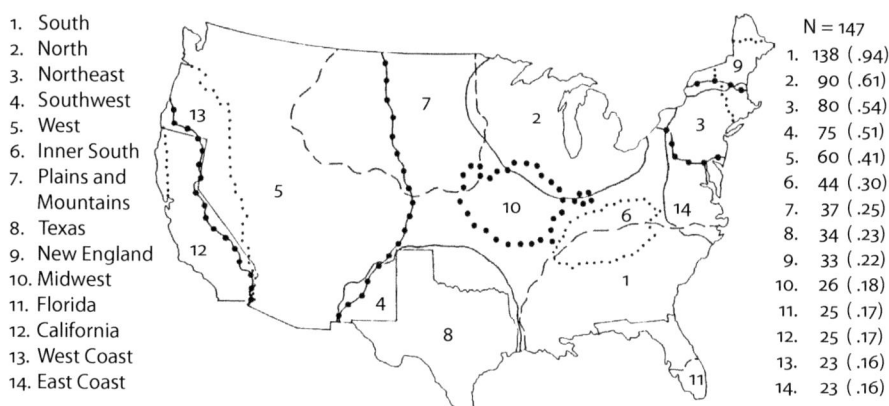

1. South
2. North
3. Northeast
4. Southwest
5. West
6. Inner South
7. Plains and Mountains
8. Texas
9. New England
10. Midwest
11. Florida
12. California
13. West Coast
14. East Coast

N = 147
1. 138 (.94)
2. 90 (.61)
3. 80 (.54)
4. 75 (.51)
5. 60 (.41)
6. 44 (.30)
7. 37 (.25)
8. 34 (.23)
9. 33 (.22)
10. 26 (.18)
11. 25 (.17)
12. 25 (.17)
13. 23 (.16)
14. 23 (.16)

Figure 17. Generalized speech regions of the US for southeastern Michigan respondents (Preston 1996b: 305)

The differences in these task results, however, also inform one another and show the importance of addressing the variability in regard by submitting such a variety of tasks rather than assuming that one has assessed the singular or uniform attitude of an individual or speech community through one task. Suppose, for example, that the results of Figure 17 are interpreted without resource to the other work described here. Look at the right-hand side of that figure to see the number of respondents who drew each speech area. #1, the US South, was drawn by 134 of 147 respondents (.94). Although that's a lot like Figure 14, where the South was the area ranked with the highest degree of difference, that will not explain the next two highest ratings, areas #2 and #3, the home (Great Lakes) area and an area focused on New York City, respectively. A glance back at correctness scores for these respondents (Figure 10) will show that the South, the local area (Michigan) and New York City are the best (local) and worst (New York City and the South) rated areas. This shows that the draw-a-map task, which asked only for areas where English is spoken differently in the US, is importantly tied to correctness, perhaps the dominating feature that gave such salience for both the local (correct) and the New York City and southern (incorrect) areas. In other words, when faced with the task of outlining those areas of the US that exhibit speech differences, the connection between "speech differences" and "language correctness" looms very large for these southeastern Michigan respondents, and we are able to see the influence of various aspects of the cognitorium.

Can a different task tease out another but related aspect of Michigan regard for language variety? I believe so. Recall that, unlike the Alabama respondents, who put such great stock in language pleasantness (Figure 13), the Michiganders seem less impressed with it (Figure 12). To approach this question of pleasantness more specifically, the well-established matched guise technique was used (e.g., Shuy & Fasold 1973), but the stimulus was a regional identification rather than a voice sample. The first step in such work is to derive the labels from local respondents, and, to accomplish this, undergraduate students (again all from Michigan) were shown a simplified version of Figure 17 and asked to write down any labels or descriptions that entered their minds when they considered the speech of these various regions. The following were the most frequent labels they offered (although several of the "opposites" were later supplied, including all the negatives of *nasal*, *drawl*, and *twang*):

slow – fast	formal – casual	educated – uneducated
smart – dumb	polite – rude	snobbish – down-to-earth
nasal – not nasal	normal – abnormal	friendly – unfriendly
drawl – no drawl	twang – no twang	bad English – good English

Another set of similar respondents (N=85) were then shown the same map used to elicit the labels and asked to evaluate each of the regions shown in Figure 17 on a six-point scale for each of these twelve traits. The results are shown in Table 1.

Table 1. Ratings for the North (the local area) and the South for twelve traits by southeastern Michigan respondents on a one-to-six scale (Preston 1999b: 366)

	Means scores (ordered) South				Means scores (ordered) North		
Factor	Mean	Attribute	Rank	Rank	Factor	Mean	Attribute
–1&2	4.66	Casual	1	12	–1&2	3.53	Casual
2	4.58	Friendly	2	9.5	2	4.00	Friendly
2&–1	4.54	Down-to-earth	3	6	2&–1	4.19	Down-to-earth
2	4.20	Polite	4	9.5	2	4.00	Polite
ø	4.09	Not nasal	5	11	ø	3.94	Not nasal
1&2	3.22	Normal [Abnormal]	6	3	1&2	4.94	Normal
1	3.04	Smart [Dumb]	7	4	1	4.53	Smart
1	2.96	No twang [Twang]	8	2	1	5.07	No twang
1	2.86	Good English [Bad English]	9	5	1	4.41	Good English
1	2.72	Educated [Uneducated]	10	8	1	4.09	Educated
1	2.42	Fast [Slow]	11	7	1	4.12	Fast
1	2.22	No drawl [Drawl]	12	1	1	5.11	No drawl

It's fairly straightforward to classify many of these attributes as ones associated with language standardness (or correctness, Factor 1), or solidarity (or pleasantness, Factor 2). If this is the case, then the North or local area will outpace the South for those qualities associated with both correctness and pleasantness, and they clearly do as shown in Figures 10 and 12, but Table 1 tells a slightly different story. For the standard characteristics, everything is as expected: the North is smarter, better educated, and speaks better English. (It is also more normal and has neither a drawl nor a twang, providing evidence that these features too should be linked to standardness.) The contrast with the previous tasks lies in the dimension of solidarity (pleasantness).

The South is ranked higher than the North for the qualities friendliness, down-to-earth, casual, and polite, these latter two, at least in this task, allied to solidarity. In other words, when asked to rate the states for pleasantness, Michigan respondents found their own area and a few others outside the South the best; when asked to rate specific characteristics of language variety, some of which are surely components of pleasantness, they found the South better.

There are two ways to interpret these results. The first is a uniformitarian approach that suggests Michigan respondents have *an* attitude towards speech regions (in this case, one towards the North and another towards the South) as regards pleasantness and that only one of these tasks was successful in teasing it out. The second, and I believe better way to proceed, suggests that these tasks awaken different aspects of the various attitudes that respondents have towards objects to be evaluated and that it is better to characterize that system of regard than to search for a single truth.

Is it possible to extract yet another response from the underlying set of beliefs about language varieties held by Michigan respondents? The matched-guise research just described triggered a response to the solidarity characteristics that was very different from the simple pleasantness ranking task. Surely the Michigan view of local correctness is so fundamental in the regard inventory that it cannot be challenged. Labov (1966: 332–335) introduced a measure of *linguistic insecurity* that asked respondents what the correct pronunciation of a word was and then what their personal usage was. When a respondent declared their personal use to be different from what they had just identified as the standard, each such mismatch was tallied as an instance of linguistic insecurity. Labov found the overall scores of New Yorkers on this test to be very bad, evidence of their low regard for local speech (Chapter 13), a regard Labov even calls "linguistic self-hatred" (344).

Owens and Baker (1984) replicated the New York insecurity study in Winnipeg, and found that their Canadian respondents were much more linguistically secure than Labov's New Yorkers. Preston (2013) replicated this same test among young southeastern Michigan respondents, but with an amazing result. The Michigan respondents found their own usage nonstandard, i.e., they were as insecure as the New Yorkers and considerably more insecure than the Winnipeg respondents (10). Labov is explicit about the match between regard for New York City speech and the individual: "We find that the negative attitude towards the city speech in general is directed by the respondent towards himself [sic] as well" (1966: 345).

Labov's New Yorkers appear to be a little less complex in the area of regard for local language correctness. Their cognitorium links the regard for personal performance to the regard for place. Michiganders, however, seem to have two repositories of local correctness. The first, correctness in general, gives very high regard to place for correctness; the second, regard for personal correctness, is not very high at all. In other words, it was necessary to carry out a task that revealed local as well as personal assessments of correctness to construct a more complete account of the repository for correctness regard among southeastern Michigan respondents.

I will not venture here to draw an even partial cognitorium of language regard for Michigan respondents. It will be dominated by language correctness, and such correctness will be assigned strongly to the local area, but with a component of individual deprecation. Local speech is pleasant, but, given the right circumstances, certain pleasant values (friendliness for example) may be assigned to the area usually rated quite low in other tasks (the US South). If one wants to learn the characteristics of language regard in a speech community or other delimited group, it will paint a more complete picture to proceed with various tasks that allow for a weighting of the complex elements that lie within the individual. Obviously, many more tasks could be considered, and many are exemplified in this volume.

4. So what?

Linguists will want to know what the results of regard studies offer the more central concerns of the field. For some it will not be sufficient to cite Hymes' ethnographic rationale:

> If the community's own theory of linguistic repertoire and speech is considered (as it must be in any serious ethnographic account), matters become all the more complex and interesting.   (Hymes 1972: 39)

The remainder of this chapter shows how regard sheds light on matters beyond the ethnographic, including variation and change as suggested above in the discussion of the importance of *evaluation* in Weinreich et al. 1968).

In offering this evidence, I continue to use US data, specifically responses and categorizations from the same (or similar) southeastern Michiganders discussed above. Their local vocalic system is the first object of discussion. Southeastern Michigan, like other areas around the Great Lakes of the US (particularly urban areas) supports a system known as the Northern Cities Chain Shift (NCCS), e.g., Labov et al. 2006.

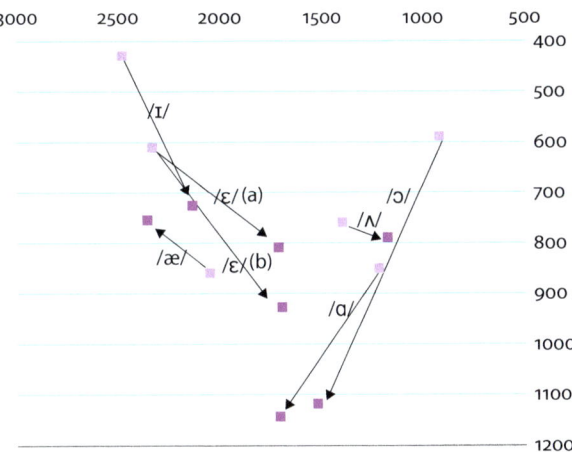

Figure 18. Northern Cities Chain Shift vowels in dark squares; a conservative US system in light squares (Peterson & Barney 1952); arrows point to the difference between the two

As Figure 18 shows, the NCCS involves (1) /æ/ raising, (2) /ɑ/ fronting and lowering, (3) /ɔ/ lowering and fronting, (4) /ɛ/ backing and lowering (along two tracks), (5) /ʌ/ backing, and (6) /ɪ/ lowering and backing.

In the first experiment presented here, NCCS vowels were presented in single-word environments to seventy young, European-American respondents from suburban southeastern Michigan, all of whom were NCCS speakers. They were asked simply to write down the word they heard. One goal of the test was to see what sorts of misclassifications might arise, and two possibilities were imagined. First, respondents might misclassify those tokens that were close to one another in the phonetic space of the NCCS (or "new") system, i.e., their own. Second, respondents might misclassify tokens that were close in phonetic space to the vowels of the more conservative (or "old") system, the ones shown in open squares in Figure 18. For example, if a respondent heard a raised and fronted NCCS (in this test, in the word "pat") with reference to the old system, Figure 18 suggests that it would be perceived as /ɛ/ or /e/, but if it was heard with reference to the "new" system, it would more likely be perceived as /ɪ/ or /e/. Here is a list of all these likelihoods, based on the proximity of the experimental vowels to the vowels of the NCCS or the conservative system:

If the "new" (NCCS) positions are targets for misclassification:
    a.   /æ/ might be confused with /ɪ/ or /e/
    b.   /a/ might be confused with /ɔ/
    c.   /ɔ/ might be confused with /a/
    d.   /ɛ/ might be confused with /ɪ/
    e.   /ʌ/ might be confused with /ɛ/ or /o/
    f.   /ɪ/ might be confused with /æ/

If the "old" (pre-NCCS, Peterson and Barney) positions are targets for misclassification:
    a.   /æ/ might be confused with /e/ or /ɛ/
    b.   /a/ might be confused with /æ/
    c.   /ɔ/ will not be confused
    d.   /ɛ/ might be confused with /ʌ/
    e.   /ʌ/ might be confused with /a/
    f.   /ɪ/ might be confused with /ɛ/

Table 2 shows the words presented to the respondents in the first column and the identity of the response in the top row. The grayed cells show the number correct, and the bold numbers show the cases in which the "old" or conservative system was the source of the error. For example, the word "tin" was heard correctly 44 times, 25 times incorrectly as /ɛ/ (an "old" system error), and only once incorrectly as /a/ (a random error). Since many single errors were phonetically and phonologically unreasonable, single errors were ignored. Misconstruings that could be attributed to the new (NCCS) system are italicized and those that can be attributed to the old (conservative) one are bolded.

As the bold numbers in Table 2 show, 103 misunderstandings were based on the older, conservative system, and only 18 were made in the direction of the new system. Why would these hearers not classify the experimental vowels in the direction of their proximity to those of their own system? The answer lies in regard. The Michigan quandary is this: How can we be the best speakers when our vowel system is different from the conservative standard? Their cognitive dissonance is resolved by their high regard for local speech, causing them to embed a phonological system that reflects a conservative positioning of the vowels rather than their actual shifted one. In this task at least, they

Table 2. Results of a Michigan NCCS comprehension test for 70 respondents (N.B.: one respondent each did not give a response for "Ben" and "boat")

	/i/	/ɪ/	/e/	/ɛ/	/æ/	/a/	/ʌ/	/ɔ/	/o/	/ʊ/	/u/
beet	70										
tin		44		25		1					
bait			68			1				1	
Ben	1			13	1	1	52			1	
pat				17	53						
hot					9	61					
done				4	1		64		1		
dawn						14	9	47			
boat									69		
boot	1	1									68

continue to reference the older system, one they have access to through speakers from other areas, older speakers in their own area, speakers in their own area less advanced in the shift, and media exposure (Evans et al. 2006). In this case, (1) the respondents attended to the words in an experimental situation, one in which the phonetic evidence was that the speakers were just like them (i.e., young, European-American speakers from southeastern Michigan); (2) auditory discrimination (detection of the phonetic signal) may have proceeded normally, but (3) classification was sometimes derailed by reference to a conservative, regard-based phonological system.

Perhaps even segment discrimination can be influenced by regard. Niedzielski (1999) presented Detroit-area southeastern Michigan respondents (all NCCS speakers) with three samples of the vowel /æ/ (in the word "last"). The first was a raised and fronted token, typical of the NCCS, the second was a conservative token (see Figure 18 for both of these), and the third was an exaggeratedly low and back version, one near the vowel space of /a/, particularly an NCCS one. The respondents first heard a model NCCS token, were asked to remember it, and were told the speaker was from Michigan; they were then asked to match it with one of the three versions just described. This should have been an easy task since the three are acoustically quite distinct, but none of the respondents (N=42) paired the NCCS model with the second NCCS token. Thirty-eight identified it with the conservative token, and four even suggested that it was the same as the exaggeratedly lowered and backed one (72). Just as Michiganders misclassify single-word items in terms of the conservative system, in this study they also incorrectly identify phonetic alternatives for exactly the same reason. They regard their variety as the most correct in the US; therefore, since Niedzielski told them the speaker was from Michigan, they refused to hear the NCCS model in the phonetic space it occupied. Instead, they identified it as the conservative (or even the exaggerated) version of US English /æ/.

Psycholinguists, speech scientists, and others interested in comprehension and/or discrimination, perhaps especially in experimental settings in which the respondents know the focus is on language, would be well-advised to be on the lookout for the influence of regard-based interference, an effect that does not ordinarily appear in everyday, contextualized speech.

Can students of language and culture who deal with the details of variation be advised by regard findings? I believe so. Plichta and Preston (2005) played a continuum of pronunciations of the word "guide" in which the vowel ranged from fully diphthongal to fully monophthongal. The monophthong ([aː]) is a well-known caricature of US southern speech,[8] and this research originally sought to discover if US respondents would be sensitive to degree of monophthongization in terms of region; i.e., they would place more monophthongal versions farther south. Male and female speakers' fully diphthongal tokens were resynthesized to exactly the same degree of monophthongization along a seven-step continuum and played for respondents in a web-based survey. For each token they were asked to identify the city they believed the speaker was from (Figure 19). The sites were assigned the values shown in Figure 19 (Saginaw = 1, Coldwater = 2, etc...), and the mean score was calculated for each of the seven-step versions of "guide." The lower the mean, the more likely the respondents thought the token was "northern"; the higher, the more "southern" it was perceived.

Table 3 shows that US respondents not only associate monophthongization of ([aɪ]) with the South but also associate greater monophthongization with more southern sites. So far, however, it is difficult to see how regard has played a major role in this discrimination. One could say only that monophthongization is associated with southern speech and that the ability to discriminate degree forces a more southern interpretation of the signal. Remember, however, that the respondents heard male and female voices, resynthesized so that their degree of monophthongization was the same at every step.

---

8.   Readers who would like to see a partial cognitorium of Northern regard for Southern speech should see Preston 2010a: 18 or several examples in Preston 2010b.

Figure 19. The nine sites in the US to which respondents assigned pronunciations of "guide" (Plichta & Preston 2005)

Table 3. Mean scores for each step in the "guide" continuum (1=completely diphthongal to 7= completely monophthongal) based on association with the regions in Figure 19

Region	Step	Mean
1. Saginaw, MI		
2. Coldwater, MI	1	2.85
3. South Bend, IN	2	3.17
4. Muncie, IN	3	3.87
5. New Albany, IN	4	4.89
6. Bowling Green, KY	5	5.99
7. Nashville, TN	6	6.58
8. Florence, AL	7	7.02
9. Dothan, AL		

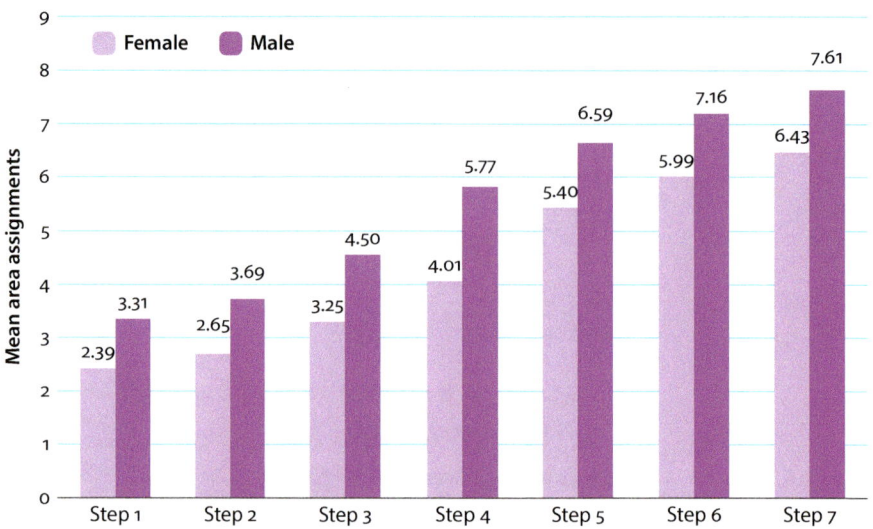

Figure 20. Perceived regional position of the seven-step monophthongized version of "guide" by sex (Plichta & Preston 2005:121)

Figure 20 shows that at every step men were heard as more southern and women as more northern. Why is a man's voice, with the same degree of monophthongization as a woman's, regarded as "more southern"? (Or why is a woman's voice regarded as more "northern"?) Recall that Figure 10 showed the southern states as worst-rated for language correctness (with the exception of New Jersey and New York City), but it is also a sociolinguistic commonplace that women are more standard speakers than men. The respondents, in this case from all over the US, not only distinguished levels of monophthongization as to region but let another of their language regard concepts (men and women differ on the standardness dimension) interfere with their discrimination of the quality of the vowel. The respondents were likely skewed in their ability to discriminate the degree of monophthongization ("southernness") on the basis of the sex of the voice due to their regard association of standard speech with women and nonstandard speech with men. Since the US South is perceived as a nonstandard or "incorrect" speech area, this additional regard factor, coupled with the sex stereotype, caused the consistent misassignment.

These discrimination findings show that the very acoustic signals linguists from many areas of the field depend on can be easily redirected by language users due to regard factors. These several examples should also make it clear that language regard concepts may have their origins in accurate or inaccurate social and linguistic stereotypes.

Finally, how will language regard factors interact with what might be viewed as purely linguistic motivations for sound change? Consider the following scenario for early stages of the NCCS. Figure 21 shows a case where the area of the low front vowel /æ/ (shaded circles) contains a single case of the /ɑ/ vowel (an unfilled square). The normal territory for this vowel in non-NCCS speakers (i.e., Peterson and Barney-like) is farther back in the vowel space, and, if one considers only the tokens in that area, the mean is shown in the center of the territory (the dark square) at 1550Hz for F1. If respondents do not hear the outlier as an example of an /ɑ/ word (i.e., they misunderstand the outlier as an /æ/ word, a plausible interpretation as shown in Table 2), then the system is probably not influenced.

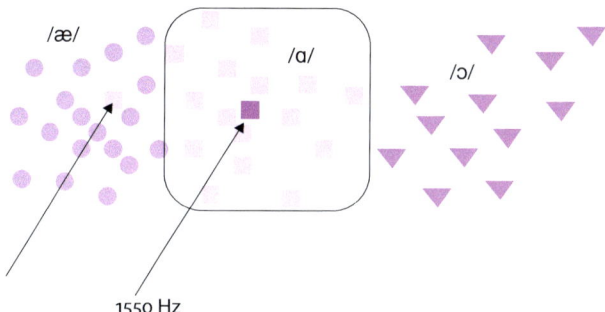

Figure 21. A fronted /ɑ/ in the /æ/ vowel space (Adapted from Labov 2002)

In Figure 22, however, the /æ/ tokens have fronted, as they do in the first stages of the NCCS, leaving the previously surrounded /ɑ/ token behind in the vowel space (the leftmost light square), one more likely to be understood as an instance of /ɑ/, and a contributor to a new mean score of 1571Hz (the dark square) for that vowel class.

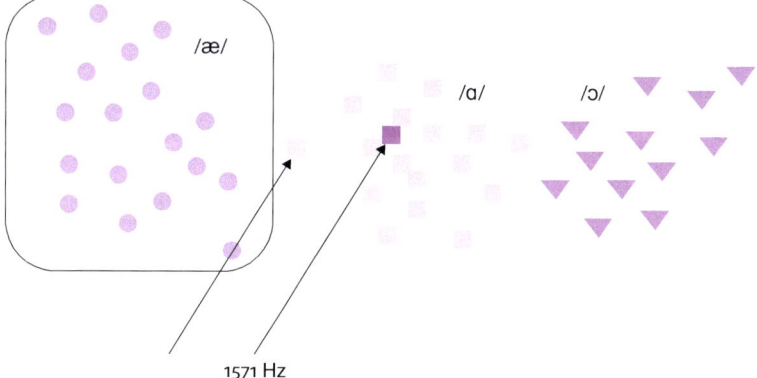

Figure 22. A fronted /ɑ/ left behind after the fronting of /æ/ and a new center of the /ɑ/ vowel space (Adapted from Labov 2002)

As the experimental work on regard discussed above shows, however, it is not the case that NCCS speakers will unerringly hear the frontmost examples of /ɑ/ as members of that vowel class. They appear to have constructed a "phantom" vowel space based on the old, conservative position of /æ/, one that ignores the fronted tokens of /æ/ as well as those of /ɑ/. Figure 23 shows this space for /æ/ (in a dashed box), a conservative one apparently invoked when the regard element of local language correctness is triggered in a respondent's cognitorium.

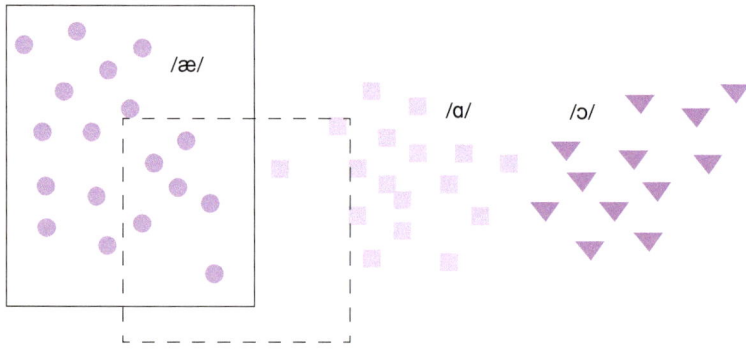

Figure 23. A "phantom" (conservative) vowel space for /æ/ (Adapted from Labov 2002)

When this phantom space is fully activated, Figure 24 shows (some of) the results. Tokens of fronted (i.e., incipient) NCCS /æ/ are pruned from the respondent's system (the Xed-out circles in the fronted /æ/ space), exactly as shown in Niedzielski 1999. The frontmost /ɑ/ tokens (indicated by arrows in Figure 24) are now within the phantom space for /æ/ and are understood as such (e.g., the nine tokens of /ɑ/ misunderstood as /æ/ in Table 2). Respondents must have also filled the phantom space with imagined tokens (the dark circles), for a few of Niedzielski's respondents matched an NCCS token with a very low and retracted one from the lower right corner of the phantom space, allowing a hearer to recognize what would have been an /ɑ/ even in the conservative system as an /æ/.[9]

To return to the characteristics of variation and change outlined in Weinreich et al. (1968) cited at the beginning of this chapter, these regard-influenced data link one characterization of the *evaluation problem* to the social side of the *embedding problem*. How can Michigan speakers embed a new vowel system which would replace a standard ("correct") one when they are so focused on their own

---

9.   I leave it up to the reader to construct the phantom space (and center) for /ɑ/ and even /ɔ/ and relate those spaces to the misunderstandings shown in Table 2.

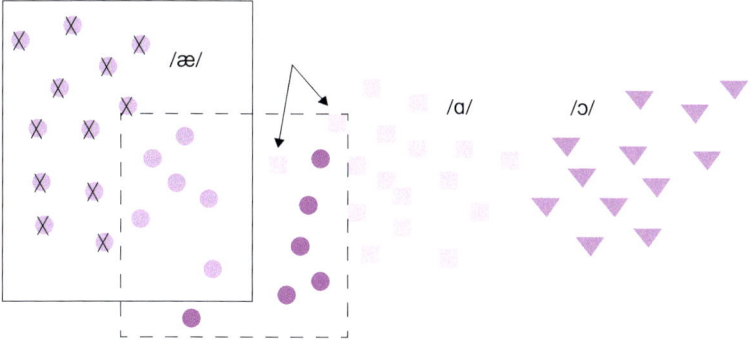

Figure 24. The phantom space in action (Adapted from Labov 2002)

correctness? The answer is a curious combination of conscious and nonconscious activities. Michiganders clearly believe that what they do is standard and correct, and that conscious evaluation accounts for the formation of a phantom, conservative system that allows them to mishear their own and others' vowel performances in the face of the rapidly advancing (and for many fully advanced) NCCS change. Activation of that system, however, is not conscious or at least not at the same level of consciousness as their overtly held belief in local correctness. It allows, therefore, change from below the level of consciousness, surely a requirement for a group that believes in its own correctness. Without this array of evidence of regard for their own speech, the full story of the steps involved in the acquisition of the NCCS, a story of language change in progress, could not be told.

5.   Conclusions

This is a story both like (and not like) the account of variety change in Denmark (Kristiansen, this volume). There residents from several locales evaluated their own variety as the one they "liked" best (most pleasant?). When presented with actual speech samples, however, they preferred modern Copenhagen speech for solidarity factors (cool, nice, etc… – called "dynamism" in Kristiansen's account) over their own varieties and conservative Copenhagen area speech for standardness characteristics (intelligent, goal-directed, etc… – Kristiansen's "superiority"). Linguistic change all over Denmark, however, shows change in the direction of modern Copenhagen speech, a variety preferred only when offered in a matched guise format, one which Kristiansen labels nonconscious and declares to be the guiding regard principle for linguistic change. Michiganders do not prefer their own speech for pleasantness in some regard tasks but do in others. They clearly prefer their own in conscious, overt evaluations. In a matched guise task without speech samples, their own speech is regarded as superior for correctness or standard features but not so highly for solidarity ones. Lacking in the Michigan test is a speech sample presentation of the conservative (older) Michigan norm and the emerging (and emerged) NCCS norm. Lacking in the Danish studies are accounts of the specific linguistic features that may be perceived (or misperceived) as local or not and the values assigned them.

In every case, a study of the regard features respondents retrieve from their beliefs about people and their language varieties can enhance the understanding of the social embedding of language change. In many cases, there is simply more to be done. At least the following facts might be considered in the collection of regard responses:

A: Setting
  1. Actual – home, laboratory, etc…
  2. Context – contextualized vs. noncontextualized
B: Stimulus
  3. Priming – primed vs. non-primed
  4. Presentation – video, written stimulus, pictures, etc…
  5. Size – global vs. specific
  6. Status – stigmatized, prestige, neutral, etc…
  7. Access – direct vs. indirect access to a linguistic stimulus
  8. Authenticity – native vs. imitated
  9. Naturalness – natural vs. (re)synthesized
  10. Presence – an actual linguistic stimulus is provided or not provided
C: Respondents
  11. Non-targeted vs. targeted
D: Response
  12. Behavior – respondent activity or task (rate, read, observe, perform, etc…)
  13. Mode – fixed (Likert scale, forced choice, etc…) vs. open-ended (discoursal, eye-tracking, etc…)
  14. Timing – present vs. absent
  15. Awareness – unaware (subconscious) vs. aware (conscious) (Preston & Niedzielski 2013)

Of course no single scholar or even team can cross-classify local data based on a manipulation of all these contexts and conditions for the collection of regard responses. They illustrate, however, the potential for differing responses to arise from the variety that is there in the cognitorium, the repository of regard beliefs.

Variation in language regard is important because linguists need to know not only how language varies and what people think about it but also what the interaction is between performance and the variability in regard. Since such variability in regard may surface in its link to performance, a cognitive foundation for language regard that admits variability will play an important part in the explanatory areas of language variation and change.

References

Albarracín, Dolores, Johnson, Blair T. & Zanna, Mark P. (eds). 2005. *The Handbook of Attitudes*. Malwah NJ: Lawrence Erlbaum Associates.

Bassili, John N. & Brown Rick D. 2005. Implicit and explicit attitudes: Research, challenges, and theory. In Albarracín et al. (eds), 543–74.

Daan, Jo. 1970[1999]. Dialekten. In *Van Randstad tot Landrand* [Bijdragen en Mededelingen der Dialecten Commissie van de Koninklijke Nederlandse Akademie van Wetenschappen te Amsterdam XXXVII]. Amsterdam: N.V. Noord, Hollandsche Uitgevers Maatschappij. (Translated as 'Dialects,' in Preston (ed.), 1999a: 9–30).

Devine, Patricia G. 1989. Stereotypes and prejudice: Their automatic and controlled components. *Journal of Personality and Social Psychology* 56: 5–18.
DOI: 10.1037/0022-3514.56.1.5

Dovidio, John F., Kawakami, Kerry, Johnson, Craig, Johnson, Brenda & Howard, Adaiah. 1997. The nature of prejudice: Automatic and controlled processes. *Journal of Experimental Social Psychology* 33: 510–540. DOI: 10.1006/jesp.1997.1331

Evans, Betsy E., Ito, Rika, Jones, Jamila & Preston, Dennis R. 2006. How to get to be one kind of Midwesterner: Accommodation to the Northern Cities Chain Shift. In *Language Variation and Change in the American Midland* [Varieties of English around the World G36], Thomas Murray & Beth Lee Simon (eds), 179–197. Amsterdam: John Benjamins.
DOI: 10.1075/veaw.g36.14eva

Fazio, Russel H., Jackson, Joni R., Dunton, Bridget C. & Williams, Carol J. 1995. Variability in automatic activation as an unobtrusive measure of racial attitudes: A bonafide pipeline? *Journal of Personality and Social Psychology* 69: 1013–1027.
DOI: 10.1037/0022-3514.69.6.1013

Fine, Elizabeth. 1983. In defense of literary dialect: A response to Dennis Preston. *Journal of American Folklore* 96: 323–330. DOI: 10.2307/540948

Fowler, Carol A. 1986. An event approach to the study of speech perception from a direct-realist perspective. *Journal of Phonetics* 14: 3–28.

Grootaers, Willem A. 1959. Origin and nature of the subjective boundaries of dialects. *Orbis* 8: 355–84.

Hockett, Charles F. 1958. *A Course in Modern Linguistics*. New York NY: Macmillan.

Hymes, Dell. 1972. Models of the interaction of language and social life. In *Directions in Sociolinguistics: The Ethnography of Communication*, John J. Gumperz & Dell Hymes (eds), 35–71. New York NY: Holt, Rinehart and Winston.

Irvine, Judith, 1989. When talk isn't cheap: Language and political economy. *American Ethnologist* 16(2): 248–267. DOI: 10.1525/ae.1989.16.2.02a00040

Irvine, Judith, 2001. "Style" as distinctiveness: The culture and ideology of linguistic differentiation. In *Style and Sociolinguistic Variation*, Penelope Eckert & John R. Rickford (eds), 21–43. Cambridge: CUP.

Kruglanski, Arie W. & Stroebe, Wolfgang. 2005. The influence of beliefs and goals on attitudes. In Albarracín et al. (eds), 323–68.

Labov, William. 1966. *The Social Stratification of English in New York City*. Arlington VA: The Center for Applied Linguistics.

Labov, William, 1972. *Sociolinguistic Patterns*. Philadelphia PA: University of Pennsylvania Press.

Labov, William. 2002. Driving forces in linguistic change. A paper presented to the International Conference on Korean Linguistics, Seoul National University, August 2.

Labov, William, Ash, Sharon & Boberg, Charles. 2006. *The Atlas of North American English: Phonetics, Phonology, and Sound Change: A Multimedia Reference Tool*. Berlin: Walter de Gruyter.

Liberman, Alvin M., Cooper, Franklin S., Shankweiler, Donald & Studdert-Kennedy, Michael. 1967. Perception of the speech code. *Psychological Review* 74: 431–361. DOI: 10.1037/h0020279

McClelland, James L. & Rumelhart, David E. 1986. A distributed model of human learning and memory. In *Parallel Distributed Processing: Explorations in the Microstructure of Cognition*, Vol. 2, James L. McClelland & David E. Rumelhart (eds), 170–215. Cambridge MA: The MIT Press.

Montgomery, Chris & Stoeckle, Philipp. 2013. Geographic information systems and perceptual dialectology: A method for processing draw-a-map data. *Journal of Linguistic Geography* 1(1): 52–85. DOI: 10.1017/jlg.2013.4

Niedzielski, Nancy. 1999. The effect of social information on the perception of sociolinguistic variables. *Journal of Language and Social Psychology* 18(1): 62–85. DOI: 10.1177/0261927X99018001005

Niedzielski, Nancy & Preston, Dennis R. 2003. *Folk Linguistics* (rev. pb. edn). Berlin: Mouton de Gruyter.

Owens, Thompson W. & Baker, Paul M. 1984. Linguistic insecurity in Winnipeg: Validation of a Canadian index of linguistic insecurity. *Language in Society* 13(1): 337–350. DOI: 10.1017/S0047404500010538

Peterson, Gordon E. & Barney, Harold L. 1952. Control methods used in a study of the vowels. *The Journal of the Acoustical Society of America* 24(2): 175–84. DOI: 10.1121/1.1906875

Plichta, Bartłomiej & Preston, Dennis R. 2005. The /ay/s have it. *Acta Linguistica Hafniensia* 37: 107–30. DOI: 10.1080/03740463.2005.10416086

Preston, Dennis R. 1982. 'Ritin' fowklower daun 'rong: Folklorists' failures in phonology. *Journal of American Folklore* 95(377):304–326. DOI: 10.2307/539912

Preston, Dennis R. 1983. Mowr bad spellun': A reply to Fine. *Journal of American Folklore* 96(381): 330–39. DOI: 10.2307/540949

Preston, Dennis R. 1985a. Southern Indiana perceptions of "Correct" & "Pleasant" speech. In *Methods/Méthodes V, Papers from the Vth International Conference on Methods in Dialectology, University of Victoria, British Columbia*, Henry Warkentyne (ed.), 387–411.

Preston, Dennis R. 1985b. The Li'l Abner syndrome. *American Speech* 60(4): 328–336. DOI: 10.2307/454910

Preston, Dennis R. 1996a. "Whaddayaknow": The modes of folk linguistic awareness. *Language Awareness* 5(1): 40–74. DOI: 10.1080/09658416.1996.9959890

Preston, Dennis R. 1996b. Where the worst English is spoken. In *Focus on the USA* [Varieties of English around the World G16], Edgar Schneider (ed.), 297–360. Amsterdam: John Benjamins.

Preston, Dennis R. (ed.) 1999a. *Handbook of Perceptual Dialectology,* Vol. 1. Amsterdam: John Benjamins. DOI: 10.1075/z.hpd1

Preston, Dennis R. 1999b. A language attitude approach to the perception of regional variety. In Preston (ed.) 1999a, 359–73. DOI: 10.1075/z.hpd1.30pre

Preston, Dennis R. 2000. Mowr & mowr bayud spellin': Confessions of a sociolinguist. *Journal of Sociolinguistics* 4(4): 614–21. DOI: 10.1111/1467-9481.00132

Preston, Dennis R. 2010a. Variation in language regard. In *Variatio delectat: Empirische Evidenzen und theoretische Passungen sprachlicher Variation, für Klaus J. Mattheier zum 65. Geburtstag,* Petre Gilles, Joachim Scharloth & Evelyn Zeigler (eds), 7–27. Frankfurt: Peter Lang.

Preston, Dennis R. 2010b. Language, people, salience, space: Perceptual dialectology & language regard. *Dialectologia* 5: 87–131. ⟨http://www.publicacions.ub.es/revistes/dialectologia5/⟩

Preston, Dennis R. 2013. Linguistic insecurity forty years later. *Journal of English Linguistics* 41: 304–33. DOI: 10.1177/0075424213502810

Preston, Dennis R. To appear. 'Whaddayaknow now?' In *Awareness and Control in Sociolinguistic Research,* Anna Babel (ed.). Cambridge: CUP.

Preston, Dennis R. & Howe, George M. 1987. Computerized generalizations of mental dialect maps. In *Variation in Language: NWAV-XV at Stanford,* Keith M. Denning, Sharon Inkelas, John R. Rickford & Faye McNair-Knox (eds), 361–78. Stanford CA: Department of Linguistics, Stanford University.

Preston, Dennis R. & Niedzielski, Nancy. 2013. Approaches to the study of language regard. In *Language (De)standardisation in Late Modern Europe: Experimental Studies,* Tore Kristiansen & Stefan Grondelaers (eds), 287–307. Oslo: Novus.

Rensink, W.G. 1955[1999]. Dialectindeling naar opgaven van medewerkers. In *Mededelingen der Centrale Commissie voor Onderzoek van het Nederlandse Volkseigen* 7, 20–3. (Translated as 'Informant classification of dialects' in Preston (ed.), 1999a: 3–7).

Rosenberg, Milton J. 1968. Hedonism, inauthenticity, and other goads toward expansion of a consistency theory. In *Theories of Cognitive Consistency,* Robert P. Abelson, Elliot Aronson, William J. McGuire, Theodore M. Newcomb, Milton J. Rosenberg & Percy H. Tanenbaum (eds), 279–349. Chicago IL: Rand-McNally.

Ryan, Ellen Bouchard, Giles, Howard & Sebastian, Richard J. 1982. An integrated perspective for the study of attitudes toward language variation. In *Attitudes towards Language Variation,* Ellen Bouchard Ryan & Howard Giles (eds), 1–19. London: Arnold.

Schmidt, Richard. 1995. Consciousness and foreign language learning: A tutorial on attention and awareness in learning. In *Attention and Awareness in Foreign Language Learning,* Richard Schmidt (ed.), 1–63. Honolulu HI: University of Hawai`i, National Foreign Language Resource Center.

Shuy, Roger W. & Fasold, Ralph W. 1973. *Language Attitudes: Current Trends and Prospects.* Washington DC: Georgetown University Press.

Sibata, Takesi. 1959[1999]. Consciousness of dialect boundaries. In Preston (ed.), 1999a, 39–62. (Translated from Hôgen kyôkai no ishiki. *Gengo Kenkyû* 36: 1–30).

Sibata, Takesi, 1971[1999]. Consciousness of language norms. In *Takesi Sibata: Sociolinguistics in Japanese Contexts,* Tetsuya Kunihiro, Fumio Inoue & Daniel Long (eds), 371–77. Berlin: Mouton de Gruyter. (Prescriptive Consciousness of Language. *Gengo Seikatsu* 236: Special Issue: *Words that Bother Us.*)

Silverstein, Michael, 1981. The limits of awareness. *Sociolinguistic Working Paper* 4. Austin TX: Southwest Educational Development Laboratory.

Stevens, Kenneth N. 2002. Toward a model of lexical access based on acoustic landmarks and distinctive features. *Journal of the Acoustical Society of America* 111(4): 1872–1891. DOI: 10.1121/1.1458026

Trudgill, Peter.1986. *Dialects in Contact.* Oxford: Blackwell.

van Bezooijen, Renée. 2002. Aesthetic evaluations of Dutch: Comparison across dialects, accents, and languages. In *Handbook of Perceptual Dialectology,* Vol. 2, Daniel Long & Dennis R. Preston (eds), 113–130. Amsterdam: John Benjamins. DOI: 10.1075/z.hpd2.07bez

Weijnen, Antonius A. 1946. De grenzen tussen de Oost-Noordbrabantse dialecten onderling (The borders between the dialects of eastern North Brabant). In *Oost-Noordbrabantse dialectproblemen* [Eastern North Brabant dialect problems]. *Bijdragen en Mededelingen der Dialectencommissie van de Koninklijke Nederlandse Akademie van Wettenschappen te Amsterdam* 8, Antonius A. Weijnen, Johannes M. Renders & Jac. van Ginneken (eds), 1–15.

Weinreich, Uriel, Labov, William & Herzog, Marvin I. 1968. Empirical foundations for a theory of linguistic change. In *Directions for Historical Linguistics*, Winifred F. Lehmann & Yakov Malkiel (eds). Austin TX: University of Texas Press.

Wyer, Robert S. Jr. & Albarracín, Dolores. 2005. Belief formation, organization, and change: Cognitive and motivational influences. In Albarracín et al. (eds), 273–322.

REACT – A constructivist theoretic framework for attitudes

Christoph Purschke
University of Luxembourg

This text is devoted to a new theoretical framework for (language) attitudes (REACT) integrating both the traditional idea of attitudes as (more or less) stable) cognitive assessment categories and the constructivist view on attitudes as situated evaluative practices. The text discusses five constitutive elements to the theory (Relevance, Evaluation, Activation, Construction, and Targeting) against the background of respective theories: a theory of actional relevance (cf. Schütz 1970), a listener judgment theory (cf. Purschke 2011), a model for cognitive activation (cf. Kroeber-Riel et al. 2009), a constructivist symbol theory (cf. Cassirer 1953–57 |1923–29|), and a model for attitude functions (cf. Katz 1960). The paper then concludes with proposing an integrative definition of attitudes as evaluation routines in social practices that conforms to the constructivist criticism of classic attitude theory, while at the same time taking account of the fundamental structuring patterns of social interaction that also determine the structure and dynamics of attitudes.

1. Introduction[1]

Since its beginnings the theory of (language) attitudes has evolved around the idea of an attitude representing a (more or less) stable "psychological tendency that is expressed by evaluating a particular entity with some degree of favor or disfavor" (Eagly & Chaiken 1993: 1).[2] Other approaches highlight the observable expression of attitudes in interaction, defining an attitude as "a favorable or unfavorable evaluative reaction toward something or someone, exhibited in one's beliefs, feelings, or intended behavior" (Myers 2006: 36). Alongside this goes the classical trichotomy of dimensions, including affective, cognitive, and behavioral aspects

---

1. A summarizing German version of the theory is presented in Purschke (2014b).

2. See Eagly & Chaiken (2007) for an actualized definition and Allport (1967) or Fishbein & Ajzen (1975) for classical definitions.

DOI 10.1075/impact.39.02pur
© 2015 John Benjamins Publishing Company

of attitudes (cf. Rosenberg & Hovland 1960), as well as the four main functions of attitudes (cf. Katz 1960; Smith et al. 1956; see below 2.5.).[3] Albarracín et al. (2005) gives a comprehensive overview on the state of the art in attitude research.

Going back to Jung's initial definition of attitude as "readiness of the psyche to act or react in a certain way" (Jung, 1971 |1921|: 415), we already find the crucial parameters present that have structured the research on attitudes since then:[4]

> To have an attitude means to be ready for something definite, even though this something is unconscious; for having an attitude is synonymous with an a priori orientation to a definite thing, no matter whether this be represented in consciousness or not. The state of readiness, which I conceive attitude to be, consists in the presence of a certain subjective constellation, a definite combination of psychic factors or contents, which will either determine action in this or that definite direction, or react to an external stimulus in a definite way.
>
> (Jung 1971 |1921|: 415)

Jung's conception directly connects to Brentano's (1995 |1874|) fundamental notion about the intentionality of human consciousness, namely the inherent directedness of the mind toward (environmental or mental) phenomena in the life-world:

> Every mental phenomenon is characterized by what the Scholastics of the Middle Ages called the intentional (or mental) inexistence of an object, and what we might call, though not wholly unambiguously, reference to a content, direction towards an object (which is not to be understood here as meaning a thing), or immanent objectivity. Every mental phenomenon includes something as object within itself, although they do not all do so in the same way. In presentation something is presented, in judgment something is affirmed or denied, in love loved, in hate hated, in desire desired and so on. This intentional in-existence is characteristic exclusively of mental phenomena. No physical phenomenon exhibits anything like it.   (Brentano 1995 |1874|: 88–89)

Following this, attitudes can be understood as intentional psychic reactions toward (mental or environmental) life-world phenomena. As such they can only be deduced indirectly from overt behavior, which is still one of the crucial problems of empirical attitude research (cf. Soukup 2012; Purschke 2015).

Starting from this conception attitude theory has clearly succeeded in defining more precisely the structure, functions, and long-term development of attitudinal reactions, but still it encounters fundamental problems when

---

3.   See Fazio (2000) for a different functional approach.

4.   See Allport (1935) for an early example and Purschke (2015) for a more detailed discussion of basic conceptions of 'attitude' in early psychology.

dealing with the interactional dynamics of attitudes (cf. Gumperz 1982). There-fore constructivist critique of classical attitude research aims at the dynamics of attitudes dependent on contextual and interactional factors (cf. Potter & Wetherell 1987, Silverstein 2003).[5] The main idea behind the constructivist view lies in the conception of attitudes as situational and instable construc-tions in "evaluative practices" (cf. Potter 1998).[6] Or as Soukup (2012: 217) puts it: "In other words, the expression of attitudes is seen as just another human meaning-making activity, similar to, for example, the negotiation of relation-ships in conversational interaction." And although the constructivist critique is crucial for a more adequate understanding of the dynamics of attitudes in practice (cf. Auer & di Luzio 1992; Eckert 2008), it seems to ignore the fact that all symbolic meaning assignment in social practice largely depends on pro-cesses of *structuration* that fundamentally shape human action and therefore human culture (cf. Giddens 1984; Purschke in prep.), namely *routinization* (of practices and evaluation patterns; cf. Giddens 1984), *sedimentation* (of routines in an individual's stock of knowledge; cf. Schütz 1970),[7] *synchronization* (of knowledge between interacting selves; cf. Schmidt & Herrgen 2011), *fixation* (of practices on specific structures in the life-world; cf. Simmel 1903), *tradition* (i.e. the passing on of cultural practices with specific rules and meanings; cf. Hall 1997),[8] and *hierarchization* (of practices, rules and meanings; cf. Bourdieu 1977).[9] Thus it seems only natural to merge the evidence from both theoretical views on the formation and structure of attitudes. Doing so holds some promise for the conceptualization of attitudes as situated constructions (or reconstruc-tions) of symbolic meaning – covering the constructivist side – that are stored in the individual's "stock of knowledge at hand" (cf. Schütz 1970) and shaped as evaluation routines in the individual's life-world orientation – upholding many aspects of classical attitude research.

---

5.   See also Markard (1984) for a fundamental critique.

6.   See Cunningham et al. (2007) and van Bavel et al. (2012) for another interactional constructivist approach that focuses on the iterative reprocessing of phenomenon-related evaluations in interaction.

7.   *Sedimentation* is a term used by Schütz (1970) to illustrate the way experiences are dispos-ited in the memory system during action.

8.   See also Hobsbawm (1983) for the term "invented tradition", describing the establishment of a new practice in a social context via rules and symbolic forms by linking it to its prior expressions within the same social group.

9.   Purschke (in prep.) discusses these six processes of structuration within the context of a comprehensive theory of cognition, communication, and culture.

2.   REACT – Attitudes as evaluation routines in social practices

The present text tries to conform to the constructivist criticism of classic attitude theory, while not ignoring the fundamental structuring patterns of social interaction that also govern the structure and dynamics of attitudes. As a consequence, a new theoretical framework – *REACT* – for attitudes is explored, that builds on evidence from sociology and psychology as well as from cultural philosophy and constructivism, leading to a new definition of attitudes as evaluation routines in social practices.[10] The structure of the text follows the five central elements of REACT, namely *Relevance, Evaluation, Activation, Construction,* and *Targeting,* with each section discussing one theoretical assumption against the background of theories connected to that assumption.

2.1   Relevance: Attitudes are relevance-driven sedimentations in the stock of knowledge

The first assumption directly leads to the relevance theory by Alfred Schütz that stands at the very center of his highly influential sociological theory of the life-world (cf. Schütz & Luckmann 1973, 1989). Although the problem of relevance is crucial to the understanding of his theory, Schütz never wrote a comprehensive account of it, except for the unfinished manuscript *Reflections on the Problem of Relevance* (Schütz 1970).[11] In this theory Schütz develops a system of three highly interdependent types of relevance that define the evaluational background of action planning, including perceptual, cognitive, and projective aspects of judgments.[12]

First, *topical* (or *thematic*) *relevance* reflects the salience-based (*imposed relevance*) and attention-based (*intrinsic relevance*) concentrations on experiential content, thus reflecting the perceptual aspect of judgments (cf. Schütz 1970: 26–35).

---

10.   Given the long tradition of attitude research this attempt inevitably builds on a lot of previous work that deals with the formation and structure of attitudes against the background of social practices, although the sociological and philosophical foundations of the present approach seem to be unmatched in the existing literature. For a different tracing of the cognitive organization in an attitudinal response see Preston (2011) for example; for a socio-semiotic approach to indexicalization of life-world phenomena see Silverstein (1981) for example.

11.   See also Schütz & Luckmann (1973: 182–242).

12.   In doing so he builds on ideas of Bergson (1896). The term *projective* is set out to cover all types of knowledge externalization, be they linguistic, gestural, or artistic. See Purschke (2011, 55–57) for a discussion.

Second, *interpretative relevance* describes the (highly) routinized or attentive interpretation and evaluation of experiential content,[13] thus covering the cognitive aspect of judgments (cf. Schütz 1970: 35–45).[14] And third, *motivational relevance* contains "the chain of motivations determined by the project for future action" as well as "the biographical 'attitude' determined by sedimented motives" (Schütz & Luckmann 1973: 209), thus defining the projective aspect of judgments in the planning of action (cf. Schütz 1970: 45–52).[15]

All three types of relevance have to be seen as closely intertwined aspects of judgments about life-world phenomena.[16] As such, they define the relevance-driven shape of action planning, with attitude expression being one type of relevance-driven action. As for the first assumption, Schütz (1970: 53–74; see also Schütz & Luckmann 1973: 223–229) develops a six-step model that outlines the relevance-based shape of judgments about experiential content in action planning:[17]

> Strictly speaking, one must distinguish the following levels of operation for the interdependent relevance structures. *First*, the thematic relevances which in connection with the structures of interpretative and motivational relevance determine the originary constitution of an experience. *Second*, the motivational relevances which in connection with the structures of the thematic and interpretative kinds can make an experience problematic. *Third*, the interpretative relevances which in connection with the structures of thematic and motivational relevance determine the 'direction' of the processes of explication. *Fourth*, the motivational relevances which in connection with the structures of the

---

13.   This distinction, which originates in the work of William James (1890), is systematically elaborated in the theory of judgment by Kahnemann (2011).

14.   This strict distinction between perception and cognition primarily serves the purpose of descriptive precision, but can also be justified from a judgment-theoretic viewpoint: perception means realizing a problem, cognition means getting to a solution. See Purschke (2011) for a discussion.

15.   In this chapter Schütz also introduces his famous distinction of "in-order-to and because motives" (Schütz 1970: 45), that are directly linked to the two defining aspects of motivational relevance: "Whereas the in-order-to relevances motivationally emanate from the already established paramount project, the because relevances deal with the motivation for the establishment of the paramount project itself." (Schütz 1970: 50)

16.   See Schütz & Luckmann (1973: 208) and Purschke (2014a) for a detailed discussion.

17.   "The interrelationships among the types of relevances should not be taken as chronological, that 'first' the one, 'then' the other, 'then' the last type becomes established. All three types are concretely experienced as inseparable, or at least as an undivided unity, and their dissection from experience into three types is the result of an analysis of their constitutive origin." (Schütz 1970: 66)

interpretative and thematic relevance cause the conclusion or discontinuance of the processes of explication. *Fifth*, the three mutually interdependent relevance aspects not 'devalued' in the course of explication which guide the sedimentation of the result of the explication in the structure of the stock of knowledge. *Sixth*, the relevance structures which bring out the application of the sedimented element of knowledge in the mastery of new actually present situations.

(Schütz & Luckmann 1973: 228)

As we can see from this, attitudes (understood as a constitutive element of motivational relevance) play a crucial role for the question of why (*Second* above) and to what end (*Fourth* above) we evaluate experiential content in the course of action. Still, they are not the sole aspect of action-related relevance that constitutes the evaluation of experiential content as a whole. Especially when considering the fact that we are not goldfish-like evaluators (i.e. we do not forget every single evaluation we have made due to memory constraints),[18] it becomes apparent that relevance-based evaluations sediment in the individual's stock of knowledge, thus becoming a "habitual possession of certain motives, latent for the time being but always ready to be actualized" (Schütz 1970: 54) as an effect of routinization processes (see 2.2). In this regard, an attitude can be seen as

a potential set of typical expectations to be actualized under typical circumstances leading to typical reactions or [...] to the building up of a paramount project of possible action involving the whole chain of in-order-to motives relating to the carrying out of the paramount project as, if, and when needed.

(Schütz 1970: 54)

In conclusion we can state that according to Schütz's theory of relevance, attitudes are in fact relevance-driven evaluation patterns that sediment in the individual's stock of knowledge and can be actualized at any time needed.

2.2   Evaluation: Attitudes are routinized evaluations of life-world phenomena

Explicitly building on Schütz's action-theoretic approach to relevance, Purschke (2011) carries forward the idea of a relevance-driven theory of judgment to his *listener judgment theory*. Grounded in evidence from perceptual psychology, this theory sets out to explain the internal structure of listener judgments about life-world phenomena (e.g. regional linguistic variation) by dint of judgment-theoretic and socio-pragmatic aspects of action. The key subject of such a perception-based

---

18.   Actually, feeding experiments with goldfish by Gee et al. (1994) indicate that even goldfish dispose of a trainable memory, so that the goldfish-metaphor might be nothing more than a myth.

approach consists in listener judgments about language understood as constitutive element of social practice. Consequently Purschke (2011:75) defines listener judgments as complexly shaped processes of evaluation about phenomena in the life-world dependent on situational, perceptual, cognitive, and projective aspects.[19] Starting from this definition Purschke (2011:80–87 and 307–310) identifies two fundamental categories of listener judgments that reflect the two constitutive elements of judgments about experiential content: the perception of conspicuous phenomena on the one hand (= *salience*) and the evaluation of the subjective life-world relevance of such phenomena (= *pertinence*) on the other hand.[20]

In this regard salience can be defined as the contextual conspicuity listeners attach to the usage of speech phenomena as a result of processes of perception. As such, salient phenomena differ from the individual's situational norm horizon, and that insofar as phenomenon-specific features become conspicuous to a listener contingent on listener-specific and contextual parameters (cf. Purschke 2011:84). But since the perception of salient phenomena alone doesn't allow for conclusions about the socio-pragmatic (symbolic) meaning of these phenomena, it is necessary that listeners evaluate salient phenomena to be subjectively relevant for their purposes in practice by granting them a specific situational significance. For this type of relevance, Purschke (2011:87) uses the term pertinence. Thus, pertinence is operationalized as the subjective relevance listeners attach to the usage of salient speech phenomena as a result of processes of cognition. As such pertinent phenomena form the precondition for the reevaluation of the individual's knowledge and action, and that insofar as contextual characteristics are judged to be relevant by a listener contingent on phenomenon-specific and listener-specific parameters. As against Schütz's system of relevances pertinence has the status of an umbrella term: it can also be defined as the sum of active subjective relevance structures in a specific context of action.

Building upon Schütz's action-theoretic six-step-model of relevance processing Purschke (2011:85–86 & 2014) develops a theory of judgment deductive scheme in order to explicate the role of salience and pertinence as fundamental categories and crucial evaluational substeps of listener judgments in the context of socio-pragmatic meaning construction (Table 1).

---

19. See Purschke (2011:45–87) for a detailed discussion of the comprehensive theoretical framework.

20. See Purschke (2014a) for a detailed discussion of (judgment-)theoretic aspects of salience and pertinence.

Table 1. Schematic structure of listener judgments based on salience and pertinence processing

A. Salience processing
    1. Categorization of the *perceptual distinctness*
       Perceptual evaluation of the salience of a stimulus with respect to the category
       conspicuous/inconspicuous

B. Pertinence processing
    2. Categorization of the *interactional acceptability*
       Cognitive evaluation of the problematicity of a salient stimulus with respect to
       categories like *comprehensible/incomprehensible* and *familiar/unfamiliar*
    3. Categorization of the *situational significance*
       Cognitive evaluation of the situational remarkableness of an (in)acceptable stimulus
       with respect to categories like *typical/untypical, appropriate /inappropriate,* or *decisive/
       indecisive*
    4. Evaluation of the *pertinence*
       Cognitive evaluation of the subjective relevance of a significant stimulus with respect
       to the category *relevant/irrelevant*

C. Consequence processing
    5. *Sedimentation* in the stock of knowledge (by modification or stabilization)
    6. *Application* in the course of action (continuity or discontinuity)

The starting point of listener judgments consists in the perception of (linguistic) phenomena that have to be processed with respect to (at least) three evaluation criteria – distinctness, acceptability, and significance – leading to a concluding pertinence evaluation that essentially impacts the further course of action. So the relationship of pertinence and salience is complementary: The outcome of perception processes consists in the salience that listeners attach to linguistic phenomena, while the outcome of cognitive evaluation processes relating to these consists in the pertinence that listeners assign to these phenomena related to the modification or stabilization of the stock of knowledge.

As for the second assumption, we can now state that attitudes are (conscious or unconscious) evaluations of life-world phenomena. As such, they sediment in the individual's stock of knowledge. Given the fact that in everyday-life we encounter numerous recurrent phenomena that lead to such evaluations, we also have to account for the role of routinization in the formation of attitudes. While at the very first encounter with a specific phenomenon the individual might have to build an attitude towards it (see 2.4), the next time he/she encounters the very same phenomenon he/she already can refer to the sedimented evaluation pattern in his/her stock of knowledge, thus actualizing it – and this goes on with every new corresponding evaluation he/she has to make. Such habitualization of judgments about specific life-world phenomena is reflected in the concept of *routinization* mentioned above.

The concept of *routinization*, as grounded in practical consciousness, is vital to the theory of structuration. Routine is integral both to the continuity of the personality of the agent, as he or she moves along the paths of daily activities, and to the institutions of society, which *are* such only through their continued reproduction.   (Giddens 1984:60)

It is by sedimentation that we store the outcome of evaluation processes in our stock of knowledge, and by routinization we structure these sedimentations leading to habitual evaluation patterns we can call attitudes.

2.3   Activation: Attitudes demand a high level of cognitive activation

Given the fact that in everyday-life judgments normally are not emotionless logical assessments, a theoretical framework for attitudes also has to deal with the affective core of such evaluations. Out of the many available, the concept of activation levels as developed by Kroeber-Riel et al. (2009) seems to fit well into the constructivist approach taken here. Basically, *activation* covers all processes of psychophysical excitation that give rise to the individual's readiness for action. *Tonic activation* determines the long-lasting alertness and general performance ability, whereas *phasic activation* describes the short-term variation in activation that indicates the specific performance ability of the individual when reacting to a given stimulus. Phasic activation is closely linked to the concept of selective attention (cf. Kroeber-Riel et al. 2009:60–61).[21]

The authors then distinguish between three ascending levels of activation covering different aspects of emotional involvement (cf. Kroeber-Riel et al. 2009:59): An *emotion* is defined as *central nervous arousal pattern + cognitive interpretation,* a *motivation* then consists of an *emotion + cognitive targeting,* and finally an *attitude* is a *motivation + cognitive evaluation.* As for the third assumption, this trichotomy serves two functions: First, it sheds light on the emotional core of attitudes as well as on the contribution of motivational relevance to evaluations. And second, it mirrors the three common components of attitudes without claiming a clear-cut distinction between the affective, cognitive, and behavioral dimension (cf. Rosenberg & Hovland 1960), so that we can conclude that attitudes imply a high level of activation.[22] As such, they consist of cognitively reshaped emotion patterns in relation to an object of evaluation emerging from the action situation.

---

21.   See also Pfaff (2006).

22.   With this said, there seems to be a certain tension between the concepts of routinization and activation within the REACT framework: The routinization of judgment processes normally leads to a lower level of cognitive activation needed during processing (cf. Eysenck

2.4   Construction: Attitudes are situated (re-)constructions of symbolic meaning

This assumption, the constructivist view on attitudes, directly leads to basic problems of culture theory, and a theory of cognition that cannot be treated in principle at this point.[23] The theoretical approach taken here essentially originates from the highly influential *Philosophy of Symbolic Forms* developed by Ernst Cassirer, that – like many influential philosophers and theorists in the 20th century (e.g. Schütz) – builds on Husserl's (1982 |1913|) phenomenology. The main claim of Cassirer emerges from the idea that reality ('Wirklichkeit') as experienced by the self is not merely a product of passive perception, but rather of construction in action ('Tun'). "It is not mere meditation but action which constitutes the center from which man undertakes the spiritual organization of reality." (Cassirer 1953–57 |1923–29|: II 157). For Cassirer, action – in the sense of shaping, constructing – is the defining root of all human existence. Concerning perception this basically means that every act of perception already is of a constructive kind, because an act of perspectivation, i.e. the dissociation of focal perceptual content, is already inherent to it.

Then, there is the core mechanism of all human action in the construction of reality: *symbolic pregnance*. "By symbolic pregnance we mean the way in which a perception as a sensory experience contains at the same time a certain nonintuitive meaning which it immediately and concretely repesents." (Cassirer 1953–57 |1923–29|: III 202). The act of relating a specific sensual experience to a nonintuitive meaning is what we can call *symbolization*. Following Cassirer's idea, every aspect of human action is structured by such symbolic relations, leading to a multitude of different *symbolic forms* (e.g. myth, language, or science).[24] Thus symbolization does not only include the (perceptual, cognitive, or projective) shaping of phenomena, but also gives meaning to these phenomena. And this, the construction of symbolic forms in action for Cassirer is the defining root of human culture.

The consequence of this for the understanding of attitudes is that we have to conceptualize every single judgment listeners make (e.g. about linguistic

---

1982). Still, that doesn't affect the basic structure of attitudinal judgments as related to the two subprocesses.

23.   See Purschke (in prep.) for a detailed discussion.

24.   "Under a 'symbolic form' should be understood each energy of spirit through which a spiritual content or meaning is connected with a concrete, sensory sign and is internally adapted to this sign." (translation in Bayer 2001: 15) ["Unter einer 'symbolischen Form' soll jene Energie des Geistes verstanden werden, durch welche ein geistiger Bedeutungsgehalt an ein konkretes sinnliches Zeichen geknüpft und diesem innerlich zugeeignet wird." (Cassirer 1923 |1910|: 15)]

phenomena) as acts of symbolic meaning construction. But since in most cases these judgments do not concern the primary function of language – communication –, we are dealing with a second-order indexical meaning of linguistic variation here (cf. Silverstein 2003), one that carries specific social meaning (cf. Eckert 2008). Purschke (2014a, 43–45) calls the product of this practical construction of second-order social meaning *socio-pragmatic indexicality*.

So as for the fourth assumption we can now state that attitudes are (routinized) acts of symbolization (i.e. the attachment of second-order indexical meaning to phenomena) that are constructed in interaction. Since the outcomes of such acts of symbolization sediment in the individual's stock of knowledge, they do not have to be constructed from scratch each time; instead they are merely reconstructed from the stock of knowledge, leading to an actualization (modification or stabilization) of the corresponding evaluation routine.

2.5   Targeting: Attitudes serve specific targeting functions for the life-world-orientation toward goals of action

The last assumption concerns the specific functions attitudes serve for the individual alongside their relevance-based and activation-driven construction and structuration. According to Katz (1960: 170) there are four major functions that focus on different aspects of self-organization and social positioning of the individual: "the instrumental, adjustive, or utilitarian function", "the ego-defensive function", "the value expression function", and "the knowledge function". Katz's typology of functions is well established and covers the main structuring domains of the life-world from the perspective of the self, so that for REACT we can maintain the four-functions-model. Yet we have to adjust the structural perspective on these attitudinal domains, since REACT is all about the practical construction of evaluational responses to life-world phenomena. So while keeping up the four dimensions, we need to reshape them from a constructivist and action-theoretic viewpoint.

As for the adjustment function, it is primarily

> a recognition of the fact that people strive to maximize the rewards in their external environment and to minimize the penalties. [...] Attitudes acquired in the service of the adjustment function are either the means for reaching the desired goal or avoiding the undesirable one, or are affective associations based upon experiences in attaining motive satisfactions.   Katz (1960: 170–71)

Since the main objective of REACT is to provide a theoretical framework for the practical construction of attitudes in interaction, namely the intentional pursuit of specific purposes by dint of appropriate means, in line with the culturalist theory of action (cf. Hartmann 1996),[25] this function shall be named the *pragmatic intention function* of attitudes.

The ego-defensive function deals with the perceptual and evaluational routines the individual develops in order to maintain a consistent self-image. "They include the devices by which the individual avoids facing either the inner reality of the kind of person he is, or the outer reality of the dangers the world holds for him." (Katz 1960:172). Since it focuses on the construction and continuance of the self, this function shall be named the *self-maintenance function* of attitudes.

The value-expression function has

> the function of giving positive expression to his central values and to the type of person he conceives himself to be. [...] The reward to the person in these instances is not so much a matter of gaining social recognition or monetary rewards as of establishing his self-identity and confirming his notion of the sort of person he sees himself to be.   Katz (1960:173)

Since it is mainly concerned with ego-expression and the socio-symbolic meaning of action, this function shall be named the *social identity function* of attitudes.

Last, the knowledge or cognitive orientation function according to Katz (1960:170) is

> based upon the individual's need to give adequate structure to his universe. The search for meaning, the need to understand, the trend toward better organization of perceptions and beliefs to provide clarity and consistency for the individual.

All these examples directly reflect Cassirer's idea of how the self organizes reality by dint of symbolic forms constructed by assigning meaning to phenomena. Thus, this function shall be named the *symbolic structuring function* of attitudes.

With these four functions of attitudes – self-maintenance, symbolic structuring, pragmatic intention, and social identity – it is now possible to differentiate all relevant attitudinal targeting domains that structure the way attitudes impact action: the self, the life-world, the intentional core and the socio-symbolic meaning of action.

3.   Consolidation – a pragmatic constructivist definition of attitude

As a last point, we can now combine the evidence from all five assumptions, leading to a new definition of attitudes as evaluational routines in social practices within the framework of REACT:

---

25.   An (actualized) English version of the culturalist theory of action can be found in Kasper (2015).

- *Relevance*: First, the analysis of Schütz's theory of relevance has shown that attitudes originate from complex relevance structures in practice, that sediment in the individual's stock of knowledge.
- *Evaluation*: Second, according to Purschke's listener judgment theory attitudes can be seen as routinized evaluations of life-world phenomena.
- *Activation*: Third, the examination of different levels of activation prompts the conclusion that attitudes are high-level activation constructs grounded in emotional and motivational processes.
- *Construction*: Fourth, in line with Cassirer's idea of symbolic forms, we provided evidence for the constructive nature of attitudes as (re)constructions of symbolic meaning in interaction.
- *Targeting*: Fifth, Katz's typology of functions of attitudes, reshaped against the background of constructivism, has proven successful in order to qualify the main targeting domains of attitudes.

As a consequence, the definition of attitude within the REACT theoretical framework is as follows: *Attitudes are relevance-driven targeting and evaluation routines on a high level of activation that sediment in an individual's stock of knowledge and are situationally (re)constructed in interaction.* As such, attitudes are mental constructs (cf. Brentano 1995 |1874|), so that they cannot be measured directly, but only indirectly via explicit reactions towards life-world phenomena.[26]

Starting from this definition, a lot of work still needs to be done in order to specify the quality and interrelationship between the five discussed dimensions to the theory. Also the prognostic strength of the theoretic assumptions has to be tested in empirical studies, especially regarding the interactional dynamics of attitudes as well as the "attitude-behavior-link" (cf. Soukup 2012). Nonetheless the framework has already proven fruitful for the analysis of the (socio-)psychological, action-theoretic, and philosophical nature of attitudes, especially when taking into account constructivist criticism of the classical socio-psychological attitude research without neglecting the achievements of the latter.

Building on the theoretical evidence from REACT, Purschke (2014b) discusses methodological consequences for a quantitative approach to attitude research within the context of a new attitude measurement experiment. The basic idea of this approach is strictly in line with the theoretical assumptions discussed in the present text: While the experiment uses common 7-point rating-scales for the quantification of the judgments, the statements to be judged are constructed

---

26. Direct observable *externalizations* of evaluative reactions are rather seldom in social practice. Jaffe (2013, 1) discusses such externalizations of attitudes in the context of communicative interaction under the term *stancetaking* ("taking up a position with respect to the form of or the content of one's utterance").

in a way that directly reflects the evaluative practice of everyday-life, implementing situations that individuals encounter and evaluate in the life-world (e.g. "The news presenters in nation-wide television should speak Standard German."). As a consequence, in most cases respondents will already have prior experience with the type of judgment to be made, so that they only need to reconstruct the corresponding attitude from their stock of knowledge, while for most other quantitative experiments, this is not the case (e.g. the highly problematic adjective pairs items used in the semantic differential).

Another aspect related to REACT theory concerns an adequate action-theoretic embedding of the (judgment-)theoretical assumptions made in the present text. Since the main idea behind REACT theory consists in a strict orientation of theoretical statements (and experimental designs) to social practice in the life-world, a comprehensive framework for attitudes needs to be clear about the (often disputed) connection between attitudes and action. Purschke (2015) discusses this connection against the background of culturalist theory of action (cf. Hartmann 1996), resulting in an additional characterization of attitudes as routinized cognitive action schemes (preparing or accompanying the actualization of observable actions) that (a) establish or maintain the action ability of the individual and (b) indicate suitable means for the achievement of purposes.

Subject to the results of empirical studies, it can already be stated that REACT theory, in line with its new approach to the experimental study of (language) attitudes and action-theoretic embedding, provides a comprehensive and strictly practice-oriented framework for attitude research that integrates the classic understanding of attitudes originating from early psychology with the constructivist critique of the latter, thus presenting a viable solution for the ongoing discussion about attitudes.

References

Albarracín, Dolores, Johnson, Blair T. & Zanna, Mark P. (eds). 2005. *The Handbook of Attitudes.* Mawah NJ: Lawrence Erlbaum Associates.

Allport, Gordon. 1935. Attitudes. In *A Handbook of Social Psychology*, Carl Murchison (ed.), 789–844. Worcester MA: Clark University Press.

Allport, Gordon. 1967. Attitudes. In *Readings in Attitude, Theory and Measurement*, Martin Fishbein (ed.), 1–13. New York NY: Wiley & Sons.

Auer, Peter & di Luzio, Aldo (eds). 1992. *The Contextualization of Language* [Pragmatics & Beyond New Series 22]. Amsterdam: John Benjamins. DOI: 10.1075/pbns.22

Bayer, Thora Hin. 2001. *Cassirer's Metaphysics of Symbolic Forms. A Philosophical Commentary.* New Haven CT: Yale University Press. DOI: 10.12987/yale/9780300083316.001.0001

Bergson, Henri. 1896. *Matière et mémoire. Essai sur la relation du corps à l'esprit.* Paris: F. Alcan.

Bourdieu, Pierre. 1977. *Outline of a Theory of Practice*. Cambridge: CUP. DOI: 10.1017/CBO9780511812507

Brentano, Franz. 1995[1874]. *Psychology from an Empirical Standpoint*. London: Routledge.

Cassirer, Ernst. 1953–57[1923–29]. *Philosophy of Symbolic Forms*, 3 Vols. New Haven CT: Yale University Press.

Cassirer, Ernst. 1923[1910]. Der Begriff der symbolischen Form im Aufbau der Geisteswissenschaften. In *Vorträge der der Bibliothek Warburg*, Vol. 1, Friedrich Saxl (ed.), 11–39. Leipzig: Winter.

Cunningham, William, Zelazo, Philip David, Packer, Dominic J. & Van Bavel, Jay J. 2007. The iterative reprocessing model: A multilevel framework for attitudes and behavior. *Social Cognition* 25(5): 736–760. DOI: 10.1521/soco.2007.25.5.736

Eagly, Alice & Chaiken, Shelly. 1993. *The Psychology of Attitudes*. Fort Worth TX: Harcourt Brace & Company.

Eagly, Alice & Chaiken, Shelly. 2007. The advantages of an inclusive definition of attitude. *Social Cognition* 25(5): 582–602. DOI: 10.1521/soco.2007.25.5.582

Eckert, Penelope. 2008. Variation and the indexical field. *Journal of Sociolinguistics* 12(4): 453–476. DOI: 10.1111/j.1467-9841.2008.00374.x

Eysenck, Michael. 1982. *Attention and Arousal. Cognition and Performance*. Berlin: Springer. DOI: 10.1007/978-3-642-68390-9

Fazio, Russel H. 2000. Accessible attitudes as tools for object appraisal: Their costs and benefits. In *Why We Evaluate: Functions of Attitudes*, Gregory Maio & James Olson (eds), 1–36. Mahwah NJ: Lawrence Erlbaum Associates.

Fishbein, Martin & Ajzen, Icek. 1975. *Belief, Attitude, Intention, and Behavior: An Introduction to Theory and Research*. Reading MA:Addison-Wesley.

Gee, Philip, Stephensen, David & Wright, Donald E. 1994. Temporal discrimination learning of operant feeding in goldfish (*Carassius auratus*). *Journal of Experimental Analysis of Behavior* 62: 1–13. DOI: 10.1901/jeab.1994.62-1

Giddens, Anthony. 1984. *The Constitution of Society. Outline of the Theory of Structuration*. Cambridge: CUP.

Gumperz, John. 1982. *Discourse Strategies*. Cambridge: CUP. DOI: 10.1017/CBO9780511611834

Hall, Stuart. 1997. *Representation: Cultural Representations and Signifying Practices*. London: Sage.

Hartmann, Dirk. 1996. Kulturalistische Handlungstheorie. In *Methodischer Kulturalismus – Zwischen Naturalismus und Postmoderne*, Dirk Hartmann & Peter Janich (eds), 70–114. Frankfurt: Suhrkamp.

Hobsbawm, Eric. 1983. Introduction: Inventing traditions. In *The Invention of Tradition*, Eric Hobsbawm & Terence Ranger (eds), 1–14. Cambridge: CUP.

Husserl, Edmund 1982[1913]. *Ideas Pertaining to a Pure Phenomenology and to a Phenomenological Philosophy – First Book: General Introduction to a Pure Phenomenology*. Translated by Fred Kersten. The Hague: Springer.

Jaffe, Alexandra. 2013. Introduction. In *Stance: Sociolinguistic Perspectives*, Alexandra Jaffe (ed.), 1–28. Oxford: OUP.

James, William. 1890. *The Principles of Psychology*, 2 Vols. New York NY: Henry Holt & Company. DOI: 10.1037/11059-000

Jung, Carl. 1971[1921]. *Psychological Types* [The collected works of C. G. Jung 6]. Princeton NJ: Princeton University Press.

Kahnemann, Daniel. 2011. *Thinking, Fast and Slow.* New York NY: Farrar, Straus & Giroux.

Kasper, Simon. 2015. *Instruction Grammar. From Perception via Grammar to Action* [Trends in Linguistics: Studies and Monographs 293]. Berlin/Boston: de Gruyter.

Katz, Daniel. 1960. The functional approach to the study of attitudes. *Public Opinion Quarterly* 24: 163–204. DOI: 10.1086/266945

Kroeber-Riel, Werner, Weinberg, Peter & Gröppel-Klein, Andrea. 2009. *Konsumentenverhalten,* 9th edn. München: Vahlen.

Markard, Morus. 1984. *Einstellung. Kritik eines sozialpsychologischen Grundkonzepts.* Frankfurt: Campus.

Myers, David. 2006. *Social Psychology,* 9th edn. New York NY: Basic Books.

Pfaff, Donald. 2006. *Brain Arousal and Information Theory: Neural and Genetic Mechanisms.* Cambridge MA: Harvard University Press. DOI: 10.4159/9780674042100

Potter, Jonathan. 1998. Discursive social psychology: From attitudes to evaluative practices. *European Review of Social Psychology* 9(1): 233–66. DOI: 10.1080/14792779843000090

Potter, Jonathan & Wetherell, Margaret. 1987. *Discourse and Social Psychology: Beyond Attitudes and Behaviour.* London: Sage.

Preston, Dennis R. 2011. The power of language regard – Discrimination, classification, comprehension and production. *Dialectologia* 2: 9–33. Special issue, *Production, Perception and Attitude,* John Nerbonne, Stefan Grondelaers & Dirk Speelman (eds).

Purschke, Christoph. 2011. *Regionalsprache und Hörerurteil. Grundzüge einer perzeptiven Variationslinguistik* [Zeitschrift für Dialektologie und Linguistik. Beihefte 149]. Stuttgart: Steiner.

Purschke, Christoph. 2015. Das Holz, die Axt, der Hieb. Über den Zusammenhang von Einstellung und Handeln am Beispiel des Handlungsschemas 'Holz hacken.' In *Sprache, Literatur, Raum. Festgabe für Willy Diercks,* Robert Langhanke (ed.), 145–162. Bielefeld: Verlag für Regionalgeschichte.

Purschke, Christoph. 2014a. "I remember it like it was interesting." Zur Theorie von Salienz und Pertinenz. In *Die Vermessung der Salienz(forschung),* Helen Christen & Evelyn Ziegler (eds). *Linguistik Online* 66: 31–50.

Purschke, Christoph. 2014b. REACT – Einstellungen als evaluative Routinen in sozialen Praxen. In *Sprechen über Sprache: Perspektiven und neue Methoden der linguistischen Einstellungsforschung,* Christina Cuonz & Rebekka Studler (eds), 123–142. Tübingen: Stauffenberg.

Purschke, Christoph. In preparation. Kognition, Kommunikation, Kultur – Eine Philosophie der Selbstbehauptung. Habilitation, University of Luxemburg.

Rosenberg, Milton & Hovland, Carl. 1960. Cognitive, affective, and behavioral components in attitudes. In *Attitude Organization and Change: An Analysis of Consistency among Attitude Components,* Carl Hovland & Milton Rosenberg (eds), 1–14. New Haven CT: Yale University Press.

Schmidt, Jürgen Erich & Herrgen, Joachim. 2011. *Sprachdynamik. Eine Einführung in die moderne Regionalsprachenforschung.* Berlin: Erich Schmidt.

Schütz, Alfred. 1970. *Reflections on the Problem of Relevance,* edited, annotated, and with an introduction by Richard Zaner. New Haven CT: Yale University Press.

Schütz, Alfred & Luckmann, Thomas. 1973. *The Structures of the Life-world,* Vol. 1. Evanston IL: Northwestern University Press.

Schütz, Alfred & Luckmann, Thomas. 1989. *The Structures of the Life-world,* Vol. 2. Evanston IL: Northwestern University Press.

Simmel, Georg. 1903. Soziologie des Raumes. *Jahrbuch für Gesetzgebung, Verwaltung und Volkswirtschaft im Deutschen Reich* 27(1): 27–71.

Silverstein, Michael. 1981. *The Limits of Awareness* [Sociolinguistic Working Paper 84]. Austin TX: ERIC.

Silverstein, Michael. 2003. Indexical order and the dialectics of sociolinguistic life. *Language & Communication* 23: 193–229. DOI: 10.1016/S0271-5309(03)00013-2

Smith, Brewster, Bruner, Jerome S. & White, Robert W. 1956. *Opinions and Personality*. New York NY: Wiley & Sons.

Soukup, Barbara. 2012. Current issues in the social psychological study of 'language attitudes': Constructionism, context, and the attitude-behavior link. *Language and Linguistics Compass* 6(4): 212–224. DOI: 10.1002/lnc3.332

van Bavel, Jay J., Xi, Jenny Xiao & Cunningham, William A. 2012. Evaluation is a dynamic process: Moving beyond dual systems models. *Social and Personality Psychology Compass* 6(6): 438–454. DOI: 10.1111/j.1751-9004.2012.00438.x

Mixing methods in the study of language attitudes

Theory and application

Barbara Soukup
University of Vienna

Mixed methods research (MMR) is currently on the rise in the social sciences. This paper provides a theoretical discussion and a practical illustration of MMR in the social psychological study of language attitudes. First, I review perceived obstacles to MMR - in particular, the 'incompatibility thesis', whereby quantitative and qualitative methods are assumed to clash epistemologically. I propose an alternative account by which QUAL and QUAN research on language attitudes can be integrated on a common theoretical basis that holds attitudes to constitute interactionally processed 'human epistemological constructs' (HECs). I apply this approach in MMR on Austrian German, where I integrate a QUAL analysis of language-attitudinal HECs found in discourse data with a QUAN speaker evaluation experiment designed to corroborate the QUAL exegesis.

1.   Introduction[1]

As the 21st century advances, social sciences research that integrates both qualitative and quantitative methods of data collection and analysis (i.e. what is commonly referred to as 'mixed methods research' – MMR) is gaining considerable ground. This is attested, for example, in the foundation of a new *Journal of Mixed Methods Research* in 2007 (see Tashakkori & Creswell 2007) and a host of recent (re-)editions and monographs (e.g. Bergmann 2008; Tashakkori & Teddlie 2010; Creswell & Plano Clark 2011; Kuckartz 2014; Morgan 2014). The central purpose, interest, and contribution of MMR lie in generating a deeper understanding of complex and multidimensional phenomena through approaching them

---

1.   I very cordially thank Nikolas Coupland, Alexei Prikhodkine, and Henry Widdowson for their insightful and inspiring feedback on an earlier version of this paper. I am, of course, responsible for all remaining shortcomings.

DOI 10.1075/impact.39.03sou
© 2015 John Benjamins Publishing Company

from different perspectives that can complement each other in meaningful ways (Bryman 2006; Creswell & Zhang 2009; Teddlie & Tashakkori 2010; Kuckartz 2014). Miles and Huberman (1994:310), for example, exhort their readers to "entertain" MMR under the argument of

> avoiding polarization, polemics, and life at the extremes. Quantitative and qualitative inquiry can support and inform each other. Narratives and variable-driven analyses need to interpenetrate and inform each other. [...] Think of it as hybrid vigor.

In this vein, MMR is also an important avenue in the social psychological study of language attitudes. Yet, here, the progress of methods mixing appears to be particularly hampered by an assumption that continues to challenge MMR at large (see Bryman 2007): the assumption that quantitative and qualitative research operate on entirely different sides of a fundamental epistemological and ontological divide.

In this contribution, I begin by reviewing this assumption and its implications in general as well as in the context of language attitude study. Then, I propose a theory of (language) attitudes that can arguably overcome the issue by providing a shared, common epistemological basis for integrating quantitative and qualitative research. I subsequently apply my argumentation in a study on the social meanings of varieties of Austrian German which aligns data, analyses, and findings of both kinds – QUAL and QUAN (to be represented by speaker evaluation and interaction analytic approaches respectively).[2] Thus, I aim to provide on the one hand a theoretical foundation for mixed methods research in the social psychological study of language attitudes, and on the other hand a practical example of it. The goal is to boost such research down the line, in the conviction that it is only through integrating a variety of methods that we can maximally account for the inherent variability, complexity, and multidimensionality, but also for the real-life manifestations and consequences of the kinds of phenomena we routinely investigate as 'language attitudes'.

---

2.   See Hyrkstedt & Kalaja (1998) and Tophinke & Ziegler (2006) for two more critical discussions of approaches to language attitude study that use speaker evaluation studies as representative for quantitative language attitude research. See furthermore Liebscher & Dailey-O'Cain (2009) for an overview of qualitative (discourse analytic) approaches.

In terms of theoretical lineage, my study of the social meanings of varieties of Austrian German relates to work on the agentive, interactional use of sociolinguistic 'styles' along the lines of i.a. Schilling-Estes (2004), Coupland (2007), Eckert (2008), and Johnstone & Kiesling (2008). See Schilling (2013) for a general review of research on sociolinguistic style.

2.   The 'divide'; and how to conquer it

The postulation that quantitative and qualitative research are by their very nature incompatible is rooted in the presupposition of an intrinsic link between methods and epistemological paradigms (see Howe 2003:29f., who calls this the "incompatibility thesis"). Specifically, it is frequently assumed in the social sciences that QUAN methods are an operationalization of a (post)positivist epistemology, and QUAL methods of a constructivist one (see also Morgan 2007; Creswell 2011). Yet, such a "correspondence theory" (Kuckartz 2014:43, my translation) of method and knowledge paradigm is not a natural law; it merely represents one particular position in a controversy. In fact, "what counts as a paradigm and how the core content of a paradigm is portrayed involves a series of ongoing struggles between competing interest groups" (Morgan 2007:61). Such competing interest groups arose especially in the late 20th century 'paradigm wars' between (radical) positivists and constructivists (see e.g. Creswell 2011, 2014; Denzin & Lincoln 2011). Pitted against each other were, on the one hand, the dominant mainstream of social sciences research with its orientation towards the natural sciences and dogma of the rigorous experiment as the best pathway to objective knowledge, and, on the other hand, the subversive force of critical, interpretative approaches to knowledge generation that openly questioned the possibility of objectively establishing facts, especially via experimentation (e.g. Denzin & Lincoln 2011). The QUAL vs. QUAN methods debate was one of the war zones here.

Again, in this debate, the 'incompatibility thesis' is just one possible stance. Howe (2003:29) advances the "compatibility thesis" as an alternative – "the view that a thoroughgoing integration of quantitative and qualitative methods is advisable and involves no epistemological incoherence". As Kuckartz (2014:38) argues, the case can be made that the use of a particular method of data gathering and analysis, its design and application, is not automatically a commitment to a particular theory about knowledge, or vice versa. Specifically, just because the use of QUAN methods has so far shown a strong correlation with a positivistic ontology and interpretation of data, this does not mean that it is intrinsically linked to a positivist stance. In other words, QUAL and QUAN methods do not necessarily investigate ontologically different things from epistemologically different vantage points – they can be cast as different ways of generating knowledge about the same thing, from a shared perspective (see also Howe 2003:29; Richards 2005:36). I return to this point further below.

Under the compatibility thesis, what are then the remaining essential differences between QUAN and QUAL that warrant their distinction, and ultimately the usefulness of a mixed methods design? Following Dörnyei (2007: ch. 2), one major difference is that QUAN research and its methods are geared towards a "'meaning in the general' strategy" (Dörnyei 2007:27), by which typically large-scale samples of informants are investigated for overall patterns of commonalities in their responses (as operationalized via 'variables'). Preference is thus given to average results, over the study of individual cases. By contrast, QUAL research typically abstains from general descriptions averaged across large samples of informants, and rather subscribes to a "'meaning in the particular'" strategy (Dörnyei 2007:27). The goal is a 'rich', multifaceted account of an issue established on the basis of an emergent, thorough exploration of individual cases in all their variability and contextual situatedness.

Further, and quite vitally, QUAN methods are heavily geared towards generating numerical data that can be statistically processed and analyzed, thus enabling probability checks on the general patterns found across samples (i.e. to what extent they are likely to be a mere matter of chance). While QUAL methods may also generate data that lend themselves to counting and statistical processing, its hallmark are interpretative, narrative analyses that hinge on researchers' scrupulous application of their expertise and skills for a convincing data exegesis (see again Dörnyei 2007 for further discussion).

At the same time, QUAL and QUAN methods also share significant ground. Thus, what they both draw on is

> eine Reihe von Basics [...], die quasi zur anthropologischen Grundausstattung gehören: etwa die Bildung von Begriffen; die Fähigkeit, Regelmäßigkeiten zu erkennen, wobei mehr oder weniger explizit mit Mengenbegriffen und Zahlen gearbeitet wird; und ferner die Fähigkeit, Äußerungen der Mitmenschen und der Umwelt zu interpretieren, mit mehreren Wahrscheinlichkeiten und verschiedenen Lesarten zu arbeiten – manche Interpretationen sind dann wahrscheinlicher als andere.   (Kuckartz 2014:43)[3]

The delimitation of strategies and goals is therefore not as neat as some would have it (see also Dörnyei 2007). In fact, both kinds of research quite necessarily also deal in what could otherwise have been called the other's prerogatives. Thus, Howe (2003:34) argues that "even highly quantitative studies require that the context be made intelligible by use of some sort of narrative ('qualitative') history of events." And if qualitative studies are to transform future practice and events, as is a frequently voiced aspiration (e.g. Denzin & Lincoln 2011; see also Scollon & Scollon

---

3.   "a series of basics [...] that pertain to the standard anthropological equipment: for example, the formation of concepts, the ability to identify regularities, whereby sets and numbers play a more or less explicit role; and furthermore the ability to interpret the discourses of fellow-humans and the environment, to work with multiple probabilities and readings – so that some interpretations become more plausible than others." [my translation]

2004), they in turn must promote at least *some* level of generalization of identified patterns; otherwise, they risk being dismissible as idiosyncratic, anecdotal, and trivial (Dörnyei 2007; see also Miles et al. 2014: ch. 1).

My point here is to underline that QUAL and QUAN, while not automatically entailing different epistemologies, still constitute a noticeably different methods toolbox. At the same time, they are compatible or even not neatly separable, to the point where their integration is possible and can generate a multi-perspective view on a given issue (i.e., a 'meaning in the general' *plus* a 'meaning in the particular' view). As can be gleaned from the literature, this is exactly the argument underlying much MMR.

Yet, revoking the incompatibility thesis should certainly not be understood as a wholesale dismissal of epistemological and ontological concerns. All research entails *some* theory and assumptions about the nature of the phenomena under study. In the current post-postmodern era of social science, these cannot be eschewed, but rather should be made explicit, to provide proper grounds for the evaluation of the undertaking (see also Denzin & Lincoln 2011).

But what's more, for MMR, the very idea that one can investigate an issue from multiple perspectives and then interlace the findings in a comprehensive account arguably hinges on the condition that this issue be conceptualized in a consistent fashion *across the entire design*. Otherwise, the effect would be like in the parable of the six blind men examining an elephant, each grabbing a different piece and unable to derive a coherent picture.[4] Thus, a common epistemological and ontological basis for MMR research must be established, to ensure the coherence and success of the enterprise (see also Morgan 2007). In the following, I develop such a basis for MMR on language attitudes, which I will then operationalize in a study in the context of Austrian German.

3. A theoretical basis for MM language attitude research

As mentioned at the outset, methods mixing in the realm of language attitude study appears to be particularly hampered by the incompatibility thesis, which 'naturally' links QUAL and QUAN methods to different, competing epistemological paradigms. The main point of contention here is the ontological status of

---

4. The most famous rendition of this story is probably John Godfrey Saxe's 19th century poem (e.g. Saxe & Galdone 1963), which appears in the public domain – for example under ⟨http://en.wikisource.org/wiki/The_poems_of_John_Godfrey_Saxe/The_Blind_Men_and_the_Elephant⟩ [15 November 2014].

the phenomena under study, attitudes (i.e., what they are). The concomitant debate has in fact trickled down from the 'mother discipline' of language attitude study – the social psychology of attitudes at large. There, scholars writing from a constructionist perspective[5] and promoting qualitative research (most notably Potter & Wetherell 1987) have denounced the quantitative mainstream for its positivistic tendency to cast attitudes as cohesive, stable, underlying evaluative dispositions that constitute objects amenable to scientific 'discovery'. Such reification is seen as problematic (or even as "wholly gratuitous" – Gergen 2008: 355), because it stands in apparent contradiction to findings that show people's attitudinal responses to be subject to situational variation and relativity, which suggests a more ad hoc, bricolage-type evaluative process. Furthermore, findings from quantitative experiments (the data source for most mainstream research) have time and again been found to map poorly onto people's real-life behavior in concrete situations, thus casting doubt on their external validity and explanatory usefulness (see also Hyrkstedt & Kalaja 1998). This is all the more problematic, because the explication of human behavior has been proclaimed as the very raison d'être of attitude research (e.g. Meinefeld 1988; Eagly & Chaiken 2005).[6]

Constructionists' proposed and preferred alternative is to conceptualize attitudes as locally situated 'evaluative practice' or activity (Potter & Wetherell 1987; Potter 1998). This conceptualization follows from general social constructionist accounts of human meaning-making. As the term suggests, social constructionism conceives of such meaning-making as an emergent, online, productive social activity, rather than as the epiphenomenal surface symptom of underlying mental structures and dispositions. Interactional processes are the focus, and thus also the basis for the ontology of the phenomena under study. And because discourse is the central medium for interactional processes, discourse analysis is the constructionist approach of choice.

Indeed, the force of a constructionist conceptualization of social life and human communication, the knowledge and insights gained in its progress, as well as the pertinence of its approach and findings to the exegesis of real-life

---

5. See Raskin (2002) for differentiation of the terms 'construc**tivism**' and 'construc**tionism**'. Raskin designates the former as an umbrella term for non-positivistic ontology and epistemology, and the latter as *a certain kind of* constructivism that stresses the interactive, discursive, inherently social nature of human meaning-making.

6. For the first salient statement of the attitude/behavior problem see LaPiere's famous study from 1934. For further review and discussion see e.g. Ajzen & Fishbein (2005).

phenomena shall not be disputed here, but rather firmly embraced.[7] Social constructionism has managed to cast valid doubt on positivistic pursuits of underlying mental 'dispositions' for the explication of human meaning-making. Thus, in our current state of knowledge, casting attitudes as emergent, agentive evaluative practice appears to be the best way forward.

Yet conceptualizing (language) attitudes as evaluative practice can only be part of the story. It still requires some further specification of terms and approach. This, because even the most hardened proponents of constructivism are unlikely to suggest that evaluative practice does not draw on *any* kind of stored entities of experience, but would time and again be done 'from scratch'. A comprehensive constructionist ontology of attitudes therefore has to account for *two* properties of its term: for the processual quality of attitudes within interactional activity, but also for the fact that we find some kind of evaluative constructs that show continuity of existence, content, and shape *across* locally and individually situated interactions.

The upshot is a dualism problem somewhat akin to how quantum physics has to account for light both in its particle and in its wave form. An epistemologically coherent solution is needed. This cannot be to push a constructionist account of attitudes regarding their discursive *expression* ('Einstellungs*äußerung*'), but then to fall back on positivist notions of evaluative *dispositions* to capture the situationally and chronologically stable property of attitudes 'themselves' ('Einstellungen') – in the sense that it is such underlying dispositions that get activated in locally situated evaluative practice (see e.g. the proposal of Arendt 2011). Rather, a unified conceptualization of attitudes is needed that is able to draw together the process and the entity properties in one and the same account. For this purpose, I find it useful to apply Scollon's (2003) notion of 'human epistemological constructs', which he develops within the framework of 'critical realism'.

Based on the writings of Bhaskar (1989, 1991, 1997) as well as on Korzybski's famous adage "a map *is not* the territory" (Korzybski 1994 [1933]: 750; italics in original), Scollon (2003: 78) describes critical realism as endorsing "a realist ontology coupled with a constructivist epistemology". In other words, the assumption is that there does exist a tangible world/reality/'territory' out there. At the same time, human knowledge about it is inevitably mediated through 'human epistemological constructs' (HECs) or 'maps' – representations of the

---

7. Here, I am in particular referring to work that draws on the writings of Bakhtin (e.g. 1986 [1952–53]), Garfinkel (e.g. 1967), Goffman (e.g. 1959, 1981), and Gumperz (e.g. 1982) on human communication and interaction.

territory that are 'partial' in both senses of the word (and as such are necessarily historically and culturally situated and relative). The social sciences and humanities, then, are in the business of investigating not the territory or world itself (as do the natural sciences), but these very maps, or the ways in which people make sense of the world. The resulting analyses therefore constitute "maps of maps, human epistemological constructs *about* or *of* other human epistemological constructs, not about 'the world' in any direct sense" (Scollon 2003:79; italics in the original). Positivist reification of the primary 'lay' constructs (maps) as 'reality' is indeed a fallacy ('a map is not the territory') – just as it is misguided, however, to apply in reverse a constructivist ontology indiscriminately to the world that actually *is* out there.

According to Scollon (2003:78), the concept of the HEC comprises "languages, mathematical characterizations, photographs, road maps,[8] cultures, semiotic codes", or, in other words, 'discourses' (see p. 79). The latter can be specified as 'big-D Discourses' in Gee's (1999) sense:

> that is, different ways in which we humans integrate language with non-language 'stuff,' such as different ways of thinking, acting, interacting, valuing, feeling, believing, and using symbols, tools and objects in the right places and at the right times so as to enact and recognize different identities and activities, give the material world certain meanings, distribute social goods in a certain way, make certain sorts of meaningful connections in our experience, and privilege certain symbol systems and ways of knowing over others   (Gee 1999:13).[9]

For my present concerns, I propose to conceptualize language attitudes also as HECs – as discourse constructs featuring the 'social meanings' related to language use (including evaluative meanings).[10] Under a constructionist perspective, such

---

8.   The road map probably serves best to illustrate the point about 'maps' vs. 'territories'. It is a depiction of the environment driven by purposes of orientation and navigation, and thus features landmarks like towns, streets, crossroads, mountains, and rivers, *selectively*. What it is not is an exact, all-encompassing, faithful copy of the real-life natural environment (the territory) it refers to. Besides being virtually unfeasible, such a thing would actually run counter to the intended purpose, which is to make (a particular kind of) sense of a territory.

9.   Note that Gee (1999) differentiates "big-D Discourses" from "little-d discourses". The latter refer to concrete utterances or 'language in use' (Gee 1999:6–7). Blommaert (2005:3) provides a definition of Discourse similar to Gee's, holding that it "comprises all forms of meaningful semiotic human activity seen in connection with social, cultural, and historical patterns and developments of use".

10.   See Soukup (2013a) for a detailed discussion and recast of language attitudes as 'social meanings of language'. Throughout the present paper, I use the term 'language attitudes' in the sense of this recast (unless otherwise indicated).

HECs are formed, applied, developed further, and appropriated in the course of social interactions – i.e., in concrete instances of locally situated dialogical practice.[11] *Across* concrete instances, HECs, as discourse constructs, may be propagated via mechanisms of *intertextuality*. This view is based on Bakhtin's work, who elaborates as follows:[12]

> [A]ny speaker is a respondent to a greater or lesser degree. He [sic!] is not, after all, the first speaker, the one who disturbs the eternal silence of the universe. And he presupposes not only the existence of the language system he is using, but also the existence of the preceding utterances – his own and others' – with which his given utterance enters into one kind of relation or another (builds on them, polemicizes with them, or simply presumes that they are already known to the listener). Any utterance is a link in a very complexly organized chain of other utterances.   (Bakhtin 1986 [1952–53]: 69)

Becker (1995: 9) describes the same process, which he calls 'languaging', as "taking old texts[13] from memory and reshaping them into present contexts", which inherently combines "shaping, storing, retrieving, and communicating knowledge", in an emergent and ongoing fashion.

Thus, in keeping with the constructionist epistemology and ontology that are expedient for current social science (see above), the dualism of language attitudes as interactional process and transferrable construct can be resolved as follows. Attitudes emerge and evolve in locally situated moments of interactional, discursive activity where language use is assessed, discussed, and evaluated. Just as such discourse references previous moments of interaction,[14] it may itself 'sediment' and thus be stored for future reference. In short, human epistemological

---

11.   For reference on the inherent dialogicality of all discourse see Bakhtin (1986 [1952–53]), Erickson (1986), Tannen (1989). See furthermore Goffman's (1959: 15) definition of 'interaction' as "the reciprocal influence of individuals upon one another's actions when in one another's immediate physical presence". The work of Vygotsky (e.g. 1978) also relates here, with its account of learning as a social enterprise.

12.   According to Fairclough (1992) the term 'intertextuality' itself was first used by Kristeva in her discussion of Bakhtin's writings (e.g. Kristeva 1986 [1966]).

13.   N.B.: For my present concerns, I propose to substitute 'texts' with 'HECs' or 'discourse constructs'. See also Fairclough (1992) for development of the term 'interdiscursivity' to go beyond the textual.

14.   In Gumperz's (1982) terms, such referencing can be called 'contextualization', whereby any language use indexes certain aspects of context as relevant to the 'inference' of meaning. These aspects of context include any knowledge brought to an interaction, such as HECs of the social meanings of language.

construction morphs into human epistemological *constructs* and vice versa, in an ongoing, evolutionary cycle.

It is now time to return to my primary concern and to address the question of how this line of reasoning promotes MMR on language attitudes. My claim is that *both* QUAL and QUAN research can be conceptualized as capturing instances of language-use-related HEC processing – of interactionally constructing, referencing, developing, and appropriating language attitudes. This is the shared, consistent epistemological and ontological basis I suggest for our mixed methods research and for interlacing its findings.

QUAL approaches typically elicit or collect instances of HEC processing via interviews, conversational discussions, or textual artifacts that turn on the theme of language (use), and subject these to forms of discourse analysis. In turn, QUAN designs typically elicit such instances via (quasi)experimental set-ups in which informants are presented with linguistic stimuli and asked to rate these on scales, and the outcome is subjected to statistical probability analysis to check on general patterns. Thus, there is no apparent reason for which language-use-related HECs should only emerge in QUAL data, like in interviews, or in conversations and textual documents that occur 'naturally' (i.e. are not elicited by an analyst). Rather, *any* situation that involves language-evaluative practice features the attitudinal HEC cycle, and thus can serve as data source for constructionist attitude study – including the activity in which informants engage during speaker evaluation experiments: contrastively assessing speech samples. Such experiments are also a type of social interaction involving HECs, namely one that takes place between informants, investigators, and stimulus speakers.[15]

Of course, a fundamentally interactional conceptualization of language attitudes is also subject to the constructionist postulation that all interactional activity and meaning-making is contextually situated and relative (see e.g. Gumperz 1982). In other words, any corresponding analysis must take into account that language attitudinal HEC processing and its outcome necessarily relate to a specific 'frame of reference' (Goffman 1974, 1981). It is inevitably within such a frame, or sense of "what is going on" (Tannen & Wallat 1993: 59), that interactants make and negotiate meaning.[16]

---

15.   See Giles & Coupland (1991: ch. 2) for an early version of the proposal that language attitude experiments can be seen as interactional events; similarly, see also Garrett et al. (1999).

16.   Certainly, frames of reference can also be regarded as HECs. However, a comprehensive identification and classification of HECs outside of language attitudes goes beyond my present scope. See Tannen & Wallat's (1993) differentiation of 'interactive frames' vs. 'knowledge schemas' as a potential starting point for such discussion. See furthermore Widdowson

The inherent contextual relativity of findings may appear like another important obstacle for MMR, especially in the sense that quantitative experimental methods, for one, set up contexts for data elicitation that seem to differ vastly from those that QUAL methods typically draw on. Under these circumstances, how can QUAN and QUAL findings possibly be integrated? I propose that the answer lies in exploiting a quintessential principle of the experimental approach for the design of MMR: the principle of scientific 'control'. It holds that, in order to properly gauge the influence that one particular aspect ('variable') has on producing different experimental outcomes across different groups or conditions, the influence that any other 'extraneous' or 'confounding' variables could have must be neutralized ('controlled'). One way to neutralize such influence is by a 'ceteris paribus' strategy, which is to keep all aspects of the experiment constant ('equal') across groups, except for the one whose effect is being investigated (for further discussion see e.g. Huber 2013). The underlying tenet is that *similar conditions generate similar outcomes*. If a change in conditions from similar to different in one particular aspect goes along with a change in the outcome, it is at least very likely that the one altered aspect was the driving force for this.

It is in fact the very idea that similar conditions generate similar outcomes that can be put to use in designing truly integrated MMR. Under a constructionist perspective on human interaction, this idea can be taken to signify that if the frames of reference are similar across communicative situations, then the meaning-making processes involved are also similar. Developed further, this means that if both a QUAL and a QUAN study are devised so as to feature a similar frame of reference within which informants 'make sense' (here: process language-use-related HECs), then the outcomes (here: which HECs they process) are also likely to be similar, to a point where findings can mutually inform each other.

Of course, the question arises of 'how similar would be similar enough' for the frames of reference involved, to legitimize the interlacing of MMR outcomes.[17] I return to this point further below, where I choose an empirical way out. But first, a solution is needed for how to align frames of reference across QUAL and QUAN studies to begin with. For this, I propose to use Dell Hymes' SPEAKING grid – a heuristic that has been successfully applied in

---

(2004) on discourse and schemas. Soukup (2014) discusses attitudinal HECs in additional data and contexts.

17.   This question was justly raised by Nikolas Coupland in response to the first version of this paper (p.c.).

anthropological linguistic research (in the ethnography of communication) to describe interactional contexts.[18]

Hymes (1972) identifies a set of eight 'components' that typically configure the context of an interaction. He used the mnemonic acronym SPEAKING to list these components: Settings (time and place, physical circumstances, but also 'psychological' setting), Participants, Ends (outcomes as well as goals), Act sequences (relating to activities and speech acts), Keys (tone, mood), Instrumentalities (including modes/media of communication), Norms (expectations regarding behavior and its interpretation), and Genre (the type of event) – (see also Schiffrin 2014: 199–200). A particular moment of human social interaction can thus be characterized by a particular configuration of these parameters (with the understanding that these necessarily overlap and mesh, and cannot be neatly delimited). Their inventorying also allows for comparison and contrasting across different situations of interaction.

The idea is now to use the SPEAKING grid as an instrument to capture and align central contextual features of QUAL and QUAN datasets which are to be integrated in MMR. Crucially, informants/interactants draw on interactional context in order to establish the frame of reference for their meaning-making, or their sense of 'what is going on', 'what game is being played' (see Tannen & Wallat 1993: 60, with reference to Ortega y Gasset 1959). The alignment of SPEAKING parameters is therefore used as a proxy to establish that the frames of reference can be expected to be construed similarly across interactions, and hence that the informants'/interactants' emergent meaning-making is also likely to be similar. Again, I propose that this is a basis on which MMR findings can then inform each other across different methods and datasets.

Below, I now apply the theoretical considerations I have just laid out in an MMR study that focuses on language-attitudinal HECs in relation to Austrian German. I first present the QUAL component, where I analyze and discuss some conversational data from an Austrian TV discussion show, in which HEC processing features in the form of strategic style-shifting ('Speaker Design' – Schilling 2013), as I claim. To support this claim, I follow up with a related QUAN component in the form of a speaker evaluation experiment, whose design was tailored to the QUAL data. As mentioned at the outset, my goal is to provide a hands-on example of how I envision MMR on language attitudes to proceed in order to generate a 'rich', multidimensional, and compelling account of the phenomena under investigation. I review my undertaking in the final, concluding section of this paper.

---

18.   See for example Schiffrin (1994) and Cameron (2001) for illlustrations of how the SPEAKING grid can be used in analysis.

4.   The QUAL component: Strategic style-shifting in an Austrian TV discussion

The data I draw on here come from an episode of the Austrian TV discussion show *Offen gesagt* ('Openly said'), produced and broadcast by the Austrian national television company ORF from 2002–2007. Under the show's format, changing groups of four to six participants discussed a hot public-interest topic of the week, live, for about an hour, hosted by a TV journalist.[19] The expected, 'default' language variety on the show, as on Austrian public TV in general, is standard Austrian German (see e.g. Steinegger 1998). However, in the heat of what is oftentimes a political debate, linguistic shifting out of the standard and into some form of Austrian dialect can also be observed. Some of this shifting clearly serves a rhetorical purpose, and hence can be labeled and analyzed as 'Speaker Design' – strategic, agentive use of linguistic styles (see Schilling 2013).[20]

Passage 1 below constitutes my 'anchor example' of the phenomenon and comes from a show episode broadcast in 2004 on the topic of imminent Austrian presidential elections (for further examples see Soukup 2009). In this episode, five invited guests discuss the two remaining presidential candidates. Two guests each represent one camp; the fifth is a comedian who is taking a supposedly 'neutral' stance. In Passage 1, then, journalist and political activist AT is relating an occurrence involving the Austrian Foreign Minister, who incidentally is the presidential candidate he himself opposes. In the course of the tumultuous 2001 G8 summit in Genoa, Italy, an Austrian leftist theater group was arrested by the police. AT is claiming that the Foreign Minister subsequently committed a big, 'disqualifying' gaffe because she did not immediately intervene with Italian authorities on behalf of the incarcerated Austrians. (Note that in Passage 1, features of Bavarian-Austrian dialect are rendered in eye-dialect and bold print.)

---

19.   This type of show has in various incarnations been a staple of Austrian public broadcasting almost from its beginning, and still is today, albeit currently under the name *Im Zentrum* ('In the center').

20.   For further reference on the (socio)linguistic situation in Austria see e.g. Dressler & Wodak (1982); Ebner (2008); Lenz and Glauninger (2015); Moosmüller (1991); Scheuringer (1997); Soukup (2009); Wiesinger (2006). In this paper, my use of the term 'dialect' henceforth refers to Bavarian-Austrian varieties, which vastly dominate in Austria. The sociolinguistic situation in the Alemannic-speaking dialect areas in the westernmost part of Austria is known to have different properties, which are not my topic here. See e.g. Kaiser & Ender (2012) for reference.

Passage 1 (*Offen gesagt*, 'Wer soll in die Hofburg', ORF2, 01/18/2004)

a AT: Da geht es nämlich um nicht mehr um nicht weniger
b   als dass dort ein paar linke Theaterleute im Zuge
c   dieser Veranstaltung festgenommen wurden österreichische
d   Staatsbürger und Staatsbürgerinnen und dass die Frau
e   Außenminister nichts anderes zu tun hatte als zu sagen najo und
f   zwar öffentlich nachzulesen auf der Homepage des
g   Außenministeriums der Text steht fest najo des **san kane** Guatn
h   gegen die liegt **eh** sozus- gegen die liegen **eh** sozusagen
i   Anzeigen vor im Innenministerium und denen wird **scho** recht
j   **gsche**hn das war ihre Ant- das war ihre Reaktion zum Schutz
k   österreichischer Staatsbürger die im Ausland verhaftet werden

(English near-text/line-by-line translation:)

a AT: Because this is about nothing more nothing less
b   than that there a few leftist theater people in the course of
c   this event [the G8 summit] were arrested Austrian
d   citizens men and women and that the Madam
e   Foreign Minister did not have anything better to do than to say **well** and
f   this in public can be checked on the homepage of the
g   Foreign Ministry the text is fixed there **well those are no good people**
h   against them are **anyway** so to s- against them are **anyway** so to say
i   charges recorded in the Interior Ministry and **thus** right
j   will them **be served** that was her ans- that was her reaction to protect
k   Austrian citizens who are arrested abroad

What is noticeable in Passage 1 is the fact that AT shifts from standard Austrian German to using dialect features specifically in those parts of his monologue where he is allegedly 'quoting' the Minister, in lines e through j. In line e, he produces the dialectal [ɔ] in *najo* [naˈjɔ] (vs. std. [naˈja] 'well'); then, in line g, a second [naˈjɔ], as well as dialectal [d̥e:s] (vs. std. [das] 'those'); [san] (vs. std. [sind] 'are'); [a:] in *kane* [ˈka:ne] (vs. std. [ˈkaɛne]– 'no'); and [ʊɐ] in *Guatn* [ˈgʊɐd̥n̩] (vs. std. [ˈgu:ten] – 'good people'). In line h, he produces two instances of the dialectal discourse marker *eh* ('anyway'), and then further phonological dialect features in line i (*scho* [ʃɔ:] vs. std. [ʃo:n] 'thus/already'), and line j (a *ge*-reduction in *gschehn* [kʃe:n] vs. std. [geˈʃe:n] – 'be served').[21]

The upshot of AT's narrative is that he condemns the Minister's reaction to the incident. On the one hand, this is clear from the content of his monologue (which he in fact previewed in previous talk as reporting a 'big blunder' – "ein Megafettnapf"). On the other hand, it can be argued that AT's antagonistic

---

21. For further linguistic details and descriptions see Moosmüller (1991), Soukup (2009).

message is also indexically embodied in his strategic use of dialect when voicing the Minister. In short, it constitutes an instance of 'evaluative practice'.[22]

As stated earlier, human communicative meaning-making is an online, emergent, interactional process in which all kinds of information is referenced and negotiated. In evaluative practice, part of this information is constituted by the language attitudinal HECs commonly associated with the linguistic variety used in an utterance (see Gumperz' 1982 notion of 'contextualization'). Now, as the literature shows (e.g. Moosmüller 1988, 1991; Steinegger 1998), the social meanings commonly found to be associated with dialect use in Austria are in fact that it sounds less educated, less intelligent, and less refined, but also more natural and emotional to Austrian native speakers than standard Austrian German. By the above line of reasoning, AT's use of dialect when 'quoting' the minister indexes these associations, but, due to the overall antagonistic set-up, particularly with a negative slant. And because the Minister is supposedly the originator of the quote (the 'deictic center' – Schiffrin 2002: 317), these associations are projected onto her, casting her, by extension, as a less educated, less intelligent, less refined person. It is in this way that AT's 'Speaker Design' (strategic language use) embodies his negative stance towards the Minister, and ultimately constitutes a form of 'evaluative practice' – of processing language attitudinal HECs.

The type of rhetorical maneuver exhibited in Passage 1 can be encountered quite frequently and systematically across various episodes of the discussion show *Offen gesagt* (see Soukup 2009). Time and again, participants shift into dialect when quoting or commenting on somebody they do not agree or align with – a pattern that is evident in a statistically significant rise of dialect rates in such contexts. This further corroborates the claim that there is Speaker Design at work. Yet, what is crucial to the success of this (like any) rhetorical strategy, is, of course, whether or not the audience/listeners actually and actively follow along in their interpretation of the message. In other words, AT will only ever really have projected an antagonistic alignment between himself and the Minister via his dialect use, if his audience indeed calls up and integrates the relevant language attitudinal HECs when inferencing meaning in this particular situational context – in other words, if they engage in similar evaluative practice. And from

---

22. In fact, we can safely assume that this dialect use is strategic (rhetorical), because it is highly improbable that the original utterance (if such there was) would actually have been in dialect: the (then-)Minister is a known standard speaker, especially in public, and any 'homepage of the Foreign Ministry' would publish exclusively in standard German (this being the written norm in Austria). The untruthfulness of language use in the 'quote' is indeed very obvious to Austrian listeners (see Soukup 2009).

an empirical perspective, this cannot simply be assumed or presupposed, based on general research. Rather, evidence should ideally be found 'live'. Put differently, an empirical test is needed to show that an Austrian audience, when confronted with dialectal vs. standard speech in a TV discussion context, is really likely to reference the kinds of language-attitudinal HECs which AT seems to be banking on.

This is precisely the point at which an MMR design is useful, in that a QUAN speaker evaluation experiment can be harnessed to generate processual evidence for the QUAL data exegesis. A carefully designed experiment allows us to check up on what social meanings and associations (what HECs) an Austrian audience actually comes up with in concrete situations in which they hear standard and dialect in juxtaposition, like in the style-shifts occurring in the TV broadcast.[23] In the light of my previous discussion, 'careful design' here means that the experiment needs to be aligned as closely as possible with the conversational data it is called on to illuminate, in terms of the frame of reference within which informants/interactants make sense of the evaluative activity involved.

Table 1 is an instrument for such alignment. It presents the typical contextual set-up of the TV discussion show *Offen gesagt*, using Hymes' SPEAKING heuristic.[24] As mentioned before, the SPEAKING configuration serves as an indicator of the frame of reference likely to be construed by interactants (here: discussion participants and audience).

In Table 1, call-outs indicate aspects in which the design of my speaker evaluation experiment emulates the set-up of the show. In other words, they show specific, deliberate points of engagement where the QUAN latches onto the QUAL study component. While most aspects of the experimental protocol and procedure for the QUAN component are thus already incorporated in Table 1 and the ensuing explication, the findings from the experiment are presented in a separate section further below.

---

23. For reasons of scope, I am omitting here any discussion of the role that perception, particularly perceptual differentiation of standard and dialect, plays in the process. See Soukup (2011) for discussion and an empirical approach to that issue. Note also that the use of an *indirect* language attitude elicitation technique (in the form of a speaker evaluation task) for gathering empirical evidence regarding interactional inferencing is particularly expedient, as it seems unlikely that such inferencing happens at a level of awareness accessible to direct reflection (see also Gumperz 1982:ch. 4).

24. This typical set-up also applies in the particular case of the TV show episode from which Passage 1 is taken.

Table 1. The contextual configuration of the TV discussion show *Offen gesagt* outlined via Hymes' SPEAKING grid, with points of engagement for the design of the speaker evaluation experiment

TV show *Offen gesagt*		Speaker evaluation experiment
Settings	– Make-shift TV studio in Vienna, Austria (actually a café) – Sunday night (ca 10-11pm), live broadcast – Armchairs in a circle, small side-tables – Cameras in the background – No live studio audience – Main audience is at home in front of TV (and thus removed and anonymous, no direct interaction with show participants)	Pre-recorded speakers; Removed and anonymous audience
Participants	On camera: – One journalist/ host – 4–6 experts/ politicians/ activists/ eyewitnesses; males and females; typically well-educated, public-speaking experience 'Backstage': studio technicians Off camera: – Audience at home: mainly Austrian; typically upper (middle) class, highly educated, older	Male and female speakers, well educated; introduced as 'participants in a rhetoric seminar' Austrian students as informants (> highly educated); Rating scales based on pre-study interviews with similar sample that also included older informants
Ends	Overall purpose of the show: – to illuminate a hot topic of the week, present and confront different viewpoints; 'infotainment' Goals of the invitees: – to present their opinion/ perspective authoritatively and convincingly – to argue and make their points – to comprehend and engage with others' points – politicians: to represent their party's position, score sympathy with the audience at home Goals of the host: – to elicit opinions and ask topic-relevant questions, generate a lively discussion – to assign turns, referee, keep control – to deliver an interesting TV program Goals of audience at home: – to be informed on different positions on a hot topic – to make sense, via assessment of participants and what they are saying – infotainment	Task set-up (incl. for speakers): presenting an opinion convincingly to a public audience Audience/ informants: make sense within the task of assessing the speakers

(Continued)

Table 1. (Continued) The contextual configuration of the TV discussion show *Offen gesagt* outlined via Hymes' SPEAKING grid, with points of engagement for the design of the speaker evaluation experiment

TV show *Offen gesagt*		Speaker evaluation experiment
Act sequences	Show:	
	– Pre-recorded introductory sequence	
	– Greeting by the host, presentation of today's topic	
	– Introduction of the participants	
	– Start of the discussion >	
	– Host: assigns turns, monitors, asks follow-up questions, keeps order	
	– Discussion participants: present arguments and opinions, often in long stretches of monologual talk, answer questions, address and confront others' arguments and opinions, present party ideology (politicians)	Text = presentation of an opinionated argument (on genetically engineered food); monologue
	– Closing of discussion, thanks and leave-taking (host)	
	Audience at home:	
	– Turn on TV	
	– Follow and make sense of discussion	Judge speakers as presenters of an argument, rate speakers on scales
	– Interpret talk, form opinions, judge effectiveness of speakers	
Keys	– Serious but with occasional banter and humor	Anonymous, distant, formal, polite (both virtual and real setting of university classroom), serious argument
	– Formal, distant, and polite	
	– Depending on the topic: somber, belligerent, competitive, sensationalist, or purely centered on facts	
Instrumentalities	– Broadcasting technology	Spoken language; Std AG and Bavarian-Austrian dialect; 'style-shifting' by same speakers between samples ('open guise')
	– Occasional graphics inserts	
	– Spoken discourse	
	– Standard Austrian German (dominant) and occasionally dialect (mostly Bavarian-Austrian) > style-shifting	
	– Currently relevant contextual knowledge (including language-attitudinal HECs)	language-attitudinal HECs prompted/ elicited via rating scales
Norms	– Recognition of the host as 'referee' authority	
	– Orderly turn-taking (often assigned, one speaker at a time), limited speaking time (at host's discretion)	Monologue (one speaker at a time); standard first, then dialect
	– Language norm: standard is expected on national TV	
	– Common norms for behavior in public (for show participants)	

(*Continued*)

Table 1. (Continued)

TV show *Offen gesagt*		Speaker evaluation experiment
Genre	– Live discussion show on public television > 'public speaking' > 'high performance' (Coupland 2007)	Virtual setting: 'public speaking' -presenting an argument as if in a public discussion > high performance

As Table 1 shows, points of engagement between the QUAL and QUAN study components were established for each of the SPEAKING parameters listed by Hymes (1972). Thus, where the TV show setting of my QUAL data causes the main audience to be physically removed from and anonymous to the discussion participants, the same holds for the speaker evaluation experiment, where speakers and informants are in fact removed by physical distance and time, and are not personally known to each other. (The experiment was carried out in two rounds in university classrooms using pre-taped recordings.)

The participants of the TV show comprise politicians, activists, and experts, as well as one host, an ORF journalist. They usually have some degree of rhetorical training, or at least experience in public speaking; they are mostly Austrian, well-educated, at least middle class, and older (30+). The TV show audience is also mostly Austrian; and the upper class and upper middle class (which commonly include the highly educated in Austria), as well as the generation of 50–59 year-olds are typically overrepresented, compared to the general Austrian population (source: ORF media surveys for the show, p.c.).

In the experiment, the participant parameters of the show are paralleled in that the one male and two female speakers recording the linguistic stimuli are all Austrians, between thirty and thirty-five years of age, of middle class background, and with at least some tertiary education. Two of them have teaching (and hence in a sense public speaking) experience. In turn, the informants are 123 students of higher education at an Austrian university, born and raised in Austria (from all regions). 76% of the informants are (self-identified) females (n=94) and 24% males (n=29).[25] They range in age from 18 to 30 (median: 21). While the audience

---

25. This skewed gender distribution is due to the fact that the informants were recruited in female-student-dominated courses (though a broad array of subjects of study were represented). My experience with speaker evaluation studies suggests, however, that informant gender has typically a negligible effect on ratings, and, if any, a predictable one, namely that females tend to give 'kinder' ratings across the board. I cordially thank all my informants for their participation, and Manfred Glauninger at the University of Vienna for facilitating access.

demographics of the show and the experiment thus do not match in age, they do in educational background, so that the student informants could be argued to constitute the future audience of the show (later in their lives). Because the show format is a well-known, classic staple of Austrian public TV, it can furthermore be expected to be familiar to them.[26]

A central point of engagement regarding the 'Ends' and 'Act sequences' of the TV discussion and the experiment is the presentation of opinionated stretches of talk with the goal of sounding authoritative and convincing. In the experiment, the speakers were instructed accordingly, and their 'opinions' were presented in the form of a text that both in topic (genetically engineered food) and form (a monologue) was closely modeled on typical occurrences on the show. Further, for both 'audiences', an immediate goal is to make sense of and evaluate the ongoing discourse and its originators. In the experiment, this is the vital aspect of the 'Act sequences' during the rating task.

Both on the show and in the experiment, the tone ('Key') is predominantly formal, serious, distant, and polite.[27] In both settings, spoken language is the main 'Instrumentality', in the form of standard Austrian German and (Bavarian-)Austrian dialect.[28] And crucially, sense-making in both contexts requires reference to shared sociocultural knowledge, including reference to language-attitudinal HECs for the interpretation of language use and style-shifts. In other words, both the TV show's home audience as well as the experiment's informants need to draw on and process language attitudinal HECs if they are, in the one case, to make sense of Speaker Design as exemplified in Passage 1, and in the other case, to make sense of the task of speaker evaluation posed in the experiment.

Speaker Design (strategic style-shifting between Austrian standard and dialect) is, of course, the evaluative practice that is the focus of the MMR expounded here. In the speaker evaluation experiment, it is operationalized by shifting speaking styles from standard to dialect *between* samples by the same speakers. Thus, each speaker is heard once in each variety. Contrary to traditional speaker evaluation protocols that are based on the matched-guise technique (following Lambert et al. 1960), in the present experiment it was *not* concealed from the informants,

---

26. A poll by show of hands subsequently conducted with a comparable group of Austrian student showed that the vast majority are indeed familiar with this type of TV show.

27. See Giles and Ryan (1982) for discussion of level of formality as an influential parameter in the evaluation of language use.

28. All Austrians can typically be assumed to have some (at least passive) competence in *both* standard and dialect (see e.g. Moosmüller 1991). This therefore applies equally to the participants/audience of the TV show, and to the experiment's informants, across the board.

but rather stated openly at the beginning, that they would hear each speaker twice 'in different versions' (without further specification). This 'open guise' technique (see Soukup 2013b) was used to emulate as closely as possible the real-life situation of hearing and evaluating one and the same speaker as he or she shifts between styles in conversation.[29]

In the experiment, the language attitudinal HECs which informants process for meaning-making were elicited via semantic differentials scales provided in a paper questionnaire.[30] In detail, the following twenty-two five-point bipolar semantic differential scales were used (here translated from German):

> *likeable – not likeable, educated – uneducated, trustworthy – not trustworthy, polite – impolite, intelligent – unintelligent, friendly – unfriendly, honest – dishonest, self-confident – not self-confident, competent – not competent, industrious – lazy, natural – artificial, good sense of humor – no sense of humor, clever – not clever, emotional – unemotional, relaxed – not relaxed, serious – non-serious, aggressive – not aggressive, strict – not strict, conservative – open-minded, rough – gentle, arrogant – non-arrogant, coarse – refined.*

These scale items were compiled on the basis of pre-study interviews and the relevant literature (Moosmüller 1988, 1991; Steinegger 1998), in view of testing commonly listed social associations of Austrian standard and dialect.

Note that the outcome of the experiment (HECs provided by the informants via the scales) is computed across many scores, thus establishing the *average* HEC profile applied (i.e., the stereotype). However, stereotypical language attitudinal HECs are also precisely what Speaker Design on the TV show relies on: idiosyncratic response is beside the point, because the only common denominator for meaning-making for both speakers like AT and their audience is broad-stroked, shared, common sociocultural knowledge.[31]

---

29.   Of course, the anchor example of Passage 1 involves a participant speaking 'in another's voice' and thus not as himself, so that additional complexities of 'production format' (Goffman 1981) are involved. A fuller exploration of strategic style-shifting in Austrian German shows, however, that it also occurs in interactional moves outside of quoting – particularly in (negative) comments on a preceding speaker's contribution (see Soukup 2009). In these cases, no 'other-voicing' is involved.

30.   See again Soukup (2013a) for a discussion of how semantic differential scales are particularly apt to elicit the social meanings of language use, going back to the original agenda of Osgood et al. (1957), which was *The Measurement of Meaning* (as their book title reads).

31.   I am stressing this point because it encounters criticism of quantitative methods that holds the concomitant loss of individual response patterns in the process of results computation to be a shortcoming. Here, in my MMR, it is a desirable affordance. I return to this point in my conclusion. Notice also in this context that whether or not the audience or speakers

Returning to the points of engagement between conversational interaction and experimental design, another one lies in the norm that only one person is (supposed to be) speaking at a time. And finally, the genre of both kinds of inter-action is 'public speaking'. Following Coupland (2007: 146–148, with reference to Baumann 1992), this constitutes a 'high performance', in the sense that the rhetori-cal function of language use plays a central role, the show (display) character of the interaction is foregrounded, talk is particularly tailored for and directed at a large, anonymous audience, and the stakes (in terms of public scrutiny) are rather high.

That said, in the speaker evaluation, the most immediate genre is of course that of an experiment. To superimpose on this the genre of public speaking, rel-evant information was deliberately introduced, such as that the speakers were pre-sented as participants in a practical course on rhetoric. Furthermore, the nature of the speech samples (involving an argument on a public-interest topic), and the performer/anonymous audience set-up arguably also established a public-speak-ing (high performance) context for the speaker evaluation task.

In sum, and to recap, the protocol and procedural elements of the experi-ment as just discussed were designed in order to set up a frame of reference for meaning-making for the informants that would be similar to that within which an Austrian TV audience would make sense of Speaker Design in a TV discussion, as instantiated in Passage 1 presented further above. This should in turn license the conclusion that the processing of language attitudinal HECs would also be similar across the two datasets. This way, it is possible to find empirical evidence for the claim that, when an Austrian audience is confronted with standard and dialect in juxtaposition, their inference of meaning does follow the lines laid out in my exegesis of Passage 1. In other words, we should be able to find 'live' evidence for whether a TV audience would actually realize the projection of a negative align-ment between AT and the Minister.

This now brings me back to a point I suspended earlier on: How can we be sure that the strategy of frame alignment actually works? How similar is similar enough, for frames of reference, to facilitate similarity in the meaning-making processes? As I already intimated, I am able to provide some empirical evidence for the fact that the frame of the TV show was successfully evoked in the speaker evaluation (which, arguably, warrants the 'similar enough'). This evidence comes

---

personally and always consider the stereotypes attaching to language use to be a good or a bad thing (the actual 'attitude' in the social psychological reading of the term – see e.g. the definition by Eagly & Chaiken 2005) is also irrelevant. What is important is only that the stereotypes be widely known, and that they be referenced in the local evaluative practice and its interpretation.

from an earlier, longer, *verbal* guise take of the speaker evaluation experiment presented here, which otherwise featured the same stimulus speakers and design (see Soukup 2009). Remarkably, when prompted in the questionnaire to indicate in what kinds of settings the standard speakers would fare particularly well, one of that study's informants actually cited the show *Offen gesagt*. Similar (although less specific) references to contexts of public and TV discussions were made by a handful of other informants as well. It is highly recommended that such feedback be elicited in speaker evaluation experiments in MMR, to check on and evaluate the design, as well as the legitimacy of transposing findings from the QUAN to the QUAL component. Such feedback may be our best gauge of the success of frame alignment across MMR components.

5. The QUAN component: Findings from the speaker evaluation experiment

To briefly recap, the speaker evaluation experiment featured three speakers, who each presented the same piece (an argument concerning genetically engineered food) once in standard Austrian German, and once in Bavarian-Austrian dialect. Informants were told that the speakers were participants in a rhetoric seminar, and that they were to provide feedback on how the speakers would be assessed by a public audience. Responses were recorded in a questionnaire, via a set of 22 semantic differential scales. The informants were 123 Austrian students of higher education.

Results were computed using SPSS for Windows (v.17.0). A series of paired samples *t* tests was conducted, matching up and comparing the ratings each speaker had received for their standard and their dialect performance. Results are reported only for those items on which (1) at least two speakers show significantly different ratings across the two samples, and (2) at least one of the speakers' significant ratings differences also showed a medium or large effect size (Cohen's *d* ≥ 0.5).[32]

---

32.   Parametric tests were selected under the considerations of a sufficiently large sample and the repeated-measures design, where homogeneity of variances can be assumed. See e.g. Himmelfarb (1993) for a discussion of parametric tests in connection with attitudinal scales. See furthermore Aron et al. (2009) for discussion of the complexities of carrying out a large number of *t* tests. Details of the statistical analysis are not provided for space considerations – please contact the author for further information (barbara.soukup@univie.ac.at). Additional details are also provided in Soukup (2013b).

As it turns out, then, the informants on average rated all three speakers as significantly more *educated, industrious,* and *serious* ('ernst'), but also as more *arrogant,* when speaking in the standard (p < .5). On the other hand, they found the speakers to sound more *natural, relaxed, honest, emotional,* and as having more *sense of humor* when speaking in the dialect. Yet they also rated the dialect to sound significantly *coarser.*

While the average ratings on the above-listed items show the same trend for all speakers, there are also some other items for which the outcome is inconsistent.[33] First, both female speakers were rated as sounding much *stricter* in the standard; but there is no such effect for the male speaker; and all three speakers' ratings are (statistically) the same for the dialect guise. This may suggest a possible gender effect, by which using the standard incurs a perception of sternness for women that it does not for men. However, such a claim requires much further testing.

Furthermore, there are items for which the ratings of the two female speakers diverge significantly. The overall patterning of the results actually suggests that one of the female speakers encountered a considerable negative bias when speaking in the standard, which lowered her average scores across the board (meaning, the informants seemed to indiscriminately dislike her standard guise). Because of the consistency of this pattern, it seems legitimate to consider what the results look like with her taken out of the picture. What they look like is, in fact, that an additional trend appears whereby standard language use is perceived to sound more *intelligent, competent, clever,* and tendentially more *polite* than the dialect.

All in all, the results from the speaker evaluation experiment indicate that speaking in the standard enhances positive perceptions of 'competence' (e.g. education, industriousness, intelligence, cleverness, sophistication), while the dialect evokes more strongly perceptions of what could be labeled 'down-to-earthness' (naturalness, honesty, emotionality, humor). This way, the outcome of the speaker evaluation experiment clearly supports the exegesis I provided for Passage 1: AT's shifting from Austrian standard into dialect when quoting his 'opponent', the Foreign Minister, is very likely to successfully index negative HECs regarding competency (low education, low intelligence, low sophistication), in the sense that an audience is likely to inference a corresponding interpretation. And again, because the Minister is the 'deictic center' of the quote, or its supposed originator ('author' and 'principal' – Goffman 1981), these perceptions fall back on her (and not on AT), projecting a negative impression. More positive social associations of dialect,

---

33.   The items concerned were investigated using post-hoc repeated-measures ANOVAs and paired-samples *t* tests in hierarchical order of means. Only those for which statistically significant differences were found are reported here.

such as its 'honesty', are likely to be suppressed within the immediate local inter-actional frame of reference, given, for one, that AT has introduced his 'quote' in a way (as a 'big blunder') that leaves very little doubt about his unfavorable opinion of the Minster's alleged behavior. If any trace of such positive HECs regarding dialect use should remain, the interpretation that the Minister makes the cruel statement attributed to her in an 'honest' and 'natural' fashion (see the findings of the experiment) is only a further detriment to her projected persona.

6. Discussion and conclusion(s)

My point of departure in this paper was the claim that MMR projects can lead to a rounder and richer view of multifaceted phenomena in social science, by illuminating them from the different but complementary perspectives of QUAL and QUAN research. In my present case, the phenomena in focus were the social meanings of varieties of Austrian German and the interactional use to which these can be (and have been) put. Integration of a QUAL and a QUAN component has now allowed me to corroborate a meaning-in-the-particular finding, namely that stereotypical social meanings of Austrian dialect vs. standard Austrian German can be used strategically to project (negative) interactional alignments, via a meaning-in-the-general approach, which attested that the interactional inferencing (interpretation) required for the success of this strategy can indeed be expected from an average Austrian audience. In this respect, at least, we have come to a fuller understanding of how language attitudinal HECs may feature in Austrian sociocultural linguistic meaning-making, and thus, ultimately, in Austrian social life.

But in a sense, my opening claim can also be read such that MMR not only benefits from complementarities of QUAL and QUAN approaches in terms of their strengths and affordances. MMR can also serve to compensate for their comple-mentary weaknesses. For QUAN research, the fact that the meaning-in-the-general approach glosses over individual and situational variability of response has been proclaimed as such a weakness, in the sense that the usefulness and applicabil-ity of QUAN findings to the explication of complex, variable, real-life situations of human meaning-making has been questioned. But in my present study, a QUAN approach was harnessed and adapted successfully to corroborate the exegesis of actual, real-life, situated instances of language use (Speaker Design) where meaning-in-the-general is of vital import. This illustrates how a QUAN study can be given a very concrete purpose, usefulness, and direction for instance by tailor-ing its design to the exigencies of a QUAL data analysis where (crucially) a similar level of phenomenon is at play.

In turn, the harshest criticism voiced against QUAL researchers has probably been that their interpretative accounts constitute "fiction, not science," and that they allegedly have no way of verifying most of their statements (see Denzin & Lincoln 2011: 2). It seems that this kind of criticism could be most compellingly refuted by basing the claim that one kind of QUAL data exegesis is more plausible than others on large-scale, systematic, empirical evidence whose patterning is statistically confirmed. Such evidence is precisely what a judiciously designed QUAN study can contribute to a QUAL analysis.

Meaning-in-the-particular and meaning-in-the-general need not be mutually exclusive – they can be mutually informing and supportive. In the context of language attitude study, this is what I hope to have shown here.

Fitting all these claims best, as I have argued, is a theory of knowledge and ontology of language attitudes that conceptualizes them as human epistemological *constructs* sedimenting from human epistemological *construction* and (re-)flourishing interdiscursively in emergent interaction – whether it be interaction arising within QUAL or within QUAN studies. 'A map is not the territory' – once we have fully internalized the implications of this adage in our practice, the road is wide open for thoroughly integrated mixed methods research on language attitudes.

References

Ajzen, Icek & Fishbein, Martin. 2005. The influence of attitudes on behavior. In *The Handbook of Attitudes*, Dolores Albarracín, Blair T. Johnson & Mark P. Zanna (eds), 173–221. Mahwah NJ: Lawrence Erlbaum Associates.

Arendt, Birte. 2011. Laientheoretische Konzeptionen von Sprache und Dialekt am Beispiel des Niederdeutschen: Eine kontextsensitive Analyse von Spracheinstellungsäußerungen sowie ihre methodologische Fundierung. *Niederdeutsches Wort: Beiträge zur niederdeutschen Philologie* 51: 133–162.

Aron, Arthur, Aron, Elaine N. & Coups, Elliot J. 2009. *Statistics for Psychology*, 5th edn. Upper Saddle River NJ: Pearson.

Bakhtin, Mikhail. 1986[1952–53]. The problem of speech genres. In *Speech Genres and Other Late Essays*, Vern W. McGee (transl.), Caryl Emerson & Michael Holquist (eds), 60–102. Austin TX: The University of Texas Press.

Baumann, Richard. 1992. Performance. In *Folklore, Cultural Performances, and Popular Entertainments*, Richard Baumann (ed.), 41–49. Oxford: OUP.

Becker, Alton L. 1995. *Beyond Translation*. Ann Arbor MI: University of Michigan Press.

Bergmann, Manfred M. (ed.). 2008. *Advances in Mixed Methods Research*. London: Sage.

Bhaskar, Roy. 1989. *Reclaiming Reality: A Critical Introduction to Contemporary Philosophy*. London: Verso. DOI: 10.1515/lity.2000.4.1.55

Bhaskar, Roy. 1991. *Philosophy and the Idea of Freedom*. Oxford: Basil Blackwell. DOI: 10.1075/cilt.330.01gul

Bhaskar, Roy. 1997. *A Realist Theory of Science*. London: Verso.

Blommaert, Jan. 2005. *Discourse*. Cambridge: CUP.

Bryman, Alan. 2006. Integrating quantitative and qualitative research: How is it done? *Qualitative Research* 6(1): 97–113. DOI: 10.1177/1468794106058877

Bryman, Alan. 2007. Barriers to integrating quantitative and qualitative research. *Journal of Mixed Methods Research* 1(1): 8–22. DOI: 10.1177/2345678906290531

Cameron, Deborah. 2001. *Working with Spoken Discourse*. London: Sage.

Coupland, Nik. 2007. *Style: Language Variation and Identity*. Cambridge: CUP. DOI: 10.1017/CBO9780511755064

Creswell, John W. 2011. Controversies in mixed methods research. In *The SAGE Handbook of Qualitative Research*, Norman K. Denzin & Yvonna S. Lincoln (eds), 269–283. Thousand Oaks CA: Sage.

Creswell, John W. 2014. Die Entwicklung der Mixed-Methods-Forschung. In *Introduction to Mixed Methods*, Udo Kuckartz (ed.), 13–26. Wiesbaden: Springer.

Creswell, John W. & Plano Clark, Vicki L. 2011. *Designing and Conducting Mixed Methods Research*, 2nd edn. Thousand Oaks CA: Sage.

Creswell, John W. & Zhang, Wanqing. 2009. The application of mixed methods designs to trauma research. *Journal of Traumatic Stress* 22(6): 612–621.

Denzin, Norman K. & Lincoln, Yvonna S. 2011. Introduction: The discipline and practice of qualitative research. In *The SAGE Handbook of Qualitative Research*, Norman K. Denzin & Yvonna S. Lincoln (eds), 1–19. Thousand Oaks CA: Sage.

Dörnyei, Zoltan. 2007. *Research Methods in Applied Linguistics*. Oxford: OUP.

Dressler, Wolfgang U. & Wodak, Ruth. 1982. Sociophonological methods in the study of sociolinguistic variation in Viennese German. *Language in Society* 2: 339–370. DOI: 10.1017/S0047404500009350

Eagly, Alice H. & Chaiken, Shelly. 2005. Attitude research in the 21st century: The current state of knowledge. In *The Handbook of Attitudes*, Dolores Albarracín, Blair T. Johnson & Mark P. Zanna (eds), 743–767. Mahwah NJ: Lawrence Erlbaum Associates.

Ebner, Jakob. 2008. *Duden – Österreichisches Deutsch*. Mannheim: Dudenverlag.

Eckert, Penelope. 2008. Variation and the indexical field. *Journal of Sociolinguistics* 12(4): 453–476. DOI: 10.1111/j.1467-9841.2008.00374.x

Erickson, Frederick. 1986. Listening and speaking. In *Languages and Linguistics*, Deborah Tannen & James E. Alatis (eds), 294–319. Washington DC: Georgetown University Press.

Fairclough, Norman. 1992. *Discourse and Social Change*. Cambridge: Polity Press.

Garfinkel, Harold. 1967. *Studies in Ethnomethodology*. Englewood Cliffs NJ: Prentice-Hall.

Garrett, Peter, Coupland, Nik & Williams, Angie. 1999. Evaluating dialect in discourse: Teachers' and teenagers' responses to young English speakers in Wales. *Language in Society* 28: 321–354. DOI: 10.1017/S0047404599003012

Gee, James Paul. 1999. *An Introduction to Discourse Analysis*. London: Routledge.

Gergen, Kenneth J. 2008. On the very idea of social psychology. *Social Psychology Quarterly* 71(4): 331–337. DOI: 10.1177/019027250807100403

Giles, Howard & Coupland, Nik. 1991. *Language: Contexts and Consequences*. Buckingham: Open University Press.

Giles, Howard & Bouchard Ryan, Ellen. 1982. Prolegomena for developing a social psychological theory of language attitudes. In *Attitudes Towards Language Variation*, Ellen Bouchard Ryan & Howard Giles (eds), 208–223. London: Edward Arnold.

Goffman, Erving. 1959. *The Presentation of Self in Everyday Life*. New York NY: Doubleday.

Goffman, Erving. 1974. *Frame Analysis*. Cambridge MA: Harvard University Press.

Goffman, Erving. 1981. *Forms of Talk*. Philadelphia PA: University of Pennsylvania Press.

Gumperz, John J. 1982. *Discourse strategies*. Cambridge: CUP. DOI: 10.1017/CBO9780511611834

Himmelfarb, Samuel. 1993. The measurement of attitudes. In *The Psychology of Attitudes*, Alice H. Eagly & Shelly Chaiken (eds), 23–87. Fort Worth TX: Harcourt Brace Jovanovich.

Howe, Kenneth R. 2003. *Closing Methodological Divides*. Dordrecht: Kluwer.

Huber, Oswald. 2013. *Das psychologische Experiment*, 6th edn. Bern: Hans Huber.

Hymes, Dell. 1972. Models of the interaction of language and social life. In *Directions in Sociolinguistics*, John J. Gumperz & Dell Hymes (eds), 35–71. New York NY: Holt, Rinehart & Winston.

Hyrkstedt, Irene & Kalaja, Paula. 1998. Attitudes toward English and its functions in Finland: A discourse-analytic study. *World Englishes* 17(3): 359–368. DOI: 10.1111/1467-971X.00108

Johnstone, Barbara & Kiesling, Scott F. 2008. Indexicality and experience: Exploring the meanings of /aw/-monophthongization in Pittsburgh. *Journal of Sociolinguistics* 12(1): 5–33. DOI: 10.1111/j.1467-9841.2008.00351.x

Kaiser, Imtraud & Ender, Andrea. 2013. Diglossia or dialect–standard continuum in speakers' awareness and usage: On the categorisation of lectal variation in Austria. In *Variation in Language and Language Use*, Monika Reif, Justyna A. Robinson & Martin Pütz (eds), 273–298. Frankfurt: Peter Lang.

Kristeva, Julia. 1986[1966]. Word, dialog and novel. In *The Kristeva Reader*, Toril Moi (ed.), 34–61. New York NY: Columbia University Press.

Korzybski, Alfred. 1994[1933]. A non-Aristotelian system and its necessity for rigour in mathematics and physics. In *Science and Sanity*, 5th edn, 747–761. Fort Worth TX: Institute of General Semantics.

Kuckartz, Udo. 2014. *Mixed Methods*. Wiesbaden: Springer. DOI: 10.1007/978-3-531-93267-5

Lambert, Wallace E., Hodgson, Richard, Gardner, Robert C. & Fillenbaum, Samuel. 1960. Evaluational reactions to spoken languages. *Journal of Abnormal and Social Psychology* 60(1): 44–51. DOI: 10.1037/h0044430

LaPiere, Richard T. 1934. Attitudes vs. actions. *Social Forces* 13(2): 230–237. DOI: 10.2307/2570339

Lenz, Alexandra N. & Glauninger, Manfred M. (eds). 2015. *Standarddeutsch in 21. Jahrhundert* [Wiener Arbeiten zur Linguistik 1]. Vienna: Vienna University Press.

Liebscher, Grit & Dailey-O'Cain, Jennifer. 2009. Language attitudes in interaction. *Journal of Sociolinguistics* 13(2): 195–222. DOI: 10.1111/j.1467-9841.2009.00404.x

Meinefeld, Werner. 1988. Einstellung. In *Handwörterbuch der Psychologie*, 4th edn, Roland Asanger & Gerd Wenninger (eds), 120–126. Munich: PVU.

Miles, Matthew B. & Huberman, A. Michael. 1994. *Qualitative Data Analysis*, 2nd edn. Thousand Oaks CA: Sage.

Miles, Matthew B., Huberman, A. Michael & Saldana, Johnny. 2014. *Qualitative Data Analysis*, 3rd edn. Thousand Oaks CA: Sage.

Moosmüller, Sylvia. 1988. Dialekt ist nicht gleich Dialekt: Spracheinschätzung in Wien. *Wiener Linguistische Gazette* 40–41: 55–80.

Moosmüller, Sylvia. 1991. *Hochsprache und Dialekt in Österreich*. Vienna: Böhlau.

Morgan, David L. 2007. Paradigms lost and pragmatism regained: Methodological implications of combining qualitative and quantitative methods. *Journal of Mixed Methods Research* 1(1): 48–76. DOI: 10.1177/2345678906292462

Morgan, David L. 2014. *Integrating Qualitative and Quantitative Methods*. Thousand Oaks CA: Sage.

Ortega y Gasset, José. 1959. The difficulty of reading, Clarence E. Parmenter (transl.). *Diogenes* 7(28): 1–17. DOI: 10.1177/039219215900702801

Osgood, Charles E., Suci, George J. & Tannenbaum, Percy H. 1957. *The Measurement of Meaning*. Urbana IL: University of Illinois Press.

Potter, Jonathan. 1998. Discursive social psychology: From attitudes to evaluative practices. *European Review of Social Psychology* 9(1): 233–266. DOI: 10.1080/14792779843000090

Potter, Jonathan & Wetherell, Margaret. 1987. *Discourse and Social Psychology*. London: Sage.

Raskin, Jonathan D. 2002. Constructivism in psychology: Personal construct psychology, radical constructivism, and social constructionism. In Jonathan D. Raskin & Sara K. Bridges (eds) *Studies in Meaning*, 1–25. New York NY: Pace University Press.

Richards, Lyn. 2005. *Handling Qualitative Data*. Thousand Oaks CA: Sage.

Saxe, John Godfrey & Galdone, Paul. 1963. *The Blind Men and the Elephant*. New York NY: McGraw-Hill.

Scheuringer, Hermann. 1997. Sprachvarietäten in Österreich. In *Varietäten des Deutschen*, Gerhard Stickel (ed.), 332–335. Berlin: Walter de Gruyter.

Schiffrin, Deborah. 1994. *Approaches to Discourse*. Malden MA: Blackwell.

Schiffrin, Deborah. 2002. Mother and friends in a Holocaust life story. *Language in Society* 31(3): 309–353. DOI: 10.1017/S0047404502020250

Schiffrin, Deborah. 2014. Discourse. In *An Introduction to Language and Linguistics*, 2nd edn, Ralph W. Fasold & Jeff Connor-Linton (eds), 183–215. Cambridge: CUP.

Schilling, Natalie. 2013. Investigating stylistic variation. In *The Handbook of Language Variation and Change*, 2nd edn, Jack K. Chambers & Natalie Schilling (eds), 327–349. Malden MA: Wiley-Blackwell. DOI: 10.1002/9781118335598

Schilling-Estes, Natalie. 2004. Constructing ethnicity in interaction. *Journal of Sociolinguistics* 8(2): 163–195. DOI: 10.1111/j.1467-9841.2004.00257.x

Scollon, Ron. 2003. The dialogist in a positivist world: Theory in the social sciences and the humanities at the end of the twentieth century. *Social Semiotics* 13(1): 71–88. DOI: 10.1080/1035033032000133517

Scollon, Ron & Scollon, Suzie Wong. 2004. *Nexus Analysis*. New York NY: Routledge.

Soukup, Barbara. 2009. *Dialect Use as Interaction Strategy*. Vienna: Braumüller.

Soukup, Barbara. 2011. Austrian listeners' perceptions of standard-dialect style-shifting: An empirical approach. *Journal of Sociolinguistics* 15(3): 347–365. DOI: 10.1111/j.1467-9841.2011.00500.x

Soukup, Barbara. 2013a. The measurement of 'language attitudes': A reappraisal from a constructionist perspective. In *Language (De)standardisation in Late Modern Europe*, 251–266. Oslo: Novus.

Soukup, Barbara. 2013b. On matching speaker (dis)guises: Revisiting a methodological tradition. In *Language (De)standardisation in Late Modern Europe*, Stefan Grondelaers & Tore Kristiansen (eds), 267–285. Oslo: Novus.

Soukup, Barbara. 2014. Konstruktivismus trifft auf Methodik in der Spracheinstellungsforschung: Theorie, Daten, Fazit. In *Sprechen über Sprache*, Christina Cuonz & Rebekka Studler (eds), 143–168.Tübingen: Stauffenburg.

Steinegger, Guido. 1998. *Sprachgebrauch und Sprachbeurteilung in Österreich und Südtirol*. Frankfurt: Peter Lang.

Tannen, Deborah. 1989. *Talking Voices*. Cambridge: CUP.

Tannen, Deborah & Wallat, Cynthia. 1993. Interactive frames and knowledge schemas in interaction: Examples from a medical examination/ interview. In *Framing in discourse*, Deborah Tannen (ed.), 57–76. Oxford: OUP.

Tashakkori, Abbas & Creswell, John W. 2007. Editorial: The new era of mixed methods. *Journal of Mixed Methods Research* 1(1): 3–7. DOI: 10.1177/2345678906293042

Tashakkori, Abbas & Teddlie, Charles (eds) 2010. *The SAGE Handbook of Mixed Methods in Social & Behavioral Research*, 2nd edn. Thousand Oaks CA: Sage.

Teddlie, Charles & Tashakkori, Abbas. 2010. Overview of contemporary issues in mixed methods research. In Tashakkori & Teddlie (eds), 1–41.

Tophinke, Doris & Ziegler, Evelyn. 2006. "Aber bitte im Kontext!" Neue Perspektiven der dialektologischen Einstellungsforschung. *Osnabrücker Beiträge zur Sprachtheorie* 1: 205–224.

Vygotsky, Lev S. 1978. *Mind in Society*. Michael Cole, Vera John-Steiner, Sylvia Scribner & Ellen Souberman (eds). Cambridge MA: Harvard University Press.

Widdowson, Henry G. 2004. *Text, Context, Pretext*. Malden MA: Blackwell. DOI: 10.1002/9780470758427

Wiesinger, Peter. 2006. *Das österreichische Deutsch in Gegenwart und Geschichte*. Vienna: LIT.

PART II

Implicit and/or explicit? When are attitudes "authentic"?

The primary relevance of subconsciously offered attitudes

Focusing the language ideological aspect of sociolinguistic change

Tore Kristiansen
University of Copenhagen

The chapter deals with the role of language-ideological structures in linguistic variation and change at the macro-level of societal life. It argues that we need to construe (conceptualize and operationalize) data collection contexts which allow for a clear distinction between consciously (overtly) and subconsciously (covertly) offered attitudes – because subconsciously offered attitudes appear to be a driving force in linguistic variation and change in a way that consciously offered attitudes are not. The argument is based on evidence from empirical investigations of attitudes and use in the 'standard vs. non-standard' dimension in Denmark, and in the 'national vs. English' dimension in seven Nordic communities (including the Icelandic, Faroese, Norwegian, Danish, Swedish, Finland-Swedish, and Finnish communities).

1. Introduction

All the data we gather and prepare for analysis and interpretation are constructed. As any introduction to research methodology will tell, the construction should secure that the data are valid and reliable; and it will be explained that data validity is about whether or not the constructed data are *relevant* to the question which is being asked. It goes without saying that answers which are based on data that are not relevant, must be bad answers. The problem is, however, that it is often far from obvious which data are relevant to solving a research problem, and which are not. This is not least the case when the research problem concerns the interconnecting relationship between processes of social, language-ideological and linguistic change. An endeavor to conceptualize and operationalize the investigation of this relationship will study what Nikolas Coupland calls *sociolinguistic change* – i.e. "will study language-ideological change in the context of social change, and refer

DOI 10.1075/impact.39.04kri
© 2015 John Benjamins Publishing Company

to changes in linguistic usage within that broader matrix" (Coupland 2009: 43; see also Coupland 2014). My additional claim, which will be explicated in this chapter, is that we will need to study the language-ideological aspect of sociolinguistic change at different levels of consciousness – because subconsciously offered attitudes are far more relevant than consciously offered attitudes when it comes to explaining stability/change in language use.

The latter claim is based on my own experience from projects which have addressed the role of attitudes in two rather different contexts of language contact and impact. First I discuss the issue at a national level in terms of the relational strength between varieties of Danish, based on experience from the LANCHART project.[1] Then I take the issue to an international level and discuss it in terms of influence from English on seven speech communities/languages in the Northern area of Europe, based on experience from the MIN project.[2]

In terms of methodology, approaches to the construction of attitudinal data are commonly held to fall into three different categories: (i) collection and analyses of various behavioral data, including public texts of different kinds, that shed light on *how the norm-and-variation issue is treated in the society,* (ii) collection and analyses of self-reported data obtained through various forms of *direct* questioning, and (iii) collection and analyses of self-reported data obtained through various forms of *indirect* questioning (Ryan, Giles & Hewstone 1988; Garrett 2010). In what follows, like in the studies I report from, these approaches are used to construct data which are meant to be representative of three potentially different language-ideological structures at work in a society: (i) official ideology, (ii) conscious attitudes, and (iii) subconscious attitudes.

The extent to which these ideological structures are similar or different across local communities in a country like Denmark, or across larger communities across an area like the Nordic countries, is a question which has to be answered

---

1. The LANCHART project (LANguage CHAnge in Real Time; ⟨http://www.dgcss.ku.dk⟩) is funded by the Danish National Research Foundation, grant DNRF63, to Professor Frans Gregersen, Copenhagen University, for a ten year period 2005–2015. The attitudinal data referred to in this chapter was collected in 2005–2006. For detailed presentations of the LANCHART attitudes studies, see Kristiansen 2009; Grondelaers & Kristiansen 2013).

2. The area will be referred to as 'the Nordic countries' and includes, from west to east: Iceland, The Faroe Islands, Norway, Denmark, Sweden, and Finland. The MIN project (Modern Import words in the languages in the Nordic countries; ⟨http://folk.uib.no/hnohs/MIN/⟩) was initiated by the then existing Nordic Language Council (*Nordisk Språkråd*), was led by Professor Helge Sandøy, University of Bergen, and was financially supported by various sources in the period 2000–2010. For detailed presentations of the MIN attitudes studies, see Kristiansen & Vikør 2006; Kristiansen 2006; Kristiansen 2010.

by empirical investigations (Sections 2 and 3). If the results of such investigations point to the existence of conflicting patterns of attitudes, our next step will be to look at how these conflicting attitudinal patterns relate to language use patterns. Comparisons of the various patterns will form the basis of claims about which attitudes, if any, are relevant to our understanding of the role of subjective forces in processes of language variation and change (Sections 4 and 5). To finish, an attempt will be made to understand the established ideological patterns in their socio-historical contexts (Section 6), before a few concluding remarks round off the chapter (Section 7).

2.   Denmark: Attitudes towards varieties of Danish

2.1   Official hierarchization of varieties

When one sets out to characterize the official ideology of a country like Denmark in terms of how the 'dialect vs. standard' issue is treated, one would ideally like to look as broadly and deeply as possible at all the main institutions that uphold the public sectors of society: the institutions of education, religion, business, administration, politics, and all aspects of cultural life (not least the media).

The school is probably the institution which has been subjected to the broadest and deepest investigation of how the 'dialect vs. standard' issue has been, and is being treated in Danish society – in a book-length study (Kristiansen 1990) on which the following short characterisation is based. From the introduction of compulsory schooling in 1814 until the 1960s, discourse on variation as a norm issue simply did not exist. *Rigsdansk* (the traditional term for 'Standard Danish') was the 'natural' and 'self-evident' language of the school. The norm-and-variation issue was dealt with only in terms of 'natural', 'distinct', 'clear', 'pure', 'nice' speech (the school's language) vs. 'distorted', 'indistinct', 'vulgar' speech (the youth's language). During the 1960s, the school's notion of *dannelse* ('educatedness') changed from this traditional 'bourgeois' version with its aesthetic and moral demands on language form, into a 'social democrat' version which addressed the norm issue in terms of 'normal', 'common', 'appropriate' language vs. 'special', 'group', 'inappropriate' language – i.e. as a demand for equality and situational adjustment. In the new ideology, local *dialects* were generally talked about as objects to be highly estimated – in terms of 'tolerance', 'respect', and' love'. However, as the use of 'broad' dialect potentially hampers communication, a modern society needs a shared 'standard' language in order to secure effective communication and equal possibilities for all. The required appropriation by everybody of *rigsdansk* (under the denomination of *fællessprog* 'common language') was now explicitly propagated as a means of communication to be conceived of as 'appropriate and necessary for public use in a modern society', and at the same time as 'socially neutral'. Expanding among young people, a new way of speaking 'standard' Danish – featuring some new phonetic developments together with traditionally stigmatised phonetics associated with the working class of the capital city and known as *københavnsk* ('Copenhagen speech') – was explicitly turned into a serious problem because it allegedly put communication between generations in danger. This way of speaking was negatively characterised in terms borrowed from both discourses (the 'traditional bourgeois' and the 'new social democratic')' as 'sloppy', 'indistinct', and 'inappropriate', and teachers were instructed to be observant of such speech and discourage it.

Thus, in today's official evaluative hierarchy of Danish varieties, we may say that *rigsdansk* and the *dialects* interchange in the top positions depending on the perspective (communicative effectiveness or social identity) – while *københavnsk* is generally downgraded.

2.2   Conscious hierarchization of varieties

The Danish LANCHART project studies five communities which cover the whole country from east to west (see map in Figure 1). The communities differ largely in terms of size and potential for general influence, nationally or regionally. In the east, on the island of Sealand, *Copenhagen* is the capital and only big city. In southern Sealand, *Næstved* as a middle-sized Danish town plays the role as a regional centre. On the island of Funen, the small town of *Vissenbjerg* is today more like a suburb to Odense, Denmark's third largest city. Likewise, in Jutland, the small town of *Odder* is in many ways a suburb to Århus, the second largest city of Denmark. In the far west, the small town of *Vinderup* is situated close to the middle-sized regional centre of Holstebro.

When we ask people direct questions about their views on (some aspect of) language, they will normally answer in full awareness of giving away language attitudes. Responses that are elicited in this way, I shall refer to as 'consciously offered attitudes', or 'conscious attitudes' for short. The 'label ranking task' (LRT), when administered to large audiences of people, is a simple way of collecting huge amounts of readily quantifiable attitudinal data. The method has been used for a long time in language attitudes studies, beginning with Giles (1970). In the LANCHART project, audiences of 9th graders (15–16 years old) were given a list of dialect names covering all of Denmark, and were asked to rank the dialects according to their personal preference. While the total number of names in the lists varied between seven and eleven in the five sites under study, all lists contained labels for the speech variation assumed to be relevant to social

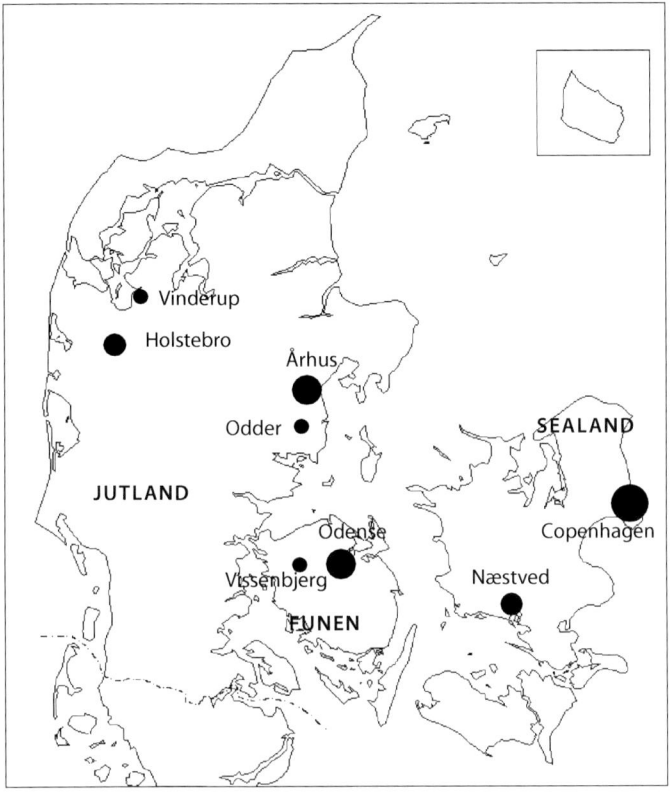

Figure 1. Map of Denmark with LANCHART sites Copenhagen, Næstved, Vissenbjerg, Odder, Vinderup – and potential linguistic norm centres Odense, Århus, Holstebro

identification processes among adolescents in their local community – namely *københavnsk*, *rigsdansk* and the name of their *local dialect*. These data were collected in 2005–2006.

Focusing the analyses on the relative ranking of these labels, we can summarize that the major ideological force involved in the task appears to be *local patriotism*. The same evaluative hierarchy emerged in all five communities (see Table 1). The local variety came out in top position, followed by the variety of the local big city, or the neighbouring dialect in cases of no local big city. As *rigsdansk* followed everywhere in third position, the adolescents seem to recognize a particular status for this variety in comparison with all other varieties. *Københavnsk* appeared further down in the rankings – with the modification that 'the principle of local patriotism' secured top position for *københavnsk* in Copenhagen itself, and second position for *københavnsk* in Næstved, where Copenhagen is the local bigger city.

Table 1. Label ranking in the five LANCHART communities

København		Næstved		Vissenbjerg		Odder		Vinderup	
københavnsk	*1,57*	*sjællandsk*	*1,50*	*fynsk*	*2,09*	*østjysk*	*2,26*	*midtjysk*	*3,00*
sjællandsk	*2,53*	*københavnsk*	*2,67*	*odenseansk*	*2,09*	*århusiansk*	*2,53*	*vestjysk*	*3,52*
rigsdansk	**3,28**	**rigsdansk**	**3,72**	**rigsdansk**	**3,54**	**rigsdansk**	**4,91**	**rigsdansk**	**4,86**
fynsk	4,78	lol-falstersk	4,14	jysk	4,48	**københavnsk**	**5,41**	nordjysk	5,01
århusiansk	5,12	fynsk	4,50	sjællandsk	5,00	nordjysk	5,57	århusiansk	5,56
jysk	5,13	jysk	5,39	**københavnsk**	**5,02**	vestjysk	5,86	østjysk	5,60
bornholmsk	5,59	bornholmsk	6,02	bornholmsk	5,89	sjællandsk	5,95	sønderjysk	6,91
						fynsk	6,73	fynsk	7,21
						sønderjysk	7,09	sjællandsk	7,27
						bornholmsk	8,73	**københavnsk**	**7,63**
								bornholmsk	9,32
p<0,001		p<0,001		p<0,001		p<0,001		p<0,001	
n=135,		n=163,		n=54,		n=172,		n=81,	
chi² =412, df=6		chi² =502, df=6		chi² =151, df=6		chi² = 645, df=9		chi² =261, df=10	

Figures are mean ranks on a 7-point scale (Copenhagen, Næstved, Vissenbjerg), a 10-point scale (Odder), and an 11-point scale (Vinderup). Significance test: Friedman. Post-hoc testing (Wilcoxon signed-rank test) shows that all differences between the varieties that are of particular interest to the research – i.e. [*local varieties*], **rigsdansk** and københavnsk – are significant in all the communities.

2.3 Subconscious hierarchization of varieties

The common way to ask people *indirectly* about their views on (some aspect of) language is to design a 'speaker evaluation experiment' (SEE) and ask listeners to evaluate short clips of audio-recorded speakers. While SEEs can be based on either the 'matched guise technique' (MGT) using the same speaker to represent different varieties or the 'verbal guise technique' (VGT) using different speakers to represent different varieties, the important point to be noticed here about both versions of the SEE approach is that responses are only indirectly about language (– at least to the extent that listeners are asked for reactions to speakers instead of speech varieties).

It should be noticed, however, that answers to such indirect questions are not necessarily 'subconsciously offered attitudes'. The SEE should not be treated as a method that automatically yields subconscious (or covert, or private, or implicit) language attitudes. In fact, it may not only be difficult but simply impossible in some contexts to design and implement a SEE so that the participants do not think 'it's about my attitudes to dialects'. Issues to be considered and solved in order to avoid such participant awareness concern, in particular, the gamut and kind of variation which can be included in the stimulus material, the kind of questions which can be included in the measurement instrument, and also the implementation of a procedure which can secure that nothing is revealed about the objective either before or during the data collection session. Such issues are not our concern here, however.

In the LANCHART project we used a SEE based on the VGT. Prior to completing the LRT described above, and still being unaware of the objective of the whole data collection session, the same adolescents from the five communities listened to and evaluated clippings of speech from twelve 16–17 year old high school students who spoke freely about *what's a good teacher like?* The clippings had been edited so as to be quite similar in length (c. 30 seconds), content and fluency. The speakers represented the three accents of Danish that are relevant to social identification processes among present-day Danish adolescents in their local communities. We call these accents CONSERVATIVE, MODERN and LOCAL, and sometimes just use c-/m-/l- to refer to this variation. (More below on how these 'names' relate to the 'names' used in the LRT.) By and large, CONSERVATIVE and MODERN differ from each other in terms of segmental features, whereas LOCAL differs from CONSERVATIVE and MODERN mainly in terms of suprasegmental features. This reflects the language situation in present-day Denmark, where regional variation is by and large reduced to suprasegmental (prosodic) features in young people's speech (more on this in Section 4 below). We used four voices representing each accent in order to control for possible other influences (than the targeted linguistic features) on assessments. In other words, the criterion for accepting accent as a main factor was that the four voices were judged in a similar way, and thus were grouped together by the assessment. (This turned out to be the case.) All four c- and all four m-speakers were from Copenhagen, and were used in the SEEs in all five communities (in Copenhagen, only these eight voices were used), whereas the four l-speakers were from the local big city or bigger town. The reason for this was that we wanted to investigate the role of these places as possible local linguistic norm centres. In Næstved, the l-voices were from Næstved itself, in Vissenbjerg from Odense, in Odder from Århus, and in Vinderup from Holstebro (see map in Figure 1). The assessment was done by ticking off on eight seven-point 'adjective scales' representing positive vs. negative personality traits ('intelligent – stupid', 'fascinating – boring', etc.).[3]

The results in Figure 2 show the same pattern for all 5 communities: l-accented speech is assessed very negatively in comparison with c- and m-accented speech

---

3. The scales are given in English translation in Figure 2. In Danish, the adjective pairs were: 1. *klog–dum*, 2. *seriøs–ligeglad*, 3. *målrettet–sløv*, 4. *til at stole på–ikke til at stole på*, 5. *selvsikker–usikker*, 6. *spændende–kedelig*, 7. *tjekket–utjekket*, 8. *flink–usympatisk*.

on all scales. As to the M/C-variation, M-speech is most strongly upgraded on 'dynamism' traits (self-assured, fascinating, cool, nice), whereas C-accented speech does just as well or even better on 'superiority' traits (intelligent, conscientious, goal-directed, trustworthy). Overall, the ranking of Danish accents by adolescents is MODERN > CONSERVATIVE > LOCAL when subconsciously offered.

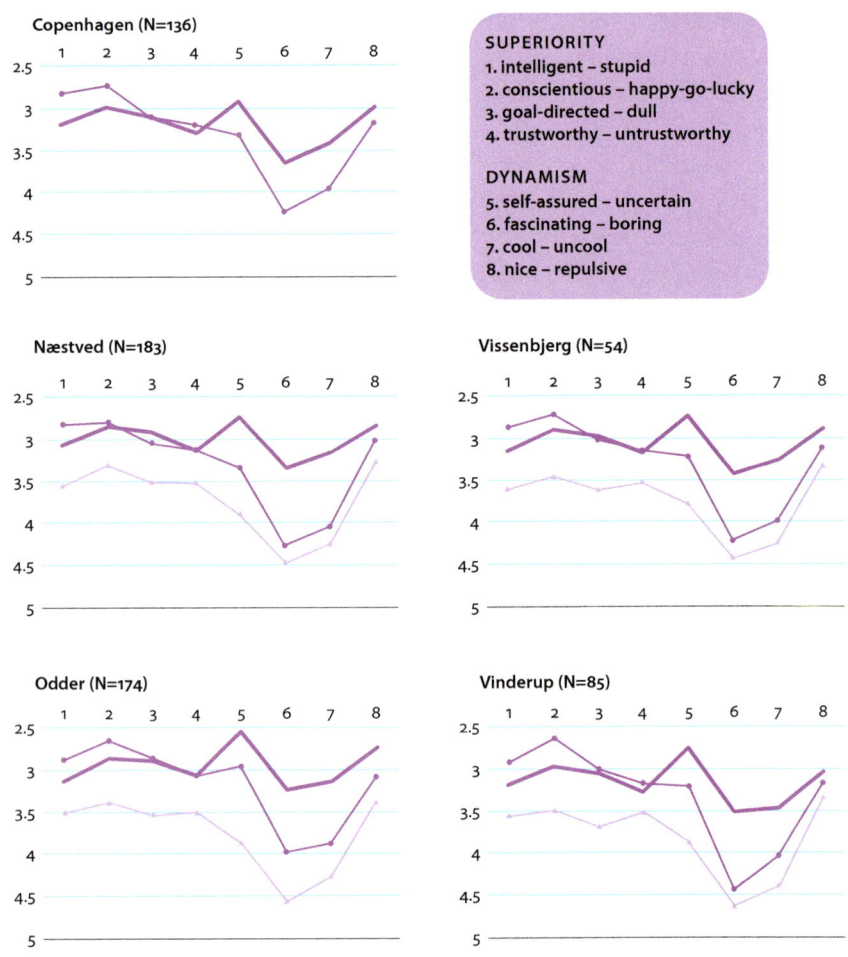

Figure 2. Results of SEEs in the five LANCHART communities showing subconscious evaluations of CONSERVATIVE (thin curve), MODERN (thick curve) and LOCAL (light curve). Entities on the X-axis are the eight measurement scales (personality traits) which – based on the evaluative patterns for CONSERVATIVE and MODERN – can be grouped into four 'superiority' scales (1–4) and four 'dynamism' scales (5–8). Values on the Y-axis are means on the seven-point measurement scales. A low value (high position in the graphs) is a more positive evaluation (in the sense that *intelligent* is positive and *stupid* negative, etc.)

2.4   Comparison of the evaluative hierarchizations

The evaluative hierarchizations of varieties that we have established for the Danish speech community can be summarized and compared as shown in Table 2.

Table 2. Ranking of…
…*rigsdansk–københavnsk–dialect/s* in Official ideology and Conscious evaluation (LRT)
…CONSERVATIVE–MODERN–LOCAL in Subconscious evaluation (SEE)

Evaluative Hierarchy	Evaluative Perspective	Ranking		
		(1)	(2)	(3)
Official	communicative efficiency/ social identity	rigsdansk/dialects		københavnsk
Conscious	liking (preference)	*own dialect*	*rigsdansk*	*københavnsk*
Subconscious	superiority	CONSERVATIVE	MODERN	LOCAL
	dynamism	MODERN	CONSERVATIVE	LOCAL

In the official evaluative hierarchy, *rigsdansk* and *dialects* (i.e. dialects in general) interchange in the top position depending on whether the evaluative perspective has to do with 'communicative effectiveness' or 'social identity' – while *københavnsk* is generally downgraded.

By and large this is also the pattern we find with the adolescents in their conscious hierarchization, which seems to be governed by a sense of 'local patriotism' in combination with an acceptance or recognition of a special status for *rigsdansk* (the 'local patriotism' principle ensured, though, that *københavnsk* was ranked better than *rigsdansk* in both Copenhagen and Næstved).

In a second phase of the SEEs, participants listened to the stimulus recordings once more and assessed the twelve speakers in terms of how '*rigsdansk*' they sounded, and in terms of whether they were 'from Copenhagen or the local city'. The results showed CONSERVATIVE to be predominantly associated with *rigsdansk*, MODERN to be predominantly associated with Copenhagen, and LOCAL to be predominantly associated with the local city. We take it that these documented associations form a fairly solid basis for comparing rankings of LRT data and SEE data, and for claiming that the subconscious ranking of varieties turns the consciously offered hierarchy upside down. Any trace of local patriotism (as expressed in LRT) evaporates as non-Copenhagen youngsters everywhere strongly downgrade the L-accented speech (in SEE), which in most cases will be their own speech. No trace of the overt denigration of *københavnsk* (in LRT) survives in the general upgrading of M-accented speech (in SEE), which is particularly manifest on dynamic personality traits.

Whether they emerge as very similar (as in the case of official and conscious hierarchizations) or very different (as in the case of conscious and subconscious hierarchizations), it is far from obvious how we can account for these language-ideological structures. We shall return to that issue in Section 6.

3.   The Nordic communities: Attitudes towards the influence from English

3.1   Official ideology: Purism vs. laissez-faire

The speech communities which were studied in the MIN project included (from west to east): the Icelandic, Faroese, Norwegian, Danish, Sweden-Swedish, Finland-Swedish, and Finnish communities. Historically, these communities have been and still are linked to each other in multiple ways that engender much similarity, but also a lot of difference. Official language politics and policies in relation to foreign influence is one ideological domain which exhibits huge differences.

The clarity of this ideological differentiation is such that linguists and other learned people with interest in language politics and policies readily agree on how the Nordic communities rank relatively to each other as far as external purism is concerned. Such rankings, based on general acquaintance with the official language policies of the communities, can actually be found in the literature (Lund 1986: 35; Vikør 1995: 181). Thus, the *learned people's purism profile* ranks the Nordic communities as follows (from more to less purist): ICELANDIC – FAROESE – NORWEGIAN – FINNISH – FINLAND-SWEDISH – SWEDEN-SWEDISH – DANISH.

Also lay people agree on these language-ideological differences. MIN data include answers from interviewees to a question about how they think 'imported words' are treated in the other Nordic communities, as well as in their own. The answering format offered five options: most of them are translated, the greater part is translated, fifty–fifty, a lesser part is translated, almost none is translated. We allocated values from 1 to 5 to these options and computed mean values in order to compare the 'purism level' that each of the communities estimated for their own and the other communities. As the results were by and large the same in all communities (see Figure 2 in Kristiansen & Sandøy 2010a: 4), we can present a total *lay people's purism profile* of the Nordic communities (from more to less purist): ICELANDIC – FAROESE – FINNISH – NORWEGIAN – SWEDISH – DANISH (the interview question did not ask specifically about Finland-Swedish).

The lay profile differs from the learned profile only in the ranking of the Norwegian and Finnish communities. Contrary to the experts' view, lay people hold the Finnish community to be somewhat more purist than the Norwegian community. The explanation for this difference is probably to do with the Norwegian two-languages situation. Lay people may have thought of the more commonly used Bokmål (written language with roots in the Danish written language), whereas Nynorsk (written language with roots in the Norwegian dialects) is likely to be more salient to the expert mind when purism is on the agenda. When he includes both Norwegian languages, Vikør's ranking looks like this (from more to less purism): ICELANDIC – FAROESE – NYNORSK – FINNISH – FINLAND-SWEDISH – BOKMÅL – SWEDEN-SWEDISH – DANISH (Vikør 2010).

3.2 Conscious attitudes towards English influence

Consciously offered attitudes were obtained in telephone interviews, conducted by professional poll institutes, with representative population samples in all of the seven participating communities (total N about 6000). The same questions were asked in all seven communities (to the extent that it is possible to ask different communities the same question). The English influence issue was addressed both 'abstractly' (subjects were asked to express degree of agreement with four statements, e.g. 'far too many English words are being used today') and 'concretely' (subjects were presented with three pairs of presumed synonymous word pairs and asked about their preference for either the English or national word, e.g. *e-mail* or *tölvupóstur* in the Icelandic community).

When scores are pooled together for the four abstract items, and for the three concrete approaches, the two resulting rankings of the speech communities appear as shown in Table 3. The only difference between the two rankings consists in a change of positions as number (2) and (3) for the Faroese and Finnish communities. In general, the Icelandic, Faroese, and Finnish communities emerge as the more purist ones in consciously offered answers to direct questioning, the Danish and Swedish communities are the more open ones, the Norwegian and Finland-Swedish communities are in-between.

Table 3. Seven Nordic communities rank-ordered according to degrees of consciously expressed external purism by lay people in 'abstract' and 'concrete' approaches to the English-influence issue

	(1)		(2)		(3/4/5)		(6)		(7)
abstract	Ic	/	Fa	>	No/FS/Fi	>	SS	>	Da
concrete	Ic	>	Fi	>	FS/No/Fa	>	SS	>	Da

Ic = Icelandic, Fa = Faeroese, No = Norwegian, FS = Finland-Swedish, Fi = Finnish, SS = Sweden-Swedish, Da = Danish. > = significant, / = non-significant

If we collapse the results from both approaches (abstract and concrete) into one general ranking, it looks like this (from more to less purist): ICELANDIC – FAROESE/FINNISH – FINLAND-SWEDISH/NORWEGIAN – SWEDEN-SWEDISH – DANISH. If we limit ourselves to looking at the Scandinavian-language communities (which we will do in the comparison between consciously and subconsciously offered attitudes, for reasons to be explained below) the rank order in both approaches is (from more to less purist): FINLAND-SWEDISH/NORWEGIAN – SWEDEN-SWEDISH – DANISH.

3.3   Subconscious attitudes towards English influence

The speaker evaluation experiment (SEE) that was designed for the MIN project used the matched-guise technique (MGT), and we made strong efforts to design the experiment in accordance with the previously mentioned guidelines for securing collection of subconsciously offered data (Section 2.3). The idea of the MGT is to measure differences in reaction to speech which is varied in form and controlled for impact of speaker characteristics and content. Thus, the same speaker appeared twice (in two 'guises') on the stimulus recording – in both a 'pure' guise and an 'English-coloured' guise – dispersed among 3 filler-voices. Control for impact from content was obtained by having the speakers read or perform the same text.

The MG voice had six-seven English features in her English-colored guise and none in her pure guise. A couple of the alternated features related to phonology and morphology (e.g. *hackning* vs. *hacking*), but most of them were lexical in kind (e.g. *kreditkort* vs. *credit card*). Much effort was put into making the English coloring of the text the 'same' in all languages. Three filler voices had various combinations of the English features. In all seven communities, the five speech samples (four speakers) were women aged around 30, and they spoke for about fifty seconds each. Audiences were told that a radio station was interested in their help in choosing between five applicants for a position as newsreader. The applicants had been given the same short text from a news agency. Their task had been, during ten minutes, to make whatever changes they wanted to the text and prepare for reading it aloud. The text itself was taken from a Danish newspaper and dealt with an issue – online shopping – which made the use of some English words seem 'natural'. In brief, this whole cover-up story aimed at construing a plausible situation for five slightly different performances of one and the same text. The performances were assessed from 'not at all' to 'very much' on eight seven-point scales representing (what was assumed to be) positive personality traits. (Finally the applicants were to be ranked from one to five according to their suitability for the job.)

It goes without saying that the construction of English-coloured guises capable of eliciting comparable data for six different languages across seven different speech communities[4] is no easy matter; and it takes a good cover story to make this whole set-up probable as something else than a readily recognizable attitudes-towards-English experiment. I shall not delve into these problems here, but underline that we feel assured – on the basis of responses given in debriefing sessions in immediate continuation of the SEEs – that our data from the Scandinavian-language communities (Norwegian, Danish, Sweden-Swedish, and Finland-Swedish) represent subconsciously offered attitudes. As our purpose is to compare consciously and subconsciously offered attitudes, only results for these communities are included in the following.[5]

The results are based on responses from samples of around 600 informants in each of the communities, broadly recruited in terms of background factors. The results for the Danish community showed a strong favoring of the pure guise on all evaluative items. Favoring of the pure guise was also true for the Sweden-Swedish community – but far less so with regard to items that normally are said to reflect competence and status (*ambitious, intelligent, independent, efficient*) than with regard to items that are assumed to reflect sociability and solidarity (*pleasant, trustworthy, interesting, relaxed*). In contrast, the Finland-Swedish and Norwegian communities showed tendencies of upgrading the English-colored guise in comparison with the pure guise. In the Finland-Swedish community, the English guise was judged more *efficient* and *interesting*; in the Norwegian community it was judged more *ambitious, independent* and *relaxed*.

Two mean values, one for the pure guise and one for the English-colored guise, were calculated for each community by adding the values for all eight personality items and dividing by eight. The difference between the two mean values was taken as a measure of relative 'English-positivity/-negativity' in the communities – or to stay with the terminology we have used so far in this chapter: a measure of 'more or less purism'. Based on this difference the communities rank as follows (from more to less purist): DANISH – SWEDEN-SWEDISH – FINLAND-SWEDISH/ NORWEGIAN.

---

4.   Seven different communities but six different languages because the same stimulus material was used in both Sweden and Sweden-language Finland.

5.   In the Icelandic and Faroese communities, the SEEs did not succeed in the crucial sense that unawareness was maintained, as reactions and responses during experiment as well as debriefing session clearly told that the informants had become aware of our experimental goal. To a lesser extent, this problem also occurred in the Finnish community. This experience may in itself be indicative of a stronger external purism.

3.4 Comparison of official, conscious, and subconscious attitudes towards the influence from English

Our various rankings of the Nordic speech communities/languages in terms of external purism can be summarized and compared as shown in Table 4.

Table 4. Rankings of Nordic speech communities in terms of external purism based on...
...(1) estimated level of purism in official ideology – by learned (a and b) and lay (c)
...(2) measured level of purism in lay people's consciously (a) and subconsciously (b)
   offered attitudes towards English influence in their speech communities/languages

	more purist .... less purist							

(1) estimated level of purism in official ideology...									
by learned (a)	Ic	– Fa	– No	– Fi	– FS	–	SS	– Da	
(b)	Ic	– Fa	– NN	– Fi	– FS – BM	– SS	– Da		
by lay (c)	Ic	– Fa	–	Fi	–	No – Sw	– Da		
(2) measured level of purism in lay evaluations offered...									
consciously (a)	Ic	–	Fa/Fi	–	FS/No	– SS	– Da		
subconscious (b)					Da	– SS	– FS/No		

Ic=Icelandic, Fa=Faroese, No=Norwegian (NN=Nynorsk, BM=Bokmål), Fi=Finnish, Sw=Swedish (FS=Finland Swedish, SS=Sweden Swedish), Da=Danish

In the upper part of the table, we might be surprised by the fact that lay people, when asked how they think the Nordic communities treat 'imported words', produce exactly the same ranking (1c) as the experts in these matters (when these focus on Bokmål instead of Nynorsk) (1b).

In the lower part of the table, it seems not only surprising but almost mysterious that representative samples of lay people, being telephone-interviewed about how they relate to the English influence on their own community/language, respond in a way that makes their community appear in the rank position (2a) where it 'should be' according to both learned (1b) and lay (1c) estimations of language-ideological differences in matters of external purism.

Finally, it certainly comes as a surprise when the ranking of the Scandinavian-language communities resulting from lay people's consciously offered evaluation (2a) is reversed in the ranking resulting from their subconsciously offered evaluation (2b) (see the two shadowed rankings).

Like in the case of the Danish community, the total picture is one of coexisting strong similarity (official and conscious hierarchizations) and radical difference (conscious and subconscious hierarchizations), and, again, it is far from obvious how we can account for these language-ideological structures – an issue we shall return to in Section 6 below.

4.   Which attitudinal pattern, if any, is likely to be relevant to the understanding of contemporary changes in the relational strength between Danish varieties?

The attitudinal patterns that were summarized for the Danish speech community in Table 2 above may no doubt give rise to interesting interpretations and further explorations in many directions. My own main interest, however, and the one I shall focus on here, concerns the role of attitudes in language variation and change. So, now that we have established, in empirical investigations, what the Danish community looks like at the social macro-level of language-ideological structuring, and furthermore have established the existence of conflicting ideological structures, we will need to consider and decide which one of the attitudinal patterns, if any, is relevant to our efforts to understand how the relative strength of Danish varieties has developed and continues to develop.

It is descriptively well-documented that all Danish speech has become very similar to Danish as heard in Copenhagen – at all linguistic levels except for prosody. No matter where they live, young Danes speak accents of *rigsdansk*, which historically speaking is 'Copenhagen dialect spread to the whole country' (Brink & Lund 1975: 769). As far as we can judge, the radical de-dialectalisation of Denmark took off in the 1960s, and the traditional dialects were dead or moribund around 1980, in the sense that the everyday speech of children and adolescents was much closer to Copenhagen speech than to the local traditional dialect. This was found to be the case in the far-western town of Vinderup already in the first variationist study in Denmark in the 1970s (Kristensen 1977), and variationist studies based on data from the 1980s showed that young people in Odder (Jul Nielsen & Nyberg 1993) and Næstved (Jørgensen & Kristensen 1994) appropriated Copenhagen speech more in its 'low' variety than in its 'high' variety. As the associations that go with the variation in Copenhagen speech are no longer a matter of social class, at least not in the same sense as 30–40 years ago, we found it timely in the LANCHART project to drop the terms 'low Copenhagen' and 'high Copenhagen' (Brink and Lund's terminology) and use MODERN and CONSERVATIVE instead, although some of the linguistic variation involved is still the same.[6]

---

6.   For overviews (with further references) that document the radical transformation of Denmark from a traditional European 'dialect society' to, arguably, Europe's 'standard

Thus, a ranking of Danish varieties in terms of their relative strength (their 'production vitality') among adolescents yields the pattern: MODERN > CONSERVA-TIVE > LOCAL.

This relative strength pattern for use corresponds well with the subconsciously offered SEE pattern, but not at all with either the consciously offered LRT pattern or the official ideology (see Table 2). Therefore – on the assumptions that language attitudes do influence language use and, furthermore, that relative attitudinal positivity towards a variety favors its use whereas relative attitudinal negativity disfavors use – our conclusion for the Danish community must be that *subconsciously offered attitudes influence language use in a way that consciously offered attitudes do not*. Theoretically, it is still possible of course that evaluative support is a companion rather than a motor of production vitality. We do have some empirical indication, however, that the evaluative upgrading of MODERN Copenhagen speech does precede its geographical diffusion. Firstly, the issue has been studied in terms of prediction in real time data. In the 1980s data from Næstved adolescents, boys used more MODERN features than girls, while girls were subconsciously more positive than boys towards MODERN-accented speakers. Taking this pattern as their outset, Kristiansen and Jørgensen (2005) ventured the prediction that Næstved girls would be found to use more MODERN features than Næstved boys if the issue were to be studied in the future. Later, a study by Kammacher et al. (2011) confirmed the prediction. Secondly, while the subconscious social evaluation of Copenhagen speech (MODERN and CONSERVATIVE) has spread in a copy-like way across the whole of Denmark (see Figure 2), the innovative features seem to diffuse with some time delay depending on geographical distance and/or size in terms of population (Maegaard et al. 2013).

5.   Which attitudinal pattern, if any, is likely to be relevant to the understanding of English influence in the Nordic communities?

Just as with Danish varieties (Table 2) it is clear that language-ideological structures with regard to English influence may be very different 'things' depending on whether attitudes are consciously or subconsciously offered (Table 4 rows 2(a) and (b)). However, in the case of English influence, it is less clear to what extent it can also be claimed that it is the subconsciously offered attitudes which yield the better correspondence with empirically established strength patterns concerning use.

In the MIN project, the occurrence of English influence was quantitatively measured and compared across the Nordic communities at the levels of words,

---

language society' par excellence, see Kristiansen & Jørgensen (1998: 239–241); Pedersen (2003); Kristensen (2003); Maegaard et al. (2013).

orthography and morphology for written language, and at the levels of phonology and morphology for spoken language. Newspaper texts (from the same days and years in all communities) made up the main material for the studies of written language, whereas the spoken language material was elicited from informants. A calculated total ranking of the communities on the basis of these results looks as follows (from most to least purist): ICELANDIC – FINNISH – FAROESE – FINLAND-SWEDISH – SWEDEN-SWEDISH – NORWEGIAN – DANISH (see Sandøy & Kristiansen 2010, which also gives the more detailed results). This corresponds well with the rankings which result from consciously offered attitudes (Table 3) – except that the Norwegian community comes out as generally less purist than both Swedish-language communities, second in terms of 'laissez-faire' only to the Danish community.

In fact, at the level of words, the MIN results showed the Norwegian 'openness' to join or even outdo the Danish community. In editorial newspaper texts from the year 2000, the measured frequencies of imported words (the large majority of which were English) gave the following ranking of the Nordic communities (number of imported words per 10.000 running words in parentheses): ICELANDIC (12) – FAROESE (27) – FINNISH (35) – FINLAND-SWEDISH (68) – SWEDEN-SWEDISH (70) – DANISH (82) – NORWEGIAN (88). It was furthermore established, in an analysis which compared with the same text genre from the year 1975, that the frequency of imported words had risen from a lower level, and thus faster, in the Norwegian newspaper (from 21 to 88/10.000) than in the Danish newspaper (from 31 to 82/10.000).

Restricting ourselves to the four Scandinavian-language communities for a further discussion of the relative impact on language use from conscious and subconscious ideological structures, let us look at how these communities relate to each other in terms of English influence on language use on the six parameters studied in the MIN project (Figure 3).

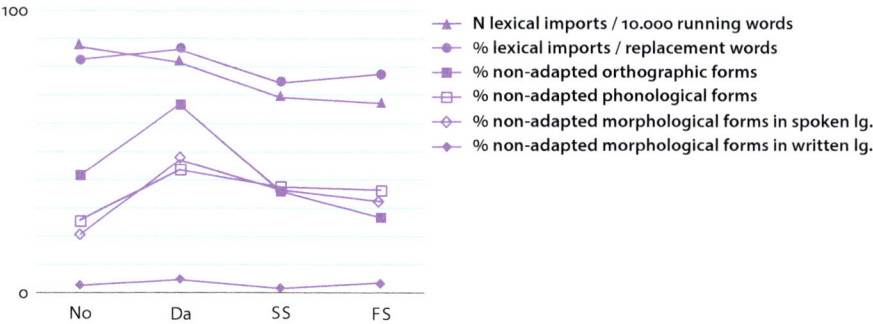

Figure 3. Language use on six parameters in the four Scandinavian-language communities (No = Norwegian, Da = Danish, SS = Sweden-Swedish, FS = Finland-Swedish)

The bottom curve in the figure reveals that (i) there is no difference between the four communities with regard to morphology in written language. Moving up to the other curves, we notice that (ii) the relationship between the two forms of Swedish (SS and FS) is generally a relationship of little or no difference, that (iii) Swedish is generally more purist than Danish, while (iv) Norwegian changes rank order position in comparison with the other communities, from the most purist position on the two spoken-language parameters (cf. curves with non-filled symbols), through a less purist position than Swedish on the orthographic parameter, to the position as the most 'open' community in the lexical domain. (For further information on the MIN language use studies, see Kvaran 2007; Jarvad & Sandøy 2007; Omdal & Sandøy 2008; Selback & Sandøy 2007; Kristiansen & Sandøy 2010b).

The results in the figure illustrate clearly that purism should be studied at different linguistic levels separately (Thomas 1991). In our connection, the different results at the different levels of use have the following implication: in order to answer our question about whether, and which, attitudinal data are relevant to our understanding of what happens at the level of use, we first need to consider the relevance of the different usage data. Which of the patterns (curves) in Figure 3 should be taken into account?

Is it possible to decide on this? Well, I think an attempt in that direction will have to begin by considering the conditions under which the usage data behind the patterns in Figure 3 was produced. In that respect, two important issues can be raised: – did the producer have a choice or not, – and was the producer aware of English influence as an issue?

To take the *choice* issue first, I guess it is a fact about codified writing systems like the ones we are dealing with here that the choice between 'own language vs. English' alternatives is very limited at the levels of morphology and orthography.[7] We can take for granted that the analysed written newspaper texts were produced by people who just followed the orthographic norm (including morphology) as best they could. Thus, comparisons of community results at these linguistic levels will be indicative of the levels of purism in official orthography policies, but will not shed any light on the question of whether and how attitudes influence language use simply because the data producers could not make choices. In consequence, we leave the patterns for orthography/morphology in written texts out of consideration as irrelevant.

At the level of words, however, it was of course possible to make choices when the newspaper texts were written. Also in the case of the spoken data, choice was

---

7.   This holds true even for the orthographies of Nynorsk and Bokmål which otherwise go unusually far in building on a 'free choice principle', allowing for many alternative spellings which reflect dialectal differences in phonology and morphology.

part of the game, as these data were elicited in interviews which used experimental-type approaches ('guess-a-word' and 'cloze-test'; see Jarvad & Sandøy 2007; Svavarsdóttir et al. 2010) and thus made 'own language vs. English' a salient feature of the production context.

Therefore, with regard to the second issue about producer *awareness*, it goes without saying that the people who produced the spoken data were aware that influence-from-English was the focus of interest. This may well have influenced the data production. If we compare the purism differences for spoken language in Figure 3 (from more to less purist: NORWEGIAN – FINLAND-SWEDISH/SWEDEN-SWEDISH – DANISH), we see that the pattern corresponds fairly well with the patterns for official ideology and conscious attitudes (see Table 4), in particular in what concerns the relatively strong purism performed in the Norwegian data. One might argue that the purism profile emerging in the spoken data, produced by interviewees being aware of the English-influence focus of the interview, says little about real purism differences in usage, but quite a lot about the impact of official ideology on lay conscious attitudes. The pattern is just another example of how lay people (are surprisingly able to) reproduce, or literally perform, the level of purism which distinguishes their own community from the others in official ideology.

In contrast, the newspaper data is quite another matter with regard to the issue of producer awareness, because no one knew, of course, at the time of production, that these texts would be made the object of studies of English influence on their authors' language. It is interesting to notice that the relatively stronger Norwegian 'openness' to English influence is to be found for exactly newspaper texts at the level of words – that is: in data which were produced by people who could freely choose between words from 'own language or English'. For that reason, these data might in fact be seen as a relevant usage correlate to the more open (less purist) attitudes which were subconsciously expressed by the Norwegians in the SEE (Table 4 row 2(b)). In brief: Norwegians are subconsciously more positive to English influence than what is stereotypically expected and consciously expressed, and this greater positivity is reflected in use.

At the end of analysis, then, our investigation of English influence, which compares perception and production data across seven Nordic communities, lends support to the claim that *subconsciously offered attitudes influence language use in a way that consciously offered attitudes do not.*

6. Why are language-ideological structures the way they are?

I have several times suggested that the patterns we have found in comparing conscious and subconscious evaluations are rather surprising. It may therefore be appropriate to finish by reflecting on the issue of 'why': How come that official ideology is the way it is? And why is official ideology reproduced by lay attitudes when consciously offered, but contradicted when subconsciously offered?

6.1   Reflections on the 'why' of official language ideology

In order to understand why societies have the official language ideologies they have, we need to take a closer look at the socio-historical conditions under which these ideologies developed. Here we can only give summary sketches of what is involved in the two cases discussed.

6.1.1   *The Danish case*

As mentioned (Section 2.1), the valorization of Danish varieties in official ideology changed radically in the 1960s and 1970s (at least as represented and studied in the educational system): the traditional 'bourgeois' notion of *dannelse* ('educatedness') – with its aesthetic and moral demands on language form (acquire 'nice and proper Danish'!) – was replaced by a 'social democratic' notion which addressed the linguistic norm-and-variation issue as a demand for equality and situational adjustment (Danish is 'many things' to be used and valued differently dependent on context!).

This language-ideological change was the subjective correlate of a whole series of objective societal changes which gained momentum from the 1960s. We can group these, highly interlinked, changes under headlines such as *increased geographic and social mobility* and *new relationships between public and private life*: urbanization of the population, physically as well as mentally (more and more people 'move to town', and 'the town moves to the countryside'), mobilization of the 'working force reserves' (a general political aim in the economically booming 1960s), inclusion of women in the labor market (the majority of women 'left the kitchen' early in Denmark), institutionalization of childhood (linked to the preceding, most children begin spending their days in institutions from before they learn to talk), increased demands on the labor force in terms of qualifications and flexibility (more and more people get more and more education; talk is of 'educational explosion' and 'lifelong learning'). Last but not least, a new national public sphere developed from the 1960s onwards as the TV apparatus became the main sitting room furniture in every home.

My point is not that changes in objective societal factors necessarily lead to changes in the language-ideological sphere. Many communities have been through similar changes without developing such a mighty *standard language ideology* as we see in the Danish case (i.e. the idea that there is a best language). Probably the best testimony to this is the neighboring Norwegian community, which, in spite of paralleling Denmark on crucial objective social parameters to do with mobility and urbanization (Kristiansen 1996), has developed a strong *dialect ideology* (and vital dialects without any commonly agreed upon spoken standard).[8] In the Danish community, however, the new 'social democratic' discourse about norm-and-variation claimed that a modern society could not do without a common language if equal rights and opportunities were to be secured for all citizens, as well as communicative effectiveness in all public domains. This type of argumentation grew into an explicit as well as implicit stronghold of official ideology in the decades that followed the 1960s (Kristiansen 1990, 2003): please feel obliged to speak *rigsdansk* in public and value it as geographically and socially 'neutral', and please feel free to speak, respect and love your dialect in private! If not a necessary companion of the outlined societal changes, this was the kind of official ideology which was developed and commonly accepted. It is likely to have corroborated the effects of other societal changes that contributed to transforming Denmark from a traditional dialect society into, arguably, Europe's most standardized speech community.

6.1.2 *The Nordic case*

We saw (in Section 3.1, see also Table 4 row 1(a) and (b)) that experts easily agree on how the Nordic communities relate to each other in terms of the 'levels of purism' that characterize their official language ideologies.

In order to understand why this ideological differentiation exists, it is crucial to realize that only Denmark and Sweden have always been politically independent states – and that they have ruled over the other communities for centuries. For centuries, Danish was the language of the rulers in the west,[9] Swedish was the language of the rulers in the east. Norway, with its North Atlantic territories (including Iceland and the Faeroe Islands), came under Danish rule from the end of the 14th century. Later, as a consequence of defeat and victory in the Napoleonic wars, Norway (but not the North Atlantic territories) came under Swedish rule in 1814, and obtained full independence only in 1905. Iceland voted for full independence from Denmark in 1944. When Denmark fell to Germany in 1940, British troops moved into Iceland, but were from 1941 replaced by US troops who stayed in the country in large numbers (at one time more than 10.000) until 2006.

---

8. For a media-related discussion of the role of language ideology in shaping the very different norm-and-variation situations in Denmark and Norway, see Kristiansen (2014).

9. Henrik Ibsen, who himself wrote his plays in a slightly modified Danish (still being the main written language in Norway at the end of the 19th century), lets Peer Gynt refer to the Danish rule as *"firehundreårignatten som ruget over apekatten"* ('the four hundred years of night that brooded over the monkey'), a phrase known to every Norwegian.

Still a part of the Danish kingdom, the Faroe Islands have had a home rule system since 1948 (and permanent debates about whether to go for full independence or not). The Swedish king ruled over Finland from the 12th century until 1809, when Sweden had to cede Finland and Åland (an archipelago with a Swedish-language population in the Gulf of Bothnia between Sweden and Finland) to the Russian tsar as another offshoot of the Napoleonic wars. After more than one century as an autonomous Grand Duchy of Russia, Finland declared its full independence in the wake of the October 1917 revolution in Russia, while Åland was granted home rule status within the new Finnish republic in 1921.

Thus, it is at the end of many centuries with various forms of dominance and subordination that the official language ideologies of today's Nordic communities feature clear differences when it comes to 'external linguistic purism'.[10] This is not hard to understand. It may not come as a big surprise either that the clarity of the differentiation is such that it can easily be agreed upon by language scholars (see Table 4 rows 1a and 1b). But to my mind it is rather surprising that also lay people, similarly across seven Nordic communities, know the 'purism-profile' that emerges from the official language ideologies of these communities (see Section 3.1 and Table 4 row 1c). This must mean that the scholarly discourse about this is public in all communities in a way that makes it readily available for people to draw on when they are asked about the issue. Based on my own experience from living in the Nordic area, I would not have expected that. Surprising, indeed.

6.2   Reflections on the 'why' of consciously offered attitudes

From the perspective of language politics (or planning) in a community, it will always be an interesting question what kind of impact the propagated official ideology has on lay people's attitudes, and possibly also on their linguistic behavior. Great impact on consciously offered attitudes is a commonality of our two cases.

6.2.1   *The Danish case*

On the one hand, we found that adolescents all over Denmark seemed to adopt a 'local patriotism' perspective in ranking varieties by consistently giving top positions to their own local dialect and the neighbouring dialect – above *rigsdansk* which consistently appeared just below (Table 1). On the other hand, we found the official language-ideological discourse (regarding the school) to be interchangeably

---

10.   Among the Nordic communities which have been part of the outlined history of dominance and subordination are also the Greenlandic and Sami communities, but these were not included in the MIN project.

more positive towards either *rigsdansk* or the dialects – depending on whether the evaluative perspective was 'communicative effectiveness' or 'social identity'.

Whether these findings entitle us to claim that the adolescents' conscious ranking is to be understood as a simple reproduction of the official ideology is hard to tell. If we assume a considerable affinity between the evaluative perspectives of 'local patriotism' and 'social identity', the adolescents' consciously offered attitudes are in full harmony with the official ideology. But perhaps their 'local patriotism' should rather be seen as something that the adolescents *add on to* their performance of the official ideology.

Anyway, there can be no doubt that Danish adolescents all over the country do 'know' and follow the same ideological guidelines in their consciously offered rankings, as these yield the same basic pattern in all investigated sites. A nationwide agreement of this kind among adolescents is hard to understand except as a school product. It is not obvious, however, how the school achieves this. Does the general and consistent reproduction of the same basic pattern testify to the school's effectiveness in inculcating the value system which is attached to Danish varieties in official ideology? Or should we rather conceive of this value system as something that is around in the school discourse, readily available to be drawn on by students when they are asked to rank varieties according to their preference? While it is tempting to discard the former alternative because it smells too much of 'successful indoctrination', the latter alternative is hardly more attractive as it seems to imply that adolescents just reproduce the discourse that is readily available around them.

6.2.2   *The Nordic case*

If it is surprising, as we said above, that the scholarly discourse about the Nordic purism-profile is public in all communities in a way that makes it readily available for lay people to draw on when they are asked about how they think imported words are treated in each one of the Nordic communities, it becomes rather mysterious that lay people reproduce this Nordic purism-profile when asked questions about how they relate to the English influence in their own community (Table 4, row 2(a)). How on earth does that happen? The two suggested explanations from the Danish case above are possible also here, both of which would again testify to an extreme effectiveness of official ideology: either it is the case that a particular level of language-ideological purism is inculcated in people, or it is the case that people somehow learn to answer these questions so 'correctly' that the average result earns their community exactly that very position in the Nordic purism-profile which everybody (learned and lay) agrees on. Mysterious, indeed.

One might suggest that the finding would appear less mysterious if it could be shown that the populations' levels of competence in English correspond to their communities' positions in the Nordic purism-profile. In that case, people's producing of the 'right' level of purism could be seen as resulting from personally experienced problems with English. Other MIN findings do indeed indicate that competence differences influence how subgroups in a population relate to the English influence in their community. However, regardless of the possible existence of such differences among the communities, there seems to be no reason to assume a simple connection from the realm of competence to the realm of ideology. On the contrary, the MIN telephone survey found that the Icelanders were by far the most frequent English users (according to self-reports), while at the same time being by far the language-ideological more purist of the Nordic communities (as we have seen).

There is another interesting aspect of the consciously offered reproduction of the Nordic purism-profile that deserves to be reflected upon. As outlined above (Section 6.1.2), the Nordic purism-profile is the result of relationships of dominance and subordination that existed long before English became a language with influence in the Nordic area. It is not immediately obvious why this traditional purism-profile should be of relevance to how the communities relate to the English influence that has characterized the Post World War II period. Shouldn't we rather expect the English-related ideologies and attitudes to reflect the fact that the Nordic communities have been differently coupled to the power structures that have existed on the European and global scene after World War II, in particular concerning NATO membership (Icelandic, Faroese, Norwegian, Danish) or not (Swedish, Finland-Swedish, Finnish), and EU membership (Danish, Swedish, Finland-Swedish, Finnish) or not (Icelandic, Faroese, Norwegian)? Or, perhaps we should expect no difference in attitudes towards English at all, since English is associated with the same socio-historical changes (globalization) in all of the Nordic communities?

It turns out, however, that the traditional hierarchy of more or less strong feelings towards external language influence reappears in the consciously expressed attitudes towards English at the beginning of the 2000s. Seemingly, these historically deep-rooted traditions reproduce across major restructurings of fundamental socio-historical contexts – and live on in the era of globalization. In that sense, the results of the MIN study testify to the relative independence of language ideology from changing historical circumstances. (A more detailed discussion of the MIN telephone survey data in this perspective can be found in Kristiansen 2005.)

6.3   Reflections on the 'why' of subconsciously offered attitudes

If the great impact of official ideologies on consciously offered attitudes is clear enough in both the Danish and Nordic cases – even if it may not be that clear how the great impact happens – it is also a clear enough commonality of our two cases that there is little or no impact of official ideology on subconsciously offered attitudes. Where then do the subconscious attitudes come from; how can we explain them?

6.3.1   *The Danish case*

We have seen that when the response condition changes from 'awareness' to 'non-awareness', the ranking LOCAL > CONSERVATIVE > MODERN is turned upside down into MODERN > CONSERVATIVE > LOCAL, with the specification that MODERN does particularly well on 'dynamism' values while CONSERVATIVE does as well or better on 'superiority' values (see Section 2.3 and Table 2). Why does this happen?

If we assume that it takes dynamism values (self-assured, fascinating, cool, nice) to be successful in the late-modern public sphere of broadcast media, while success in the more traditional public sphere of school and business is associated more with 'superiority' values (intelligent, conscientious, goal-directed, trustworthy), the subconsciously offered attitudes may be seen, arguably, as the result of a newly developed 'split' in the representation of what 'the best language' is – an ideological split which results from the addition of a new public sphere, the modern broadcast media, to societal life (Kristiansen 2001; Grondelaers & Kristiansen 2013). In these media, the use of (some) traditional capital-city 'low' features seems to be an important means to construe 'casual, relaxed, laid-back' ways with language. From the 1960s on, TV in particular has exposed the Danish people not only to more Copenhagen speech than before, but also to increasingly greater quantities of the MODERN accent of Copenhagen speech (including traditional 'low' features).

However, the split evaluative pattern which singles out ('focuses') the two accents – 'superior' CONSERVATIVE and 'dynamic' MODERN – is not the main argument for linking the found subconscious evaluative pattern to the development of the modern broadcast media. The main argument is the copy-like similarity of the patterns across all sites which appears clearly from the graphs in Figure 2. The consistent uniformity of the patterns testifies to the existence of a strong subconscious value system among young people. Adolescents across the whole of Denmark have a precise 'knowledge' not only of the relatively negative social values which adhere to their own LOCAL accent in comparison with Copenhagen speech, they also have a precise 'knowledge' of the relatively positive social values which adhere to the MODERN and CONSERVATIVE accents of Copenhagen speech. Where in the world did that 'knowledge' come from? A value system which downgrades LOCAL and upgrades MODERN in particular is something the adolescents certainly did not acquire in school. It is hard to see how Figure 2 can be explained without referring to *shared experience resulting from exposure to broadcast media.*

6.3.2   *The Nordic case*

Also the reverse purism-ranking which emerged for the Scandinavian-language communities as they offered attitudes subconsciously instead of consciously (see shadowed cells in Table 4) is probably best understood as a media effect – but this time as the effect of *different experience* resulting from exposure to broadcast media. Recall that the SEE used in the MIN project was framed as an assessment of applicants for a position as newsreader at a radio station (see Section 3.3).

With regard to the amount of linguistic variation which figures on the national broadcast waves, our four Scandinavian-language communities clearly fall into two groups. In the Swedish and Danish communities, the linguistic variation 'made public' by the broadcast media is very limited, especially so in the Danish community, and especially in broadcasted news reading.

In contrast, as all Norwegian broadcast media are full of dialectal variation and the Finland-Swedish community is a bilingual minority (6% of Finland's population), Norwegians and Finland-Swedes are accustomed to living with linguistic variation as a natural element of everyday-life. Even though we are referring here to a 'sense of variation' which basically has nothing to do with English-influence, we find this difference between the communities to be the most likely reason why the Norwegians and Finland-Swedes assessed the English-colored guise on par with the pure guise, or even slightly better, while the Swedes and the Danes, in particular the latter, expressed a strong preference for the pure guise.

7.   Concluding remarks

The main focus of this chapter has been on the logic behind our approach to the problem of constructing valid attitudinal data in investigations of linguistic variation and change – i.e. data which are relevant to the issue of whether and how attitudes influence use – and we have presented our results from two large-scale survey studies (concerning Danish varieties and English influence in Nordic communities, respectively) as evidence for the existence of two language-related value systems – one of which emerges in consciously offered attitudes and seems to have little or no influence on use, while the other one emerges in subconsciously offered attitudes and seems to have much influence on use.

We are not claiming any general-principle status for this conclusion. On the contrary, we have repeatedly stressed that it is an empirical question whether language-ideological structures are similar or different across local communities in a country like Denmark, or across larger communities across an area like the Nordic countries. It might be noticed, though, that recent findings in other European countries actually show similar contrastive patterns for conscious and subconscious attitudes in investigations where efforts were made to theorize and operationalize the distinction (see chapters on Bosnia and Herzegovina, Flanders, Germany, Ireland, Lithuania, and Norway in Kristiansen & Grondelaers 2013).

As for the explanation for the existence of the two value systems, we argued that our results for consciously offered attitudes indicate a strong impact from official ideology, whereas our results for subconsciously offered attitudes indicate a strong impact from experiences with the broadcast media. In both cases, the nature of the impact is an interesting issue: what does actually happen to children and adolescents as they grow up and experience how the language norm-and-variation issue is being treated in school, in the media, in the community in general? Do they just learn a way to talk about the issue when need be, or are they being formed or indoctrinated in a deeper psychological sense? In this respect, our results strongly suggest that there is a difference between consciously and subconsciously offered attitudes. About attitudes which are offered consciously in direct questioning, we can be reasonably certain that they do have an existence at least as shared 'ways of talking' about language norm-and-variation issues (even if the general availability of these 'ways of talking' may appear surprising for some of the established patterns). In contrast, attitudes which are offered subconsciously clearly contradict the ideology of public discourse, and it therefore seems reasonable to assume that the similarity and consistency of subconscious patterns in a community must be psychologically rooted in something else than 'ways of talking'. (I take it that this assumption is supported by results obtained in experimental research using the Implicit Association Test (IAT) technique, an experimental tool developed to probe deep and automatic perceptual reactions; see e.g. Preston & Niedzielski 2013; Campbell-Kibler 2013).

However, no matter how interesting the discussion about the cognitive nature of attitudes is in itself (as developed in discourse-oriented social psychology in particular, following Potter & Wetherell 1987), it may be of less importance when the interest concerns the role of attitudes in linguistic variation and change. In that research perspective, which is ours, I see no reason not to go for agnosticism regarding 'the nature of attitudes' issue. Regardless of the mode of existence of attitudes, the lesson from our studies is that we need to elicit both consciously and subconsciously offered attitudes – and compare the resulting evaluative patterns with patterns of use.

Conversely, it goes without saying that agnosticism is not an option in our perspective when it comes to 'the precedence issue': what come first, attitudinal change or linguistic change? A solution to that issue must be an essential ingredient of any attempt to answer the fundamental question about the role of attitudes in the processes of linguistic variation and change: are attitudes a major driving force in these processes, or mainly a concomitant? Against the agnostic claim that we cannot tell, I think our results support another conclusion: subconscious attitudes lead to changes in use and are a major driving force in linguistic variation and change in a way that conscious attitudes are not. Granted, this can hardly be more than a tentative conclusion based on the Nordic case data, but based on the Danish case data I take the conclusion to be fairly secure.

References

Brink, Lars & Lund, Jörn. 1975. *Dansk rigsmål*. Copenhagen: Gyldendal.
Campbell-Kibler, Kathryn. 2013. Connecting attitudes and language behaviour via implicit sociolinguistic cognition. In Kristiansen & Grondelaers (eds), 307–329.
Coupland, Nik. 2009. Dialects, standards and social change. In *Language Attitudes, Standardization and Language Change*, Marie Maegaard, Frans Gregersen, Pia Quist & J. Normann Jørgensen (eds), 27–49. Oslo: Novus.
Coupland. Nik. 2014. Sociolinguistic change, vernacularization and broadcast British media. In *Mediatisation and Sociolinguistic Change*, Jannis Androutsopoulos (ed.), 67–96. Berlin: Mouton de Gruyter.
Garrett, Peter. 2010. *Attitudes to Language*. Cambridge: CUP. DOI: 10.1017/CBO9780511844713
Giles, Howard. 1970. Evaluative reactions to accents. *Educational Review* 22: 211–227.
    DOI: 10.1080/0013191700220301
Grondelaers, Stefan & Kristiansen, Tore. 2013. On the need to access deep evaluations when searching for the motor of standard language change. In Kristiansen & Grondelaers (eds), 9–52.
Jarvad, Pia & Sandøy, Helge (eds). 2007. *Stuntman og andre importord i Norden. Om udtale og bøjning* [Moderne importord i språka i Norden 7]. Oslo: Novus.
Jul Nielsen, Bent & Nyberg, Magda. 1993. Talesprogsvariationen i Odder kommune. II. Yngre og ældre rigsmålsformer i sociolingvistisk belysning. *Danske Folkemål* 35: 249–348.
Kammacher, Louise, Stæhr, Andreas & Jørgensen, Jens Normann. 2011. Attitudinal and sociostructural factors and their role in dialect change: Testing a model of subjective factors. *Language Variation and Change* 23: 87–104. DOI: 10.1017/S0954394511000019
Kristensen, Kjeld. 1977. Variationen i vestjysk stationsby-mål. En kvantitativ sociolingvistisk dialektundersøgelse i Vinderup, Ringkøbing Amt. *Dialektstudier* 4(2): 29–109.
Kristensen, Keld. 2003. Standard Danish. Copenhagen sociolects, and regional varieties in the 1900s. *International Journal of the Sociology of Language* 159: 29–43.
Kristiansen, Tore. 1990. *Udtalenormering i skolen*. Copenhagen: Gyldendal.
Kristiansen, Tore. 1996. Det gode sprogsamfund: det norske eksempel. *NyS* 21: 9–22.
Kristiansen, Tore. 2001. Two standards: One for the media and one for the school. *Language Awareness* 10(1): 9–24. DOI: 10.1080/09658410108667022
Kristiansen, Tore. 2003. Language attitudes and language politics in Denmark. *International Journal of the Sociology of Language* 159: 57–71.
Kristiansen, Tore. 2005. The power of tradition, a study of attitudes towards English in seven Nordic communities. *Acta Linguistica Hafniensia* 37: 155–169.
    DOI: 10.1080/03740463.2005.10416088

Kristiansen, Tore (ed.). 2006. *Nordiske sprogholdninger. En masketest.* [Moderne importord i språka i Norden 5]. Oslo: Novus.

Kristiansen, Tore. 2009. The macro-level social meaning of late-modern Danish accents. *Acta Linguistica Hafniensia* 41: 167–192.

Kristiansen, Tore. 2010. Conscious and subconscious attitudes towards English Imports in the Nordic countries: evidence for two levels of language ideology. *International Journal of the Sociology of Language* 204: 59–95.

Kristiansen, Tore. 2014. Does mediated language influence immediate language? In *Mediatisation and Sociolinguistic Change*, Jannis Androutsopoulos (ed.), 99–126. Berlin: Mouton de Gruyter.

Kristiansen, Tore & Jørgensen, Jens Normann. 1998. Sociolinguistics in Denmark. *Sociolinguistica* 12: 230–250.

Kristiansen, Tore & Jørgensen, Jens Normann. 2005. Subjective factors in dialect convergence and divergence. In *Dialect Change. Convergence and Divergence in European Languages*, Peter Auer, Frans Hinskens and Paul Kerswill (eds), 287–302. Cambridge: Cambridge University Press.

Kristiansen, Tore & Grondelaers, Stefan (eds). 2013. *Language (De)standardisation in Late Modern Europe: Experimental Studies.* Oslo: Novus.

Kristiansen, Tore & Sandøy, Helge. 2010a. Introduction. The linguistic consequences of globalisation: the Nordic laboratory. *International Journal of the Sociology of Language* 204: 1–7. DOI: 10.1515/ijsl.2010.027

Kristiansen, Tore & Sandøy, Helge. (eds). 2010b. The linguistic consequences of globalization: the Nordic countries. *International Journal of the Sociology of Language* 204.

Kristiansen, Tore & Vikør, Lars S. (eds). 2006. *Nordiske språkhaldningar. Ei meiningsmåling* [Moderne importord i språka i Norden 4]. Oslo: Novus.

Kvaran, Guðrún (ed.). 2007. *Udenlandske eller hjemlige ord? En undersøgelse af sprogene i Norden* [Moderne importord i språka i Norden 6]. Oslo: Novus.

Lund, Jørn. 1986. Det sprogpolitiske klima i de nordiske lande. Kommentarer og påstande. *Sprog i Norden* 1986. 34–45.

Maegaard, Marie, Jensen, Torben Juel, Kristiansen, Tore & Jørgensen, Jens Normann. 2013. Diffusion of language change: Accommodation to a moving target. *Journal of Sociolinguistics* 17(1): 3–36. DOI: 10.1111/josl.12002

Omdal, Helge & Sandøy, Helge (eds). 2008. *Nasjonal eller internasjonal skrivemåte? Om importord i seks nordiske språksamfunn.* [Moderne importord i språka i Norden 8]. Oslo: Novus.

Pedersen, Inge Lise. 2003. Traditional dialects of Danish and the de-dialectalization 1900–2000. *International Journal of the Sociology of Language* 159: 9–28.

Potter, Jonathan & Wetherell, Margaret. 1987. *Discourse and Social Psychology: Beyond Attitudes and Behaviour.* London: Sage.

Preston, Dennis R. & Niedzielski, Nancy. 2013. Approaches to the study of language regard. In Kristiansen & Grondelaers (eds), 287–306.

Ryan, Ellen Bouchard, Giles, Howard & Hewstone, Miles. 1988. The measurement of language attitudes. In *Sociolinguistics. An International Handbook of the Science of Language and Society*, Ulrich Ammon, Norbert Dittmar & Klaus J. Mattheier (eds), 1068–1081. Berlin: Walter de Gruyter.

Sandøy, Helge & Kristiansen, Tore. 2010. Conclusion. Globalization and language in the Nordic countries: conditions and consequences. *International Journal of the Sociology of Language* 204: 151–159.

Selback, B. & Sandøy, Helge (eds). 2007. *Fire dagar i nordiske aviser. Ei jamføring av påverknaden i ordforrådet i sju språksamfunn.* [Moderne importord i språka i Norden 3]. Oslo: Novus.

Svavarsdóttir, Ásta, Paatola, Ulla & Sandøy, Helge. 2010. English influence on the spoken language – with a special focus on its social, semantic and functional conditioning. *International Journal of the Sociology of Language* 204: 43–58.

Thomas, George. 1991. *Linguistic Purism.* London: Longman.

Vikør, Lars S. 1995. *The Nordic Languages. Their Status and Interrelations,* 2nd edn. Oslo: Novus.

Vikør, Lars S. 2010. Language purism in the Nordic countries. *International Journal of the Sociology of Language* 204: 9–30.

Applying the Implicit Association Test to language attitudes research

Andrew J. Pantos
Metropolitan State University of Denver

Incorporating concepts from the domain of Implicit Social Cognition (ISC), this quantitative study measured participants' implicit attitudes (through an audio Implicit Association Test) and explicit attitudes (through self report questionnaires) toward foreign and U.S. accented speech stimuli. The study's results revealed a pro-U.S. accent bias on the implicit measure, but a pro-foreign accent bias on explicit measures, supporting the conclusion that these are separable attitude constructs resulting from distinct mental processes. This distinction in attitude type explains previous inconsistencies in language attitudes research and is supported theoretically by the Associative Propositional Evaluation Model, a dynamic dual processing conceptualization of the attitude formation process consistent with ISC.

1. Introduction

Over the past 45 years, an extensive body of language attitudes research has provided a wealth of information about listener reactions to a multiplicity of nationalities and accents. Some of these studies have pointed to the existence of a general negative affect toward foreign ('nonstandard') accents (e.g., Lambert 1967; Rubin & Smith 1990; Ryan 1983). At the same time, other researchers have recognized that listener attitudes towards an identified foreign accent can vary, in some instances being negative but in other instances positive. This variation in reactions to specific accents has been attributed to a number of factors including reaction type (e.g., *affective* versus *evaluative* reactions), speaker trait (e.g., *solidarity* versus *status*) (Ryan 1982; Cargile & Giles 1997), the aggressiveness of the message (Cargile & Giles 1997), stereotypes associated with the speaker's nationality (Frumkin 2007; Kristiansen 2001), and the degree of 'nonstandardness' of the speaker's accent (Brennan & Brennan 1981; Bresnahan et al. 2002). While this extensive body of research has yielded an abundance of information about attitudes towards specific accents, it has neither reconciled the findings of a general bias with those of specific attitude variation nor established a quantitatively based

DOI 10.1075/impact.39.05pan

link between the posited variation factors and attitude type. In addition, it has failed to establish a consistent theoretical conceptualization of the attitude formation process (Lambert 1967; Ryan 1982; Gluszek & Dovidio 2010). To address these open questions, the present study of attitudes towards foreign accented speech incorporates concepts and methods from the domain of *Implicit Social Cognition* (ISC; Greenwald et al. 2002) and, specifically, its recognition of a distinction between *implicit attitudes* (immediate reactions) and *explicit attitudes* (thoughtful reactions; Greenwald & Banaji 1995). Because implicit attitudes are inaccessible to the individual and are thus difficult to observe directly using traditional self report measures, the ISC framework requires that implicit attitudes be measured using methods that do not necessitate the introspection involved in traditional language attitudes methodologies. Accordingly, the present study measured participants' explicit attitudes with a traditional methodology – self report – but measured their implicit attitudes with a methodology that does not involve introspection – the Implicit Association Test (IAT; Greenwald, McGhee & Schwartz 1998; Cargile & Giles 1997; Chaiken & Stangor 1987), a computer-based sorting task that measures relative reaction times between distinct pairings of concepts and/or attributes.

Specifically, this study addresses the application of the ISC framework to language attitudes research through the investigation of two research questions: (1) whether participants' implicit attitudes are biased in favor of the U.S. accented speech, indicating an immediate negative reaction to foreign accented speech relative to US accented speech; and (2) whether participants' explicit (e.g., self-reported) attitudes toward US accented speech differ from their implicit attitudes, supporting the conclusion that the two types of attitudes represent distinct modes of cognitive processing, consistent with models such as the Associative-Propositional Evaluation (APE) Model (Gawronski & Bodenhausen 2006; 2007), which explains attitude formation as resulting from either an associative (immediate, affective) or propositional (thoughtful) cognitive process.

> Accordingly, this study tests the following two hypotheses:
> (H1) Participants' implicit attitudes will be biased in favor of the US accented speech, indicating a negative immediate response to foreign accented speech relative to US accented speech.
> (H2) Participants' explicit attitudes, which are subject to cognitive control and self-presentation concerns, will show no significant bias in favor of either speaker, indicating that implicit and explicit attitudes can diverge, and supporting the conclusion that implicit and explicit attitudes are the result of different cognitive processes.

This second hypothesis was based, in part, on the results of a nationwide (US) Web-based pilot study (Pantos & Franklin 2009) that tested the same stimuli as those used in the explicit attitudes measures tasks in the present study. The pilot study found no significant explicit bias in favor of either speaker in the binary measure of which doctor participants would side with in 'case outcome' (a = .05; χ^2 (1, N=59) = 2.98). Additionally, this hypothesis was based on the belief that the context of the present study – a civil court case in which the facts presented for each side were equally plausible and participants were asked to imagine themselves as jurors – would result in overall impartiality in explicit responses.

1.1 Characterizing attitudes

The origins of ISC are found in cognitive psychology. Two distinct theoretical and methodological threads, each with its own terminology, underlie ISC: the *selective attention model* and the *implicit memory model*. Schiffrin & Schneider (1977) describe attitude formation in terms of selective processing (Posner & Snyder 1975), which is accomplished either in an automatic or controlled mode. Automatic processing requires little attention and is difficult to suppress, while controlled processing demands attention and is voluntary. Perhaps most importantly, automatic processing is characterized as inescapable but never as unconscious. In fact, consciousness is rarely mentioned in selective attention literature. Sequential priming (measuring the effect of exposure to selected stimuli on subsequent participant responses) and bogus pipeline (encouraging truthful responses by tricking participants into believing their responses are being monitored by a lie detector) are the two methodologies most closely associated with this theoretical tradition.

The present study is instead situated within the implicit memory model, which is supported by a large body of literature relating to associated methodologies and attitude processing theories. This theoretical perspective, put forth by Banaji and others (2001), conceptualizes attitude processing in terms of implicit memory. Under this approach, attitudes are defined based on the type of cognitive processes involved in their formation: *implicit* attitudes are formed as a result of a person's automatic, immediate reactions to an attitude object based on pre-existing stereotypes and cognitive connections, and *explicit* attitudes as reactions formed through additional controlled cognitive processing (Wittenbrink & Schwarz 2007). Importantly, implicit memory characterizes the processing of implicit attitudes as unconscious and the processing of explicit attitudes as conscious. Both implicit and explicit attitudes can be held simultaneously and both can affect behavior and/or judgment (Perkins & Forehand 2010; Greenwald & Banaji 1995). However, because implicit attitudes, by definition, are introspectively unidentified (or inaccurately identified) traces of past experiences that are inaccessible to the individual, they are difficult (perhaps impossible) to assess using traditional self-reflective methods, such as self report measures or interviews–the two primary methods used historically in quantitative language attitudes studies. Instead, implicit attitudes can be captured only through indirect methods that do not rely on personal introspection.

One measure closely identified with implicit memory is the Implicit Association Test (IAT; Greenwald, McGhee & Schwartz 1998), which measures response latencies in sorting tasks of stimulus exemplars from four concepts using two response options. The IAT is based on the assumption that greater association strengths are evidenced by faster performance in tasks requiring sorting into paired category labels that are consistent in the participant's mind (Nosek, Greenwald & Banaji 2005; 2007; Greenwald, McGhee & Schwartz 1998). For example, in a hypothetical IAT used to measure relative implicit attitudes toward hamburgers versus hot dogs, participants who prefer hamburgers should sort visual stimuli representing hamburgers and hot dogs into the categories labeled *hamburger + good* and *hot dog + bad* more easily (e.g., more quickly and with less error) than into the categories labeled *hamburger + bad* or *hot dog + good*. For participants who prefer hot dogs, the opposite should be true. Thus, while explicit self-report tasks measure an individual's accessible, thoughtful reactions to a stimulus object, the IAT is thought to measure an individual's immediate, affective reaction based on pre-existing cognitive associations.

According to the implicit memory tradition, implicitness is equated with *unconsciousness*. This characterization contrasts with the selective attention approach's characterization of the same reactions as *automatic*. Some ISC adherents complain that researchers subsequent to Greenwald and Banaji have expanded the original intent of the selective attention theoretical approach by conflating consciousness of the formative source experience with consciousness of the attitude itself (Payne & Gawronski 2010). For present purposes, it is not vital that implicit be defined as unconscious. That is, it is not important that the participant be unaware of his or her implicit attitude. It is only important that, whether characterized as unconscious or automatic, implicit attitudes are not controllable and thus are measurable only by methods that do not permit thoughtful revision. These methods include measures like the IAT, as well as sequential priming and go/no go (characterizing individually presented stimuli as one of two options) tasks. The present study employs the IAT, the method most consistently and closely identified with the ISC framework (Banaji 2001).

Another question raised about the ISC framework asks whether implicit reactions are personally held attitudes or merely reflections of social realities. This question stems, in part, from a belief that the almost universal IAT findings of racism are implausible. Even before the IAT was developed, both Devine (1989) and Fazio and colleagues (1995) argued that automatic responses would reflect well learned associations and that poorly learned associations, which would require more effort – and thus take more time – to retrieve, would be reflected only in tasks that permitted thoughtful contemplation. According to this view, well learned associations necessarily include those that reflect social realities, such as racial stereotypes. Devine further characterized automatic responses as the demonstration of the *knowledge* of social attitudes, to be distinguished from the *personal endorsement* of those attitudes as reflected in measures of more thoughtful reactions. This view called into question exactly what was being accessed through automatic measure tasks: the participant's own attitude or the participant's knowledge of society's attitude. Subsequent research, however, has shown significant individual differences in automatic measures on a number of topics among participants from the same society and culture meaningful enough to predict behavior. Consequently, automatic measures are today thought to reveal personal and not social attitudes; that is, automatic measures disclose personally formed attitudes and do not simply reflect an individual's acknowledgement of general social values (Perugini, Richetin & Zogmeister 2010). It is argued here that this distinction between implicit and explicit attitudes explains the seemingly contradictory findings in previous language attitudes studies of the existence of a general negative affect towards foreign accent (an implicit attitude) yet individual variation in attitudes towards specific, identified foreign accents (explicit attitudes).

1.2   Explaining the cognitive processing of language attitudes

The implicit-explicit attitude distinction and the IAT methodology are supported by a theoretical framework that explains the attitude formation process. The Associative-Propositional Evaluation (APE) Model (Gawronski & Bodenhausen 2006; 2007) describes attitude formation as the result of a dynamic dual processing system in which evaluation responses – attitudes – are formed as a result of two distinct yet potentially interacting cognitive processes in memory, *associative* or *propositional*. Associative processes are characterized as immediate or affective reactions to an object in the environment resulting from the automatic or unconscious retrieval of previously existing information in memory, and generally correspond to implicit attitudes. Propositional processes, in contrast, are those that attempt to determine the validity of evaluations and beliefs by assessing their consistency with other relevant propositions. The Implicit Social Cognition framework thus links the nature of an attitude to its formation process and provides a consistent means for explaining attitude formation through the Associative-Propositional Evaluation Model, a cognitive model not limited to language attitudes (Gluszek & Dovidio 2010; Cargile et al. 1994) or persuasive messages (Petty & Cacioppo 1986), but that is a comprehensive and consistent explanation of attitude processing, in general (Pantos 2012).

2.   Method

2.1   Overview

Applying the Implicit Social Cognition theoretical framework to the context of language attitudes, the present study measured participants' reactions to audio stimuli using two distinct methods. First, immediate, associative reactions were measured by IAT in Task 1. Second, thoughtful, propositional reactions were measured to determine the participants' explicit attitudes toward the stimuli through self report in Task 2. Because the Associative-Propositional Evaluation Model suggests that propositional and associative processes can interact throughout, an additional explicit measure was employed in Task 3 to test the robustness of the explicit finding in Task 2 (Gawronski & Bodenhausen 2006; 2005). A schematic summary of the experiment structure is depicted in Figure 1.

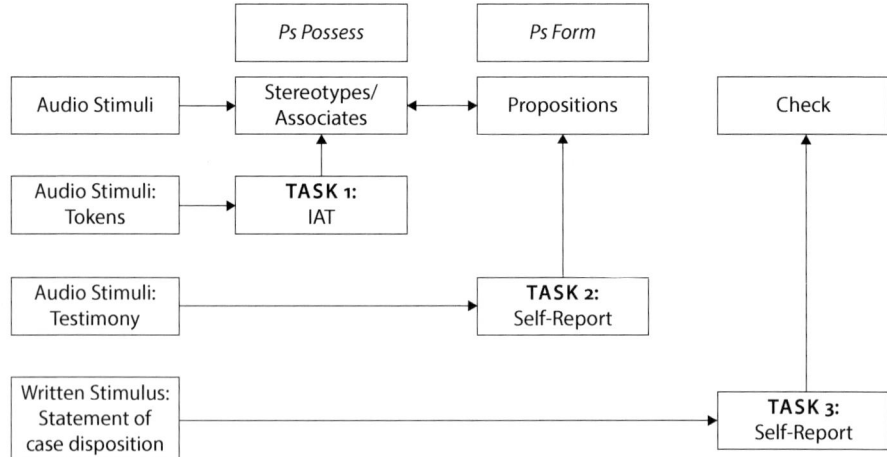

Figure 1. Schematic representation of the experimental procedure
Note: *Ps* stands for 'participants'

2.2   Participants

A total of 165 participants took part in this study. Participants were sought from a university's graduate and undergraduate population. Participation was voluntary, and a fee of $10 per participant was paid in compensation. Participants ranged in age from 17–22 years of age, with an average age of 20. Of the participants, 114 were women and 51 were men; 63 self identified their race as 'Caucasian/white/European', 40 as 'Asian/Chinese/Taiwanese', 20 as 'Hispanic/Mexican/Latino', and 17 as 'African/African American/Black'. The majority of participants self identified their nationality as 'US/American' (131); 34 participants designated their nation-ality as foreign (16 as 'Chinese'; 4 as 'Korean'; 4 as 'Mexican'; 2 as 'El Salvadoran', 2 as 'English', and 6 as 'other'). Although all participants were proficient enough in English to attend a US university, 35 indicated their native language to be some-thing other than English (14 as 'Chinese/Mandarin/Cantonese', 8 as 'Spanish', 6 as 'Korean', and 7 as another language).

2.3   Task procedure

Because the order of testing has been shown to have no effect (Lane et al. 2007; Nosek, Greenwald & Banaji 2005), the three tasks were administered in the same order to each participant. The tasks took a total of approximately 25 minutes to complete: approximately ten minutes for Task 1 (the IAT), ten minutes for Task 2 (the first self report), and five minutes for Task 3 (the second self report). A dis-traction task was inserted between Tasks 1 and 2, which consisted of a Rational Evaluation Inventory (Pacini & Epstein 1999) that asked participants to rate the degree to which they emotionally or thoughtfully answer questions. In addition, participants were required to answer demographics questions after Task 3.

The entire study was computer based. Each participant sat in a private, sound-controlled room. Each room was equipped with a Windows™ based laptop computer with a standard keyboard, a track pad, an external mouse, and a set of headphones (Sennheiser™ HD 201) connected to the computer's headphone port. All tasks were created using Inquisit™ software (Draine 1998).

2.4   Task 1: Implicit Association Test (IAT)

Task 1 consisted of an audio IAT designed to provide a means to measure partici-pants' immediate, associative responses to the audio tokens presented. The use of audio stimuli was deemed essential to the linguistic nature of the study and repre-sents an expansion of the IAT methodology, which in published studies to-date has relied on visual stimuli such as printed words and images.[1] The audio stimuli were excerpts, including lexical items and collocations, taken from the audio recordings (in .mp3 format) used in Task 2. These excerpts were equalized for loudness using SoundForge™ and trimmed to assure that there was no silent lead at the start of each clip. Each audio stimulus consisted of three iterations of the same token. One second of silence was inserted between iterations.

---

1.   An unpublished study using an audio IAT was part of a dissertation (Vande Kamp 2002). That dissertation, however, did not provide sufficient details about its methodology to allow for replication.

In order to reduce the risk of introducing a confound based on non-relevant reactions to the content meaning of the audio stimuli, the semantic valence of the content of each audio stimulus (*at 2:25, 2 options, perform charting*, etc.) was prescreened. Only those stimuli that exhibited no significant variance in semantic valence were used. This prescreening consisted of an on-line written survey in which participants rated the semantic valence of 20 potential stimuli on three dimensions (bad-good, unpleasant-pleasant, and negative-positive) on a seven-point scale, with a score of 7.00 indicating the extreme of positive semantic valence, a score of 1.00 indicating the extreme of negative semantic valence, and 4.00 indicating neutral semantic valence. The stimuli ultimately selected for use in the study indicated neutral semantic valence within a variance of 0.5.

As visual attribute stimuli, positive and negative valence words were used. The visual lexical stimuli consisted of attributes that were chosen as emblematic of either obviously positive or obviously negative concepts. The positive attributes selected were: *marvelous, superb, pleasure, beautiful, joyful, glorious, lovely,* and *wonderful.* The negative attributes selected were: *tragic, horrible, agony, painful, terrible, awful, humiliate,* and *nasty.* These specific attributes have been used in previous IAT studies and are a combination 2 to 4 syllable nouns, verbs, and adjectives that are easily and quickly identifiable as representing only one of the categories presented (e.g., Nosek 2007).

Both audio and visual stimuli were randomized across participants. Participants were told stimuli would be presented either audibly through the headphones, or visually on the computer screen. Participants were instructed to categorize each stimulus as belonging to the category shown in the upper left or upper right of the computer screen by pressing the appropriate computer key ('E' for left or 'I' for right). The four categories were: *US* and *Foreign* (target concepts), and *good* and *bad* (target attributes). Participants were instructed to work quickly without sacrificing accuracy. Participants were able to categorize the audio stimuli immediately upon the start of the recorded stimulus. A list of all stimuli and the organization of the IAT are set out in Table 1.

The IAT was presented in five blocks, or stages. The first block was a practice stage, in which participants were presented with each of the four positive and four negative visual attribute stimuli twice, for a total of 16 trials. The second block was also a practice stage, in which participants were presented with each of the four audio stimuli spoken by the US accented physician and the four audio stimuli spoken by the Korean accented physician twice, for a total of 16 trials. In the third block, a total of 32 trials were created from the combination of the first two test blocks. The fourth block repeated block two, but with the screen position of the attribute stimuli reversed. In the fifth block, the 32 trials from block three were repeated, but with the reversed screen positions for the attributes, as shown in

Table 1. The IAT stimuli and testing blocks

Block	Upper left of screen	Stimuli	Upper right of screen
Block 1 (Training)	Good	marvelous, superb, pleasure, beautiful, joyful, glorious, lovely, wonderful tragic, horrible, agony, painful, terrible, awful, humiliate, nasty	Bad
Block 2 (Training)	Foreign	*at 2:25; 2 options; assistance first; training and experience; it is my opinion; I have frequently encountered; perform charting; probability*	American
Block 3 (Measurement)	Foreign Good	*at 2:25; 2 options; assistance first; training and experience; it is my opinion; I have frequently encountered; perform charting; probability* marvelous, superb, pleasure, beautiful, joyful, glorious, lovely, wonderful tragic, horrible, agony, painful, terrible, awful, humiliate, nasty	American Bad
Block 4 (Training)	American	*at 2:25; 2 options; assistance first; training and experience; it is my opinion; I have frequently encountered; perform charting; probability*	Foreign
Block 5 (Measurement)	American Good	*at 2:25; 2 options; assistance first; training and experience; it is my opinion; I have frequently encountered; perform charting; probability* marvelous, superb, pleasure, beautiful, joyful, glorious, lovely, wonderful, tragic, horrible, agony, painful, terrible, awful, humiliate, nasty	Foreign Bad

Note: Audio stimuli are in *italics*; visual stimuli are in plain text.

block four. The order of the trials within each block was randomized. If incorrect selections were made (i.e., a stimulus was mischaracterized), a red X appeared on the computer screen for 400 milliseconds. Subsequent trials started 400 milliseconds after the previous response or the disappearance of the red X. The assignment of screen position to positive or negative valence was counterbalanced for the participant pool, so that half the participants saw positive words on the left and negative on the right, and half saw them reversed.

2.5 Task 2: Self report 1

Task 2 was designed to measure the participants' explicit attitudes toward foreign accent. Accordingly, Task 2 consisted of a written self report survey, designed to measure participants' thoughtful, propositional reactions to the audio stimuli. In this task, participants heard the fictional audio testimony in English of two similarly aged male actors portraying physicians in a medical malpractice trial. Given that previous studies have established that a number of extralinguistic personal features such as physical appearance and presentation characteristics affect jurors' perceptions (DeSantis & Kayson 1997; Lavrakas & Bickman 1975; Catano 1980; Wells & Bradfield 1998; Yarmey & Kent 1980), this study limited the channel of communication to audio recordings in order to isolate accent as a variable. Additionally, in order to avoid subconscious reactions that would naturally affect determinations of speaker credibility and introduce an unwanted variable into the research (Reich 1981), two actors speaking with their natural, native accents were used instead of one actor affecting one accent or the other (as in a matched guise approach).

Speaker accent selection intended to minimize the potential that social stereotypes associated with specific foreign nationalities or US regional dialects would affect results. To that end, one of the actors is a native Korean speaker and the other a native US English speaker. Korean was selected as an appropriate foreign accent based on previous research that showed Korean accents are seldom (approximately eight percent of the time) correctly identified in the US (Lindemann 2003).[2] The US accented actor is a native US English speaker with a predominantly mid-Atlantic accent from the Philadelphia area, an accent that was chosen because of its status as a neutral prestige regional dialect in the US Frumkin 2000 and 2007). The verbal performances of the actors were analyzed to verify minimal difference in acoustic factors – such as pitch variation and fundamental frequency differences – shown to affect perceptions of pleasantness (Eadie & Doyle 2005; Fridland & Bartlett 2006) and, at least potentially, other variables in the solidarity dimension, such as likeability. To complete this analysis, Praat™ was used to measure the sound wave depictions of the actors' recorded speech for pitch and pitch range comparisons. In the recording of the first script, the US accented actor's pitch range fluctuated between a minimum of 88 Hz to a maximum of 482 Hz, and the Korean accented actor's pitch range fluctuated between 90 Hz and 457 Hz. In the recording of the second script, the US accented actor's pitch range fluctuated between a minimum of 87 Hz and 479 Hz, and the Korean accented

---

2. Participants were not asked to rate the Korean speaker's degree of accentedness in the present study. Previous research has shown that, when comparing US accented speech to foreign accented speech, the negative affective consequences attendant to the foreign accent do not necessarily vary with the degree of accentedness or level of intelligibility of the speech (Cargile & Giles 1997).

actor fluctuated between a minimum of 88 Hz and 397 Hz. These measurements were determined to be similar enough to allay concerns of having an effect on perceptions.

Each actor was recorded portraying both the defendant treating physician and the plaintiff's expert witness.[3] The physicians were presented as equally well qualified practicing physicians. No other information about the physicians was conveyed to the participants. A practicing medical malpractice attorney wrote both scripts, which are based on deposition testimony taken from an actual medical malpractice lawsuit arising from the methods employed in the course of delivering a child.[4] The scripts, which were controlled to neutralize potential differences, deliberately represent two equally plausible opinions regarding the treatment of the patient in the fact situation presented. The language in the scripts was equalized for number of technical terms and approximately matched in length.[5] In addition, the texts were analyzed using the Linguistic Inquiry Word Count software (Newman et al. 2003), which has been successfully used in credibility assessments. No significant differences were found between the texts concerning language vividness, displacement or other factors potentially relevant to perceptions of believability and credulity.[6]

Participants were assigned to one of four treatment conditions within a two (accent: American versus Korean) by two (defense versus plaintiff) experimental design. To maintain ecological validity with the trial procedure cover story, the defendant treating physician was heard first, followed by the plaintiff's expert witness. After hearing each testimony, participants were asked to rate the physicians and the testimonies they heard on a 14-item scale anchored 1 through 11(believability, credibility, trustworthiness, knowledge, expertise, intelligence, competence, likeability, friendliness, warmth, judgment, persuasiveness, presentation

---

3.   The actors were recorded with an Edirol™ flash recorder (model R-09) using unidirectional lapel microphones in a sound controlled booth. The sound files were saved in .wav format and were normalized to relative loudness using audio editing software (Audacity™) before being finalized. One final .mp3 sound file was created for each actor for each script.

4.   The names and certain identifiable facts were altered to maintain the anonymity of the parties.

5.   The treating physician's testimony was 337 words and the expert witness's testimony was 318 words long.

6.   For additional details of the methodology, including copies of the scripts, please contact the author.

style, and clarity), hereinafter referred to as *speaker trait measures*.[7] The order of the presentation of these variables was randomized across participants. After each testimony, participants were asked to identify the nationality of the speaker they had just heard in a free response format. In addition, after hearing both testimonies, participants were asked to provide their relative preference for the two expert witnesses. Specifically, participants were asked to indicate which of the two doctors they would side with in the dispute on a sliding scale from 1 to 11, the first doctor (1) to the second doctor (11).

2.6   Task 3: Self report 2

Because the Associative Propositional Evaluation Model assumes that associative and propositional processes can inform each other throughout processing, the explicit attitudes found in Task 2 were checked with a third task. Task 3 consisted of a second response that measured participants' reactions to a written statement regarding the outcome of the case. Specifically, participants were asked to imagine they were alternate jurors who did not vote on the case outcome but who heard all the testimony. They were then presented with two different outcomes, one at a time, and asked to rate on a scale from 1 (very unfair) to 11 (very fair) the fairness of each hypothetical outcome. Because Tasks 2 and 3 both involve explicit attitudes (propositional processes), it was expected that the fairness ratings in Task 3 would align with the preference ratings in Task 2.

3.   Results

3.1   Explicit results

The relative preference measure was recoded such that responses closer to 1 indicated preference for the Korean accent and responses closer to 11 indicated a preference for the American accent, with the midpoint of the scale (6 on a 1 to 11 scale) indicating no preference for either. This recoded measure was submitted to a two-tailed T-test. Across both treatment conditions, analysis revealed a significant bias in favor of the Korean accented speaker ($M = 5.40$, $SD = 1.90$, $t = -2.64$, $p = .01$). Further, a within-treatment ANOVA was not significant ($F = 2.49$, $p = .12$), suggesting that the Korean expert witness was preferred regardless of whether he

---

7.   The purpose of measuring reactions to these variables was to test the trait dimension (status versus solidarity) dichotomy maintained by language attitudes research and supported by an earlier study (Pantos & Franklin 2009). An analysis of those variables and findings is beyond the scope of this paper.

testified for the defendant or the plaintiff. No results were obtained on the fairness or speaker trait measures.

3.2 IAT results

The raw IAT data was aggregated and transformed using the D measure (Greenwald, Nosek & Banaji 2003). The D measure may be interpreted as equivalent to an effect size measure, similar to Cohen's d measure; however, Cohen's d uses a pooled within-treatment standard deviation, while the IAT's D-measure uses a standard deviation calculated from only the scores in both measurement blocks. Previous IAT studies (Greenwald et al. 2003) recommend that data be eliminated for ostensibly random responses (latencies of less than 300 ms for more than ten per cent of trials in combined task blocks) or lapses of concentration (latencies of greater than 10,000 ms). Seven participants' data were eliminated because they contained extreme numbers of sorting errors or for being extreme outliers. Following conversion to the D measure, participants' IAT responses were submitted to a two-tailed T-Test. Overall, results indicated an implicit bias in favor of the US accented speaker over the foreign accented speaker ($D_{American}$ = .32, t = 10.42, p < .001). Additionally, no differences obtained between the treatment and control conditions ($M_{TreatmentD}$ = .29, $M_{ControlD}$ = .33, F = .43, p = .51), or within the treatment conditions ($M_{KoreanFstD}$ = .29, $M_{AmericanFstD}$ = .30, F = .01, p = .91), such that all respondents revealed the same *a priori* US accent bias.

3.3 Correlations between IAT results and explicit findings

In order to examine the relationship between the IAT measure of implicit accent bias and witness preference, correlational analysis was conducted. Interestingly, a significant correlation between the IAT and witness preference obtained, such that a stronger pro-US implicit bias predicted an increased likelihood of preferring the Korean expert witness explicitly (r = .26, p = .03). This result did not obtain for the control condition that incorporated expert witnesses who both had Korean accents (r = .02, p = .89) or American accents (r = −.08, p = .62) suggesting that the relationship between implicit accent attitude and witness preference is only significant when the participant heard two different accents during the testimony.

4. Discussion and conclusion

This study's results confirm the existence of a distinction between implicit and explicit attitude constructs and thus help answer questions left open by previous language attitudes studies. First, the IAT found that the participants' implicit attitudes favor the US accented speaker over the Korean accented speaker, confirming H1. Because implicit attitudes are linked to affective reactions (Wittenbrink & Schwarz 2007; Gawronski & Bodenhausen 2007), this result is consistent with the concept of a general negative affect toward foreign accented speech as posited by traditional language attitudes studies (e.g., Ryan 1983). This study's participants sorted the audio stimuli (an average of 1.233 ms) before hearing one complete iteration of a stimulus (an average of 1.25 ms). Because accent foreignness can be determined in as few as 30 ms (Flege 1984), it appears that participants in the present study formed their implicit attitudes based on the nonnativeness of the accent, and not on the content of the statement or an identification of the accent. This result is consistent with research showing that language attitudes are formed even though listeners broadly and/or incorrectly identify the origin of a speaker's accent (Niedzielski 1999; Preston 1989).

In contrast to the IAT findings, the explicit self report measure found a bias in favor of the Korean speaker, generally confirming the study's second hypothesis (H2). H2, however, specifically posited that there would be no significant bias in favor of either speaker in any of the four explicit measures of speaker preference. This belief was based on the results from a pilot study (Pantos & Franklin 2009) and on the notion that the context of the present study–a jury trial in which participants were asked to imagine themselves as fair and impartial jurors–would encourage participants to overcome any implicit biases when forming their explicit attitudes through additional cognitive processing. Instead of impartiality, however, the present findings showed a trend favoring the Korean accent in all four explicit measures and, although not statistically significant for the binary choice (the measure of which doctor the participant would side with in the dispute), the bias in favor of the Korean accented speaker for the three scalar analyses (the measure of the extent to which the participants sided with one of the speakers in Task 2, and the two fairness of verdict measures in Task 3) proved significant. The difference between the results for the binary and the scalar evaluations for siding with a speaker might be a reflection of a higher threshold for determining bias in binary selections, or some other aspect of the methodological choices made in the experiment design, such as inserting the 14 speaker trait questions between the two witness testimonies.

It is important to note that the IAT predicted expert witness choice, such that participants that revealed a stronger pro-US bias on the IAT were more likely to choose the Korean accented speaker explicitly, regardless of whether the Korean accented speaker was the defendant treating physician or the expert witness for the plaintiff. This effect only obtained when participants heard expert testimony from both the US- and Korean accented witnesses. Because the explicit results obtained only in the accent comparison conditions, these findings indicate that the explicit preference is related to accent and not to witness role or to the order of accent presentation. Additionally, the predictive oppositional relationship between the pro-US bias on the IAT and the likelihood of favoring the Korean accent in the explicit measures suggests that listeners can hypercorrect their explicit attitude reporting if they suspect their performance on an earlier IAT might have revealed a socially unacceptable bias. It should be noted that such meta-analysis of IAT performance is quite different from implicit attitude accessibility, awareness, and controllability during the test. Participants may not be aware of any particular bias before starting the IAT. During or after the test, however, a participant may suspect his or her immediate, uncontrollable IAT answers revealed an undesirable bias that the participant could then seek to neutralize in later, cognitively controllable explicit measurement tasks. Such hypercorrection in attitude reporting has been shown to occur when participants are concerned about perceptions of their self-presentation (Lane et al. 2007; de Jong et al. 2003; Baron & Banaji 2006). The fact that participants are unable to change or construct their IAT answers during the test so that undesirable attitudes are not revealed in the first place supports the argument that the IAT measures attitudes that are beyond the participant's cognitive control.

In the present study, almost half of the participant pool was comprised of students from an introductory sociolinguistics class that was learning about the negative consequences of unfounded biases against foreign accented speech. If that is, in fact, the reason for the bias in favor of the native Korean speaker, then this result might indicate a type of hypercorrection in explicit attitude reporting. It should be noted that the proportional aspect of the predictive oppositional result (i.e., the greater the implicit bias in favor of the Korean accent, the smaller the explicit bias in favor of the U.S. accent, and vice versa) indicates that there is an interaction between the two attitude constructs and eliminates the possibility that the explicit bias in favor of the Korean speaker is related to the identification of accent, the status of the speaker, or any other factor. Accent identification or status considerations alone cannot explain a higher likelihood of explicitly favoring the Korean accented speaker when implicit reactions favor the US accented speaker.

With regard to the present study's hypotheses, the results underscore the difference between the natures of the two attitude constructs, and support the argument that explicit attitudes are cognitively controllable, while implicit attitudes are not (Botvinick et al. 2001; Nosek, Greenwald & Banaji 2007). Nonetheless, it should be emphasized that both attitude constructs are authentic attitudes, both are reflective of an individual's reactions to the stimulus, and both are cognitively formed by the individual – albeit through different cognitive processes. It is, therefore, argued here that implicit attitudes are individually held and formed and not mere reflections of social values. Furthermore, the fact that explicit attitudes may be influenced directly or indirectly by social or other external factors does not diminish their authenticity, as long as they are reported honestly. It is also important to emphasize that the difference between the implicit bias in favor of the US accented speaker and the explicit bias in favor of the foreign accented speaker does not indicate a change in attitude. It is not the case that the divergent attitudes mean that the pro-US implicit attitudes changed to the pro-foreign explicit attitudes between tasks. Implicit attitudes remain separate from, and continue to co-exist alongside, the individual's explicit attitudes (Rohner & Björklund 2006) and both can affect judgment and behavior (Perkins & Forehand 2010). For language attitudes study, these results indicate that the same individual can process different attitudes toward the same attitude object and hold them concurrently, and consequently support the measurement of both implicit and explicit attitudes to provide a more complete picture of the individual's attitudes, judgment, social perception, and potential behavior than measuring only one of these attitude constructs to the exclusion of the other (Rohner & Björklund 2006).

4.1   Conclusion

Consistent with the Implicit Social Cognition's conceptual framework, this study's quantitative findings support the conclusion that listeners' implicit and explicit attitudes are distinct attitude constructs, both with potential behavioral consequences. This study thus augments traditional language attitudes research by explaining the apparent contradiction between findings of a general negative affect toward foreign accent and variation in attitudes towards specific, identified accents. Because this study also characterizes the nature of reactions to foreign accented speech in terms consistent with broader attitudes study, the Associative-Propositional Evaluation Model and the Implicit Social Cognition framework provide the basis for a clear and comprehensive explanation of the cognitive processes underlying attitude formation and bears on certain previously unaddressed or unsettled theoretical and practical considerations, including the conceptualization of the attitude formation process and the effect of attitude on behavior. Furthermore, because this study supports the conclusion that methods involving introspection cannot capture implicit attitudes, and implicit measures do not capture explicit attitudes, this study argues that measuring both implicit and explicit attitudes using appropriate methods will provide a more complete analysis of listener reactions to speakers and their speech than will measuring explicit attitudes alone.

References

Banaji, Mahzarin R. 2001. Implicit attitudes can be measured. In *The Nature of Remembering: Essays in Remembering*, Robert G. Crowder, Henry L. Roediger III, James S. Nairne, Ian Neath & Aimée Surprenant (eds), 117–150. Washington DC: American Psychological Association.

Baron, Andrew Scott & Banaji, Mahzarin R. 2006. The development of implicit attitudes: Evidence of race evaluations from ages 6 and 10 and adulthood. *Psychological Science* 17(1): 53–58. DOI: 10.1111/j.1467-9280.2005.01664.x

Botvinick, Matthew M., Braver, Todd S., Barch, Deanna M., Carter, Cameron S. & Cohen, Jonathan D. 2001. Conflict monitoring and cognitive control. *Psychology Review* 108(3): 624–652. DOI: 10.1037/0033-295X.108.3.624

Brennan, Eileen M. & Brennan, John Stephen. 1981. Accent scaling and language attitudes: Reactions to Mexican American English speech. *Language and Speech* 24(3): 207–21.

Bresnahan, Mary Jiang, Ohashi, Rie, Nebashi, Reiko, Liu, Wen Ying & Shearman, Sachiyo Morinaga. 2002. Attitudinal and affective response toward accented English. *Language and Communication* 22(2): 171–185. DOI: 10.1016/S0271-5309(01)00025-8

Cargile, Aaron Castelan & Giles, Howard. 1997. Understanding language attitudes: Exploring listener affect and identity. *Language and Communication* 17(3): 195–217. DOI: 10.1016/S0271-5309(97)00016-5

Cargile, Aaron Castelan, Giles, Howard, Ryan, Ellen Bouchard & Bradac, James J. 1994. Language attitudes as a social process: A conceptual model and new directions. *Language and Communication* 14: 211–236. DOI: 10.1016/0271-5309(94)90001-9

Catano, Victor M. 1980. Impact on simulated jurors of testimony as a function of non-evidential characteristics of witness and defendant. *Psychology Report* 46: 343–348. DOI: 10.2466/pr0.1980.46.2.343

Chaiken, Shelly & Stangor, Charles. 1987. Attitudes and attitude change. *Annual Review of Psychology* 38: 575–630. DOI: 10.1146/annurev.ps.38.020187.003043

DeSantis, Andrea & Kayson, Wesley A. 1997. Defendants' characteristics of attractiveness, race, and sex and sentencing decisions. *Psychology Report* 81(2): 679–683. DOI: 10.2466/pr0.1997.81.2.679

Devine, Patricia G. 1989. Stereotypes and prejudice: Their automatic and controlled components. *Journal of Personality and Social Psychology* 56: 5–18. DOI: 10.1037/0022-3514.56.1.5

Draine, Sean C. 1998. *Inquisit*. Seattle WA: Millisecond Software.

Eadie, Tanya L. & Doyle, Philip C. 2005. Classification of dysphonic voice: Acoustic and auditory-perceptual measures. *Journal of Voice* 19(1): 1–14. DOI: 10.1016/j.jvoice.2004.02.002

Fazio, Russel H., Jackson, Joni R., Dunton, Bridget C. & Williams, Carol J. 1995. Variability in automatic activation as an unobtrusive measure of racial attitudes: A bona fide pipeline? *Journal of Personality and Social Psychology* 69: 1013–1027. DOI: 10.1037/0022-3514.69.6.1013

Flege, James Emil. 1984. The detection of French accent by American listeners. *Journal of the Acoustic Society of America* 76(3): 692–707. DOI: 10.1121/1.391256

Fridland, Valerie & Bartlett, Kathryn. 2006. Correctness, pleasantness, and degree of difference ratings across regions. *American Speech* 81(4): 358–386. DOI: 10.1215/00031283-2006-025

Frumkin, Lara. 2007. Influences of accent and ethnic background on perceptions of eyewitness testimony. *Psychology, Crime & Law* 13(3): 317–331. DOI: 10.1080/10683160600822246

Frumkin, Lara. 2000. The Effect of Eyewitnesses' Accent, Nationality, and Authority on the Perceived Favorability of their Testimony. Ph.D. dissertation, University of Maryland.

Gawronski, Bertram & Bodenhausen, Galen V. 2005. Accessibility effects on implicit social cognition: The role of knowledge activation and retrieval experiences. *Journal of Personal and Social Psychology* 89(5): 672–85. DOI: 10.1037/0022-3514.89.5.672

Gawronski, Bertram & Bodenhausen, Galen V. 2006. Associative and propositional processes in evaluation: An integrative review of implicit and explicit attitude change. *Psychology Bulletin* 132(5): 692–731. DOI: 10.1037/0033-2909.132.5.692

Gawronski, Bertram & Bodenhausen, Galen V. 2007. Unraveling the processes underlying evaluation: Attitudes from the perspective of the APE model. *Social Cognition* 25(5): 687–717. DOI: 10.1521/soco.2007.25.5.687

Gawronski, Bertram & Payne, B. Keith (eds). 2010. *Handbook of Implicit Social Cognition: Measurement, Theory, and Applications.* New York NY: Guildford Press.

Giles, Howard & Ryan, Ellen Bouchard. 1982. Prolegomena for developing a social psychological theory of language attitudes. In *Attitudes toward Language Variation: Social and Applied Contexts,* Ellen Bouchard Ryan & Howard Giles (eds), 208–223. London: Arnold.

Gluszek, Agata & Dovidio, John F. 2010. The way they speak: A social psychological perspective on the stigma of nonnative accents in communication. *Personal and Social Psychology Review* 14(2): 214–37. DOI: 10.1177/1088868309359288

Greenwald, Anthony G. & Banaji, Mahzarin R. 1995. Implicit social cognition: Attitudes, self-esteem, and stereotypes. *Psychological Review* 102(1): 4–26. DOI: 10.1037/0033-295X.102.1.4

Greenwald, Anthony G., Nosek, Brian A. & Banaji, Mahzarin R. 2003. Understanding and using the Implicit Association Test: I. An improved scoring algorithm. *Journal of Personal and Social Psychology* 85(2): 197–216. DOI: 10.1037/0022-3514.85.2.197

Greenwald, Anthony G., McGhee, Debbie E. & Schwartz, Jordan L.K. 1998. Measuring individual differences in implicit cognition: The Implicit Association Test. *Journal of Personal and Social Psychology* 74(6): 1464–1480. DOI: 10.1037/0022-3514.74.6.1464

Greenwald, Anthony G., Banaji, Mazharin R., Rudman, Laurie A., Farnham, Shelly D. Nosek, Brian A. & Mellott, Deborah S. 2002. A unified theory of implicit attitudes, stereotypes, self-esteem, and self-concept. *Psychological Review* 109(1): 3–25. DOI: 10.1037/0033-295X.109.1.3

de Jong, Peter J., van den Hout, Marcel, Rietbroek, Hans & Huijding, Jorg. 2003. Dissociations between implicit and explicit attitudes toward phobic stimuli. *Cognition and Emotion* 17(4): 521–545. DOI: 10.1080/02699930302305

Kristiansen, Gitte. 2001. Social and linguistic stereotyping: A cognitive approach to accents. *Estudios Ingleses De La Universidad Complutense* 392(9): 129–146.

Lambert, Wallace. E. 1967. A social psychology of bilingualism. *Journal of Social Issues* 23: 91–109. DOI: 10.1111/j.1540-4560.1967.tb00578.x

Lane, Kristin A., Banaji, Mahzarin R., Nosek, Brian A. & Greenwald, Anthony G. 2007. Understanding and using the Implicit Association Test: IV. What we know (so far) about the method. In *Implicit Measures of Attitudes,* Bernd Wittenbrink & Norbert Schwarz (eds), 59–102. New York NY: The Guilford Press.

Lavrakas, Paul J. & Bickman, Leonard. 1975. What makes a good witness? Eyewitness identification by elderly and young adults. *Law & Human Behavior* 4: 359–371.

Lindemann, Stephanie. 2003. Koreans, Chinese or Indians? Attitudes and ideologies about non-native English speakers in the United States. *Journal of Sociolinguistics* 7(3): 348–364. DOI: 10.1111/1467-9481.00228

Newman, Matthew L., Pennebaker, James W., Berry, Diane S. & Richards, Jane M. 2003. Lying words: Predicting deception from linguistic styles. *Personal and Social Psychology Bulletin* 29(5): 665–75. DOI: 10.1177/0146167203029005010

Niedzielski, Nancy. 1999. The effect of social information on the perception of sociolinguistic variables. *Journal of Language and Social Psychology* 18(1): 62–85. DOI: 10.1177/0261927X99018001005

Nosek, Brian A., Greenwald, Anthony G. & Banaji, Mahzarin R. 2005. Understanding and using the Implicit Association Test: II. Method variables and construct validity. *Personal and Social Psychology Bulletin* 31(2): 166–80. DOI: 10.1177/0146167204271418

Nosek, Brian A., Greenwald, Anthony G. & Banaji, Mahzarin. 2007. The Implicit Association Test at age 7: A methodological and conceptual review. In *Social Psychology and the Unconscious: The Automaticity of Higher Mental Processes,* John A. Bargh (ed.), 265–279. New York NY: Psychology Press.

Pacini, Rosemary & Epstein, Seymour. 1999. The relation of rational and experiential information processing styles to personality, basic beliefs, and the ratio-bias problem. *Journal of Personal and Social Psychology* 76: 972–987. DOI: 10.1037/0022-3514.76.6.972

Pantos, Andrew J. 2012. Defining the cognitive mechanisms underlying reactions to foreign accented speech: An experimental approach. *Review of Cognitive Linguistics* 10(2): 427–453. DOI: 10.1075/rcl.10.2.08pan

Pantos, Andrew J. & Franklin, Amy. 2009. *The Effect of Foreign Accent on Witness Assessment.* Cambridge: International Association for Forensic Phonetics and Acoustic (IAFPA) Conference.

Payne, B. Keith & Gawronski, Bertram. 2010. A history of implicit social cognition. In Gawronski & Payne (eds), 1–18.

Perkins, Andrew W. & Forehand, Mark R. 2010. Implicit social cognition and indirect measures in consumer behavior. In Gawronski & Payne (eds), 535–547.

Perugini, Marco, Richetin, Juliette & Zogmeister, Cristina. 2010. Prediction of behavior. In Gawronski & Payne (eds), 255–277.

Petty, Richard E. & Cacioppo, John T. 1986. *Communication and Persuasion: Central and Peripheral Routes to Attitude Change.* New York NY: Springer.

Posner, Michael I. & Snyder, Charles R.R. 1975. Attention and cognitive control. In *Information Processing and Cognition: The Loyola Symposium,* Robert L. Solso (ed.), 55–85. Hillsdale NJ: Lawrence Erlbaum Associates.

Preston, Dennis R. 1989. *Perceptual Dialectology: Nonlinguists' Views of Areal Linguistics.* Dordrecht: Foris. DOI: 10.1515/9783110871913

Reich, Alan R. 1981. Detecting the presence of vocal disguise in the male voice. *Journal of the Acoustic Society of America* 69(5): 1458–61. DOI: 10.1121/1.385778

Rohner, Jean Christoph & Björklund, Fredrik. 2006. Do self-presentation concerns moderate the relationship between implicit and explicit homonegativity measures? *Scandinavian Journal of Psychology* 47(5): 379–85. DOI: 10.1111/j.1467-9450.2006.00522.x

Rubin, Donald L. & Smith, Kim A. 1990. Effects of accent, ethnicity, and lecture topic on undergraduates' perceptions of nonnative English-speaking teaching assistants. *International Journal of Intercultural Relations* 14(3): 337–353. DOI: 10.1016/0147-1767(90)90019-S

Ryan, Ellen Bouchard. 1983. Social psychological mechanisms underlying native speaker evaluations of non-native speech. *Studies in Second Language Acquisition* 5(2): 148–59. DOI: 10.1017/S0272263100004824

Schiffrin, Richard & Schneider, Walter. 1977. Controlled and automatic human information processing: Perceptual learning, automatic attending and a general theory. *Psychological Review* 84: 127–190. DOI: 10.1037/0033-295X.84.2.127

Vande Kamp, Mark E. 2002. Auditory Implicit Association Tests. Ph.D. dissertation, University of Washington.

Wells, Gary L. & Bradfield, Amy L. 1998. Good, you identified the suspect: Feedback to eyewitnesses distorts their reports of the witnessing experience. *Journal of Applied Psychology* 83(3): 360–376. DOI: 10.1037/0021-9010.83.3.360

Wittenbrink, Bernd & Schwarz, Norbert (eds). 2007. *Implicit Measures of Attitudes*. New York NY: Guilford.

Yarmey, A. Daniel & Kent, Judy. 1980. Eyewitness identification by elderly and young adults. *Law and Human Behavior* 4(4): 359–371. DOI: 10.1007/BF01040627

Implicit attitudes and the perception of sociolinguistic variation

Brandon C. Loudermilk
University of California-Davis

We investigated individual differences in processing the social dimensions of speech, addressing whether the degree of implicit stereotypical attitude towards language variants modulates brain activity during comprehension. Subjects listened to spoken stories, in which sentence-final critical words were manipulated for ING/IN' variant which was congruent/incongruent with the variants in the preceding discourse and which was typical/atypical of speaker dialect. Subjects participated in an Implicit Association Test as a measure of language attitudes towards ING/IN' variation and were classified as high or low stereotype. Results showed that listeners with low IAT scores had higher N400-like negativities while processing word variants that violated dialectal expectancies (ING uttered by a Southern speaker and IN' spoken by a Californian). Our results provide evidence that the cognitive mechanisms that support language comprehension are sensitive not just to *what* is said, but also to *how* it is said, *who* says it, and *who* hears it.

1. Introduction

Variationist sociolinguistics concerns itself with the relationship between the language forms of a speech community and the mediation of these forms by social structures. Definitions of the speech community take as a starting point the notion of a shared set of social and linguistic norms. Gumperz (1968), for example, argues that "regardless of the linguistic differences among them, the speech varieties employed within a speech community form a system because they are related to a shared set of social norms" (p.116). Labov (1972) as well defines membership in a speech community as "participation in a set of shared norms… [which] may be observed in overt types of evaluative behavior, and by the uniformity of abstract patterns of variation which are invariant in respect to particular levels of usage" (pp. 120–121). For Labov, the defining characteristics of a speech community are illustrated by (1) a shared set of sociolinguistic norms that can be observed in linguistic behavior – for example, speakers within a community all style-shift in

DOI 10.1075/impact.39.06lou

the same direction (Fig. 1); and (2) a shared set of evaluative behavior or language attitudes to these sociolinguistic norms – for example, recognition that IN' forms are less formal than ING variants. In the present study we sought to investigate the relationship between individuals' attitudes towards (ING) variation and how these attitudes influence language processing.

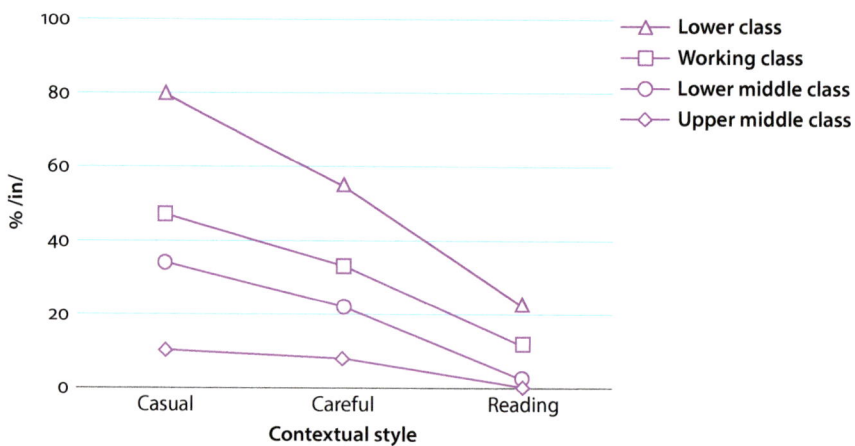

Figure 1. Style-shifting in NYC (Labov 1966). Reproduced from Labov et al. (2011)

From a socio-cultural perspective, language attitudes operate as stereotypes to justify and explain intergroup relations (Tajfel 1981), which can have real-world implications for speakers of non-standard dialects such as discrimination through "linguistic profiling" (e.g., Baugh 2000; Purnell et al. 1999). In the study of language attitudes researchers have typically relied on three broad approaches: the societal treatment approach, which typically involves participant observation and ethnography; the direct approach in which participants are directly questioned about their language beliefs and attitudes (Henerson et al. 1987); and the indirect approach, or matched-guise technique (Garrett et al. 2003). The societal treatment approach is primarily qualitative in nature and has been criticized on the grounds that the researcher is inferring attitude from behavior. Likewise, the direct approach has been criticized on "whether subjects' [overt] verbal statements of their attitudes" accurately reflect their "underlying disposition" (Knops & van Hout 1988).

The matched-guise technique (MGT) developed by Lambert and colleagues (1960) addresses these short-comings by trying to covertly elicit language attitude. In MGT studies, participants listen to repeated passages of speech read by a single speaker under different guises (e.g., language, dialect, etc.), and are asked to make judgments on some aspect of the speaker (e.g., intelligence, friendliness, etc.). Because the speaker and the content of the recording are held constant, and because the listener *believes* they are listening to different speakers, it is argued that any attitudinal differences that are elicited can only be attributed to the manipulation (i.e. guise) under study.

Although the MGT has primarily been used to investigate attitudes towards gross features of dialects and languages, it has been adopted to investigate language attitudes towards individual sociolinguistic variables. Labov et al. (2011), for example, conducted a series of MGT experiments that manipulated the frequency of (ING) variants. In their experiments, subjects were asked to rate the speech of a "newscaster-in-training" on measures of professionalism. Across these experiments, the researchers found similar overall results, namely a logarithmic progression between the relative frequency of vernacular IN' and the negative evaluation of speaker professionalism. As illustrated in Figure 2, listeners hearing passages with no IN' variants rated the speaker as the most professional, but as frequency of IN' variants increased, passages were evaluated as increasingly negative. In an additional experiment using a Southern dialect speaker, they found no differences in overall evaluation compared to the non-Southern speaker, suggesting that the frequency of the vernacular IN' variant was the determining factor in eliciting these overt attitudes.

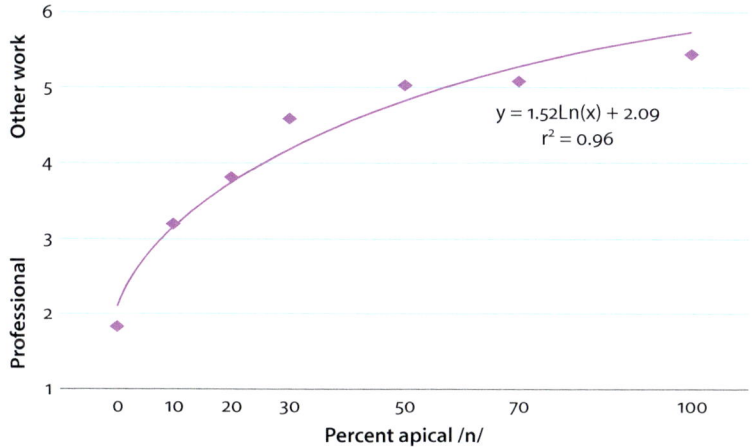

Figure 2. Frequency of vernacular IN' on ratings of newscaster professionalism. Reproduced from Labov et al. (2011)

Other researchers have used variations of the MGT to measure attitudes towards (ING) realization. Campbell-Kibler (2009), for example, played participants the spontaneous speech of Southern and West Coast dialect speakers that varied in (ING) pronunciation. Analysis revealed that the (ING) strongly affected perceptions of intelligence and education as well as the casual/formal dimension (Table 1). These effects of (ING) on listeners' attitudes towards speaker education/intelligence interacted however with the perceived social class and geographic region of the speaker. When listeners perceived a speaker to be working class, ING guises increased the perceived intelligence/education of the speaker; in contrast listening to speakers described as non-working class had no effect on listeners' judgments of speaker intelligence/education. However, as illustrated in Fig. 3, these effects were only observed when speakers were perceived to be both working class and non-Southern (so-called "anywhere" or a-regional speakers). These results illustrate the complex interplay of how listeners' perception of speakers' social and regional identities mediate attitudes towards stereotypical sociolinguistic variables such as (ING).

Table 1. Factor analysis on (ING) realization. Reproduced from Campbell-Kibler (2009)

	Factor 1	Factor 2
Educated	.815	.260
Intelligent	.844	.256
Shy/outgoing		.808
Speech rate	.126	.547
Casual/formal	.380	
Knows addressee	.152	−.233
Accented	−.171	−.292
Masculine (Feminine)		

In a subsequent study, Campbell-Kibler (2010) manipulated speaker profession in a matched guise study, asking whether perceived profession and (ING) realization influences listeners' judgments. Specifically, speakers were presented as authorities in a specific field (e.g., juvenile crime) representing one of three different professions: university professor (e.g., law professor), political candidate (e.g., district attorney), or professional (e.g., social worker). Results showed that for professors ING realization increased the perceived knowledge of the speaker. In contrast, professionals were seen as more knowledgeable in their IN' guise. No effect on perceived knowledge was observed for the politician speakers. These results suggest that variable (ING)'s "relationship to a central feature of competence may thus be not only heightened or mitigated by contextual information but also inverted" (Campbell-Kibler 2010: 218).

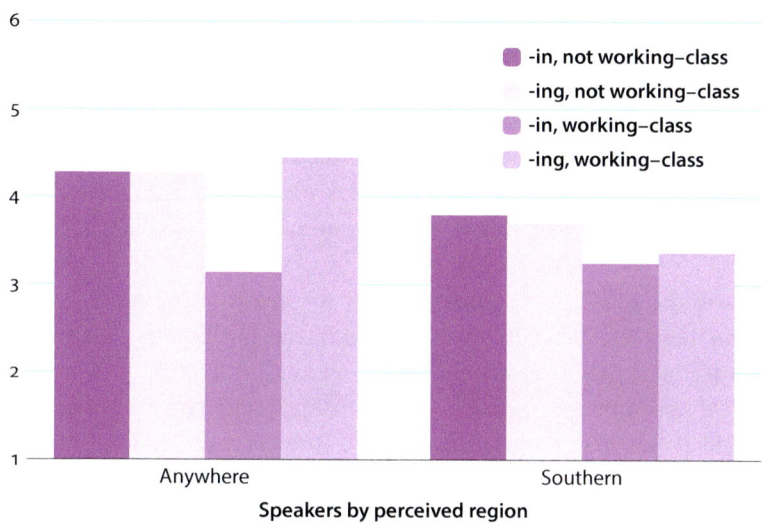

Figure 3. Perceived socio-economic status and dialect region of speaker on ratings of intelligence/education. Reproduced from Campbell-Kibler (2009)

Although single-variable MGT studies (e.g., Campbell-Kibler 2009; Campbell-Kibler 2010; Labov et al. 2011) are promising, the validity of these results remains in question. Lee (1971), for example, has argued that repeating the message forces subjects to focus on form (i.e. the linguistic features) in a manner that may not be commensurate with more naturalistic processing. Gardner and Lambert (1972) acknowledge that the measured attitudes may not accurately reflect underlying mental states, but rather what the participants *think* they should say. Moreover, it is possible that subjects have underlying attitudes which they might not be consciously aware of, nor have access to (Greenwald et al. 2002). The present study attempts to overcome these limitations by utilizing two techniques that provide more precise and more direct measures of real-time sociolinguistic cognition: the implicit association test and event-related brain potentials.

2.   The implicit association test

One promising technique that addresses some of the limitations of matched-guise studies is the implicit association test (IAT) – a chronometric technique that can measure the strength of association between concepts, attitudes, and social stereotypes (Greenwald et al. 1998). Typically, the IAT has been used to examine a wide range of social phenomena including issues of racial and gender stereotyping

(Amodio & Devine 2006; Dasgupta et al. 2000). For example, Greenwald et al. (1998), in examining attitudes towards marginalized social groups, showed that individuals show a tendency to associate black faces with negative concepts and white faces with positive concepts. Although the IAT has primarily used visual stimuli (e.g., written words and pictures), recent work shows promise for linguistic audio stimuli (e.g., Babel 2010; Pantos 2010). This is important because it provides a new tool for studying implicit attitudes towards spoken sociolinguistic variation.

Because the IAT uses response latency to measure the implicit strength of association between concepts, it circumvents the limitations of end-state self-report procedures like the matched-guise technique. During IAT experiments, subjects sort stimuli representing four concepts into two response categories (Greenwald et al. 2003). For example, an IAT study investigating positive/negative attitudes towards race could have subjects sort positive and negative words (e.g., *good, happy, beautiful* versus *bad, horrible, sick*) and pictures of black and white faces. As illustrated in Table 2, the IAT consists of seven experimental blocks. In block #1, subjects practice categorizing positive and negative words. In block #2, subjects practice sorting photos of black and white faces. Block #3 is another practice block, but here subjects must sort both positive/negative words and black/white faces. Block #4 is a test block for the compatible condition (Positive/White mapped to one key, Negative/Black mapped to another key). Block #5 is another practice block for positive and negative words, but with the key mappings reversed relative to block #1. Block #6 is a combined sorting task, but with an incompatible pairing of race and valence (i.e. Negative/White versus Positive/Black). Block #7 is the test block for the incompatible condition.

Table 2. Illustration of IAT to measure implicit associations between race (black/white) and valence (positive/negative)

Block	No. of trials	Function	Items assigned to left-key response	Items assigned to right-key response
1	20	Practice	Positive Words	Negative Words
2	20	Practice	White Faces	Black Faces
3	20	Practice	Positive or White	Negative or Black
4	20	Test	Positive or White	Negative or Black
5	20	Practice	Negative Words	Positive Words
6	20	Practice	Negative or White	Positive or Black
7	20	Test	Negative or White	Positive or Black

Subjects' D scores – a measurement of strength of association – are calculated by taking the difference in mean reaction times to the compatible and incompatible conditions (e.g., block #4 and block #7, in this example), divided by the pooled standard deviations. A positive D score indicates an association in the predicted direction (i.e. a subject responds faster for the compatible condition Positive/White versus Negative/Black) compared to the incompatible condition (Negative/White versus Positive/Black). The magnitude of the D score indicates the relative strength of this stereotypical association, ranging from -2 to 2. A strong association is D > 0.5, a moderate association is D > 0.35, and a weak association is D > 0.15.

Greenwald and colleagues (1998) have demonstrated that the IAT technique can measure valence differences for attitudes that are believed to be (almost) universal as well as attitudes that are culturally specific. Their first experiment showed that subjects responded significantly faster with compatible mappings (flowers or pleasant words and insects or unpleasant words) versus incompatible mappings (flowers or unpleasant words and insects versus pleasant words). Experiment #2 used two different subject groups, Korean Americans and Japanese Americans, who sorted Korean and Japanese surnames and pleasant and unpleasant words. Each group was significantly faster when the sorting groups were consistent with their own ethnicity. These studies additionally demonstrated that the IAT was free from several possible sources of procedural artifact including hand mapping and ISI, which are comparable between 150 ms to 750 ms. Subsequent studies have shown that the IAT measurement is not influenced by stimulus familiarity (Dasgupta et al. 2000; Ottaway et al. 2001; Rudman et al. 1999). Test-retest reliability of the IAT across a number of different studies has averaged approximately $r =.6$ (Greenwald et al. 2002). The IAT typically shows moderate to strong correlations in the expected direction with other explicit and implicit measures of attitude (Greenwald et al. 1998).[1]

In the attitude literature, depending on the particular study and type of stimuli being employed, IAT effect sizes vary considerably. The Korean-Japanese study mentioned previously reported very strong effects, D=1.88 (Greenwald, et al., 1998). Other domains show smaller effects, for example male-female/math-arts (D=.37) and black-white/weapons-gadgets (D=.30) (Sriram & Greenwald 2009). In a study measuring racial attitude, Dasgupta et al. (2000) reported significantly

1.   Among social psychologists it is believed that automatic measurements (e.g., evaluative priming and the IAT) measure the stored evaluative association, whereas more deliberate measures (e.g., semantic differentials and the MGT) tap both the stored evaluative association as well as downstream cognitive processes (Petty, Brinol & DeMarree 2007). Thus there exist theoretically motivated reasons why implicit and explicit measurements might diverge, for example, in measuring pervasive social stereotypes.

different effect sizes depending on the stimuli (i.e. racially stereotypical names, D=.93 versus pictures of Black and White faces, D=.53).

Recently, Campbell-Kibler (2012) used the IAT technique to measure associations between single sociolinguistic variables and their typical social and linguistic correlates. For example, she tested participants using written (ING) forms (e.g., *making/makin'*) contrasted with northern/southern states, white/blue collar professions, and news anchors/country singers. Results showed significant D values in the predicted direction, indicating weak to moderate associations between orthographic ING/IN' variants are their common social correlates (Fig. 4).

		D mean	*p*-Value
(ING) vs.	States	0.38	<0.001
	Professions	0.44	<0.001
	Singers/anchors	0.24	0.002

Figure 4. IAT results for written (ING) vs. states, professions, and singer/anchors. Reproduced from Campbell-Kibler (2012)

In a subsequent experiment, Campbell-Kibler used audio (ING) tokens in lieu of orthographic variation, and contrasted them with northern/southern states, /ay/ monophthongization, and /t/ release. Results showed significant associations in the predicted direction between (ING) and States and /ay/ monophthongization, but not with /t/ release (Fig. 5). These results show that the IAT is sensitive enough to capture associations between (ING) and its common social and linguistic correlates.

		D mean	*p*-Value
(ING) vs.	States	0.30	0.002
	/ay/	0.18	0.004
	/t/	0.09	NS

Figure 5. IAT results for audio (ING) vs. States, /ay/, and /t/. Reproduced from Campbell-Kibler (2012)

3.   The event-related potential technique

Another method which has shown promise in recent years for measuring aspects of sociolinguistic cognition is the event-related potential (ERP) technique. This approach entails recording participants' EEG while they perform some task – typically listening to language, reading words, making semantic/phonological judgments, etc. The EEG signal, which has been time-locked to stimulus onset, is then averaged across experimental conditions, thus increasing the signal-to-noise ratio, providing a spatially and temporally distributed waveform. The resulting ERP components are argued to reflect specific cognitive computations involved in processing the language stimuli (e.g., phonological, syntactic, and semantic processing). One such well-studied ERP component is the so-called N400 – a broad negative deflection of the waveform that peaks 400 ms after the visual or auditory presentation of a word, that is typically maximal over centro-parietal electrode sites (Holcomb & Neville 1991; Kutas & Hillyard 1980). Although all content words elicit an N400 component, the ERP response is larger for words that are semantically anomalous or less expected (Hagoort & Brown 1994; Kutas & Hillyard 1984). For example, listening to the sentence 'I like my coffee with cream and *sugar/sweetener/socks*', the expected word *sugar* elicits the smallest N400, the plausible but less expected *sweetener* elicits a larger waveform, and the semantically anomalous *socks* elicits the largest N400 response. Thus the N400 is often interpreted as an index of ease or difficulty in semantic conceptual integration (Brown & Hagoort 1993; Hagoort & Van Berkum 2007).

Consistently, studies over the past three decades have shown that the closer a word's meaning fits with the prior context (broadly construed), the greater the reduction in N400 amplitude. Importantly, however, N400-like effects show differences in amplitude distributions and latency depending on modality (visual/aural), stimulus characteristics, and task (Kutas & Federmeier 2011). Recently, a number of studies have demonstrated that the N400 response can be modulated by specific contextual factors such as discourse, pragmatics, and world knowledge (Camblin, Gordon & Swaab 2007; Hagoort et al. 2004; Nieuwland & Van Berkum 2006; St. George, Mannes & Hoffman 1994; Van Berkum, Hagoort & Brown 1999; Van Berkum, Zwitserlook, Hagoort & Brown 2003). Given this evidence, one interpretation of the N400 is that it is an index of "effort" or difficulty in integrating the meanings of individual words into higher-order units of meaning (e.g., sentence-level interpretation).

Unfortunately, relatively little is known about how measures of implicit attitude relate to electrophysiological measures such as ERPs. It is only recently that studies have begun to employ both techniques simultaneously. The most thorough of these is Williams and Themanson (2011) who used a group bias IAT (i.e. gay/straight) while recording participants' EEG in order to better understand the effects of compatible and incompatible conditions on early and late ERP components. Specifically, they examined the following ERP components: the N1, P2, N2, N400, and LPP, looking for ERP modulation by IAT condition. Results showed no modulation by compatibility for the early components (i.e. N1, P2, and N2), but they did observe a frontal N400-like effect, with incompatible trials eliciting greater negativities than compatible trials. This finding suggests greater semantic incongruity for incompatible compared to compatible IAT trials, and that "both semantic and affective properties of the stimuli... contribute to the stronger association of the compatible items" (Williams & Themanson 2011:74).

4.   Predictions

In the present study, we sought to investigate individual differences in processing the sociolinguistic aspects of speech, asking whether the degree of implicit stereotypical attitude to (ING) differentially modulates brain activity during language comprehension. In distinction to Williams and Themanson (2011), we did not record ERPs while subjects performed an IAT, but rather used the IAT as a separate measure in order to assess the role of implicit attitude towards (ING) variation during perception of (ING) variants during real-time language comprehension. In order to address this question, we divided participants into two groups using a median split on IAT D score: low stereotype and high stereotype.

We consider three possible accounts of the relationship between implicit attitude towards variation and perception of variation.

1. Implicit attitudes are *not* involved in lexical semantic processing as indexed by the N400. This could be due to latency differences in these two processes (e.g., attitudes are only evoked post semantic processing). This account predicts no differences in N400 modulation between the low and high stereotype groups, though group differences might be observed before or after N400 effects.
2. Individuals that show a *large* IAT effect for (ING) will show heightened sensitivity to conditions that violate (ING) stereotypes. This account predicts heightened N400-like negativities for the high stereotype listeners compared to the low listeners for conditions where the dialect of the speaker conflicts with the register and variant uttered. This account supports the proposition that the emotional valence of spoken words is processed concurrently with word meaning and the sociolinguistic aspects of language use.
3. Individuals that show a *small* IAT effect for (ING) will show heightened sensitivity to conditions that violate (ING) stereotypes. This account predicts larger N400-like negativities for the low stereotype listeners compared to the high listeners. Such a pattern of results would be consistent with the proposition that strong implicit attitudes towards variation block or attenuate normal spoken language processing. This account suggests that the emotional valence of words is processed concurrently with word meaning, but that these mechanisms are partially distinct and that listeners with high stereotypes of

(ING) do not process the sociolinguistic aspects of speech as deeply as individuals with low (ING) stereotypes.

5. Methods

5.1 ERP experiment and participants

In this study, subjects listened for comprehension to short, semantically rich stories which varied in (ING) realization (Fig. 6). Half the critical words were realized with ING and half realized as IN'. All sentence final words were highly predictable, as established by a previous cloze probability task (mean cloze probability 74.9%, range 20.7% – 100%). The time-locked critical words were either preceded by a formal register context containing four embedded ING words or by an informal context containing four IN' words. In addition, however, half of the passages were read by Californian speakers and half were read by Southern speakers. In summary, we used a 2×2×2 factorial design: Variant (ING/IN') × Register (Formal/Informal) × Speaker Dialect (Californian/Southern).

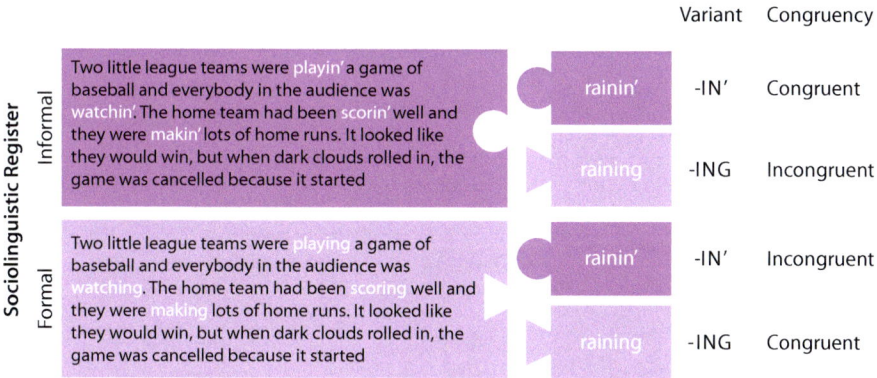

Figure 6. Stimuli conditions

EEG data was collected from 19 native-speaker participants (female = 11). These participants ranged in age from 19 to 24 years and all were raised in Northern California (primarily the Bay Area and Central Valley). Because we used a median split on D value, we removed the median subject to have 9 subjects in each group.

5.2 IAT design and procedure

After recording participants' ERPs during the main experiment, subjects were given a single seven block IAT task designed to measure individuals' strength of stereotypical response to (ING) variation. During IAT pilot testing, we pitted (ING) variation against several well-known correlates, including intelligence/education, gender, and socio-economic status. Preliminary results showed effects in the predicted direction for all correlates; however, the IAT effect for intelligence/ education was the largest and we chose this version for the actual experiment. The basic IAT design is illustrated in Table 3. In order to reduce block and handedness effects, we developed four versions of the basic design, balancing block order and left-right key mappings, and randomly assigned participants to one of the four designs.

Category items were determined by a word association task given to 20 under-graduate students who did not participate in the experiment. Given the category label Intelligent, participants were asked to write down as many associated words as they could in two minutes. The eight most frequently listed items for each cat-egory were chosen. Intelligent words: *smart, bright, educated, genius, brilliant, clever, quick,* and *wise.* Stupid words: *dumb, moron, ignorant, slow, idiot, imbecile, dopey,* and *uneducated.* Although these word groups differ in written frequency, orthographic length, and number of syllables, these factors should not bias indi-viduals' D scores, as this measure is calculated by taking the difference between the compatible and incompatible blocks, thus mitigating this potential confound. The ING/IN' words were: *doing/doin', feeling/feelin', looking/lookin', moving/movin', running/runnin' taking/takin' training/trainin',* and *working/workin'.*

Table 3. IAT design for (ING) variation

Block	No. of trials	Function	Items assigned to left-key response	Items assigned to right-key response
1	20	Practice	Educated Words	Uneducated Words
2	20	Practice	ing	in'
3	20	Practice	Educated or ing	Uneducated or in'
4	20	Test	Educated or ing	Uneducated or in'
5	20	Practice	Uneducated Words	Educated Words
6	20	Practice	Uneducated or ing	Educated or in'
7	20	Test	Uneducated or ing	Educated or in'

The IAT effect (D score) for each participant was calculated by taking the difference between test block means (blocks 4 and 7) divided by the standard deviation of all latencies in the test blocks. This algorithm outperforms candidate algorithms in terms of (a) correlations with self-reports, (b) resistance to speed of response artifacts, (c) internal consistency, (d) sensitivity to known influences, and (e) resistance to known procedural influences (Greenwald et al., 2003). This procedure removes individual trials with reaction times greater than 10,000 ms and removes participants that have more than 10% of reaction times shorter than 300 ms. Trials with an incorrect response are assigned the RT for the mean block plus a 600 ms penalty.

The participants were given the following task instructions:

In this experiment you will both listen to words and read words and press a key to indicate what type of word it is.

1. In the first block, you will see the categories ING and IN' at the top left and right of your screen. You will hear spoken words that alternate in their -ing pronunciation. If you hear the word ending in ING, you hit the left key button (E); if you hear the word with a missing g, you will hit the right key (I). For example, if you heard the word *workin'* you would press the key that corresponds to the IN' category. You should go as fast as you can while making as few mistakes as possible.
2. In the second block you will see the categories Intelligent and Stupid at the top left and right of the screen. Now you will read words and categorize them (e.g., the word smart, for example, should be categorized as Intelligent).
3. Eventually, you will get a more difficult task where you will both read words (meaning Intelligent or Stupid) and listen to words (ING or IN'). Remember to always read the instructions before starting a block, and look at the top left and right to see what the categories are. The entire experiment takes about 10 minutes to complete.

5.3 Analysis

In order to study the role of implicit attitude in modulating the ERP response, we conducted a repeated measures ANOVA, Variant (ING/IN') x Congruency (Congruent/Incongruent) x Dialect (Californian/Southern), adding listener D value as a between groups factor with two levels (low/high).

6. Results

6.1 IAT results

Participants were evenly split into two groups, High D (n=9) and Low D (n=9) based on the median D value (D =.675) of subjects with sufficient ERP trials for statistical analysis. The Low D group had a mean D value of 0.40 (min 0.11, max 0.65) and the High D group had a mean D score of 0.83 (min, 0.7, max 1.05).

A single-tailed T-test showed statistically significant differences between groups (p < 0.001). Results show that all subjects had an IAT effect in the expected direction (i.e. stronger associations of ING with intelligence and IN' with stupidity than with ING with stupidity and IN' with intelligence).

6.2   ERP results

Variant × Dialect × D (180–290 ms)
Between 180–290 ms we observed a significant interaction of Variant × Dialect × D [F(1,16)= 7.796, MSE 173.2, p = 0.013]. Pairwise comparisons revealed increased negativities for High D listeners compared to Low D listeners for IN' words spoken in a Southern dialect (p = 0.043, 2.20 mV) and ING words spoken in a Californian dialect (p = 0.069. 1.63 mV). For Low D listeners, but not High D listeners, IN' words elicited greater negativities than ING words by Californian speakers (p = 0.005, 2.83 mV difference, Fig. 7).

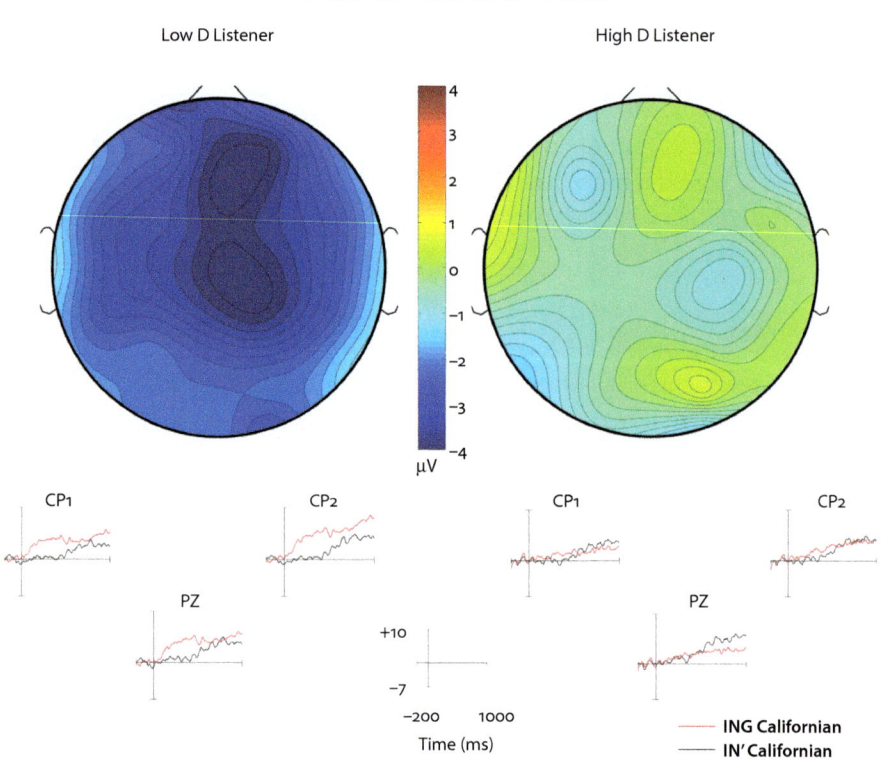

Figure 7. Californian vernacular IN' effect for low and high stereotype listeners. Positive plotted up

For Low D listeners, hearing IN' words spoken by Californian speakers elicited greater negativities than when spoken by Southern speakers (p = 0.023, 2.21 mV difference, Fig. 7, left). In distinction, for Low D listeners, hearing ING words spoken by Southern speakers elicited greater negativities than those spoken by Californian speakers (p = 0.022, 1.50 mV difference, Fig. 8, right).

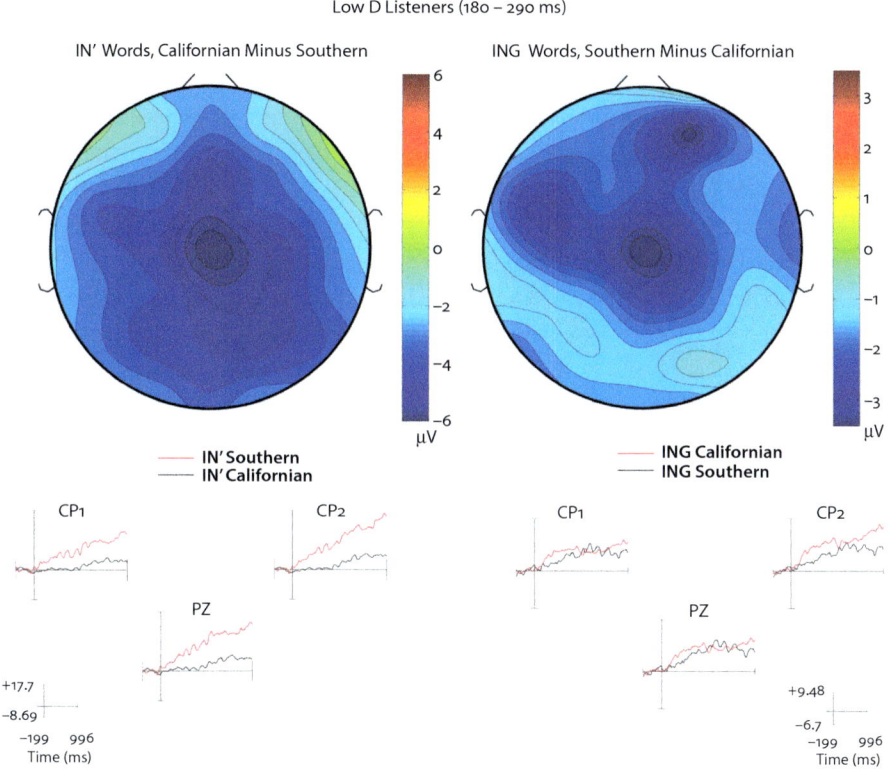

Figure 8. Variant dialect effect for low stereotype listeners. Positive plotted up

Dialect × LR × D (180–290 ms)
Within the 180–290 ms window, we observed a statistically significant Dialect × LR × D interaction [F(1,16) = 5.584, MSE .664, p = 0.031]. For Southern speakers, High D listeners showed greater negativities than Low D listeners in the left (p = 0.041, 1.35 mV difference) and right (p = 0.060, 1.24 mV difference) hemispheres. For Low D listeners, Californian speakers elicited greater right hemispheric negativities (p = 0.051, .41 mV difference).

Congruency x AP x LR (180–290 ms)
Between180-290 ms, Congruency x AP x LR interacted [F(1,16)=6.550, MSE .381, p = 0.021]. Pairwise comparisons showed that critical words that were congruent with the preceding sociolinguistic register elicited greater right hemispheric negativities at anterior sites (p = 0.001, .56 mV difference).

7. Discussion

The purpose of this experiment was to investigate the relationship between individuals' strength of stereotypical association towards variation and characterize the neural bases of sociolinguistic cognition. In the current analysis, we added participants' IAT D score as a between groups factor, with participants categorized as high or low (ING) stereotype. We observed several novel findings. Between 180–90 ms after the acoustic onset of the ING/IN' allomorph, we observed that: (1) for dialect typical variants (i.e. Southerner IN' and Californian ING) High D listeners showed greater negativities than Low D listeners; (2) Low D listeners, but not High D listeners, showed an N400-like effect of vernacular variant for Californian speakers; (3) Low D listeners showed increased negativities for IN' words spoken by Californians compared to Southerners; and (4) Low D listeners showed increased negativities for ING words spoken by Southern speakers compared to Californian speakers. No additional effects were observed for either group of listeners.

In this analysis, we observed modulation of N400-like potentials based on individuals' strength of implicit stereotypical attitude towards (ING). The significant differences in waveform amplitude between conditions and groups as well as the timing of these effects suggest that attitudinal processing occurs concurrently or in parallel with lexical semantic processing. Contrary to the proposal that high stereotype listeners should have the largest N400 response to sociolinguistic violations, we observed these effects only in the group of listeners with relatively smaller stereotypical response. Only the low stereotype listeners showed sensitivity to mismatches of dialect and sociolinguistic variant.

Williams and Themanson (2011), measuring participants' ERPs during an IAT task, reported a correlation of N400 amplitude with subjects' IAT effect size. Rather than a straight linear relation between the two measures, the authors report a curvilinear relationship: for participants with low IAT effect scores, N400 amplitude increased as RT differences between incompatible and compatible trials increased; however, for participants with larger IAT effects, N400 amplitude differences decreased as RT differences increased. We too observed a similar pattern: participants with low stereotypical bias towards (ING) variation showed increased

N400 negativities for conditions where speaker dialect was incongruent with the ING/IN' variant uttered; in contrast, participants with relatively larger IAT effects showed no such N400 modulation (Fig. 6 and 7).

The question that emerges is why do only the low stereotype listeners show sensitivity to the social aspects of language? One plausible interpretation of these results is that dual processes are involved in language comprehension. In addition to lexical semantic processing, we speculate that both word meaning and the emotional or attitudinal aspects of words are processed concurrently perhaps relying upon a single shared limited capacity resource. For listeners with little attitudinal bias to variation, emotional processing is minimized compared to listeners that hold strong implicit attitudes towards variation. For these high stereotype listeners, who show difficulties with incompatible IAT trials, we speculate that additional neural resources are recruited for processing the emotional and attitudinal aspects of language. As more cognitive resources are deployed for attitudinal processing, fewer can be devoted to the lexical semantic aspects of language processing, resulting in an attenuation of the N400 response compared to the low attitude listeners.

Future work will need to determine what are the exact components of cognition which are taxed under these conditions. Two possible candidates for future investigation are attention and working memory, both of which are typically conceived as limited capacity cognitive processes. Attention, the ability to selectively attend to or concentrate on a stimulus while ignoring other sources of information, is one such candidate. In language processing, the role of attention can be observed in the so-called "cocktail party" problem (Cherry 1953) – how does an individual selectively attend to the message of a single speaker while ignoring the cacophony of voices around her. One of the fundamental bases of attention is the processing tradeoffs that occur when multiple "sources" of information are presented – "better processing of one source seems to require poorer processing of another" (Kinchla 1992). Similarly, the observed results could be due to limitations of working memory, conceived of as "a limited capacity system that provides the temporary storage and manipulation of information for performing a wide range of cognitive activities" (Baddeley 2012: 7). Could the high stereotype listeners be attending more to the emotional and attitudinal aspects of speech at the cost of shallower lexical semantic processing? Future work will need to address such concerns.

Whatever the precise interpretation of these effects, the results from the present study show that the attitudinal aspects of sociolinguistic variation can influence real-time language processing. Individuals with strong negative stereotypes to variation show less sensitivity to the dialectal and sociolinguistic aspects of speech as indexed by the N400. In contrast, individuals with relatively little attitudinal bias appear to more deeply process the social dimensions of language.

8. Conclusion

This present study testifies to the importance of including independent measures of implicit language attitude while investigating language perception. Differences in brain activity masked through aggregate analysis were revealed by taking into account the strength of stereotypical attitude of the listeners. Results from this study revealed increased N400 negativities for listeners with low attitudinal bias towards variable (ING), suggesting that language processes may be blocked or attenuated for individuals with strong implicit biases towards variation.

References

Amodio, David M. & Devine, Patricia G. 2006. Stereotyping and evaluation in implicit race bias: Evidence for independent constructs and unique effects on behavior. *Journal of Personality and Social Psychology* 91(4): 652–661. DOI: 10.1037/0022-3514.91.4.652

Babel, Molly. 2010. Dialect convergence and divergence in New Zealand English. *Language In Society* 39: 437–456. DOI: 10.1017/S0047404510000400

Baddeley, Alan. 2012. Working memory: Theories, models, and controversies. *Annual Review of Psychology* 63: 1–29. DOI: 10.1146/annurev-psych-120710-100422

Baugh, John. 2000. Racial identity by speech. *American Speech* 75: 362–364.
DOI: 10.1215/00031283-75-4-362

Brown, Colin & Hagoort, Peter. 1993. The processing nature of the N400: Evidence from masked priming. *Journal of Cognitive Neuroscience* 5: 34–44. DOI: 10.1162/jocn.1993.5.1.34

Camblin, Christine C., Gordon, Peter C. & Swaab, Tamara Y. 2007. The interplay of discourse congruence and lexical association during sentence processing: Evidence from ERPs and eye tracking. *Journal of Memory and Language* 56(1): 103–128.
DOI: 10.1016/j.jml.2006.07.005

Campbell-Kibler, Kathryn. 2009. The nature of sociolinguistic perception. *Language Variation and Change* 21: 135–156. DOI: 10.1017/S0954394509000052

Campbell-Kibler, Kathryn. 2010. The effect of speaker information on attitudes toward (ING). *Journal of Language and Social Psychology* 29(2): 214–223. DOI: 10.1177/0261927X09359527

Campbell-Kibler, Kathryn. 2012. The Implicit Association Test and sociolinguistic meaning. *Lingua* 122(7): 753–763. DOI: 10.1016/j.lingua.2012.01.002

Cherry, Colin. 1953. Some experiments on the recognition of speech, with one and with two ears. *J. Acoust. Soc. Am.* 25(5): 975–979. DOI: 10.1121/1.1907229

Dasgupta, Nilanjana, McGhee, Debbie E., Greenwald, Anthony G. & Banaji, Mahzarin R. 2000. Automatic preference for White Americans: Eliminating the familiarity explanation. *Journal of Experimental Social Psychology* 36: 316–328. DOI: 10.1006/jesp.1999.1418

Gardner, Richard G. & Lambert, Wallace E. 1972. *Attitudes and Motivation in Second-language Learning*. Rowley MA: Newbury House.

Garrett, Peter, Coupland, Nik & Williams, Angie. 2003. *Investigating Language Attitudes: Social Meanings of Dialect, Ethnicity, and Performance*. Cardiff: University of Wales Press.

Greenwald, Anthony G., Banaji, Mahzarin R. & Nosek, Brian A. 2003. Understanding and using the implicit association test: I. An improved scoring algorithm. *Journal of Personality and Social Psychology* 85(2): 197–216. DOI: 10.1037/0022-3514.85.2.197

Greenwald, Anthony G., McGhee, Debbie E. & Schwartz, Jordan L.K. 1998. Measuring individual differences in implicit cognition: The Implicit Association Test. *Journal of Personality and Social Psychology* 74: 1464–1480. DOI: 10.1037/0022-3514.74.6.1464

Greenwald, Anthony G., Rudman, Laurie A., Nosek, Brian A., Banaji, Mahzarin R., Farnham, Shelley D. & Mellot, Deborah S. 2002. A unified theory of implicit attitudes, stereotypes, self-esteem, and self-concept. *Psychological Review* 109(1): 3–25. DOI: 10.1037/0033-295X.109.1.3

Gumperz, John J. 1968. The speech community. *International Encyclopedia of the Social Sciences* 9(3): 382–386.

Hagoort Peter, Hald, Lea A., Bastiaansen, Marcel & Petersson, Karl Magnus. 2004. Integration of word meaning and world knowledge in language comprehension. *Science* 304: 438–441. DOI: 10.1126/science.1095455

Hagoort Peter & Brown, Colin M. 1994. Brain responses to lexical-ambiguity resolution and parsing. In *Perspectives on Sentence Processing*, Charles Clifton Jr., Lyn Frazier & Keith Rayner (eds), 45–81. Hillsdale NJ: Laurence Erlbaum Associates.

Hagoort, Peter & van Berkum, Jos J.A. 2007. Beyond the sentence given. *Philosophical Transactions of the Royal Society B: Biological Sciences* 362(1481): 801–811. DOI: 10.1098/rstb.2007.2089

Henerson, Marlene E., Morris, Lyn L. & Fitz-Gibbon, Carol T. 1987. *How to Measure Attitudes.* Newbury Park CA: Sage.

Holcomb, Philip J. & Neville, Helen J. 1991. The electrophysiology of spoken sentence processing. *Psychobiology* 19: 286–300.

Kinchla, Ronald A. 1992. Attention. *Annual Review of Psychology* 43(1): 711–742. DOI: 10.1146/annurev.ps.43.020192.003431

Knops, Uus & van Hout, Roland. 1988. Language attitudes in the Dutch language area: An introduction. In *Language Attitudes in the Dutch Language Area,* Roland van Hout & Uus Knops (eds). Dordrecht: Foris. DOI: 10.1515/9783110857856

Kutas, Marta & Federmeier, Kara D. 2011. Thirty years and counting: Finding meaning in the N400 component of the Event-Related Brain Potential (ERP), *Annual Review of Psychology* 62: 621–647. DOI: 10.1146/annurev.psych.093008.131123

Kutas, Marta & Hillyard, Steven A. 1980. Event-related potentials to semantically inappropriate and surprisingly large words. *Biological Psychology* 11: 99–116. DOI: 10.1016/0301-0511(80)90046-0

Kutas, Marta & Hillyard, Steven A. 1984. Brain potentials during reading reflect word expectancy and semantic association. *Nature* 307: 161–163. DOI: 10.1038/307161a0

Labov, William. 1966. *The Social Stratification of English in New York City.* Washington DC: Center for Applied Linguistics.

Labov, William. 1972. *Sociolinguistic Patterns.* Philadelphia PA: University of Pennsylvania Press.

Labov, William, Ash, Sharon, Ravindranath, Maya, Weldon, Tracey, Baranowski, Maciej & Nagy, Naomi. 2011. Properties of the sociolinguistic monitor. *Journal of Sociolinguistics* 15(4): 431–463. DOI: 10.1111/j.1467-9841.2011.00504.x

Lambert, Wallace, Hodgson, Ricard C., Gardner, Robert C. & Fillenbaum, Samuel. 1960. Evaluational reactions to spoken languages. *Journal of Abnormal and Social Psychology* 60: 44–51. DOI: 10.1037/h0044430

Lee, Richard R. 1971. Dialect perception: A critical review and re-evaluation. *Quarterly Journal of Speech* 57: 410–417. DOI: 10.1080/00335637109383086

Nieuwland, Mante S. & van Berkum, Jos J.A. 2006. When peanuts fall in love: N400 evidence for the power of discourse. *Journal of Cognitive Neuroscience* 18(7): 1098–1111. DOI: 10.1162/jocn.2006.18.7.1098

Ottaway, Scott A., Hayden, David C. & Oakes, Mark A. 2001. Implicit attitudes and racism: Effect of word familiarity and frequency on the Implicit Association Test. *Social Cognition* 19: 97–144. DOI: 10.1521/soco.19.2.97.20706

Pantos, Andrew. 2010. Measuring Implicit and Explicit Attitudes toward Foreign-accented Speech. Ph.D. dissertation, Rice University.

Petty, Richard E., Briñol, Pablo & DeMarree, Kenneth G. 2007. The meta-cognitive model (MCM) of attitudes: Implications for attitude measurement, change, and strength. *Social Cognition* 25(5): 657–686. DOI: 10.1521/soco.2007.25.5.657

Purnell, Thomas, Idsardi, William J. & Baugh, John. 1999. Perceptual and phonetic experiments on American English dialect identification. *Journal of Language and Social Psychology* 18: 10–30. DOI: 10.1177/0261927X99018001002

Rudman, Lea A., Greenwald, Anthony G., Mellott, Deborah S. & McGhee, Debbie E. 1999. Measuring the automatic components of prejudice: Flexibility and generality of the Implicit Association Test. *Social Cognition* 17: 437–465. DOI: 10.1521/soco.1999.17.4.437

St. George, Marie, Mannes, Suzanne & Hoffman, James E. 1994. Global semantic expectancy and language comprehension. *Journal of Cognitive Neuroscience* 6(1): 70–83. DOI: 10.1162/jocn.1994.6.1.70

Sriram, N. & Greenwald, Anthony G. 2009. The brief implicit association test. *Experimental Psychology* 56(4): 283–294. DOI: 10.1027/1618-3169.56.4.283

Tajfel, Henry. 1981. *Human Groups and Social Categories*. Cambridge: CUP.

van Berkum, Jos J.A., Hagoort, Peter & Brown, Colin M. 1999. Semantic integration in sentences and discourse: Evidence from the N400. *Journal of Cognitive Neuroscience* 11(6): 657–71. DOI: 10.1162/089892999563724

van Berkum, Jos J.A., Zwitserlood, Pienie, Hagoort, Peter & Brown, Colin M. 2003. When and how do listeners relate a sentence to the wider discourse? Evidence from the N400 effect. *Brain Res. Cogn. Brain Res.* 17: 701–718. DOI: 10.1016/S0926-6410(03)00196-4

Williams, John K. & Themanson, Jason R. 2011. Neural correlates of the implicit association test: evidence for semantic and emotional processing. *Social Cognitive and Affective Neuroscience* 6(4): 468–476. DOI: 10.1093/scan/nsq065

PART III

What factors awaken attitudes?

Got class? Community-shared conceptualizations of social class in evaluative reactions to sociolinguistic variables

Laura Staum Casasanto[1], Stefan Grondelaers[2] &
Roeland van Hout[2]
[1]University of Chicago / [2]Radboud University Nijmegen

In recent years, researchers have successfully used information about cultural identity and consumption behavior to uncover class-based variation in linguistic production data. Is this variation reflected in implicit class-related language attitudes, of which listeners may not even be aware? And which types of evaluative conceptualizations of class membership do listeners in fact use? In a two-alternative forced choice task, we compared how listeners associate linguistic variables with both more classic and newer conceptualizations of class membership. High social class responses were significantly more likely for standard linguistic variants than for nonstandard linguistic variants (for all five types of social class conceptualizations we used). The fact that there was no difference between the class conceptualizations indicates that conceptualizations in terms of economic production, culture, and consumption were equally successful in probing evaluative reactions to class-based linguistic variation in the region investigated.

1. Introduction

Investigations of language as it relates to social class are a cornerstone of variationist sociolinguistics (Rickford 1986). Social class, in its many incarnations, is inextricably bound to how people produce language in the communities they live in. This makes it equally important to study language perceptions in those communities in order to investigate how language is evaluated in relation to social class values and memberships.

There are two major challenges in investigating evaluative reactions about relationships between linguistic behavior and social class in a community. One is a challenge common to all evaluation or attitude research: directly asking people

DOI 10.1075/impact.39.07cas

to discuss their language attitudes does not always result in accurate information about how language use is perceived in a community (see Garrett [2005] about the disadvantages of direct elicitation in attitude research). This raises the question of how we can study language-related evaluative reactions and attitudes in a way that will result in an accurate and valid picture. The other is a challenge common to all sociolinguistic investigations involving social class: how can we operationalize this social variable such that our ways of classifying and representing it are suited to the way our communities are organized and conceptualize it in everyday life?

As far as the latter point is concerned, the methods used to operationalize social class in production studies may not always be perfectly suited for perception studies. Observing people's linguistic and other behavior and proposing social categories that capture locally important distinctions may not automatically lay the foundation for questions about evaluative language reactions and attitudes if these distinctions are not part of the public discourse about language. Unless community members are explicitly aware of such categories, they may not respond helpfully to questions that depend upon them. In this paper, we build on *indirect* methods as well as different types of indices of social class (or, to use a word which better profiles the processing character of attitudes, *conceptualizations* of social class).

In response to the first challenge, obtaining unbiased evaluations, researchers have developed many different elicitation methods. While the most traditional attitudes studies involve directly asking participants about their attitudes towards language varieties or usages, this approach has several potential pitfalls. As Mallinson and Dodsworth put it, "However robust our ethnographic methods, speakers are generally unable or unwilling to verbalise anything like a comprehensive model of class distinctions in their own communities, even those distinctions that are critical to the use of locally meaningful linguistic variables" (2010: 267–8). Studies of explicit attitudes may not uncover the truth about attitudes because respondents are unaware of their own biases and opinions, or because respondents do not wish to be identified with their true biases or opinions, fearing that they are politically incorrect.

The concern that direct strategies for assessing attitudes may not be tapping into our true object of interest has been expressed by many researchers over the years (concerning attitudes about many subjects, not just language attitudes). Greenwald & Banaji (1995) argued that in view of the fact that people in general are not consciously aware of their attitudes, we need to use *indirect* measures to assess them. But explicit and implicit attitudes may both be deserving of attention. Strack & Deutsch (2004) argued that explicit and implicit attitudes are two separate but interacting systems, and we need ways to assess them both in order to fully understand attitudes. Pantos & Perkins (2013) showed that measuring implicit and explicit language attitudes in the same participants can produce divergent results, reinforcing the legitimacy of this concern. Squires (2014) also found that when participants respond directly (choosing a picture to represent the speaker of an utterance), they may not distinguish between categories that appear distinct when compared using an indirect response measure (mouse trajectories to make this choice). In sociolinguistically oriented work on language (de)standardization, explicit and implicit language attitudes suggest diametrically different hierarchies (see the studies in Kristiansen & Grondelaers 2013): while explicit value systems typically uphold the prestige of the conservative standard variety promoted by the cultural establishment and formal education, implicit attitude investigations increasingly confirm the (dynamic) prestige of "modern" standard varieties which are explicitly rejected.

So, what methods, then, should we use to assess language attitudes? There are two aspects of a language attitudes task that can vary on the continuum between direct/explicit and indirect/implicit: the presentation of linguistic material, and the ways of collecting responses. Some methods, such as the Matched Guise Technique, are intended to mask the linguistic variable that is being investigated via the presentation method. By presenting speech samples that are produced by a single speaker and vary along a single critical linguistic dimension (ranging from whole language varieties [Lambert et al. 1960] to phonetic variants [Campbell-Kibler 2007, 2008]) as though they are from different speakers, this method obscures the linguistic object of study. However, many matched guise studies are still accessing explicit attitudes in the sense that they ask listeners to evaluate the social or personal characteristics of the speakers. After hearing the speech samples, respondents provide reactions or opinions via open-ended questions or respond on Likert scales to questions about speaker traits such as intelligence or sincerity. The purpose of the experiment remains hidden, as respondents are not aware that the study focuses on language, but it can only query social characteristics and categories that listeners can interpret and are explicitly aware of.

Existing methods leave open the question *how* to elicit associations between social class and linguistic variables without directly referring to social class. More importantly, how can we represent social class in such a way that people can make judgments about it on the basis of their implicit evaluations? Researchers have developed increasingly complex and locally defined ways of operationalizing social class in studies of sociolinguistic production in recent years. Rather than focusing on the traditional measures of "education level, family income, and occupational rank" (Dodsworth 2009: 1315), sociolinguists are turning to information about cultural identity and consumption behavior, among other things, to uncover class-based linguistic variation that is not predicted by classic measures such as education, income, and occupation (Dodsworth 2009; Mallinson and Dodsworth 2010).

This change in focus helps to resolve theoretical concerns about, for example, the marginalization of members of society without paid employment. It also adds more practice-based criteria to the operationalization of social class, consistent with the notion of linguistic behavior as an integral component of social practice (Eckert 2000).

Eckert demonstrated that among adolescents, groups that reproduce the adult social class distinction do not do so perfectly, and the critical dimensions on which they vary are behavioral, rather than strictly economic. In some communities, the standard dimensions of income, education, and occupation are not sufficient to separate groups from one another, even among adults (Mallinson 2007). What seems to matter for predicting linguistic behavior is other symbolic behavior. That is, linguistic behavior is part of a package of symbolic behavior that expresses social allegiances and belonging in a community. So, if we want to identify the groupings of individuals that will correspond best to linguistic behavior, we should look to other types of symbolic behavior for guidance. As Dodsworth points out, we should define our categories "primarily in social terms, and secondarily in economic terms, because our objects of study are linguistic practices that have meaning within social rather than purely economic space" (2009: 1321).

Of course, symbolic behavior is not entirely separable from economic behavior. For example, the kind of job that someone has (their occupation) has both symbolic and economic value. The "church ladies" in Mallinson's study of Texana, North Carolina have jobs that differ in symbolic value from the jobs held by the "porch sitters," despite having very similar education and income levels. These occupations might be ranked similarly in a system of socioeconomic indexing, because they require similar levels of skill and education, but they have different symbolic value – the church ladies have occupations that are consistent with their identities as proper ladies, such as working for the Department of Social Services, whereas the porch sitters have occupations that would not be consistent with such an identity, such as working at a tool-making plant. Mallinson argues that these identity differences are not separate from class, but rather they are part of what makes up class in Texana. Indeed, these symbolic differences are good predictors of linguistic behavior, suggesting that the symbolic, rather than economic, value of someone's occupation may be the most relevant dimension for sociolinguistic analysis. This proposal is consistent with the idea that someone's engagement in the standard language market is a better predictor of their linguistic behavior than their income (Labov 1966), but it goes beyond that to predict that even among people whose jobs show very low engagement in the standard language market, differences in the cultural interpretations of these jobs may predict the linguistic behavior of those who hold them better than intrinsic properties of the jobs and their standard language associations.

Advances in the way social class is conceived and measured have been made primarily in the area of community studies of sociolinguistic production (e.g. Mallinson & Dodsworth 2010). However, more nuanced approaches to social class may also be valuable to the study of language attitudes. For example, when we ask participants to rate the speaker of a clip on a scale from 1 to 9, we have to choose what the scale represents. Do we ask participants to rate someone's "social class" from "low" to "high"? Do we ask them to rate someone's "education level" from "low" to "high" or from "less than high school" to "graduate or professional degree"? Most of the ways in which traditional language attitudes studies (such as matched guise studies) approach social class are restricted to these kinds of class representations, because more symbolic ways of representing class, as embodied in porch sitting or church singing, do not lend themselves to assessment with Likert scales.

As discussed above, the study of language attitudes has expanded to include a wide variety of approaches, including more indirect measurement techniques. Some of these indirect approaches lend themselves more easily to investigating sociolinguistic consequences of class using symbolic representations. Probing attitudes on the basis of locally defined or symbolic representations of social class has the additional advantage that such representations tend to require less explicit consideration of class differences. Or, to reverse the logic, using indirect response-eliciting techniques may allow us to include a wider variety of conceptualizations of social class in our research. A practical concern is whether judgments about symbolic and locally appropriate conceptualizations of class are robust enough to be used in the investigation of class-based language attitudes. In this paper, we explore the possibilities of investigating language attitudes and evaluations using five ways of expressing social class through symbolic means: personal appearance; first names; occupations; workplaces; and cars.

These conceptualizations also have non-symbolic components; for example, someone's personal appearance is made up not only of symbolic components such as body hexis, hair style and dress, but also of physical components such as skin color and face shape. The symbolic components of personal appearance may influence the way these physical characteristics are interpreted, but the physical characteristics exert some constraint over the symbolic content also.

Likewise, occupations and workplaces have obvious economic components that are not inherently symbolic, and can be interpreted in their own right (as ways of estimating more traditional notions of class like education, income and wealth). However, as discussed above, occupations have symbolic value above and beyond their economic value. Workplaces provide a good example of the extent to which occupations can have symbolic value. People who work in the same place may have very different educations and incomes: imagine a secretary, a paralegal, a first-year associate, and a partner who all work at a law firm. On a first date, all can give the same answer to the initial question, "Where do you work?" And this answer holds some value, at least sociolinguistically, as demonstrated by the results of Labov's famous department store study, in which speakers with very similar job titles and earnings used sociolinguistic variables differently depending on the prestige of the store in which they worked (Labov 1966).

First names also have a great deal of symbolic value. Perhaps one reason for this is that they are something that, by and large, our parents choose for us, rather than something we choose for ourselves. Thus they become the repository for our parents' hopes and dreams for us, and can symbolize those aspects of our social class that we inherit and that are dependent upon the opportunities available to us at a young age. First names may be a good index of how likely someone is to have taken horseback riding lessons, or to have worked a part-time job as a teenager – factors that reflect our upbringing more than our adult achievements.

Lastly, cars represent our consumer behavior. While income and wealth constrain consumer behavior somewhat, they do not correlate with it perfectly. Other factors also influence what and how much we buy, including our explicit and implicit desires to construct a particular type of consumer identity. What type of car a person drives can thus be a symbolic representation of his or her self-identified social class. It can also identify someone as a member of a smaller sub-group of people, which may be more specific than social class but still be informative about it. For example, if you have a souped-up sports car, it may identify you as a member of the drag-racing subculture, which places you as a most likely working class or middle class individual who nonetheless does not aspire to climb the class hierarchy and achieve higher status in the same way that someone who drives an equivalently valued BMW might want to. Cars are informative about values as well as means, which makes purchasing and driving cars a form of symbolic behavior that may be expected to correlate well with linguistic behavior.

Because these categories of symbols represent a diverse array of conceptualizations of social class, they may not all be equally effective at eliciting evaluative reactions or attitudes about language and social class. Broadly, the symbols fall into two larger categories, which we will be able to compare: the workplace and occupation categories represent social class primarily via information about economic production and education, whereas the names, cars, and appearance categories represent consumption patterns, culture, and other indirect aspects of social class. If both of these kinds of symbols are an effective way for individuals to express or mark social class membership, then they should all be accessible for listeners to use in assessing the social meanings of linguistic behavior.

2. Methods

2.1 Participants

Forty members of the Radboud University community participated in exchange for payment.

2.2 Materials

Four sets of 80 words were created, each representing a well-studied socio-phonetic variation pattern in Netherlandic standard Dutch (e.g. van de Velde 1996; van de Velde, Gerritsen & van Hout 1997; van de Velde & van Hout 1999; Jacobi 2009; van den Berg & van Bezooijen 2004). In all four cases, the standard variant is in competition with a newly emerging non-standard variant.

The long mid vowel (ee) has a standard variant that is slightly diphthongized [e.^{i}] (cf. van de Velde 1996; Adank, van Hout & van de Velde 2004) and a stronger diphthongized, lower variant [ɛi]. The diphthong (ij) has a standard variant [ɛi] and a newly emerging lower, nonstandard variant [ai] (cf. Jacobi 2009). The two other variables are consonants. The fricative (z) originally was a voiced [z], but it has a nonstandard devoiced variant [s] (van de Velde, Gerritsen & van Hout 1996). The (r) has a lot of variants, the tap or flap being the most frequent standard variant in coda [ɾ]. A recent innovation is the non-standard retroflex/bunched approximant [ɹ] (a mid vocalic approximant, occurring in coda position, known as the 'Gooise r') (van de Velde & van Hout 1999; van den Berg & van Bezooijen 2004).

The two vocalic variables always appeared in the primary stressed syllable of the stimulus words, which ranged from one to four syllables. Two trained phoneticians (both male) were recorded producing two versions of each of the words: the standard variant (which we predict to be associated with higher social class membership in the Netherlands) and the non-standard variant (predicted to converge with lower social class membership in the Netherlands) of the relevant sociolinguistic variable.

It should be noticed that the restriction of the stimulus materials to single phonetic variables in isolated content words also represents an important innovation in Dutch perceptual sociolinguistics. While the study of native speaker attitudes has always been at the forefront of sociolinguistic attention in The Netherlands and Belgium (Grondelaers 2013), a recurrently voiced concern (see for instance Knops 1984) is that experimental speech samples as they are used in speaker evaluation research [i.e. audio-recorded fragments of prose containing multiple perception triggers – LSC, SG and RVH] do not allow the researcher to correlate perceptions with specific linguistic features Grondelaers 2013: 591 ff).

While Knops (1988) addressed this concern by investigating the relative impact of phonological vs. phonetic deviations from standard speech on the basis of neutral prose fragments *and* isolated content words, almost nothing is known about the perceptual impact of specific phonetic features represented in single words in Dutch. In view of the standard practice to elicit attitudes and evaluations on the basis of 10 to 20 second speech clips, it is worthwhile to find out whether phonetically untrained listeners are perceptually sensitive to tiny manipulations in single words.

In addition to the word sets, we created five sets of class markers: names, occupations, portraits, cars, and workplaces. Each set consisted of eight high Socioeconomic status (SES) examples and eight low SES examples. All examples were suited to male potential speakers, since the recordings of the words containing the sociolinguistic variables were made by male speakers.

The names category consisted of names that high-SES Dutch speakers tend to have (e.g. Jan Peter), and names that low-SES Dutch speakers tend to have (e.g. Matt). The occupations category consisted of occupations that high-SES Dutch speakers tend to have (e.g. surgeon), and occupations that low-SES Dutch speakers tend to have (e.g. construction worker). The portraits category consisted of photographs that showed plausibly Dutch adult males who were dressed in a manner consistent with being high SES or low SES. The cars category consisted of photographs that showed cars that were likely to be owned by high SES people (e.g. a Rolls Royce) or low SES people (e.g. a rusty Honda). The workplaces category consisted of photographs that showed locations where a high SES individual would be likely to work (e.g. an office) or where a low SES individual would be likely to work (e.g. an automotive shop). Lists of class markers were created by the first two authors in consultation with a native Dutch-speaking research assistant.

2.3   Procedure

Participants were seated in front of a computer screen and heard one of the recorded words after which two of the visual class markers appeared side-by-side. Participants were asked to make a two-alternative forced choice between the two items, answering the question, "Which of these two items goes best with the speaker of this word?" The five different types of class markers were displayed in blocks, with all the cars together in one block, all the names together in another block, etc. The order of the blocks was counterbalanced between subjects, so that some participants did the names first, others did the cars first, etc. Each word was heard only once by each listener. The speaker in the recording was counterbalanced across items, so that each item was spoken by Speaker 1 for half of the participants and by Speaker 2 for the other half of the participants. The variant used in the recording was also counterbalanced across items, so that each item contained the standard variant for half the participants, and the non-standard variant for the other half of the participants (crossed with the speaker, so that these were not conflated). In order to obfuscate the purpose of the experiment, half of the trials were filler trials in which both class markers came from the same class category (high or low). The remaining half of the trials, in which the class markers came from different categories, were target trials. Both the participants' responses and their response times were recorded. The experiment lasted for about half an hour.

3. Results

High SES class choices were classified as positive outcomes (a score of 1), low SES class choices as zero outcomes (a score of 0). High scores for a variant mean it is valued as a high SES class marker, indicating high standard language prestige, low scores meaning that the variant is rejected as a marker of high SES class and that the variant is marked as nonstandard. We will use proportions to indicate how frequently high class choices occurred.

We started by analyzing the outcomes per linguistic variable by logistic generalized mixed modeling. The variables included were speaker (1 and 2), variant (standard vs. non-standard variant), SES class marker (five categories), plus word and participants as random factors. The factor SES class marker was never significant as a main effect, nor in any interaction with the other two explanatory variables. The significant effects found were related to speaker, to variant and to their interaction. We simplified the statistical analysis by using mean scores aggregating over words, computing the proportion of high SES class choices, keeping the variables of speaker, variant, and SES class marker as explanatory variables.

We used repeated measures ANOVAs to analyze and estimate the effects for speaker, variant and SES class marker. We started by including the SES class markers, but we never found any significant difference between the five categories. In the final analyses we left out the SES class markers as an explanatory variable. The five categories apparently cover the same conceptualization of social class.

We found, for all four variables, significant effects of either speaker, variant or their interaction. The (r) variable gave only one significant outcome, i.e. for speaker ($F(1,39) = 9.457$, $p = .004$, $\eta_p^2 = .195$), speaker 2 being evaluated higher in general, for both variants. Variant did not yield a significant result ($F(1,39) = 2.180$, $p = .148$, $\eta_p^2 = .053$), nor the interaction between speaker and variant ($F(1,39) = 0.670$, $p = .418$, $\eta_p^2 = .017$). The (z) variable returned a significant effect for variant ($F(1,39) = 20.120$, $p = .000$, $\eta_p^2 = .341$) but not for speaker as a main effect

$(F(1,39) = 2.500$, $p = .122$, $\eta_p^2 = .060)$. There was a significant interaction effect between speaker and variant $(F(1,39) = 5.417$, $p = .025$, $\eta_p^2 = .122)$, indicating that the nonstandard variant of speaker 1 was evaluated lower than the nonstandard variant of speaker 2.

The two vowel variables showed strong effects for the variant variable. The (ee) had a significant effect for variant with a high effect size $(F(1,39) = 91.015$, $p = .000$, $\eta_p^2 = .700)$. The variable speaker was significant as well $(F(1,39) = 15.600$, $p = .000$, $\eta_p^2 = .286)$, as well as the interaction of speaker by variant $(F(1,39) = 19.994$, $p = .000$, $\eta_p^2 = .339)$. The low variants of speaker 2 were evaluated lower than the low variants of speaker 1. The (ij) had a highly significant effect for variant $(F(1,39) = 318.987$, $p = .000$, $\eta_p^2 = .891)$. Speaker was significant as well $(F(1,39) = 26.842$, $p = .000$, $\eta_p^2 = .408)$, but not the interaction between variant and speaker $(F(1,39) = 0.022$, $p = .882$, $\eta_p^2 = .001)$. Speaker 1 was evaluated higher in general than speaker 2.

The three variables with a significant variant effect all had lower scores for the nonstandard variants (as predicted). Figure 1 gives the means and standard errors for the standard and nonstandard variants of the four sociolinguistic variables.

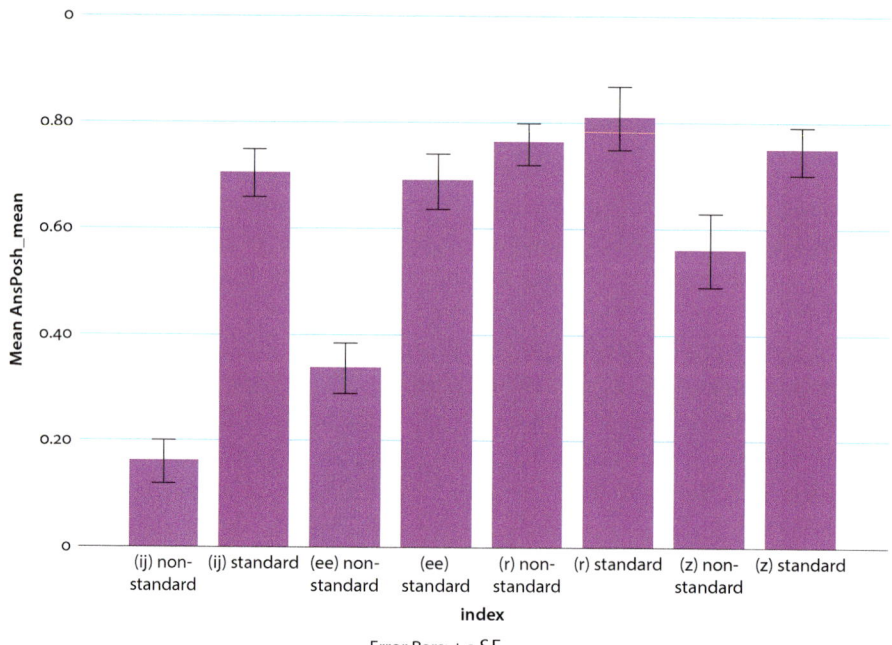

Figure 1. Means and standard errors of the SES class scores of the non-standard and standard variants of four sociolinguistic variables

Figure 1 reveals that all standard variants were positively evaluated (all scores above .70) which seems quite high given the forced choice between pictures and the different social class categories used. Non-standard variants were evaluated positively as well in the case of (z) and (r), with no significant distinction between the two variants of the (r). This matches the findings in van Bezooijen & van den Berg (2004), who obtained positive evaluations for the nonstandard (r) variant. They conclude that the nonstandard variant is no longer evaluated as nonstandard, but as a new standard variant typical of younger generations. The two nonstandard variants of the (e) and the (ij) have scores below .50, indicating that they are associated stronger with low SES class markers. Especially the scores for the (ij) show a sharp distinction between the standard and nonstandard variant.

4. Discussion

To our knowledge, the findings in the previous paragraphs are the first to confirm the social stratification of socio-phonetic variables on the basis of symbolic representations. Our data suggest that linguistic laymen strongly converge in their perception and evaluation of the social (class) meaning of minimally embedded single vowels and consonants. In a research paradigm which increasingly makes use of naturalistic multi-word stretches of spontaneous, non-controlled speech (see Knops's 1984 concern above), it is encouraging to notice that isolated word stimuli, which afford much greater experimental control, are just as efficient to probe language-triggered evaluative reactions.

In addition, our findings suggest that relatively diverse symbolic class markers afford similar access into the social stratification of phonetic variables. Judgments on occupations and workplaces were not statistically distinguishable from judgments on names, cars and personal appearances. Thus it appears that it is feasible to investigate language attitudes in this community using indicators of either production or consumption. When these two facets of social class go together (as they seem to in The Netherlands), relationships between language and social class can be investigated equally well by asking listeners to make judgments about production- and consumption-based aspects of identity.

Beyond their methodological implications, our results have theoretical implications for the interpretation of language attitudes data, as well. Even in a community where production, consumption, and other cultural aspects of social class tend to pattern together, there are differences in how things like cars, names, occupations, workplaces, and personal appearances relate to language variation. Yet these differences were not evident in our implicit language attitudes task. This suggests that participants were drawing on a core notion of social class which underlies the individual symbolic markers when making their assessments in the task, rather than estimating likelihoods of different types of linguistic behavior based on each individual pairing they responded to. While this response pattern may be specific to the task at hand, it's consistent with the idea that somewhat stereotyped notions of class underlie people's evaluative reactions, attitudes and expectations about language and social class.

At the end of this section, there are a number of caveats to be reported. Observe, to begin with, that the effects reported here need not be universal: social class aspects may correlate differently with linguistic behavior in other speech communities with more complex class landscapes. Language attitudes researchers may uncover previously invisible relationships between class and language by tuning their instruments to the variables and speakers they are investigating. Our results show that it is feasible to steer clear of explicitly articulated class distinctions and to build on the more implicit evaluations afforded by symbolic representations.

In addition, it should be noticed that in their capacity as trained phoneticians, our two experimental speakers were inevitably privy to some of the social and linguistic conditioning on the variables when making the recordings. Because of this, it would be reasonable to wonder whether the guises we created really differed exclusively with respect to the particular variables we intended them to. Could the speakers have been doing something differently in the two guises beyond the production of the four variables (such as for instance, change their voice quality)? While we cannot exclude that there were non-intended differences, we know that these cannot be the source of the social class effect, because the variables did not elicit identical effects. This indicates that rather than a general difference between the guises, it was the production of the variables themselves that produced the effect of interest.

A somewhat more serious concern is the fact that the bipartite social model ("high" vs. "low") which underlies this experiment is overly one-dimensional and binary, and that it builds on a view of society in which distinct variables automatically coincide. As far as the latter point is concerned, a growing class of wealthy but uneducated entrepreneurs belie the historical correlation between education, income, and social status. Somewhat more problematic, however, is the automatic association on which this experiment builds between traditional notions of (high) SE class, prestige and standard language. The past decades have seen the emergence of a new type of dynamic prestige (see Grondelaers & Kristiansen 2013 for an elaborate discussion) which draws heavily on media cool and the casual image of low-status urban speech. This dynamic prestige has been found to motor the emergence and vitality of non-standard phenomena in a number of European languages (including Belgian and Netherlandic Dutch – see Grondelaers & Kristiansen 2013; Grondelaers & Speelman 2013). In a perception study into the publicly downgraded but highly vital dissemination of the non-standard object form *hun* ("them") as a subject in Netherlandic Dutch, the standard subject form *zij* ("they") triggered traditional high class prestige, whereas the non-standard object form *hun* was awarded the new dynamic prestige which may account for its vitality. A non-standard pronunciation of *zij* which was included as a third variant in the experiment, and which equates the non-standard variant of the (ij) variable included in the present experiment, elicited more or less the same upper class associations as the standard pronunciation *zij*. Interestingly, this nonstandard [ai]-pronunciation has previously been reported to index "intellectualism, commercialism, and pop culture" in Smakman (2006: 50), and might well have triggered symbolic representations of "dynamic" social categories (cheap but "cool" cars, "lofty" work places) if these had been included in the experiment. The fact that the non-standard pronunciation of the (ij)-variable is downgraded as low class in this experiment does not, however, invalidate our design: the lowered [ai]-pronunciation of (ij) clearly is an upwardly mobile marker in social terms, but it is *not* received standard (yet). While a more-dimensional social stratification model may have better accommodated the change in progress, the present design with its isolated variables and binary forced choice categorization appears to bring out somewhat more conservative evaluations in our listener-judges.

5. Conclusion

Language attitudes research has many challenges, but some of them may be best approached by trying to solve them together. Creating more implicit ways of investigating listeners' attitudes may allow people to be honest about their attitudes at the same time that it allows researchers to explore (hidden) attitudes about specific aspects of social identity. Beyond social class, many different types of social variables can be operationalized in ways that are sensitive to what is important in local communities, not just for studies of language production, but also for studies of attitudes and perception. As our understanding of social categories and their relationship to language variation becomes more nuanced, studies of language attitudes will be needed to discover how social distinctions are 'translated' through the lens of language to those who interpret them.

References

Adank, Pati, van Hout, Roland & van de Velde, Hans. 2004. An acoustic description of the vowels of Northern and Southern Standard Dutch. *Journal of the Acoustical Society of America* 116(3): 1729–1738. DOI: 10.1121/1.1779271

Campbell-Kibler, Kathryn. 2007. Accent, (ING), and the social logic of listener perceptions. *American Speech* 82(1): 32–64. DOI: 10.1215/00031283-2007-002

Campbell-Kibler, Kathryn. 2008. I'll be the judge of that: Diversity in social perceptions of (ING). *Language in Society* 37(5): 637–659. DOI: 10.1017/S0047404508080974

Dodsworth, Robin. 2009. Modeling socioeconomic class in variationist sociolinguistics. *Language and Linguistics Compass* 3(5): 1314–1327. DOI: 10.1111/j.1749-818X.2009.00167.x

Eckert, Penelope. 2000. *Linguistic Variation as Social Practice.* Malden MA: Blackwell.

Garrett, Peter. 2005. Attitude measurement. In *Sociolinguistics: An International Handbook of the Science of Language and Society*, Ulrich Ammon, Norbert Dittmar, Klaus Mattheier & Peter Trudgill (eds), 1251–1260. Berlin: Mouton de Gruyter.

Greenwald, Anthony G. & Banaji, Mahzarin R. 1995. Implicit social cognition: Attitudes, self-esteem, and stereotypes. *Psychological Review* 102: 4–27. DOI: 10.1037/0033-295X.102.1.4

Grondelaers, Stefan. 2013. Attitude measurements in the Low Countries. In *Language and Space: Dutch*, Johan Taeldeman & Frans Hinskens (eds), 586–602. Berlin: Mouton de Gruyter.

Grondelaers, Stefan & Kristiansen, Tore. 2013. On the need to access deep evaluations when searching for the motor of standard language change. In Kristiansen & Grondelaers (eds), 9–52.

Grondelaers, Stefan & Speelman, Dirk. 2013. Can speaker evaluation return private attitudes towards stigmatised varieties? Evidence from emergent standardization in Belgian Dutch. In Kristiansen & Grondelaers (eds), 171–191.

Jacobi, Irene. 2009. On Variation and Change in Diphthongs and Long Vowels of Spoken Dutch. Ph.D. dissertation, University of Amsterdam.

Knops, Uus. 1984. Taalattitudes in Vlaanderen en Nederland (Language attitudes in Flanders and The Netherlands). *Tijdschrift voor Taal- en Tekstwetenschap* 4: 335–353.

Knops, Uus. 1988. Attitudes towards regional variation in Dutch pronunciation. In *Language Attitudes in the Dutch Language Area*, Roeland van Hout & Uus Knops (eds), 105–120. Dordrecht: Foris. DOI: 10.1515/9783110857856

Kristiansen, Tore & Grondelaers, Stefan (eds). 2013. *Language (De)standardisation in Late Modern Europe: Experimental Studies.* Oslo: Novus.

Labov, William. 1966. *The Social Stratification of English in New York City.* Washington DC: Center for Applied Linguistics.

Lambert, Wallace E., Hodgson, Richard C., Gardner, Robert C. & Fillenbaum, Samuel. 1960. Evaluational reactions to spoken languages. *The Journal of Abnormal and Social Psychology* 60(1): 44–51. DOI: 10.1037/h0044430

Mallinson, Christine. 2007. Social class, social status, and stratification: Revisiting familiar concepts in sociolinguistics. *Penn Working Papers in Linguistics* 13(2): 149–163.

Mallinson, Christine & Dodsworth, Robin. 2010. Revisiting the need for new approaches to social class in variationist sociolinguistics. *Sociolinguistic Studies* 3(2): 253–278. DOI: 10.1558/sols.v3i2.253

Pantos, Andrew J. & Perkins, Andrew W. 2013. Measuring implicit and explicit attitudes toward foreign accented speech. *Journal of Language and Social Psychology* 32(1): 3–32. DOI: 10.1177/0261927X12463005

Rickford, John R. 1986. The need for new approaches to social class analysis in sociolinguistics. *Journal of Communication* 6: 215–221.

Smakman, Dick. 2006. *Standard Dutch in the Netherlands. A Sociolinguistic and Phonetic Description*. Utrecht: LOT.

Squires, Lauren. 2014. Processing, evaluation, knowledge: Testing the perception of English subject–verb agreement variation. *Journal of English Linguistics* 42(2): 144–172. DOI: 10.1177/0075424214526057

Strack, Fritz & Deutsch, Roland. 2004. Reflective and impulsive determinants of social behavior. *Personality and Social Psychology Review* 8: 220–247. DOI: 10.1207/s15327957pspr0803_1

van de Velde, Hans. 1996. Variatie en Verandering in het Gesproken Standaard-Nederlands. Ph.D. dissertation, University of Nijmegen.

van de Velde, Hans & van Hout, Roland. 1999. The pronunciaton of (r). In *Linguistics in the Netherlands*, Renée van Bezooijen & René Kager (eds), 177–188. Amsterdam: John Benjamins. DOI: 10.1075/avt.16.16van

van de Velde, Hans, van Hout, Roeland & Gerritsen, Marinel. 1997. Watching Dutch change: a real time study of variation and change in Standard Dutch pronunciation. *Journal of Sociolinguistics* 1(3): 361–393. DOI: 10.1111/1467-9481.00021

van den Berg, Rob & van Bezooijen, Renée. 2004. De Gooise *R*: Wie ziet er wat in en waarom? *Taal en Tongval* 17: 86–108.

Perceived foreign accent as a predicator of face-voice match

Kathryn Campbell-Kibler and Elizabeth A. McCullough
The Ohio State University

This study examines perceived accentedness as a predictor of perceived match between faces and voices. 85 pictures were rated for the likely education, masculinity and accentedness of the person depicted. Independently, 300 recordings of disyllabic English words from native speakers of English, Hindi, Korean, Mandarin and Spanish were rated for degree of perceived foreign accent. The highest and lowest rated tokens from each of three male speakers from each language background (30 total tokens) were selected, as were 15 pictures, maximizing the variability in perceived accentedness while avoiding extremes of education or masculinity. All pairwise combinations of these 15 faces and 30 voices were rated for perceived match. The results show that listeners have clear and structured perceptions of "fit" between faces and voices which are based in part, but not entirely, on the congruence of key social attributes such as perceived accentedness and local understandings of ethnolinguistic groupings.

1. Introduction

One of the ways in which language attitudes play a role in day-to-day language use is by influencing listeners' perception of speakers as a result of the forms they use. Crucial to this process is the integration of linguistically-triggered social concepts with the overall perception of the speaker. One of the most common non-linguistic sources of social information is the human face, an information channel humans are particularly adept and rapid at analyzing. Despite its central role in social perception, the face has received little direct attention in sociolinguistics, other than as a tool to manipulate contextual information.

In this chapter we examine the perceived match between face and voice, and specifically how a single social feature, foreign accent, influences matching between faces and voices which vary along that dimension. We find that perceived accentedness is a crucial factor in the perceptual harmony of face and voice, and further, that the similarity space created by high matching with common faces provides a tool for understanding listeners' implicit ethnolinguistic models.

DOI 10.1075/impact.39.08cam

2.   Integrating audio and visual cues

A key question in sociolinguistic cognition is how indexical information in the speech stream is integrated into the larger social perception of a speaker. Sociolinguists have investigated how indexical information from different language cues is combined (Campbell-Kibler 2011; Levon 2007) and how the social meaning of variation is shifted by other information (Campbell-Kibler 2010). The integration of socially informative visual and auditory cues has been less studied, but there is every reason to believe that faces and voices work together to prompt social perceptions. We know that the linguistic processing of speech uses visual information, for example cues to consonantal place of articulation are integrated with auditory cues (McGurk & Macdonald 1976). Listeners are also able to match spoken with visual cues, even for sine wave speech (Kamachi, Hill, Lander & Vatikiotis-Bateson 2003). Building on this work, Strand (1999) showed that even still pictures can influence speech perception, through their effects on the social perceptions of the speakers.

A handful of studies have incorporated pictures of people in sociolinguistic perception tasks, typically using pictures as a tool for manipulating the sociolinguistic context of listening. Hay, Warren, and Drager (2006) used pictures to present the same speech tokens as uttered by either older or younger speakers or by working class or middle class speakers. They found that perceived age and social class impacted listeners' ability to distinguish tokens of New Zealand's NEAR/SQUARE merger, which in production correlates with age and social class. In addition, the photos themselves improved the linguistic perception abilities of the participants, apparently by allowing them to formulate more stable and quickly accessed person memories. Likewise, Koops, Gentry, and Pantos (2008) showed that age manipulations via face photos significantly affected listeners' processing of the pin/pen merger. In the Houston area, older speakers are likely to be more merged than younger speakers. Listeners viewing older photos showed a higher proportion of eye gaze movements to a competitor (e.g. *pen* when the speaker said *pin*) than those viewing younger photos.

Despite the use of face pictures as a methodological tool, little attention has been paid in sociolinguistics to how faces and voices are integrated into percepts of single, unified people. This is of particular concern given that the effects of such manipulations depend on participants accepting the face-voice pairings as believable and coherent speaker percepts. None of the work to date has reported techniques for assessing the success of these manipulations in creating such percepts, despite awareness that some pairings are more plausible than others. For instance, Koops et al. (2008) noted that they were unable to carry out the ideal 3×3 set of pairings of young, middle-aged and older faces and voices, since the extremes on each end would not have been plausible together. But despite the need for believable pairings, methodological strategies have been limited to brief norming tasks or to researchers' own intuitions.

Some work in social psychology has examined face-voice integration, particularly in the realm of emotion perception. De Gelder & Vroomen (2000) showed that listeners are able to integrate emotional information from the face and the voice simultaneously, with greater weight being given to the vocal information. More intriguingly, information gleaned from the face appears to have a special status in emotion processing. De Gelder, Pourtois, and Weiskrantz (2002) tested detection of emotion in the voice in two patients with lesions preventing them from consciously processing visual stimuli in portions of their visual range ("blindsight"). They found that incongruent emotional pairings of face and voice (happy/fearful) prompted EEG responses even when the participants were unable to consciously view the image, an effect that was not present for incongruent pairings of voices with non-face visual stimuli (pictures of happy/scary scenes). Similar effects are seen in judgments related to speaker identity. For example, the gender of a simultaneous voice influences the process of gender judgments of ambiguous faces, in terms of the judgments themselves as well as reaction times and EEG patterns (Masuda, Tsujii, and Watanabe 2005). This work suggests that studies of the attitudes towards language in use would be strengthened by greater attention to the role of the face in person perception.

3.   Perceptions of accentedness

One of the more famous findings regarding the influence of faces on language attitudes is Rubin (1992), who showed that the presence of an East Asian-appearing face prompted American listeners to increase ratings of accentedness for a simultaneous (native English-speaking) voice, and to perform more poorly in a cloze test of the delivered material. This work suggests not only that visually prompted social information contributes to the percept of a foreign accent, but that either the triggered accent or the process of more effortful integration comes with a processing cost which impacts the success of other goals such as comprehension.

This work has largely stood alone, however, with the bulk of research on perception of foreign accent focusing on auditory stimuli only. This tradition has shown that listeners consistently find non-native speech less intelligible than native speech, that they are skilled at distinguishing native from non-native speakers on the basis of auditory samples only, including very brief ones (Flege 1984; Park 2013), and that their ratings of degree of accentedness can be quite sensitive (Masuda, Tsujii, and Watanabe 2005).

Many efforts have been made to explain foreign accent by finding relationships between listeners' perceptions and other measurable properties. Flege and his colleagues have identified various demographic details about speakers that correlate with perceived foreign accentedness, such as age of learning the second language and length of residence in an environment where the second language is dominant. Piske, MacKay, and Flege (2001) provide a thorough overview of this literature.

Another vein of research has focused on the speech signal itself. Various segmental acoustic properties have been shown to correlate with perceived foreign accentedness, including VOT and static and dynamic measures of vowel quality. McCullough (2013) reviews relevant previous work. Other investigations have highlighted the apparent role of prosodic and global temporal information in listeners' perceptions (Anderson-Hsieh, Johnson and Koehler 1992; Boula de Mareüil & Vieru-Dimilescu 2006; Kang 2010; Munro, Derwing and Burgess 2010; van Els & de Bot 1987). While all these studies were restricted to the information to which their participants had direct access – the acoustic signal – many interactions with non-native speakers in day-to-day life do, in fact, involve visual information. The present investigation involved both auditory and visual input to better approximate such interactions.

4.   Methods

4.1   Visual stimuli

The faces used in the current study were selected on the basis of pilot ratings. 85 face pictures of men, with varying backdrops, were selected from a publicly available database.[1] 25 undergraduate students took part in this rating task for partial course credit. The task consisted of three blocks. In each block, participants were instructed to rate all 85 faces, based on where they thought the person pictured fell along one of three social dimensions: "accented," "masculine" or "educated," although the current discussion will focus exclusively on the "accented" dimension. Each rating was accomplished using a visual analog scale (VAS) paradigm, wherein a face appeared on the screen above a horizontal line, with a slider bar positioned in the center. Participants were asked to use their mouse to drag the

---

1.   Collection of Facial Images, maintained by Dr. Libor Spacek. ⟨http://cswww.essex.ac.uk/mv/allfaces/index.html⟩

slider bar to anywhere on the line to indicate their response. The ends of the line were labeled with "Not at all ⟨ADJECTIVE⟩" and "Very ⟨ADJECTIVE⟩," with the high versus low sides counterbalanced across participants. Each rating was recorded as an integer from 0 to 100, representing the distance from the low end of the rating scale.

For the current study, a subset of 15 faces was selected on the basis of the pilot ratings. The goal was to ensure as wide a range of perceived accentedness as possible, while minimizing variability in perceived masculinity and education. The selected faces ranged in accentedness from 17 to 83 (on a 0–100 scale), from 53 to 74 in masculinity and from 59 to 71 in education. No pairwise correlations were found among the three qualities.

The resulting men's faces represent a range of facial phenotypes, primarily faces which present, in common US cultural understandings of race, as European, East Asian and Indian in origin. Due to the composition of the original photo set, no pictures were included which read clearly as African or indigenous American in descent. Actual national or ethnic origins were not included in any analysis. This was partly a logistical issue, given that background data was not available on the particular photo set we chose to use. More fundamentally, however, the relationship between family history or national origin on the one hand and facial phenotype on the other is complex and tenuous. While observers may experience perceptions of race as straightforward, there is little to no evidence supporting race as a meaningful classification of people (see, for example, Smedley & Smedley 2005; American Anthropological Association 1998). Since our focus is on the perception of race, we chose to work exclusively with perceptions of the faces used.

4.2 Auditory stimuli

The speech stimuli for this study were taken from the larger pool of stimuli collected and rated in McCullough (2013), which examined the acoustic correlates of perceived foreign accentedness. Disyllabic English words produced by native speakers of American English, Hindi, Korean, Mandarin, and Spanish were used as stimuli in two tasks. In the rating task, participants were instructed to rate 300 auditory stimuli (10 words from each of 6 speakers from each of the 5 language backgrounds) on a VAS scale ranging from "no foreign accent" to "strong foreign accent." The intended target word was displayed on the computer screen immediately prior to each auditory stimulus, and the slider bar began at the left end of the scale ("no foreign accent") for all trials and all participants. Each rating was recorded as an integer from 0 to 100, representing the distance from the left (low) end of the rating scale. In the free classification task, listeners heard a single unique word produced by each of the 30 talkers and were asked to arrange icons on the computer screen so that speakers from the same language background were grouped together. 20 participants took part in this study for partial course credit, and the order of the two tasks was counterbalanced across participants.

In the present study, only speech stimuli from the male speakers were used, to match the pictures described above. From the 10 productions by each of the 15 male speakers, the tokens with the lowest and highest mean accentedness ratings across listeners were selected, giving 30 tokens total: 2 from each of 3 native speakers of American English, Hindi, Korean, Mandarin, and Spanish.

4.3   Procedure

A new set of 34 undergraduate students participated in the matching task for partial course credit. Each participant rated each of the 15 pictures paired with 10 speech tokens for a total of 150 ratings per subject, one-third of the 450 total pairings. Each pairing was thus rated by roughly one-third of participants. In each trial, the computer screen showed a picture of a face, the target word and the VAS scale, with the ends labeled "Definitely different" and "Definitely the same." Participants were instructed to use the scale to indicate how well the face and voice went together. As in the face rating task, the slider bar was positioned in the center of the VAS scale at the start of each trial. Each single word token was played once only, and participants were asked to drag the slider bar along the line to indicate their response.

4.4   Analysis

For statistical analysis, the mean accentedness rating across pilot judges was found for each face and voice stimulus, based on the ratings received in the solo rating tasks. Next, the distribution of the goodness-of-match ratings was examined to determine the appropriate modeling approach. Figure 1 shows a density plot of the match ratings.

In addition to the bounded nature of the VAS scale, which compromises normality, the structure of the task prompted a multimodal distribution in the data, precluding linear models. We noted that the task involved two decision points for each trial: when the participant clicked the mouse button and moved the mouse either to the left or the right, leading to a rating above or below the midpoint of the scale, and a second when the participant released the mouse button at a specific point, leading to a rating closer to or farther from the midpoint on that side. We modeled the data based on these two hypothesized decision points. We first created a binary variable which reflected whether the matching rating was above or below the scale midpoint, and fit a logistic mixed-effects regression model for this binary variable. Two linear mixed-effects regression models were also fit, one

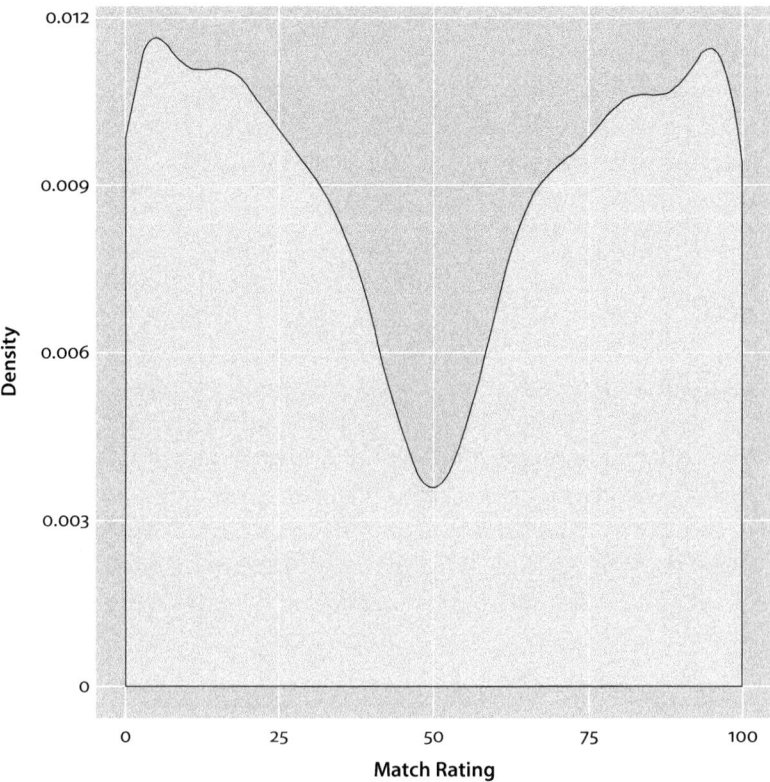

Figure 1. Density plot of ratings of face/voice match

predicting the match rating for ratings above the midpoint and another predicting match ratings for those below the midpoint. All predictors tested for the binary model were also tested for the linear models, and none were significant. We will not discuss the linear models further.

For the binary model, our predictor of interest was the interaction between the perceived accentedness of the face and that of the voice. An interaction between these two variables and the L1 of the speaker was also tested, but did not show a significant effect. In addition, random effects were included with the following grouping factors: talker, speech token (nested within talker), face and participant. Following Barr, Levy, Scheepers, and Tily (2013) would suggest maximal random slopes called for by our design, including the interaction between voice accent and face accent as a random slope for participant, face accent as a slope for speech token and talker, and voice accent as a slope for face. This full model would overfit the data, so a reduced slope model was tested which included only the main effect slopes for subject, voice rating for face picture, face rating for speech token and none for talker. The model presented below includes all the random effects with variance greater than 0.0000001, which left the intercept and both face accentedness and voice accentedness slopes for the grouping factor participant and the slope of voice accentedness for the grouping factor face. The interaction effect discussed below remains significant at the 0.001 level for all tested models with reduced random effects as well.

5.   Results

Our central question was whether the independently-rated perceived accentedness of the face and the voice influenced the perceived match between the two. We were thus looking for an interaction between the two ratings of accentedness, such that when both elements were high or both low, match ratings were high relative to when the two diverged. We found a significant interaction between the two in the prediction of the large-scale binary choice, whether the rating fell above or below the midpoint of the scale. The regression model is given in Table 1.

Table 1. Matching experiment results

Grouping factor	Slope	Variance	Std. Dev.	
Random effects:				
Participant	(Intercept)	0.15	0.39	
Participant	Face Accentedness	0.08	0.29	
Participant	Voice Accentedness	0.30	0.55	
Face	Voice Accentedness	0.02	0.14	
Predictor	**Estimate**	**Std. Error**	**z-value**	**p-value**
Fixed effects:				
(Intercept)	−0.020	0.073	−0.28	0.783
Face Accentedness	−0.072	0.058	1.25	0.212
Voice Accentedness	−0.116	0.105	−1.11	0.269
Face/Voice Interaction	0.183	0.0469	3.91	<0.0001

Table 1 shows that for the faces with low perceived accentedness, voice accent is negatively associated with above-midpoint match ratings, but this relationship becomes more positive as the perceived accentedness of face increases, as predicted. A visual depiction of the bottom is given in Figure 2. The plot on the top shows the relationship between perceived matching and perceived accentedness of voice for the 10 faces whose perceived accentedness ratings were below

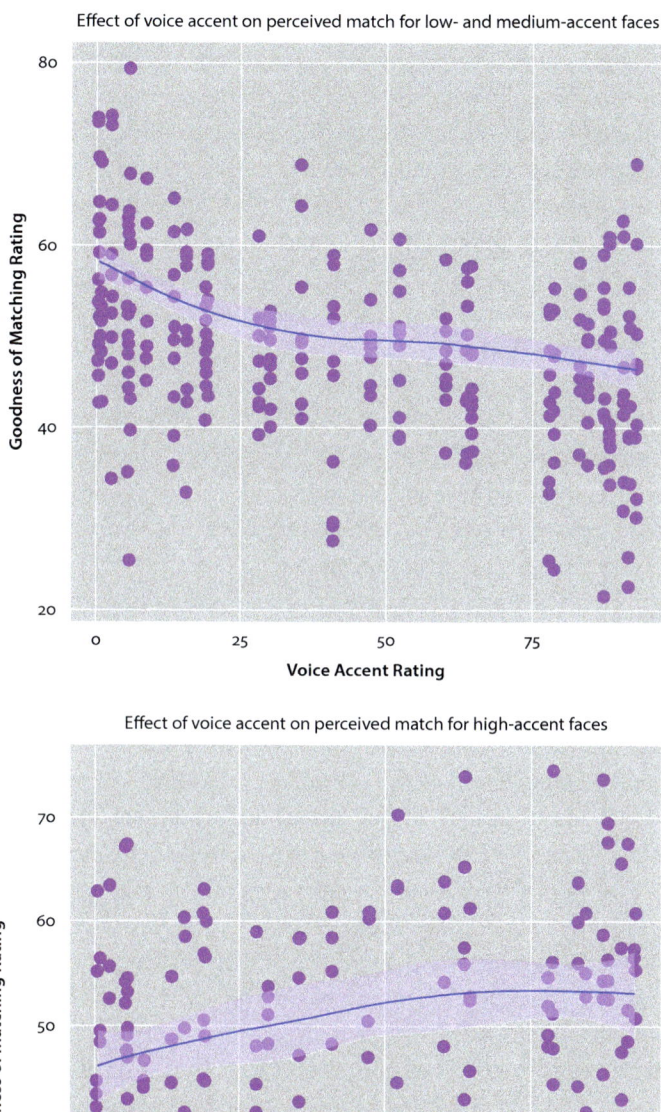

Figure 2. Matching ratings against voice accentedness for low- and medium-accent (top) and high-accent (bottom) faces

the midpoint. The plot on the bottom shows the same relationship for the 5 faces whose perceived accentedness ratings were above the midpoint of the scale. If the lower-accent faces are split between the 5 with the lowest rating (below 30) and the 5 medium-low ratings (between 30 and 50), the negative association remains the same, so the combined data for all 10 faces is presented on the top here.

While the perceptual task for both the matching and the pilot accentedness ratings limited participants to a simple continuum, perceptions of accent are not solely concerned with high vs. low, but also types of accent. Both the faces and the voices used in this study came from an apparent range of backgrounds, concentrated in European and Asian origins, allowing more complex questions about whether L1 of speakers predicts the types of faces they are likely to be matched to and what those patterns of matching can tell us about listeners' implicit models of ethnolinguistic variation. While explicit classification of both voices and faces can be revealing, we hypothesized that face-voice matching might be freer of constraints due to desires to seem socially appropriate, the availability of commonly used grouping terms (i.e. *Asian*) or participants' knowledge of languages. We thus sought to compare the similarity spaces created by the two approaches, to examine whether they yield similar results. If so, face-voice pairing might offer an alternative to explicit categorization of voices in the future in cases where explicit classification might be dispreferred for methodological reasons.

We used multi-dimensional scaling (MDS) to examine the similarity structure between the voices based on which were rated as matching well with the same faces. This approach allowed us to examine how L1 categories were conceptualized in this space of face-voice matching. It also allowed us to probe the secondary question of how stable individuals' voices were across recordings. Figure 3 shows the first three dimensions of the MDS. Examination of a scree plot supported an analysis with three dimensions. While we present all three here for the sake of completeness, the conceptual meaning of the third dimension was not clear, and we focus our discussion on the first two dimensions.

The first thing to note in this plot is that listeners' perceptions of two tokens of the same speaker are variable. Some voices show similar patterning for both tokens, but for others the tokens are quite different, even appearing at almost opposite ends of the plot. This is likely due at least in part to the selection of voice tokens that were maximally distinct in terms of perceived accentedness.

The second thing to note is that listeners do seem to differentiate based on language background, distinguishing English from Hindi from Mandarin and Korean native speakers. Dimension 1 largely distinguishes native speakers from non-native speakers. Further, Dimension 1 values correlate with voice accentedness ratings ($r = 0.75$, $p < 0.001$), even when the native English speakers are excluded ($r = 0.66$, $p < 0.001$). Thus, Dimension 1 seems to correspond roughly to

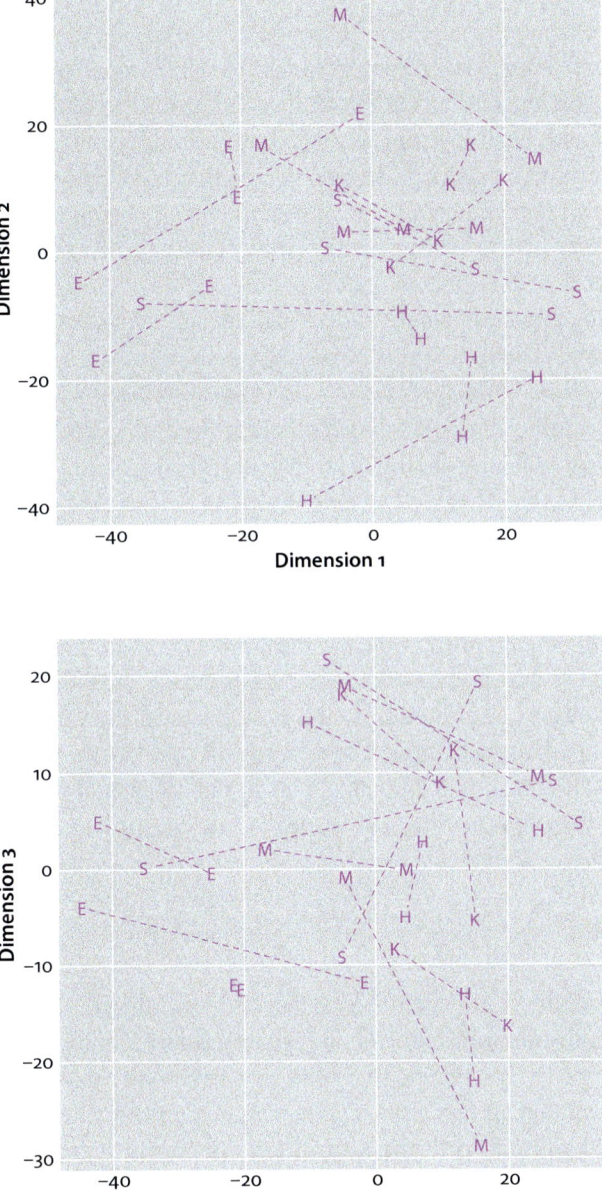

Figure 3. 1st and 2nd (top) and 1st and 3rd (bottom) dimensions of similarity between voices, based on common match scores across faces. Closer tokens showed more similar profiles of which faces they matched. Native language of speaker is marked by letter: English, Hindi, Korean, Mandarin and Spanish. Tokens from the same speaker are connected with dashed lines

accentedness, supporting our early hypothesis that in data from non-native speakers, degree of accentedness is a key dimension of variability that listeners attend to.

In contrast, Dimension 2 appears at first to reflect some kind of ethnolinguistic structure, distinguishing the Hindi speakers from the Mandarin and Korean speakers, who are nearly completely intermixed. Mapping the dimension to the face pictures using a weighted average, we see that Dimension 2 correlates moderately with perceived education ($r = 0.52$, $p = 0.047$), suggesting that it may also be connected to status, commonly the first dimension of variation in ratings of native speakers.

Comparison of these results to free classification results (McCullough 2013) shows similarities and differences between face-voice matching and explicit voice-based classification. In the free classification task described by McCullough (2013), listeners made groups based on which speakers they perceived as having the same language backgrounds. A dissimilarity matrix was constructed by calculating, for each pair of speakers, the percentage of listeners who placed them into different groups. A three-dimensional MDS analysis was carried out on this data for comparison to the matching data above, and is shown in Figure 4.

Note that the classification task was carried out on a separate set of speech stimuli from the match rating task, so similarities speak to the general perception of these speakers and their native language groups, while differences are more ambiguous, as they could be due to the differences in the tasks or to the differences in specific stimuli. Overall, the patterns for the two are quite similar. In the classification-based MDS, Dimension 1, as in the other analysis, separates native English speakers from the non-native speakers, suggesting that it may represent a similar accentedness percept. Dimension 2, again like the match-based analysis, appears to distinguish between different ethnolinguistic groupings and so may also be related to assessments of status, a construct which is tightly intertwined with race.

The treatment of the native Spanish speakers differs, however, from the face-based MDS. Instead of varying along Dimension 1, which appears to be the accentedness-related dimension, the Spanish speakers all cluster at the high end of that scale, spread out along Dimension 2, which, as in the other matrix, otherwise distinguishes the Hindi from the Korean and Mandarin speakers. We tentatively suggest that the distribution of the Spanish speakers in the face-voice matching analysis may be due in part to cultural assumptions about phenotypes, combined with the particular selection of face pictures available. None of the faces included in the study were likely to read as indigenous to the Americas, suggesting that to the extent that the Spanish speakers are perceived as such, they might be perceived as European rather than Latin American, or Latin American of European descent and thus less impacted by anti-Latin American bias. Further work probing

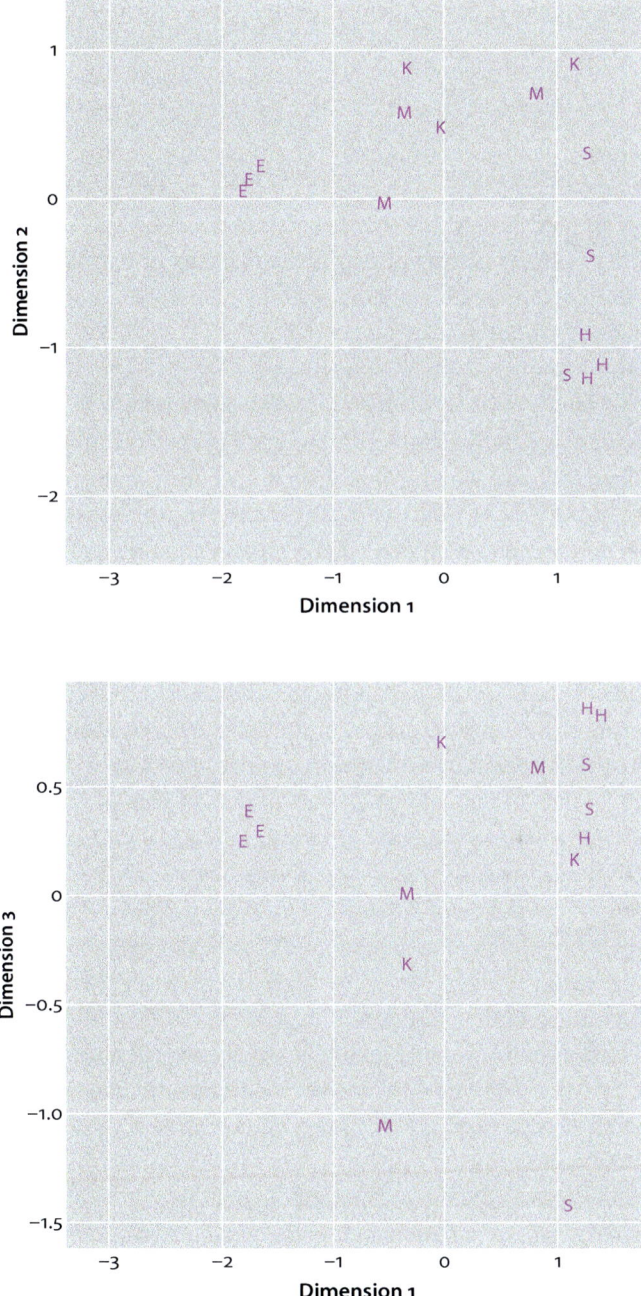

Figure 4. 1st and 2nd (top) and 1st and 3rd (bottom) dimensions of similarity between voices, based on free classification responses. Closer tokens showed more frequent inclusion in the same classification groups. Each letter represents a single speaker, coded for native language: English, Hindi, Korean, Mandarin and Spanish

categories of face types and their perceptual relationships to language types would be useful.

6. Discussion

The results presented here show that listeners have clear and structured perceptions of "fit" between faces and voices which are based in part, but not entirely, on the congruence of key social attributes such as perceived accentedness and local understandings of ethnolinguistic groupings.

One caution in our results is that the task here, to explicitly rate the believability of the match, is likely to have primed participants to the possibility of bad matches, perhaps increasing their tendency to reject unlike pairings as false. However, while the task may have had such an effect, assessment of face-voice match is not unknown in daily life. Commentary on face-voice mismatch is common, particularly in situations where voices are heard before faces are seen, as for radio personalities. Common discourses about such matching suggest that this process of assessing face-voice match is a spontaneous phenomenon. Absent the explicit task of assessing match, listeners may be less likely to question it directly. This is not to say, however, that face-voice conflicts then have no effect. Perhaps they induce distortion of listeners' perceptions of face and/or voice to increase the perceived integration of the person as a whole, as found by Rubin (1992).

The question of ethnolinguistic grouping is raised, but not answered by the data presented here. The similarity space among voices based on the match ratings shows a strong resemblance to hegemonic cultural norms in the US about structures of ethnicity, in which "East Asian" and "Indian" represent more distinguishable and coherent groupings of people than "Korean speakers" and "Mandarin speakers." This suggests that assessment of voice fit, while a relatively simple task, is likely inflected with local social ideologies. Another possible influence on these implicit similarity judgements is, of course, inherent similarity in the stimuli used. We did not analyze acoustic similarity here, but for some acoustic analyses of these data, see McCullough (2013).

The results shown here have a methodological implication. Given the use of pictures to manipulate social information, the perceived fit between voice and face has the potential to impact the results. To date, linguists using this technique have reported no formal piloting approaches to ensure the believability of such matches, although strategies for improving match have been reported. For example, Koops et al. (2008) omitted some possible combinations of face and voice, due to the lack of believability of the combination of the youngest voice with the oldest photo and vice versa. Nonetheless, no process for assessing the success of this tactic was given other than the authors' own judgments of match. Our results suggest that believability of match should be more thoroughly piloted by researchers using faces and voices together.

References

American Anthropological Association. 1998. Statement on 'race'. ⟨http://www.aaanet.org/stmts/racepp.htm⟩

Anderson-Hsieh, Janet, Johnson, Ruth & Koehler, Kenneth. 1992. The relationship between native speaker judgments of nonnative pronunciation and deviance in segmental, prosody, and syllable structure. *Language Learning* 42(4): 529–555. DOI: 10.1111/j.1467-1770.1992.tb01043.x

Barr, Dale J., Levy, Roger, Scheepers, Christoph & Tily, Harry J. 2013. Random effects structure for confirmatory hypothesis testing: Keep it maximal. *Journal of Memory and Language* 68: 255–278. DOI: 10.1016/j.jml.2012.11.001

Boula de Mareüil, Philippe & Vieru-Dimilescu, Bianca. 2006. The contribution of prosody to the perception of foreign accent. *Phonetica* 63: 247–267. DOI: 10.1159/000097308

Campbell-Kibler, Kathryn. 2010. The effect of speaker information on attitudes toward (ING). *Journal of Language and Social Psychology* 29(2): 214–223. DOI: 10.1177/0261927X09359527

Campbell-Kibler, Kathryn. 2011. Intersecting variables and perceived sexual orientation in men. *American Speech* 86(1): 52–68. DOI: 10.1215/00031283-1277510

De Gelder, Beatrice, Pourtois, Gilles & Weiskrantz, Lawrence. 2002. Fear recognition in the voice is modulated by unconsciously recognized facial expressions but not by unconsciously recognized affective pictures. *Proceedings of the National Academy of Sciences of the USA* 99(6): 4121–4126. DOI: 10.1073/pnas.062018499

De Gelder, Beatrice & Vroomen, Jean. 2000. The perception of emotions by ear and by eye. *Cognition and Emotion* 14(3): 289–311. DOI: 10.1080/026999300378824

Flege, James Emil. 1984. The detection of French accent by American listeners. *Journal of the Acoustical Society of America* 76: 692–707. DOI: 10.1121/1.391256

Flege, James Emil, Munro, Murray & MacKay, Ian. 1995. Factors affecting strength of perceived foreign accent in a second language. *Journal of the Acoustical Society of America.* 97: 3125–3134. DOI: 10.1121/1.413041

Hay, Jennifer, Warren, Paul & Drager, Katie. 2006. Factors influencing speech perception in the context of a merger-in-progress. *Journal of Phonetics* 34: 458–484. DOI: 10.1016/j.wocn.2005.10.001

Kamachi, Miyuki, Hill, Harold, Lander, Karen & Vatikiotis-Bateson, Eric. 2003. 'Putting the face to the voice': Matching identity across modality. *Current Biology* 13: 1709–1714. DOI: 10.1016/j.cub.2003.09.005

Kang, Okim. 2010. Relative salience of suprasegmental features on judgments of L2 comprehensibility and accentedness. *System* 38(2): 301–315. DOI: 10.1016/j.system.2010.01.005

Koops, Christian, Gentry, Elizabeth & Pantos, Andrew. 2008. The effect of perceived speaker age on the perception of PIN and PEN vowels in Houston, Texas. *University of Pennsylvania Working Papers in Linguistics* 14(2): 93–101.

Levon, Erez. 2007. Sexuality in context: Variation and the sociolinguistic perception of identity. *Language in Society* 36(4): 533–554. DOI: 10.1017/S0047404507070431

Masuda, Sayako, Tsujii, Takeo & Watanabe, Shigeru. 2005. An interference effect of voice presentation on face gender discrimination task: Evidence from event-related potentials. *International Congress Series* 1278: 156–159. DOI: 10.1016/j.ics.2004.11.193

McCullough, Elizabeth A. 2013. Acoustic Correlates of Perceived Foreign Accent in Non-native English. Ph.D. dissertation, The Ohio State University.

McGurk, Harry & Macdonald, John. 1976. Hearing lips and seeing voices. *Nature* 264: 746–748. DOI: 10.1038/264746a0

Munro, Murray J., Derwing, Tracey M. & Burgess, Clifford. 2010. Detection of nonnative speaker status from content-masked speech. *Speech Communication* 52: 626–637. DOI: 10.1016/j.specom.2010.02.013

Park, Hanyong. 2013. Detecting foreign accent in monosyllables: The role of L1 phonotactics. *Journal of Phonetics* 41: 78–87. DOI: 10.1016/j.wocn.2012.11.001

Piske, Thorsten, MacKay, Ian R.A. & Flege, James Emil. 2001. Factors affecting degree of foreign accent in an L2: A review. *Journal of Phonetics* 29: 191–215. DOI: 10.1006/jpho.2001.0134

Rubin, Donald L. 1992. Nonlanguage factors affecting undergraduates' judgments of nonnative English-speaking teaching assistants. *Research in Higher Education* 33(4): 511–531. DOI: 10.1007/BF00973770

Smedley, Audrey & Smedley, Brian D. 2005. Race as biology is fiction, racism as a social problem is real: Anthropological and historical perspectives on the social construction of race. *American Psychologist* 60(1): 16–26. DOI: 10.1037/0003-066X.60.1.16

Strand, Elizabeth A. 1999. Uncovering the roles of gender stereotypes in speech perception. *Journal of Language and Social Psychology* 18(1): 86–99. DOI: 10.1177/0261927X99018001006

van Els, Theo & de Bot, Kees. 1987. The role of intonation in foreign accent. *The Modern Language Journal* 71(2): 147–155. DOI: 10.2307/327199

Is Moroccan-flavoured Standard Dutch standard or not? On the use of perceptual criteria to determine the limits of standard languages

Stefan Grondelaers, Paul van Gent & Roeland van Hout
Radboud University Nijmegen

In view of the fact that Netherlandic Standard Dutch has been found to be stratifying – i.e. incorporating regional accent variation to allow speakers to profile local group membership in addition to their national affiliation – an evident question is whether non-Dutch accents are also tolerated in private conceptualizations of the standard: is Moroccan-flavoured Dutch Netherlandic Standard Dutch? In a speaker evaluation experiment designed to answer that question, 212 male and female listener-judges rated 8 short clips of spontaneous speech produced by native and Moroccan Dutchmen on 12 measures selected in function of 5 dimensions of accent attitude architecture (Status, Dynamism, Personal Integrity, Solidarity and Accent Norm); listener-judges also rated speech clips in terms of how beautiful they found them. Principal Component Analysis demonstrated that ratings on the 12 measures correlated into a Status and an Attractiveness dimension. The fact that Moroccan Dutch was systematically downgraded on the status dimension, and the fact that the Moroccan accent was deemed significantly less beautiful than the native accents, strongly suggests that a Moroccan accent is *not* acceptable as an ingredient of Standard Dutch; neither are there any indications of imminent change in these evaluations.

1. Introduction

According to a growing number of school teachers, journalists, publishers, and policy makers, things are not going well for Netherlandic Standard Dutch (NSD). Inasmuch as these professionals are the defenders of a uniform, invariant norm, they have reason to be concerned. It is well-documented (for overviews, see the volumes Deumert & Vandenbussche 2003; Kristiansen & Coupland 2011; Kristiansen & Grondelaers 2013) that all European standard languages are currently undergoing extensions which are considered a threat to the uniformity in their use. Professional linguists are increasingly attesting systematic variability – in

DOI 10.1075/impact.39.09gro

the form of, for instance, regional or social accents – in standard speech produced by the 'best speakers' (such as news anchors of official broadcasting institutions) in the most formal contexts.

The following quote bears testimony to the fact that ordinary language users are just as concerned about the "destandardization" observed in present-day Dutch:

> "Some refer to the decreasing level of education, others to spelling mistakes, there is controversy about what the norm should be, and about the fact that nobody abides by that norm, there is resistance against the influx of English loan words, there are complaints about sloppy pronunciation, about the fact that young people no longer read books, about the fact that fewer newspapers are being read, that text messaging style is on the increase, and that the tolerance against linguistic variation has gone too far. Everywhere in Europe, interestingly, the same issues are being raised."   (Van der Horst 2009: 14; our translation)

The cited changes engender panic and unease on the part of the non-professional user, and this public concern is sustained and intensified by announcements of the imminent demise of the standard language in popular volumes such as Van der Horst (2009, the book from which the quote was extracted) or Stroop (2010). It is revealing to notice that (lay) qualifications of standard language change as "norm degradation" or "norm falsification" typically invoke *ethical* arguments, pertaining to the peril and perversion inherent in "violating the arrangements that were made with respect to a common language" (Grondelaers & van Hout 2011b; Grondelaers & van Hout 2012).

On a somewhat more descriptive note, Grondelaers & van Hout (2011a) and Grondelaers, van Hout, and Speelman (2011) propose three causes for the progressing variability in NSD. In addition to the increasing informalization of our society and its concomitant anti-authoritarian sentiments (see Kristiansen 2009; Jaspers 2001: 132–133; Goossens 2000: 5; Stroop 1998: 227; Geeraerts 1993: 352; and Vandenbussche 2008: 190), dialect loss in the Netherlands has also been cited as a factor for the increasing variability in the standard. The demise of the dialects, the most important vehicle for communicating regional affiliation, has put pressure on the standard to incorporate regional (accent) variation, in order to allow people to profile a national and a regional identity (Willemyns 2007: 270–271; Grondelaers & van Hout 2011a; Grondelaers, van Hout, and Speelman 2011).

A third cause, which is of particular importance for the present paper, is immigration (Grondelaers & van Hout 2011a). Since the 1980s, Standard Dutch is no longer the exclusive property of the indigenous Dutch: the influx of migrants whose native language is not Dutch (inhabitants of the former colony Suriname and migrant workers of especially Turkish and Moroccan descent), has changed the linguistic landscape drastically. We will therefore investigate in this paper whether and to what extent the influx of (especially Moroccan) immigrants has changed conceptualizations of (the limits of) NSD.

The question to what extent the current innovations in NSD are (already) standard, necessitates a set of criteria which can be used to gauge the degree of standardization of language varieties and variants. When employed by linguists in a narrow sense (as in, for instance, Auer 2011), the term "standard language" is prototypically used to refer to:

- a *common* variety which is general and uniform within the territory it is used and ideally does not contain social or regional variation which indexes sub-groups in that territory;
- which has *prestige* and, hence, is appropriate to use in *formal* situations;
- which is *codified* in grammars and dictionaries which can be used as referees to decide what's "right" and "wrong".

Interestingly, this definition combines production criteria (uniformity, codification), a perception criterion (prestige), as well as a functional condition (the restriction to formal communication). Of these, codification is arguably the easiest to apply, but it is also the more conservative criterion because it "freezes" the dynamic nature of natural language into static norms. Observers who are distressed by the current state of NSD typically rely on the codification of NSD to reject the new developments as "in conflict with the norms which delimit the standard", and therefore as taking place outside or – in the hierarchical conceptualization of stratification – "below" NSD (hence the term "substandardization", which is also in vogue for the current developments).

We have repeatedly argued, however, that standardness cannot be determined exclusively in terms of uniformity on the level of language production (see especially Grondelaers & van Hout 2010a, 2011a). Apart from the well-known fact that (especially spoken) language can never be fully standardized (Milroy & Milroy 1985), there is evidence that even speech which is unquestionably and emblematically standard is still variable: Smakman (2006) found considerable phonetic divergences between Dutchmen who had been selected by a large panel of informants as the best speakers of Dutch. It is inevitable, therefore, that "the amount of variation which is allowed within the confines of the norm is not theoretically specified" (Willemyns 2003:113), "presumably because there is no way of describing or delineating it."

In view of the latter, and the fact that increasing variability is a characteristic of all European standard languages (see above), most (socio)linguists have ceased to consider standard language as a uniform, delineable variety with typi-cal speakers. If anything, standard languages are regarded as a "linguistic ideal" (Van Haeringen 1951:317), a "conviction" (Geerts 1987:165), an "abstraction" (Niedzielski & Preston 2000:18), and even as "a myth" (Lippi-Green 1997:44). In addition, standard languages are increasingly believed to owe their status as 'best language' to powerful Standard Language Ideologies – hierarchizations of lan-guage varieties based on conceptions of purity, modernity, and civilization (Van Hoof & Jaspers 2012:97) – rather than to any intrinsic homogeneity or superior-ity (see Milroy 2001:530).

As a result, our research question on the standard status of the current innova-tions in NSD entails an investigation into ideology and evaluation, and the ongo-ing changes in those. In Grondelaers & van Hout (2010a, 2011a, 2012), we have argued that the increasing variability in NSD does not challenge the idea that there should be a best language, but "stretches" the standard to include regionally and socially determined variants which manage to acquire prestige. In Grondelaers, van Hout, and Speelman (2011), we have outlined three quantitative operation-alizations of the prestige which is necessary for a language variety to be (sub-consciously) regarded as standard; more particularly, we propose that a variety is standard when there is broad consensus among the community members that this variety is more prestigious, more appropriate for formal interaction, and more beautiful than others. This claim was substantiated on the basis of a series of speaker evaluation experiments into the acceptance of regional accent variation in NSD. In the speaker evaluation paradigm (pioneered in Lambert et al. 1960), listener-judges rate recorded samples of language or accent varieties on a number of evaluative scales (the speaker is well-educated, competent, rich, dynamic, etc.). On the resulting set of ratings, factor analysis is applied to detect the basic dimen-sions of social meaning, which typically pertain to the prestige of the speaker (his socio-economic and intellectual status), and the solidarity he inspires on account of his integrity and attractiveness.

Let us briefly zoom in on each of the three prestige operationalizations and summarize the available evidence for the claim that NSD is a multi-standard language. All perceptual data come from speaker evaluation experiments into regional accent variation in NSD, which build on 20-second sound clips of unprepared spontaneous speech. Sound clips were extracted from the Nether-landic section of the Teacher Corpus, a stratified database of male and female, younger and older, Belgian and Netherlandic teacher speech (both spontane-ous and read-aloud), which was compiled to document contemporary Standard Dutch (van Hout et al. 1999), and eventually included in the Spoken Dutch Corpus (Oostdijk 2002). Materials in the Teacher Corpus were sampled in four accent zones. The central zone corresponds to the Randstad, the heavily urbanized area in the west (comprising the major cities Amsterdam, Rotterdam, The Hague, and Utrecht) which is the political and socio-economic hub of the Netherlands. Both the North zone, which corresponds with the Groningen and Drenthe provinces, and the South zone, which corresponds with the province of Limburg, are peripheral areas with a more rural character and a continuing vitality of the local dialects (van Hout et al. 1999). A fourth zone is a transitional area in the East which is situated in-between the other zones (hence our label "Mid zone").

1.1   Speaker prestige

Speaker prestige is arguably the most important indicator of a language variety's degree of standardization. Synchronically, the prestige inherent in the standard invariably surfaces in the observation that standard speakers are perceived as superior to non-standard speakers in terms of birth, education, competence, and income. Across all experiments, Randstad Dutch was always rated the most prestigious variety of Netherlandic Dutch in terms of the status of its speakers. Yet, there is no global and automatic prestige downgrading of speakers with a non-standard accent. Observe, to begin with, that accent strength plays an important role, to the extent that the milder variant of some regional accents does not automatically lead to downgrading (see Grondelaers, van Hout, and van der Harst (2015)). In Grondelaers, van Hout, and Speelman (2011), we found only marginally lower speaker prestige scores for the two mildly accented Limburg speakers than for the mildly accented Randstad speakers. Hence, the perception of a speaker's prestige is not only dependent on absolute values such as the speaker's regional descent and its associated stereotypes, but also on dynamic features such as the strength of his accent. By reducing his accent, a low prestige speaker can (partially) compensate the downgrading effect of his regional origin.

In addition, there has been a conceptual shift in the prestige domain which has been invoked in perceptual explanations for the vitality of specific non-standard variables and varieties in a standard speech habitat. Following Kristiansen (2009), who found that the high vitality in standard situations of former low class Copenhagen speech was sustained by perceptions of *new* prestige (dynamism, cool, assertiveness, etc...) instead of traditional prestige, Grondelaers and Speelman (2013) found perceptual new prestige motivations for the unstoppable vitality of Tussentaal, a publicly downgraded colloquial variety of Flemish Dutch (in the same vein, Ó Murchadha's (2013) data were reinterpreted in Grondelaers & Kristiansen (2013) as revealing dynamism perceptions sustaining the vitality of Post-Gaeltacht speech, a learner variety of Irish). According to

Kristiansen, Garrett, and Coupland (2005: 15), the main reason for the increasing importance of this "overt negativity, covert positivity" scenario as a language change determinant is

> "the development of an omnipresent media universe and this universe's remarkable turn from strict formality to ardent preoccupation with "doing informality": a performance that draws heavily on the 'casual' image of low-status urban speech" (Kristiansen et al. 2005: 15)

1.2   Accent status

In Grondelaers, van Hout, and Steegs (2010) we have argued that it is not only the speakers of a specific variety which can be accorded prestige, but also the variety itself. Moreover: accents whose speakers are traditionally deemed non-prestigious need not be found unsuitable themselves in terms of their appropriateness for formal interaction. We have routinely elicited accent status on statements such as 'you have to speak like this person when conversing with a news anchor, a diplomat, during a job interview, etc.', and in experiments in which ratings on these traits correlated into a separate dimension, Randstad speech was always judged the superior variety, Groningen speech was harshly condemned, but Limburg-flavoured speech received neutral scores (see for instance Grondelaers, van Hout, and Steegs 2010: 108). While regional accents are well below Standard Dutch in terms of accent status, there is evidence for a true competitor to Standard Dutch: in a speaker evaluation experiment similarly designed to ours, van Bezooijen (2001) found that Poldernederlands (Standard Dutch with a lowered pronunciation of the first part of a number of diphthongs, a variety/variant which originally indexed educated middle class females) was evaluated by younger listeners as only slightly less standard than regionally neutral NSD, and more standard than Randstad Dutch. While standardness and accent status represent overlapping constructs, we prefer our present implementation of accent status because it allows us to elicit standardness perceptions from linguistically naïve participants (to whom standardness need not mean very much) who can moreover be kept ignorant of the experimental goal (for the importance of participant ignorance in order to elicit "deep evaluations", see Kristiansen 2009 and Grondelaers & Kristiansen 2013).

1.3   Beauty

The perceived beauty of language varieties as an indication of their degree of standardness is a criterion which figured prominently in earlier work on the perception of standard vs. non-standard varieties (Giles 1970; Trudgill & Giles 1978), but which was taken up again in Grondelaers, van Hout, and Steegs

(2010), Grondelaers, van Hout, and Speelman (2011), and especially Latour, van Hout, and Grondelaers (2012). While all these studies corroborate van Bezooijen's (2002:13) claim that aesthetic judgments of language varieties represent "the most direct and compact means to gain access into language attitudes", they also confirm that beauty ratings in the field of accent perception are more than just prestige indicators. In fact, the perceived beauty of accent varieties functions as an "overarching evaluative judgment" which represents the proverbial "cement" between the status and integrity ingredients of accent attitudes (Grondelaers, van Hout, and Speelman 2011:212; Latour, van Hout, and Grondelaers 2013:259). The recurrently attested fact that regional accent varieties of NSD are deemed beautiful on account of *both* the status and the (personal and social) attractiveness of their speakers provides perceptual coherence between the different evaluative dimensions, as well as evaluative complementarity: while the status component represents the dimension on which prestige varieties are esteemed, the attractiveness dimension represents the dimension on which varieties which deviate from the standard can be valued positively. This distribution is borne out by all beauty evaluations hitherto observed: while prestigious Randstad Dutch is invariably deemed the most beautiful type of NSD, it has non-prestigious Limburg Dutch and (formerly non-prestigious) Poldernederlands as (close) competitors.

In addition to these three prestige operationalizations, we have proposed in Grondelaers, van Hout, and Speelman (2011:211–213) that a language variety is standardized when regionally flavoured standard speech – which indexes a dual identity of national and regional affiliation – invites national perceptions on the part of the listener, rather than regional or social in-group preferences and out-group rejections. The communal consent definition of standard language is empirically reflected in the absence of demographic (and especially regional) bias in the evaluations, which indicates that ratings are converged on by all the members of the Netherlandic Dutch standard language community rather than by specific subgroups. One of the more revealing findings of all previous research is the almost total absence of demographic effects in the evaluations of accent variation in NSD.

On the basis of all the available evidence, we propose that NSD is best conceived of as a "standard language space" which is vertically and horizontally stratified. This space is roofed by non-accented, uniform NSD, a variety which is "more of an ideal than a reality, since few people speak it in a pure form" (van Bezooijen 2001:260). Randstad-flavoured Dutch and – for younger speakers – Poldernederlands are the best 'real-life' varieties of NSD, both deemed more prestigious, functionally appropriate and beautiful than the other varieties. At the bottom of the standard language space, NSD is stratified into regional standards. Crucially, none of the varieties discussed occupies a fixed position in the stratificational "pyramid" of the standard space, except maybe for non-accented NSD at the top. For the accented varieties, the position in the space is dynamically determined by probabilistic features such as accent strength: a lower prestige variety such as the Limburg accent significantly gains in status when it becomes milder.

An evident follow-up question to the observation that NSD is stratifying to include regional accent variation, is whether non-Dutch accent variation is also accepted in NSD. If Dutchmen are not downgraded for profiling national and regional affiliation in their standard speech, to what extent are they "allowed" to signal that they, or their parents, were not born in the Netherlands? Are Dutchmen of Moroccan origin Dutch? And is their Moroccan-flavoured Dutch Netherlandic Standard Dutch? Can we find speaker evaluation evidence for Auer's (2011:502) suggestion that "[...] internal variability within the European standard variet-ies has been increasing over the last decades.", and that "[i]n addition to regional accents, the standard varieties have also come to be stratified in social, stylistic and *ethnic* terms"?

Let us, before we report the experiment carried out to answer these questions, provide some demographic context for the influx of Moroccans in Dutch soci-ety, and review the available evidence in favour of the hypothesis that Moroccan Dutchmen and their accent could be Dutch.

2. Background

On January 1, 2011, the Netherlands totalled 16,655,799 inhabitants, of which 79.4% (13,228,780 people) were of Dutch origin. There were 355,833 people of Moroccan origin, which accounted for 2.1% of the population and 10% of all the non-indigenous Dutch. In the 1960s and 1970s, Moroccan immigrants were brought to the Netherlands as temporary "guest workers". When it became clear in the 1980s that the situation was not temporary, the Dutch government introduced rules and regulations aimed at allowing the group to integrate into society as a distinct minority with its own culture. By the 1990s, the focus had shifted towards stronger integration with the aim of improving the arrears of the group in education and labour participation. Until the late 1990s, Dutch society could be characterised as an open-minded multicultural society: the two aspects of ethnocentrism, in-group support (nationalism) and negative attitude to the out-group, were not yet strongly subscribed to (Billiet, Eisinga, and Scheepers 1996) and right-wing politics were unpopular (De Witte & Klandermans 2000).

While the socio-political context in the Netherlands was conducive, therefore, to a speedy integration of minorities, the perception of (Muslim) immigrants changed considerably in the first years of the 21st century. The 9/11 attacks in 2001, the subsequent war on terror, and terrorist action on European soil (London and Madrid) negatively influenced public perception of Muslims in the entire Western world (Bleich 2009) and made people question the security risks inherent in the presence of large non-Western minorities. At the same time, populist right-wing politics became more popular in the Netherlands, initially with Pim Fortuyn, "who not only attacked the traditional patronising scheme of Dutch politics, but also what he called the defeat of multiculturalism and the danger of 'Islamisation' of Dutch society" (Buijs 2009: 423). In 2002, Fortuyn was assassinated, which further fanned the flames, and since then other right-wing politicians like Rita Verdonk, but later and more prominently Geert Wilders, have enjoyed popular support (Vervoort & Dagevos 2011). Finally, the murder of Islam-critical filmmaker Theo van Gogh in 2004 by a Dutch Muslim of Moroccan descent caused further social unrest; his assassination was regarded "as an attack on the freedom of speech" and thus affected "society in its entirety" (Buijs 2009: 434). As a result of these incidents and the subsequent political and social developments, Muslim immigrants became "highly stigmatised" (Nortier 2007: 202) in Dutch society.

In contrast to this evidence which suggests a (very) negative evaluation, there are some indications that opinions are changing. Several studies, to begin with, have pointed to a noticeably increased education level in the Dutch migrant communities, which has lead, or is leading to a better labour market participation and, in turn, a higher socio-economic status (see for instance Gowricharn 2002). In the second half of the first decade of the 2000s, education levels among minorities were still rising relatively fast (Bolt & van Kempen 2010), and this evolution is expected to sustain the further increase of their socio-economic status (Vervoort & Dagevos 2011). In addition, second-generation immigrants are less inclined to move to neighbourhoods with high migrant concentrations (Bolt & van Kempen 2010), which positively impacts social contacts with the indigenous Dutch (Vervoort & Dagevos 2011). Finally, across generations the Moroccan group is integrating better in socio-cultural terms, as evidenced by for instance increasing intermarriage rates, the adoption of gender equality values, and longer unmarried cohabitation (Crul & Doomernik 2006).

Furthermore, the Netherlands have, more so than many other European countries, seen individuals from non-Dutch minorities rise to positions associated with traditional social status. Examples include people like Ahmed Aboutaleb, mayor of Rotterdam (the second-largest town in the Netherlands), or Tofik Dibi, former MP for the Green Left. The Moroccan background of these politicians, or illustrious literary authors like Hafid Bouazza or Abdelkader Benali, clearly does not preclude full acceptance as prestigious members of the Dutch society. But Moroccan Dutchmen have also acquired (covert) prestige in the popular arts: cases in point are hip-hop artists (Ali B.), singers (Hind), comedians (Najib Amhali), athletes (Ibrahim Afellay), and actors (Touriya Haoud). All these examples suggest that prestige attribution is not absolute in the Netherlands: it is clearly possible for Dutchmen of Moroccan origin or background to gain status in their host society. In Flanders, the adjacent other Dutch-speaking community in Europe, there are no mayors of Moroccan origin and, apart from choreographer Sidi Larbi Cherkaoui, no "high art" performers of Moroccan origin either.

In sum, the available evidence with respect to the social integration of Moroccan Dutchmen seems to be inconclusive. The *linguistic* evidence on the other hand is almost univocally negative. The little data available on the Moroccan flavouring of Dutch suggest that the Moroccan ethnolect has a low social status (Hinskens 2007; and Muysken 2013 presents a more general overview of Dutch ethnolects). A hitherto unreported free response experiment carried out in 2011 confirms this conclusion. We asked a stratified sample of highly educated Dutchmen (n = 173) to give the three adjectives which first came to mind when confronted with a set of labels of regional and ethnic varieties of Dutch (see Grondelaers & van Hout 2010 for a review and a defence of this methodology). For "Dutch with a Moroccan accent", the adjectives most frequently given were *buitenlands* "foreign", *agressief* "aggressive", *asociaal* "anti-social", and *onverstaanbaar* "unintelligible". Other top ten adjectives which pertained to the accent rather than to its speakers were *lelijk* "ugly" and *onduidelijk* "unclear".

We have argued in Grondelaers & van Hout (2010b: 9) that the free response technique which elicits public perceptions is less suited to accessing "changing attitudes or even new attitudes that are not articulated yet in the explicit evaluative repertoire of a speech community". If, in other words, an attitude change towards Moroccan Dutchmen and their accent can be observed, we are more likely to find it in the deeper attitudes returned in a speaker evaluation experiment which operates with unlabelled samples.

While there are no speaker evaluation data yet on the subconscious acceptance of non-native accented Dutch in NSD, comparable evidence from other countries does not reveal (emergent) positivity towards non-native accents, especially when spoken by migrants with a Muslim background. Evidence of negative attitudes towards accented speakers of a migrant background has been widely reported in many western societies (Bresnahan et al. 2002; Eisenchlas &

Tsurutani 2011; Lindemann 2003; Lippi-Green 1994; Rubin 1992). Interestingly, there appears to be a correlation between negativity and accent strength, to the extent that the stronger the perceived accent, the more negative listener attitudes. Ryan, Carranza, and Moffie (1977), for instance, found that a Spanish accent in American English evoked negative stereotypes, but also that the evaluation of Mexican Americans grew more negative as their Spanish accent was deemed stronger (a similar correlation was obtained in a related investigation by Brennan & Brennan 1981; see Callan, Gallois, and Forbes 1983 and Lev-Ari & Keysar 2010 for evidence from other languages). Another factor which impacts the negativity of foreign accent attitudes is the listener's acquaintance with these accents: familiarity with a particular accent improves comprehension and intelligibility (Gass & Varonis 1984): people tend to favour accents familiar to them, which is observed also in regional accents (Long 1999; van Bezooijen 2002).

In European societies that are more comparable to the Netherlands, migrant accents are equally harshly downgraded. Jørgensen & Quist (2001:41) examined native speaker reactions to the L2-speech of Turkish-Danish adolescents in Denmark, which they regard as "a linguistically intolerant society". Speakers were evaluated consistently more negatively when they were hypothesized to be non-native Danes, but this tendency was somewhat less outspoken among the young respondents. Torstensson (2010) carried out a similar investigation in Sweden, a country which remarkably and recurrently self-identifies as the most open to immigrants of all Western European countries. Yet, Torstensson (2010) found that the speech of immigrants with a Muslim background was evaluated more negatively than the speech of immigrants with a Western Christian background. Speech samples which were incorrectly identified as being from a speaker with a Muslim background were downgraded as harshly as genuine Muslim migrant speech.

3. A speaker evaluation experiment into Moroccan-accented Standard Dutch

3.1 Introduction

The study we are about to report was designed to include the factors which were shown to impact evaluations of minority-accented L2-variants of majority speech in the previous sections. In order to obtain the best chance to observe emergent or ongoing attitude change towards Moroccan-accented Dutch, and in view of Jørgensen & Quist's (2001) finding that younger people were more tolerant of

L2-speech, we restricted our respondent sample to university students, who are taught to reflect critically on matters of power and dominance, including the media stereotyping of immigrants and refugees (see Jørgensen & Quist 2001:45). Given that respondents' evaluation of foreign-accented speech had been found to correlate with their familiarity with this variety, we elicited our respondents' degree of acquaintance with it in the demographic questionnaire following the actual experiment.[1]

The most important design decision to be taken pertained to the varieties of native and non-native speech to be included. Our original idea was to compare native Dutch speech with both Turkish- and Moroccan-flavoured Dutch, but for reasons we will flesh out in the next section, we eventually restricted the experiment to Moroccan-flavoured Dutch. The latter, however, is by no means a uniform variety. Observe, to begin with, that Moroccan- and Turkish-flavoured Dutch are difficult to distinguish from one another, for they both have the same phonetic-phonological and morpho-syntactic features, in addition to specific lexical choices. Building on the same speech corpus as the one from which our experimental stimuli were extracted (see below), van Meel et al. (2013) found that dentalized /z/ at the beginning of prosodic words is a typical marker of the Moroccan and Turkish ethnolect of Dutch, as well as a monophthongized /ɛi/ (van Meel et al. 2014). A well-known morpho-syntactic ethnolect feature is the absence of neuter nominal gender markers: Dutchmen of Turkish and Moroccan descent typically use the common instead of the neuter article, as in *de woord* "the word" (non-standard) instead of *het woord* "the word" (standard).

In addition, many features of the local urban dialect are also part of the Moroccan and Turkish ethnolects (Nortier & Dorleijn 2008:131). As a result, we decided not to compare the perception of Moroccan-flavoured NSD with unflavoured NSD, but to compare the perception of Moroccan-flavoured and native Dutch in Amsterdam (in the westernmost province of Holland), and Moroccan-flavoured and native Dutch in the city of Nijmegen (in the easternmost province of Gelderland, which is close to the Dutch-German border).

On January 1, 2011, Amsterdam's population of 779,808 inhabitants was 49.7% Dutch-ethnic and 9.1% Moroccan-ethnic, whereas Nijmegen's 123,704 population was 75.3% Dutch-ethnic and 2.1% Moroccan-ethnic (the latter being also the national average, (Centraal Bureau voor de Statistiek, 2011b)). Both locations offer the pivotal advantage that in urban centres, ethnic minorities are comparatively

---

1.   It is unfortunate that the accent strength variable, which turned out to have a significant impact on minority L2-accent perception in a number of preceding studies, could not be tested in the current study.

larger, as a result of which they are typically associated with the cities. The major difference between Amsterdam and Nijmegen is the fact that the former represents a stereotypical mix of local and ethnic flavouring in a large city context, while Nijmegen, a university town which predominantly attracts students from the Southern provinces, offers a more stable "local" flavour (the city is famously characterized as a 'big village' by its residents).

3.2   Study design

3.2.1   Speech stimuli

Speech stimuli were extracted from the Roots of Ethnolects corpus ⟨www.rootsof ethnolects.nl⟩,[2] which contains spontaneous speech produced in interview situations by young adolescents (age 12) and young adults (age 20) of Dutch, Moroccan, and Turkish descent coming from Amsterdam and Nijmegen. For the purposes of this study, the convenient availability of ethnically and non-ethnically accented speech recorded in similar conditions outweighed two disadvantages of the corpus, i.e. the comparatively small number of speakers per demographic cell, and the fact that even the speech of the native speakers sounded much more informal and globally less standard than that of the teachers we used in previous investigations into the perception and evaluation of accented speech.

In order to include the best possible stimuli in the eventual experiment, we first extracted a large collection of 20-second samples of running narrative from the 20-year-olds in the corpus (we preferred the older speakers in view of comparability with the adult speakers in our previous experiments). We initially included as many samples as possible which were suitable in terms of intelligibility and the absence of triggers which could cue listeners with respect to the professional occupation or social status of the speakers; in a number of cases, clips were digitally post-edited to meet these conditions, or to remove disruptive disfluencies. This first selection yielded 72 samples from the speech of 3 native Amsterdam, 5 Moroccan Amsterdam, 3 Turkish Amsterdam, 3 native Nijmegen, 3 Moroccan Nijmegen, and 3 Turkish Nijmegen speakers. (There were between 1 and 3 clips per speaker in the initial selection.)

In order to ensure that the eventual experiment included intelligible speakers whose ethnic and regional origin was well-identifiable, and in order to determine the strength of their ethnic and regional accents, we first carried out

---

2.   Roeland van Hout, the third author of this paper, is involved in the Roots of Ethnolects research project (promoters are Pieter Muijsken and Frans Hinskens). More information on the project, the research design and the speakers can be found in van Meel, Hinskens, and van Hout (2013, 2014).

a pre-experiment in which we played all 72 clips to 21 2nd and 3rd year BA-students who were familiar with the experimental goal. Participants were asked to determine the ethnic origin of the sample speakers (Dutch, Moroccan, Turkish), their city of origin (Amsterdam or Nijmegen), the strength of their accents on a bipolar 7-point scale (with Dutch translations of "very mild" on the left pole and "very broad" on the right pole), as well as the intelligibility of their speech on a bipolar 7-point scale. On a final, open-response item, participants were asked to note any comment they might have on speech characteristics and contents of the samples, and on the suitability of the samples for the eventual speaker evaluation experiment.

Analysis of this pre-experiment revealed that native Dutch speakers were effortlessly classified as such (93.9 %). While speakers of Moroccan and Turkish descent were recognized as non-native, participants found it difficult to distinguish between them: Moroccans were somewhat more often classified as Moroccans (53.7 %) than as Turks (43.5 %), but Turks were classified as Turks (42.1 %) or Moroccans (41.5 %). In view of the fact that speakers of Turkish descent were recurrently confused with native Dutch speakers (in 16.4 % of all cases), while Moroccans were almost never classified as native (in only 2.72 %), we decided to restrict non-native speech in the eventual experiment to Moroccan speakers. The regional (city) origin of the speakers was determined successfully on the whole: native and Moroccan Amsterdam speakers were correctly classified 95.2 and 73.9 % of all cases respectively, whereas native and Moroccan speakers from Nijmegen were correctly identified in 96.4 and 80.3 % of all cases.

In previous research (Grondelaers, van Hout, and van der Harst 2015), we found that phonetically untrained listeners strongly converged in their (subjective) impressions of the broadness of the regional accents of teachers of Dutch. The same result obtained for the present experiment, but the data in Table 1 indicate that while all speakers (whether native or non-native) were rated as comparatively broadly accented (all above average), the range in their accents was comparatively small:[3]

---

3. Compared to the mean strength (3.97) and the mean range (2.50) of regional accents of NSD in Grondelaers, van Hout, and van der Harst (2015), which used an identical methodology, the mean strength of the accents in the present study is much higher (4.59), but the mean interval is much smaller (1.38).

Table 1. Accent strength means and ranges as a function of speaker city and speaker ethnicity (strength means are pooled over all the clips in a cell, strength ranges are specified between the clip which was deemed the least accented, and the clip which was deemed the most accented in a cell)

City	Ethnicity	Mean	Range	
Amsterdam	Native	4.40	3.09	5.33
	Moroccan	4.99	4.38	5.52
	Turkish	4.87	3.90	5.90
Nijmegen	Native	4.09	3.48	4.67
	Moroccan	4.69	4.14	5.24
	Turkish	4.54	4.19	4.81

The small ranges in Table 1 make a valid implementation of the accent strength variable especially hazardous, but there is an additional risk. The low number (typically 3) of speakers in almost all demographic cells entails that the accent strength hierarchization of the samples in these cells pertains for the most part to different clips produced by the same speaker. We know from Grondelaers, van Hout, and van der Harst (2015) that speaker prestige impacts accent strength perceptions (with lower speaker prestige leading to broader accent strength perceptions), and that even very local prestige cues (such as speech topic or small disfluencies) have a discernible effect on accent strength perceptions. While the strength of the regional accent of a given speaker is typically regarded as a more or less stable parameter of that speaker's speech, subjective accent strength perceptions may vary wildly between the different clips produced by the same speaker. A case in point is the Moroccan Amsterdammer Abdelaziz, whose samples 5 and 10 are the least accented in the set of 19 Amsterdam Moroccan samples (occupying ranks 1 and 2 respectively), while his sample 8 occupies rank 15 (out of 19)!

In view of these considerations, we decided not to include accent strength as a perception determinant in the main experiment, although for each of four cells (native Amsterdam, Moroccan Amsterdam, native Nijmegen, Moroccan Nijmegen) we included one speaker with a somewhat milder accent, and one with a somewhat broader accent. For each of the eight resulting speakers, we included two clips. All in all, the experiment totalled 16 speech clips.

3.2.2 *Measures*

Listener-judges rated the speakers on the 13 traits included in the five factors previously confirmed as dimensions of language attitude architecture in

The Netherlands (see Van Bezooijen 2002, Grondelaers, van Hout, and Steegs 2010, and Grondelaers & Speelman 2013). The present dimension/trait set is more inclusive than in most other language attitudes investigations (which typically include traits which appear in two to three dimensions, Garrett 2005), but we want to measure speaker and speech prestige more multi-dimensionally than is usually the case. Recall that Competence and Dynamism traits are included to elicit old and new speaker prestige perceptions respectively, while Accent status is the best approximation of perceived standardness in a design which keeps participants ignorant of the experimental goal.

Each trait was presented as a Likert statement (According to you, this man x) rated on a 7-point scale with a left pole "disagree" and a right pole "agree". The Competence dimension was elicited on the traits "…would make a good manager", "…is intelligent", "…gets good grades at university". The Solidarity dimension was elicited on the traits "…is friendly", "…is cordial", and "…is spontaneous". The Dynamism dimension was elicited on the traits "…is enthusiastic", "…is confident", and "…is energetic".[4] An Accent norm dimension was elicited on the traits "The way this man speaks is appropriate when speaking with a radio news anchor", "…when delivering an official speech for the entire country", and "…during a job interview for the position of teacher in Dutch". Finally, the trait "This man's speech is beautiful" was included to elicit aesthetic perceptions.

3.2.3   Respondents

A total of 218 listener-judges initially participated in the experiment, but the data of only 212 were eventually included in the analysis (see below). The experiment was limited to native Dutch university students recruited on campus at the universities of Amsterdam ($n = 105$) and Nijmegen ($n = 107$). There were 105 male and 107 female respondents, and their average age was 22, with a range from 17 to 33. An important criterion for participation was that potential listener-judges had to have grown up in or around the city in which they participated. In order to guarantee this, student assistants who carried out the experiment were equipped with a list of municipalities within a 30 km radius of the city in which they experimented.

3.2.4   Procedure

The experiment was administered digitally in order to address the criticism that the traditional paper-and-pencil method is "error-prone, expensive, and boring"

---

4.   We did not include the evident dynamism trait "cool", because in The Netherlands, the term is especially en vogue for young teenagers, and would probably be regarded as childish by our older participants.

(see a. o. Perlman 1985), but also in order to be able to rotate sound clips. Although the experiment was Internet-based, it was not addressed to an open-ended Internet audience because web-based surveys are known to pose problems in terms of demographic balancing. Instead, the student assistants who functioned as experimenters recruited listener-judges on both university campuses who subsequently took the experiment in the presence of the experimenter. Survey software was run on various devices, like the personal laptops or tablets of the experimenters or on desktop terminals available in computer labs on the Amsterdam and Nijmegen university campuses.

After a listener-judge had been recruited, the experimenters first explained the experiment (without, of course, revealing its purpose). The listener-judge was subsequently invited to evaluate an example clip to assure the task had been understood. After this, listener-judges evaluated eight experimental samples (one speech clip per speaker). Following the actual experiment, listener-judges provided some demographic information (their age, gender, and regional origin), but they were also asked how much contact they had with speakers of Moroccan descent (elicited on a 7-point scale with a left pole "none whatsoever" and a right pole "a lot"). Finally, they answered a debriefing question ("What was this research about? What did we want to find out?") on an open response item. Six participants were eventually rejected from the analysis because they suggested that the experiment pertained to accent evaluation (n = 3) or to the perception of non-Western migrants (n = 2); one participant was rejected because she had been recruited in a town not within the 30-mile radius of Amsterdam.

4. Results

Two principal component analyses (PCA) were run on the ratings to determine the dimensions which underlay the 12 scales on which samples were evaluated (the "beauty"-scores were not included in this analysis, but see below). A PCA with factor selection criterion Eigenvalue > 1 (Kaiser's criterion) yielded a two-component solution; in this solution the trait *intelligent* loaded on both components; a subsequent analysis without *intelligent* accounted for 64.63 % of the variance in the data. On the first component, which could straightforwardly be identified as Attractiveness, both the originally intended Integrity and Dynamism traits were mapped. On the second component, which could easily be identified as Status, all the traits, which had originally been included in function of Competence and Accent norm, were mapped. This solution with 11 traits and their loadings on the two principal components is presented in Table 2:

Table 2. Factor loadings of 11 scales on 2 Principal Components after Varimax rotation

	Attractiveness	Status
confident	.611	.085
energetic	.796	.132
spontaneous	.844	.057
cordial	.789	.248
friendly	.749	.256
enthusiastic	.706	.141
manager	.369	.703
university	.303	.677
anchor	.097	.872
speech	.076	.885
teacher	.074	.889

To compare perceptions of the individual samples across the two components, an estimate was computed which averaged over the scores on the traits that received the highest loadings for a component (the bold-faced scales in Table 2); resulting measures were rescaled as z scores.[5] Figures 1 and 2 respectively show Status and Attractiveness scores for the 16 samples:

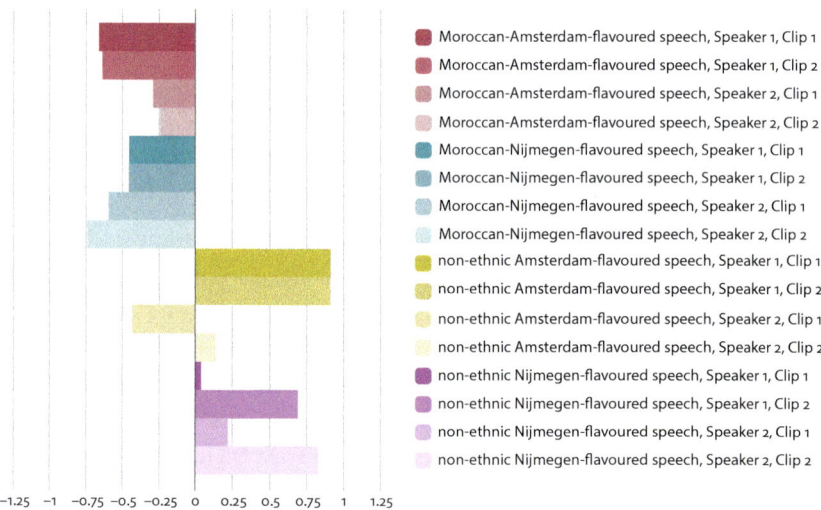

Figure 1. Z scores for 16 speech samples on the Status component

---

5.   We opted for summated scales instead of factor scores because they are easier to interpret and easier to replicate between studies (Hair, Black, Babin, Anderson, and Tatham 2006).

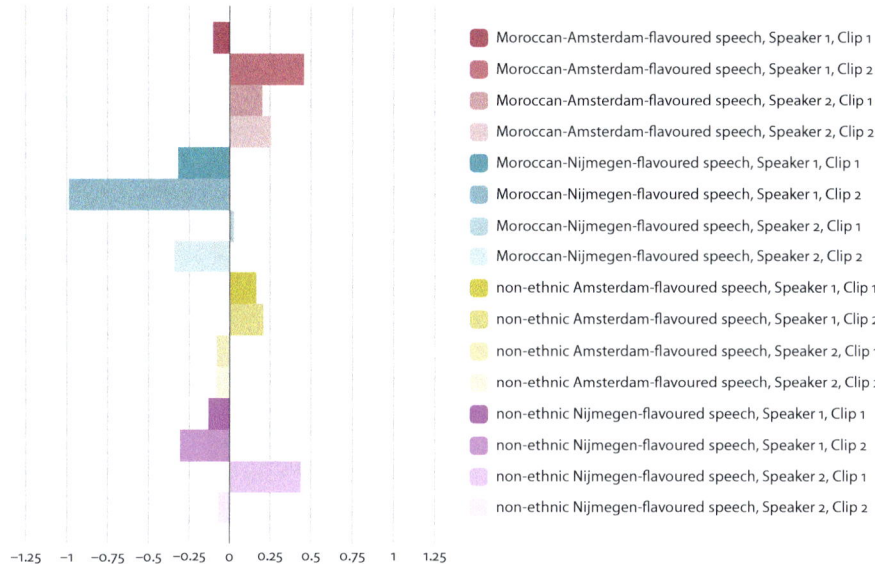

Figure 2. Z scores for 16 speech samples on the Attractiveness component

ANOVA was used to determine the significance and size of the differences between the sample scores. There was a significant main effect of *ethnicity* on the Status ratings (F(1,211) = 371.605, p < .001), with Moroccan-flavoured speech being rated lower than non-Moroccan-flavoured speech: this can be considered a very large effect (partial η^2 = .638).

There was a significant main effect of *speaker location* on the Attractiveness ratings (F(1,211) = 55.789, p < .001), with Amsterdam-flavoured speech being rated higher than Nijmegen-flavoured speech: this could be considered a large effect (partial η^2 = .209). There also was a significant interaction between *speaker location* and *ethnicity* on the Attractiveness ratings (F(1,211) = 30.656, p < .001), with Moroccan-Amsterdam speech being rated highest, followed by non-ethnic-Amsterdam, non-ethnic-Nijmegen and then Moroccan-Nijmegen speech: this can be considered a medium effect size (partial η^2 = .127).

Figure 3 shows the Beauty-ratings, which are strongly reminiscent of the Status ratings, but *not* the Integrity ratings (recall that in all research carried out so far into regional accent variation, samples were found beautiful on account of the status but also the personal or social attractiveness of their speakers). There was a significant main effect of *ethnicity* on aesthetic evaluation (F(1,211) = 212.625, p < .001), with Moroccan-flavoured speech being rated lower than non-Moroccan-flavoured speech: this can be considered a large effect (partial η^2 = .502). We also found a significant main effect of *speaker location* on aesthetic evaluation (F(1,211) = 4.512, p < .05) with Amsterdam-flavoured speech being rated higher than Nijmegen-flavoured speech: this can be considered a very small effect (partial η^2 = .021).

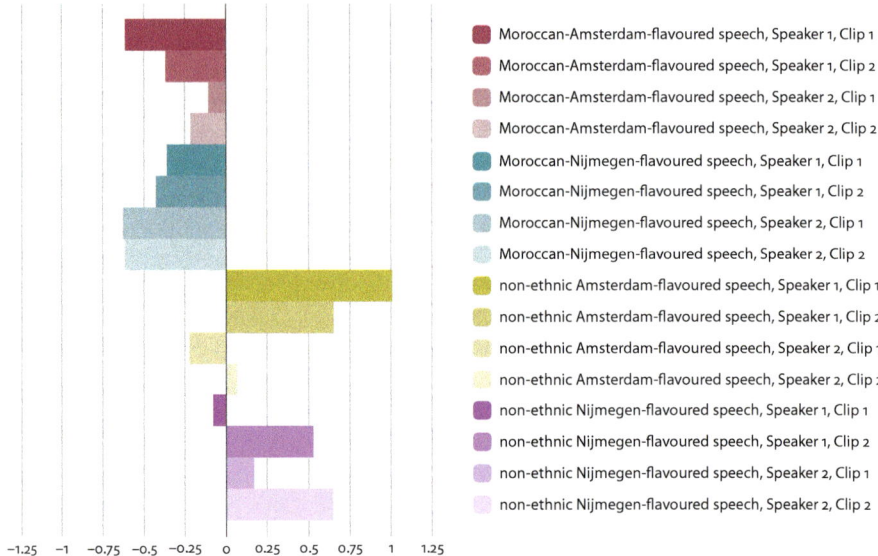

Figure 3. Z scores for 16 speech samples on Beauty

5. Discussion

In this experiment, we have looked for an answer to the question to what extent Moroccan-flavoured Dutch is a variety of Standard Dutch. Let us structure the answer in terms of the four perceptual criteria introduced in Grondelaers, van Hout, and Speelman (2011).

5.1 Speaker prestige

Do Moroccan Dutch command the prestige of typical standard speakers? In view of the findings in Figure 1, we can safely conclude that they do not: Moroccan-accented speakers are categorically downgraded on the Status component. While the variability in the lower half of Figure 1 demonstrates that a non-Moroccan accent is not the only status determinant for native Dutchmen, the consistently negative pattern for the Moroccan Dutchmen (to which only Amsterdam Moroccan speaker 2, who has a noticeably milder accent than the other Moroccans, appears to be a remarkable exception) indicates that a non-native accent is a powerful prestige determinant: for Moroccan Dutchmen, ethnic origin appears to be an absolute and insurmountable obstacle for access into the Netherlandic standard space.

Recall that Dynamism, the only dimension on which Moroccans were expected to receive some measure of prestige, did not materialize as a separate component in our experiment, which indicates that new prestige is not a parameter on which native and non-native Dutchmen are perceptually compared. If we compare native and non-native ratings on the *individual* traits were included in the dynamism function, Moroccan Amsterdammers are perceived as more dynamic on *enthusiasm*, but Moroccans of Nijmegen descent are rated the least enthusiastic ($F(1,211) = 38.258$, $p < .001$). There are no ethnic perception differences for *energetic*, and on the *confident*-trait, ethnically non-flavoured speech was regarded as even more dynamic than Moroccan-flavoured speech ($F(1,211) = 6.043$, $p < .001$).

5.2   Accent prestige

Like dynamism, the degree to which an accent is found appropriate for formal communication did not emerge as a separate component in the two-factor solution reported in Table 1.[6]

5.3   Beauty

Since the Beauty-ratings faithfully mirror the status ratings just discussed (compare Figures 1 and 3), they contain no sign of any upgrading of Moroccan-flavoured speech either. On the contrary: the speaker prestige, the accent norm, and the beauty-ratings strongly converge on the negative image of non-native Dutch speech.

Does the pronounced similarity between the Beauty and the Status ratings (but *not* the Attractiveness ratings) entail that Beauty is not, as it was before, the archetypal "synthesizer" of the different dimensions at work in the perception of accent variation? A third PCA which includes *beauty* as a trait returns a solution which is more or less identical to the one in Table 1, but shows a hitherto unattested asymmetry in the Beauty-loadings: .245 on Attractiveness but .804 on Status. These data suggest in fact, that there is a prestige condition on the operation of Beauty as an overarching concept: a comparison which involves varieties which are *too* non-standard reduces aesthetic evaluation to its standard ideological essence: a hierarchical categorization of varieties as either "good" or "bad".

Since Beauty does not function this time as the cohesive force which unites all evaluative dimensions, the fact that Moroccan-flavoured Amsterdam Dutch is rated the most attractive of all varieties is much less significant than our previous

---

6.   A PCA with factor selection criterion n = 3 yielded an Attractiveness, a Competence and an Accent norm component, but this solution was rejected on account of the fact that the Competence and the Accent norm components strongly correlated ($r = .598$). On the Accent norm component in the eventually rejected solution, Moroccan-flavoured speech from either location was categorically downgraded.

observation that Limburg-flavoured NSD is generally found an attractive variety. In the absence of an aesthetic unifier, the personality upgrading of Moroccan-flavoured Amsterdam speakers does not, or not primarily, entail a judgment on the standard language qualities of Moroccan-flavoured Dutch.

5.4   Communal consent

Participant demographics rarely affected the scores, and if they did, the effects were consistently very small. The *amount of contact*-covariate, which was found to significantly improve the perception of minority accents in other countries, did not improve our models to a degree which justified its inclusion. If anything, the Dutch community seems to agree by and large on the negative social meaning of Moroccan-flavoured Dutch.

6.   General discussion and conclusion

In this paper, we have (for the first time, to our knowledge) investigated perceptions and evaluations of Moroccan-accented Netherlandic Standard Dutch with a view to determining whether NSD is stratifying to allow ethnic accents (as it is clearly doing for regional and social accents). Can the Moroccan accent of NSD be regarded as NSD according to the prestige criteria proposed in Grondelaers, van Hout, and Speelman (2011)? In order to answer these questions we carried out a speaker evaluation experiment in which 212 university students rated unlabelled clips of spontaneous speech produced by native and Moroccan Dutchmen from Amsterdam and Nijmegen. Ratings correlated in two dimensions, viz. Status and Attractiveness. On the former, Moroccan Dutchmen were so harshly and systematically downgraded that the answer to the question whether the Moroccan accent of NSD can be regarded as NSD is categorically "no". While regionally-flavoured speech can in some cases be regarded as standard (even in the case of Limburg speech, which is traditionally associated with low prestige stereotypes), Moroccan-flavoured speech is categorically excluded from the standard language space. It is revealing to notice that increasing tolerance in a progressively stratifying standard language with strong inherent dynamics is restricted to Dutch accents: NSD is clearly a "restricted access club" to which the non-Dutch are not admitted. There is no sign of imminent change in our data.

The research presented in this paper is subject to a number of limitations. To begin with, we used speech available in the Roots of Ethnolects corpus, which (except maybe for the mild Amsterdam accent) is arguably less "standard" – as far as its production is concerned – than the teacher speech we built on in previous studies. It is unlikely, however, that this limitation affected the perception of our Moroccan speakers in any negative way. On the contrary: the regionally more flavoured, dynamic speech of the youngsters in the ethnolects corpus is a much more natural habitat for Moroccan styles and accents than a set of well-groomed, minutely accented teacher voices among which "deviant" speakers (in terms of origin or accent strength) inevitably stand out.

A design choice which *may* have affected our Moroccan speakers in a negative way was our participant sample, which consisted of university students, a population which is conspicuously more middle class in The Netherlands than our Moroccan speaker sample. The fact that the Moroccan ethnolect has sufficient (albeit covert) prestige to be appropriated as street language by non-Moroccan (Turkish but *also* originally Dutch) Dutchmen (see for instance Nortier 2001 and Nortier & Dorleijn 2008), seems to suggest that a socially more heterogeneous participant sample may have yielded (more) positive perceptions of the Moroccan Dutchmen.

A somewhat more disquieting limitation of this investigation was the limited number of speakers in the cells determined by the design variables ethnicity and city of origin, and the impossibility to implement the accent strength variable in any valid way. Another disturbing finding was that Status ratings for the second native Amsterdam speaker and both native Nijmegen speakers (viz. the lower rows in Figure 1) markedly differed for the two clips these speakers produced. While we cannot exclude the possibility that even greater care should be taken to remove or control non-relevant perception cues, we also propose an empirical reason for this inter-clip variability. We suggest that the standardization inherent in "groomed" speech also pertains to other behavioural variables than speech: people who take care of their speech – to the extent that they erase obvious linguistic triggers for (unwanted) perceptions – typically also avoid other cues (specific lexical choices, posturing, provocation, etc.) which may nurture unwanted stereotypes. As a result, the expressive bandwidth in teacher speech is noticeably smaller than that in the ethnolects corpus, and regional accent is by far the most potent perception cue (Grondelaers, van Hout, and Steegs 2010). For 3 out of 4 native Dutchmen in this study, regional accent seems to compete with other perception triggers (which may explain the perceptual differences between their clips), but *not* for the Moroccan Dutch: while there is, at first sight, no great difference between the amount of accent of the Moroccan and non-Moroccan speakers (see Table 1), and while the Moroccans do not sound more outgoing, expressive, provocative, or brutal in the clips than their non-Moroccan countrymen (we took good care to avoid these differences when preparing the speech stimuli), their Moroccan accent clearly supersedes and invalidates the non-linguistic perception cues (on the Status- and Beauty-ratings: the Attractiveness ratings appear to be more multi-dimensionally determined). A more telltale sign of the non-acceptability of non-Dutch accents in The Netherlands is hardly conceivable.

In spite of this plausible account of differences we would have liked to avoid (and in spite of the fact that they hardly impact our research findings), a number of methodological improvements suggest themselves for follow-up research. Although we are convinced that a matched guise experiment – in which the manipulated variation is produced by *one* speaker, as a result of which no "confounding" cues obtain – would unduly blow up the accent variable as a trigger (see Garrett 2005), we also believe that stimulus speech whose content is more strictly controlled could take away some of the confounds. In addition, we clearly have to be able to compare mildly and broadly accented native and non-native speech. The fact that Rotterdam's mayor Ahmed Aboutaleb has risen to native Dutch prestige is certainly due to his leadership qualities, but also – we believe – to the fact that he has almost no trace of a Moroccan accent in his formal speech. In the absence of such mild accentedness values in our experiments, we cannot hope to find any perceptual endorsement for non-native Dutch speech.

References

Auer, Peter. 2011. Dialect vs. standard: A typology of scenarios in Europe. In *The Languages and Linguistics of Europe*, Bernd Kortmann & Johan van der Auwera (eds), 485–500. Berlin: Walter de Gruyter.

Billiet, Jaak, Eisinga, Rob & Scheepers, Peer. 1996. Ethnocentrism in the low countries: A comparative perspective. *Journal of Ethnic and Migration Studies* 22(3): 401–416. DOI: 10.1080/1369183X.1996.9976547

Bleich, Erik. 2009. Muslims and the state in the post-9/11 West: Introduction. *Journal of Ethnic and Migration Studies* 35(3): 353–360. DOI: 10.1080/13691830802704509

Bolt, Gideon & van Kempen, Ronald. 2010. Ethnic segregation and residential mobility: Relocations of minority ethnic groups in the Netherlands. *Journal of Ethnic and Migration Studies* 36(2): 333–354. DOI: 10.1080/13691830903387451

Bresnahan, Mary Jiang, Ohashi, Rie, Nebashi, Reiko, Liu, Wen Ying & Sachiyo Morinaga Shearman. 2002. Attitudinal and affective response towards accented English. *Language and Communication* 22: 171–185. DOI: 10.1016/S0271-5309(01)00025-8

Brennan, Eileen M. & Brennan, John Stephen. 1981. Accent scaling and language attitudes: Reactions to Mexican American English speech. *Language and Speech* 24: 207–221.

Buijs, Frank. 2009. Muslims in the Netherlands: Social and political developments after 9/11. *Journal of Ethnic and Migration Studies* 35(3): 421–438. DOI: 10.1080/13691830802704590

Callan, Victor J., Gallois, Cynthia & Forbes, Paul A. 1983. Evaluative reactions to accented English: Ethnicity, sex role, and context. *Journal of Cross-Cultural Psychology* 14(4): 407–426. DOI: 10.1177/0022002183014004002

Centraal Bureau voor de Statistiek. 2011a. *Bevolking; kerncijfers*. Retrieved from CBS StatLine. ⟨http://statline.cbs.nl/StatWeb/publication/?DM=SLNL&PA=37296ned&D1=25–27,31& D2=l&HDR=G1&STB=T&VW=T⟩ [25 June 2012].

Centraal Bureau voor de Statistiek. 2011b. *Bevolking; ontwikkeling in gemeenten met 100.000 of meer inwoners*. Retrieved from CBS StatLine: ⟨http://statline.cbs.nl/StatWeb/publicati on/?DM=SLNL&PA=70748ned&D1=0-2,17-18&D2=0&D3=0&D4=3,19&D5=0,7-11& HDR=T,G2,G1&STB=G3,G4&VW=T⟩ [26 June 2012].

Crul, Maurice & Doomernik, Jeroen. 2006. The Turkish and Moroccan second generation in the Netherlands: Divergent trends between and polarization within the two groups. *International Migration Review* 37(4): 1039–1064. DOI: 10.1111/j.1747-7379.2003.tb00169.x

Deumert, Ana & Vandenbussche, Wim (eds). 2003. *Germanic Standardizations. Past to Present* [Impact: Studies in Language and Society 18]. Amsterdam: John Benjamins. DOI: 10.1075/impact.18

De Witte, Hans & Klandermans, Bert. 2000. Political racism in Flanders and the Netherlands: Explaining difference in electoral success of extreme right-wing parties. *Journal of Ethnic and Migration Studies* 26(4): 699–717. DOI: 10.1080/713680504

Eisenchlas, Susana & Tsurutani, Chiharu. 2011. You sound attractive! Perception of accented English in a multilingual environment. *Australian Review of Applied Linguistics* 34(2): 218–238.

Garrett, Peter. 2005. Attitude measurements. In *Sociolinguistics: An International Handbook of the Science of Language and Society*, Vol. 2, Ulrich Ammon, Norbert Dittmar, Klaus J. Mattheier, Peter Trudgill (eds.), 1251–1260. Berlin: De Gruyter.

Gass, Susan M. & Varonis, Evangeline Marlos. 1984. The effect of familiarity on the comprehensibility of non-native speech. *Language Learning* 34(1): 65–87. DOI: 10.1111/j.1467-1770.1984.tb00996.x

Geeraerts, Dirk. 1993. Postmoderne taalattitudes? *Streven* 60: 346–353.

Geerts, Guido. 1987. Variatie en norm in de standaarduitspraak. In *Variatie en Norm in de Standaardtaal*, Jaap de Rooij (ed.), 165–173. Amsterdam: Meertensinstituut.

Giles, Howard. 1970. Evaluative reactions to accents. *Educational Review* 22: 211–227. DOI: 10.1080/0013191700220301

Goossens, Jan. 2000. De toekomst van het Nederlands in Vlaanderen. *Ons Erfdeel* 4: 3–13.

Gowricharn, Ruben. 2002. Integration and social cohesion: The case of the Netherlands. *Journal of Ethnic and Migration Studies* 28(2): 259–273.

Grondelaers, Stefan. 2013. Attitude measurements in the Low Countries. In *Language in Time and Space: Dutch*, Frans Hinskens & Johan Taeldeman (eds), 586–602. Berlin: Mouton de Gruyter.

Grondelaers, Stefan & van Hout, Roeland. 2010a. Is Standard Dutch with a regional accent standard or not? Evidence from native speakers' attitudes. *Language Variation and Change* 22: 221–239. DOI: 10.1017/S0954394510000086

Grondelaers, Stefan & van Hout, Roeland. 2010b. Do speech evaluation scales in a speaker evaluation experiment trigger conscious or unconscious attitudes? *University of Pennsylvania Working Papers in Linguistics* 16(2): 93–102.

Grondelaers, Stefan & van Hout, Roeland. 2011a. The standard language situation in the Low Countries: Top-down and bottom-up variations on a diaglossic theme. *Journal of Germanic Linguistics* 23: 199–243. DOI: 10.1017/S1470542711000110

Grondelaers, Stefan & van Hout, Roeland. 2011b. The standard language situation in The Netherlands. In Kristiansen & Coupland (eds), 113–118.

Grondelaers, Stefan & van Hout, Roeland. 2012. Where is Dutch (really) heading? The classroom consequences of destandardization. *Dutch Journal of Applied Linguistics* 1(1): 41–58. DOI: 10.1075/dujal.1.1.05gro

Grondelaers, Stefan & Speelman, Dirk. 2013. Can speaker evaluation return private attitudes towards stigmatised varieties? Evidence from emergent standardisation in Belgian Dutch. In Kristiansen & Grondelaers (eds), 171–192.

Grondelaers, Stefan, van Hout, Roeland & Speelman, Dirk. 2011. A perceptual typology of standard language situations in the Low Countries. In Kristiansen & Coupland (eds), 199–222.

Grondelaers, Stefan, van Hout, Roeland & Steegs, Mieke. 2010. Evaluating regional accent variation in Standard Dutch. *Journal of Language and Social Psychology* 29(1): 101–116. DOI: 10.1177/0261927X09351681

Grondelaers, Stefan, van Hout, Roeland & van der Harst, Sander. 2015. Subjective accent strength perceptions are not only a function of objective accent strength. Evidence from Netherlandic Standard Dutch. *Speech Communication* 74: 1–11. DOI: 10.1016/j.specom.2015.07.004.

Haeringen, C. B. van. 1951. Standaard-Nederlands. *De Nieuwe Taalgids* 44: 316–320.

Hair, Joseph F., Black, William, Babin, Barry J., Anderson, Rolph E. &Tatham, Ronald L. 2006. *Multivariate Data Analysis*. Upper Saddle River NJ: Prentice Hall.

Hinskens, Frans. 2007. New types of non-standard Dutch. In *Standard, Variation and Language Change in Germanic Languages*, Christian Fandrych & Reinier Salverda (eds), 281–300. Tübingen: Gunter Narr.

Hinskens, Frans & Taeldeman, Johan (eds). 2013. *Language in Time and Space*: Dutch. Berlin: Mouton de Gruyter, 739–761.

Jaspers, Jürgen. 2001. Het Vlaamse stigma. Over tussentaal en normativiteit. *Taal en Tongval* 53: 129–153.

Jørgensen, Jens Normann & Quist, Pia. 2001. Native speakers' judgement of second language Danish. *Language Awareness* 10(1): 41–56. DOI: 10.1080/09658410108667024

Kristiansen, Tore. 2009. The macro level social meaning of late modern Danish accents. *Acta Linguistica Hafniensia* 40: 167–192. DOI: 10.1080/03740460903364219

Kristiansen, Tore & Coupland, Nik (eds). 2011. *Standard Languages and Language Standards in a Changing Europe*. Oslo: Novus.

Kristiansen, Tore, Garrett, Peter & Coupland, Nik. 2005. Introducing subjectivities in language variation and change. *Acta Linguistica Hafniensia* 37: 9–35. Thematic issue: *Subjective Processes in Language Variation and Change*, Tore Kristiansen, Peter Garrett & Nik Coupland (eds). DOI: 10.1080/03740463.2005.10416081

Kristiansen, Tore & Grondelaers, Stefan (eds). 2013. *Language (De)standardisation in Late Modern Europe: Experimental Studies*. Oslo: Novus.

Lambert, Wallace E., Hodgson, Richard C., Gardner, Robert C. & Fillenbaum, Samuel. 1960. Evaluative reactions to spoken languages. *Journal of Abnormal and Social Psychology* 66: 44–51. DOI: 10.1037/h0044430

Latour, Britt, van Hout, Roeland & Grondelaers, Stefan. 2012. De schoonheid van taal. Hoe wezenlijk is de rol van taalattitudes? *Taal & Tongval* 64: 156–194.

Lev-Ari, Shiri & Keysar, Boaz. 2010. Why don't we believe non-native speakers? The influence of accent on credibility. *Journal of Experimental Social Psychology* 46(6): 1093–1096. DOI: 10.1016/j.jesp.2010.05.025

Lindemann, Stephanie. 2003. Koreans, Chinese or Indians? Attitudes and ideologies about non-native English speakers in the United States. *Journal of Sociolinguistics* 7(3): 348–364. DOI: 10.1111/1467-9481.00228

Lippi-Green, Rosina. 1994. Standard language ideology, and discriminatory pretext in the courts. *Language in Society* 23(2): 163–198. DOI: 10.1017/S0047404500017826

Lippi-Green, Rosina. 1997. *English with an Accent. Language, Ideology, and Discrimination in the United States*. London: Routledge.

Long, Daniel. 1999. Mapping non-linguists' evaluations of Japanese language variation. In *Handbook of Perceptual Dialectology*, Vol.1, Dennis R. Preston (ed.), 199–226. Amsterdam: John Benjamins. DOI: 10.1075/z.hpd1.22lon

Milroy, James. 2001. Language ideologies and the consequences of standardization. *Journal of Sociolinguistics* 5: 530–555. DOI: 10.1111/1467-9481.00163

Milroy, James & Milroy, Lesley. 1985. *Authority in Language*. London: Routledge. DOI: 10.4324/9780203267424

Muysken, Pieter. 2013. Ethnolects of Dutch. In Hinskens & Taeldeman (ed.), 739–761.

Niedzielski, Nancy & Preston, Dennis R. 2000. Introduction. In *Folk linguistics*, Nancy Niedzielski & Dennis R. Preston, 1–40. Berlin: Mouton de Gruyter. DOI: 10.1515/9783110803389.1

Nortier, Jacomine. 2001. *Murks en Straattaal. Vriendschap en Taalgebruik onder Jongeren.* (Murkish and Streetslang. Friendship and Language Usage among Youth). Amsterdam: Prometheus.

Nortier, Jacomine. 2007. The Moroccan community in The Netherlands. In *Encyclopedia of Language and Education,* Vol. 9, Nancy Hornberger (ed.), 3079–3088. Dordrecht: Springer.

Nortier, Jacomine & Dorleijn, Margreet. 2008. A Moroccan accent in Dutch: A sociocultural style restricted to the Moroccan? *International Journal of Bilingualism* 12(1–2): 125–142. DOI: 10.1177/13670069080120010801

Ó Murchadha, Noel P. 2013. Authority and innovation in language variation: Teenagers' perceptions of variation in spoken Irish. In Kristiansen & Grondelaers (eds), 71–96.

Oostdijk, Nelleke. 2002. The design of the Spoken Dutch corpus. In *New frontiers of corpus research*, Pam Peters, Peter Collins & Adam Smith (eds), 105–112.Amsterdam: Rodopi.

Perlman, Gary. 1985. Electronic surveys. *Behavior research methods, Instruments & computers* 17(2): 203–205. DOI: 10.3758/BF03214383

Rubin, Donald L. 1992. Non-language factors affecting undergraduates' judgements of nonnative English-speaking teaching assistants. *Research in Higher Education* 33(4): 511–531. DOI: 10.1007/BF00973770

Ryan, Ellen Bouchard, Carranza, Miguel A. & Moffie, Robert W. 1977. Reactions toward various degrees of accentedness in the speech of Spanish-English bilinguals. *Language and Speech* 20: 267–273.

Smakman, Dick. 2006. *Standard Dutch in the Netherlands. A Sociolinguistic and Phonetic Description*. Utrecht: LOT.

Stroop, Jan. 1998. *Poldernederlands. Waardoor het ABN Verdwijnt*. Amsterdam: Bert Bakker.

Stroop, Jan. 2010. *Hun Hebben de Taal Verkwanseld. Over Poldernederlands, 'Fout' Nederlands en ABN*. Amsterdam: Athenaeum.

The LimeSurvey project team. (n.d.). *LimeSurvey Features*. Retrieved from LimeSurvey. ⟨http://www.limesurvey.org/en/about-limesurvey/features⟩ [28 June 2012].

Torstensson, Niklas. 2010. *Judging the Immigrant: Accents and Attitudes*. Umeå: Print & Media Umeå University.

Trudgill, Peter & Giles, Howard. 1978. Sociolinguistics and linguistic value judgments: Correctness, adequacy and aesthetics. In *Functional Studies in Language and Literature*, Frank Coppieters & Didier L. Goyvaerts (eds), 167–190. Gent: Story-Scientia.

Vandenbussche, Wim. 2008. Het einde van de standaardtaal? Een controversieel boek van Joop van der Horst. *Ons Erfdeel* 51: 188–191.

van Bezooijen, Renée. 2001. Poldernederlands: Hoe kijken vrouwen ertegen? *Nederlandse Taalkunde* 6: 257–271.

van Bezooijen, Renée. 2002. Aesthetic evaluation of Dutch. Comparisons across dialects, accents, and languages. In *Handbook of Perceptual Dialectology*, Vol. 2, Daniel Long & Dennis R. Preston (eds), 13–30. Amsterdam: John Benjamins. DOI: 10.1075/z.hpd2.07bez

van der Horst, Joop. 2009. *Het Einde van de Standaardtaal. Een Wisseling van Europese Taalcultuur*. Amsterdam: Meulenhoff.

van Hoof, Sarah & Jaspers, Jürgen. 2012. Hyperstandaardisering. *Tijdschrift voor Nederlandse Taal- en Letterkunde* 128: 97–125.

van Hout, Roeland, De Schutter, Georges, De Crom, Erika, Huinck, Wendy, Kloots, Hanne & van de Velde, Hans. 1999. De uitspraak van het Standaard-Nederlands. Variatie en varianten in Vlaanderen en Nederland. In *Artikelen van de Derde Sociolinguïstische Conferentie*, Erica Huls & Bert Weltens (eds), 183–196. Delft: Eburon.

van Meel, Linda, Hinskens, Frans & van Hout, Roeland. 2013. Ethnolectal variation in the realization of /z/ by Dutch youngsters. *Zeitschrift für Dialektologie und Linguistik* 80(3): 297–325.

van Meel, Linda, Hinskens, Frans & van Hout, Roeland. 2014. Variation in the realization of /ɛi/ by Dutch youngsters: from local urban dialects to emerging ethnolects? *Dialectologia et Geolinguistica* 22: 46–74.

Vervoort, Miranda & Dagevos, Jaco. 2011. The social integration of ethnic minorities: An explanation of the trend in ethnic minorities' social contacts with natives in the Netherlands, 1998–2006. *Journal of Ethnic and Migration Studies* 37(4): 619–635. DOI: 10.1080/1369183X.2011.545279

Willemyns, Roland. 2003. Dutch. In *Germanic Standardizations: Past to Present* [Impact: Studies in Language and Society 18], Ana Deumert & Wim Vandenbussche (eds), 93–125. Amsterdam: John Benjamins. DOI: 10.1075/impact.18.05wil

Willemyns, Roland. 2007. De-standardization in the Dutch language territory at large. In *Standard, Variation and Language Change in Germanic Languages*, Christian Fandrych & Reinier Salverda (eds), 267–279. Tübingen: Gunter Narr.

W3Counter. 2011. *Global Web Stats May 2011*. Retrieved from W3Counter. ⟨http://www.w3counter.com/globalstats.php?year=2011&month=5⟩ [3 July 2012].

Attitudes and language detail

Effects of specifying linguistic stimuli

Alexei Prikhodkine
University of Geneva

In this chapter, I explore to what extent different levels of language detail in the presentation of attitude targets have an impact on the expression of language attitudes. Results from the research carried out in the French-speaking part of Switzerland (*Suisse romande*) reveal that the evaluation of a given language variety through a global category name does not equal the sum of average evaluations of each specific feature composing that variety. Being ideologically loaded concepts, global category names (like *accent*) tend to elicit, in the *Suisse romande* context, attitudes mostly having for their target stigmatized *patois* features, while Swiss prestigious features are not mobilized by these concepts. Thus, the use of global category names for attitude elicitation in previous studies may have been a determining factor for the outcome of locating Standard French outside the Swiss community. Finally, results from my study indicate that the validity of language attitude data will be enhanced by taking into account ideology loaded in the process of sociolinguistic interpretation of global stimuli by lay persons, and by assigning to linguistic features under study the same level of specificity in terms of language regard as well as production.

1. Attitudes and language detail: Effects of specifying linguistic stimuli[1]

1.1 Introduction

One of the main interests of the study of language attitude is the role attitudes play in understanding and explaining language change (see Kristiansen 2011). In this respect, the issue of the validity of attitudinal data – to what extent do we

---

1. I would like to thank Barbara Soukup, Michel Francard, David Correia Saavedra, and Maribel Fehlmann for their helpful feedback on an earlier version of this article. Any shortcomings that may remain are, of course, my responsibility.

DOI 10.1075/impact.39.10pri

measure what we want to measure (e.g. John & Benet-Martinez 2000) – is of prime importance and provides a general theme to this volume. Concerns about this issue are not new in sociolinguistics, and doubts about the validity of language attitude data could explain, for example, a longtime lack of attitudinal surveys in variationist studies (Kristiansen & Jørgensen 2008:301–302). In contrast, relatively new to this problem is a critical reflection on the analytical depth of the "attitude" construct as well as on methodological tools involved in language attitude research (Niedzielski & Preston 2000; Garrett et al. 2003; Garrett 2010). In line with constructionist approaches, language attitudes are indeed no longer seen as stable constructs, but as context-dependent and situated evaluative reactions (see Soukup 2012, this volume). This "turning point" fostered the analytical potential of the construct, insofar as it integrated the variation. Preston (2010) systematized the various factors of language attitude variation under the label of "eliciting conditions": setting, form of the stimulus, task type, and representation of the attitude object.

There is some research today which has begun to capture the role played by a number of these factors. Thus, several speaker evaluation experiments have investigated the effect of the experimental setting for the outcome: for instance, the influence of the researcher's language variety (e.g. Price et al. 1983; Kristiansen 1997) or of the salience of inter-group conflicts relating to the different languages/ varieties tested (e.g. Bourhis & Giles 1977; Provost et al. 2003). Other experiments have investigated the impact on results of the ways in which attitudes are elicited, namely directly or indirectly (e.g. Lambert et al. 1960; Kristiansen this volume), implicitly or explicitly (e.g. Speelman et al. 2013; Pantos this volume; see also Staum Casasanto et al. this volume for a discussion of how direct/indirect are different from implicit/explicit).

A great deal of research provides evidence for the fact that the presentation of the stimuli (i.e. the attitude targets) is also an important source of variation in attitudinal responses. In this area, research has mainly focused on the interplay between social information extracted from verbal and non-verbal cues: for instance, how the social meaning of sociolinguistic variables is shifted by the social information provided by non-verbal cues such as photos (e.g. Rubin 1992; Niedzielski 1999; Campbell-Kibler this volume). However, given the large range of possibilities for the presentation of language stimuli (e.g. written or audio, isolated or combined with other verbal or non-verbal cues), more research is needed to assess to what extent the form of the stimulus itself impacts evaluative reactions delivered by respondents. Arguably, one of the interesting issues is to what extent different levels (global or specific) of language detail in the presentation of attitude targets may be responsible for language attitude variation. Although all sociolinguists are concerned with the choice of stimuli detail in their research, no critical reflection, to my knowledge, has been made about the consequences of that choice within language attitude research.

The following section aims to introduce such a reflection, especially on the validity of the data produced from global category names (like *accent*). After a presentation of the sociolinguistic background of the French-speaking part of Switzerland (*Suisse romande*) (Section 3), I report on the study I carried out in this area in order to evaluate the impact of language detail on elicited attitudes towards regional variation in Swiss French (Sections 4 and 5). The main outcome of the study suggests that the evaluation of a given language variety through a global concept does not equal the sum of average evaluations of each specific feature composing that variety. In the discussion section (Section 6), I try to explain why global category names tend to elicit attitudes having as their target only a sampling of linguistic features (the most stigmatized ones), and I also reflect on this outcome in the context of the discussion locating Standard French outside the Swiss community. Finally, a few concluding remarks regarding the outcome of the validity of language attitude data close this chapter (Section 7).

2. Language detail: Why does it matter?

Like many other objects around us, a linguistic fact can be characterized with more or less detail, or with more or less specificity. For instance, lay people can talk about accents – that is, about something very general – or they can comment on or react to very specific features, such as lexical or phonetic items (Preston 1996:41). There is extensive evidence in folk linguistics that speakers tend to spontaneously comment on global category names, such as *accent* (e.g. Niedzielski & Preston 2000; Singy et al. 2004). They also can provide details about an accent, with more or less accuracy. When providing such details, lexical features – being folk objects par excellence (Niedzielski & Preston 2000:266) – are generally more available for comment, although the stereotyped status can of course also be achieved by phonetic features (e.g. Labov 1971).[2] Language attitude studies use different levels (global or specific stimuli) of language detail in the presentation of attitude targets, and it is not uncommon that evaluative reactions to global category names (e.g. accent) stand for attitudes towards the whole variety or language (e.g. Bishop et al. 2005). This is how, in the Swiss context (Singy 1996; Singy et al. 2004), the global stimuli "local accent", "*accent vaudois*" (accent of the canton of Vaud), "your own way of speaking" tend to operationalize the analytical concept "French spoken in

---

2. I refer here to Labov's distinction between indicators, markers, and stereotypes based on the speakers' attention to the linguistic variables (Labov 1971). On this scale, stereotypes are variables that are available for conscious comment.

Switzerland", and speakers' responses to these stimuli – such as reported use of the accent, its transmission across generations, and the like – tend to be considered as the correlates of the language dynamics (i.e. forces that explain variation and change).

Such use of global stimuli in the presentation of attitude targets seems not however devoid of consequences regarding the relationship between attitude and behavior. Among the factors affecting this link, Ajzen & Fishbein (2005) attach great importance to stimulus detail and recommend that the attitude measure matches the behavior to be explicated with regard to the level of stimulus specificity. Several studies in social psychology show, in addition, that the correlation between attitude and behavior is particularly positive when the question includes specific stimuli (Leyens & Yzerbyt 1997: 107). To return to language attitudes, at least two reasons can explain why the use of global stimuli in the presentation of attitude targets by the researcher may affect the validity of the data. The first one concerns the unfeasibility of directly observing global stimuli in the form of behavior: it is obviously impossible to compute the occurrences of the category "accent". Furthermore, the respondent's cognitive processing when reacting to such stimuli can influence their expression of an attitude. Indeed, if we admit that global concepts include a number of specific features, they are in fact polysemic and multidimensional. Thus, they may activate different information for different respondents, which may even be mutually exclusive (Lorenzi-Cioldi 1997: 126).[3] But, at the same time, there is no evidence to claim an equal availability of all specific features which ideally compose a global concept. What is more likely is that certain specific features are more salient than others, because, for instance, they are more typical of a category (cf. Rosch 1978 on prototype theory).[4] However, categorization being not simply a cognitive activity, the organization of categories tends to be impacted by social norms. This can be illustrated by recent research on HIV/AIDS prevention carried out in the French-speaking part of Switzerland (Singy et al. 2006: 43–44). This study shows that when asked in an open question to explain the word "penetration", almost all respondents spontaneously mentioned

---

3. Lorenzi-Cioldi illustrates this with an example from the article of Tourangeau & Rasinski (1988). These authors have shown the complexity of respondents' reactions triggered by a general question on abortion. For example, abortion opponents indicated that the purpose of sex is reproduction, but, at the same time, they were opposed to sex outside the marriage and in favor of the death penalty for serious crimes.

4. The unequal status of different features composing a category can be illustrated by the composition of the category "bird". Thus, according to the characteristics often associated to the birds (such as feathers or ability to fly), a robin tends to be perceived by speakers as more typical of this category than a penguin (Rosch 1978).

"vaginal penetration", while only one third of them also referred with meaning "anal penetration". Interestingly, in a closed question which proposed different meanings, the former two thirds of respondents also included the meaning "anal penetration", but indicated that this feature had not immediately come to their mind. This example illustrates the appropriateness of a hierarchical conception of meaning organization: although it includes both features ('vaginal sex' and 'anal sex'), the global concept 'penetration' is primarily defined by one specific element ('vaginal'), whose availability may be explained by social norms anchored outside the survey context.

In this regard, we might assume that global category names generally used to elicit language attitudes (like *accent*) are also hierarchically organized and tend to be represented, in the minds of lay speakers, by only a portion of specific linguistic features (phonetic, syntactic or lexical), while others – with a potentially different social meaning – are not mobilized by global category names. This opens up the possibility that different levels of language detail in the presentation of attitude targets are a major source of variability in language attitude study. This is at least what seems to suggest a divergence in the results of several surveys on the prestige associated with the French spoken in Switzerland. Prior to discussing this divergence, it is necessary to give some indication on the sociolinguistic situation in the French-speaking part of Switzerland (*Suisse romande*).

3. *Suisse romande*: A sociolinguistic background

United by the dominant use of French, the *Suisse romande* consists of four officially monolingual cantons (Geneva, Vaud, Neuchâtel and Jura) and the Francophone parts of three bilingual cantons (Fribourg, Bern and Valais). One of the most important aspects of the current linguistic landscape in the *Suisse romande* is the lack of contact between French and indigenous Romance languages (or *patois*, which is a folk term for these) (Francard 2001). This is the outcome of a long process of linguistic unification, which saw the number of patois speakers decrease relatively quickly in favor of French, mainly because of the spread of public education in the first half of the 20th century. Promotion of French was accompanied by a strong purist discourse, which tended to condemn most of the marks of local variation (see Thibault 1998 for an overview). However, stigmatization focused more on linguistic features resulting from contact with indigenous languages (dialectalisms) and German (germanisms), than on archaisms (i.e. items which are still in use in the *Suisse romande*, but which are no longer used in the Standard French of France) and local innovations (i.e. items of French origin which do not exist in the Standard French of France).

Today, the distinctiveness of the local French is mostly due to phonetic and lexical features (Knecht 1996; Racine & Andreassen in press). Unique phonetic and phonological features are relatively few and often simply involve the retention of oppositions which are no longer maintained in the Standard French of France (i.e. archaisms). Thus, it is in fact the lexicon that presents the richest typology of regionalisms by including local innovations in addition to the above-mentioned archaisms, dialectalisms and germanisms (Francard 1998).

As I already mentioned, recent studies of attitudes towards the local variety of French give quite discrepant, and somewhat mutually exclusive descriptions of the sociolinguistic dynamics in the *Suisse romande*. On the one hand, several studies have found that when reacting to global category names (e.g. *local variety, Swiss French*), Swiss people assign to the French from France a better quality, while the national variety is stigmatized and has a low prestige (e.g. Singy 1996; Singy et al. 2004; L'Eplattenier-Saugy 1999). More generally, these results fit into a pattern identified as "pattern B" within the language preference model proposed by Ryan et al. (1982):[5] Swiss speakers would prefer their own variety among the group solidarity dimension but not on status, on which they would prefer the French from France. On the other hand, surveys initiated by Marie-Louise Moreau (Bouchard et al. 2004; Moreau et al. 2007) do not confirm that the standard language is located outside the Swiss community (in France) and that the local variety is stigmatized by their respondents. In fact, Swiss listeners evaluated Swiss speakers with a university degree equally well, and sometimes better than speakers from France of the same level of education. Interestingly, these results are close to findings in reviews of sociolinguistic production in the *Suisse romande*, which suggest that national variants are indeed used in the official "linguistic market" (Bourdieu 1982). For instance, the national public radio station explicitly requires their newscasters to use certain homegrown forms and emphasizes the inappropriateness of certain words of French from France (Prikhodkine 2011). Furthermore, a recent small-scale survey of news anchors shows that, on the phonetic level, one cannot accept a complete convergence toward the French from France (Armstrong & Pooley 2010: 147).

---

5.   This model includes four patterns of language preference for two contrasting language varieties (Ryan et al. 1982:8–10). The patterns contrast in terms of whether the judgments of varieties' speakers differ on two major evaluative dimensions along which attitudes generally vary (i.e. social status and group solidarity). Pattern A refers to situations in which speakers of both varieties acknowledge the superiority of one variety both on status and group solidarity. In the case of pattern B, minority speakers prefer their own variety on group solidarity dimension but not on status. Pattern C refers to situations in which each group of speakers prefers its own variety on both dimensions. Pattern D represents situations in which speakers of both varieties valorize one variety on the status dimension and the other variety on group solidarity.

This discrepancy in language attitude responses led me to consider stimuli presentation as a potential source of the variation. In particular, I was interested in exploring how far the attested variation in language attitudes could be explained by the level of language detail presented to the informants as their attitudinal target. Indeed, while studies locating the Standard outside the Swiss community elicited attitudes regarding global category names (such as *accent* or *variety*), surveys uncovering different dynamics proposed socially specified speech samples (academics with Ph.D. degree versus workers with vocational training) to listeners.[6]

In the next sections, I propose to evaluate the impact of language detail on elicited attitudes towards regional variation in Swiss French by addressing the following research questions:

– To what extent does language detail account for the language attitude variation found?
– What specific linguistic features do global category names tend to include, and what is the social meaning of these specific features?

The research questions were operationalized in the study described below.

4. Methods

4.1 Participants

The survey was carried out in French-speaking Switzerland. Data were collected through individual interviews from a quota sample (Dörnyei 2007) of 100 participants, demographically stratified according to canton of residence, age, socioprofessional category and gender. The choice of these independent variables was determined by previous research (see Prikhodkine 2011 for more details). Three cantons represented French-speaking Switzerland: Geneva (n=29), Vaud (n=53) and Fribourg (n=18). The age variable was represented by two groups: a younger group (n=51, with a range from 16 to 45 years) and an older group (n=49, with a range from 46 to 76 years). Based on the classification used by the Swiss federal office of statistics (Office fédéral de la statistique), four socio-professional categories were constructed: executives (n=23, such as lawyers, University professors), intermediate professions (n=26, such as nurses, schoolteachers), employees

---

6. Arguably, the different fashions in which the stimuli were presented in the reported studies (by global names vs. using recordings) plays only a comparatively minor role in the variation, as research in Britain suggests (Giles 1970).

(n=29, such as bank clerks, medical assistants) and manual occupations (n=22, such as horticulturalists, farmers). Finally, 45 participants were men and 55 women.[7]

4.2   Stimuli

To operationalize the research questions regarding the role of stimulus specificity for the outcome (see above), attitudes were elicited referring to two kinds of target: (1) global stimulus (the syntagm "words of local French") and (2) specific linguistic features. The latter were represented by a corpus of 45 lexical items selected from *Dictionnaire suisse romand*[8] (Thibault & Knecht 2004) according to the following main criteria: diffusion (their use should be documented in at least three cantons under investigation), frequency (items should not be labeled "rare" or "getting older"), referential equivalence (Swiss items should have a common reference with their equivalent of French from France).[9] Then, still according to the *Dictionnaire suisse romand*, the items were selected so as to represent the four main sources of distinctness of the local variety of French, namely dialectalisms, germanisms, archaisms and local innovations (see §3 for their definition). For reasons of feasibility, the corpus was divided into two sets during the experiment. The items of the first set (n=17) were investigated during the major part of the interview (see Appendix for a list). The second set features (n=28) were compared to the first set items on only some evaluative dimensions at the end of the interview. This distribution was a great time-savet, while ensuring a comprehensive representation of the local lexicon.

4.3   Procedure and measures

Each interview consisted of four parts and lasted about one hour.

The first part was designed to indirectly measure the use of lexical items. Respondents were asked to produce a word in response to a dictionary definition.

---

7.   Interaction effects in inter-respondent variation will not be presented in this chapter, insofar as numerous and systematic demographic biases have not been observed for the topics discussed in this article (see Prikhodkine 2011 for more details).

8.   Issued by the Department of dialectology of Neuchâtel University, the *Dictionnaire Suisse romand* ('Dictionary of Swiss French' – Thibault & Knecht 2004) is currently the richest lexicographical work on the Swiss features of French.

9.   The syntagm "French from France" refers here and hereafter to its standard variety, *i.e.* the one having the following characteristics proposed by Auer (2005:8): it is oriented to by speakers of more than one vernacular variety; it is considered as an H-variety and used for writing; it is subject to at least some codification and elaboration.

For instance, the sentence "device that delivers banknotes after the introduction of a magnetic card" aimed to stimulate the production of the Swiss variant "bancomat" (ATM), of the French variant "distributeur" or both at once. Importantly, the respondents were not informed of the research hypotheses; they simply knew that the study focused on oral French and concrete words they use in everyday life. Then it was stated that the informants had only three seconds to answer, and that the investigator was interested in the first word came to mind (see Oppenheim 1986: 163 for more details on the associative techniques).

The second part of the interview was conducted in a semi-directive way and was designed to elicit overt language attitudes towards, firstly, the global category name "words of local French" and, secondly, specific lexical items. For example, respondents were asked to report their personal use of the lexical items and to judge the acceptability of the latter by news anchors.

The third part of the interview aimed to obtain an assessment of the lexical variables from the first set of features on semantic differential four-point scales. Informants had to rate each lexical variant on five evaluative attributes (beautiful-ugly, pleasant-unpleasant, correct-incorrect, elegant-tough, warm-cold). These attributes were selected from the pilot study and were expected to present relevant qualifiers for our respondents. In total, 34 lexical items (17 Swiss features and their 17 French equivalents) were rated on five evaluative attributes.

The fourth part was designed to gather the ratings of the lexical variables from the second set of features through a categorization technique (Moliner et al. 2002: 119). The key feature of this technique is that it requires the speaker to make himself the object of classification, comparison or ranking, the main objective being the identification of similarity links that speakers establish between various elements. Concretely, respondents were invited to compare the second set of features (n=28) to the first set of items on the basis of the evaluative attributes used in the third part of the interview.[10]

5. Some results

5.1 Global category name

When attitudes are elicited from the global category name "words of the local French" (as opposed to the French from France) with no other details provided,

---

10. Due to space, results for the second set of items used in the study (see §4.2) are not presented here. Largely convergent with the results for the first set, they do not impact on my argument. Note that whenever specific items are mentioned, they are from the first set.

respondents perceive their speakers as mostly old (92%), rural (87%) and having a poor educational background (76%).[11] Interestingly, the emerging portrait of the local variety users as presented by the majority of the informants seems to closely parallel the dialectological notion of NORMs – "non-mobile older rural males", a well-known informant sampling bias in traditional dialect studies (Chambers & Trudgill 1998: 29).[12] Furthermore, the portrait of the local variety described earlier is similar to that produced by the Swiss respondents of previous studies, which elicited attitudes from category names such as *accent* and *variety* (e.g. Singy et al. 2004: 51–81).

Respondents were also asked to quote some words that they believe represent well the local French. Of the 59 mentioned items, four were quoted by at least ten informants: *panosse* (57%), *gouille* (20%), *s'encoubler* (17%), *cheni* (10%).[13] More than four out of five respondents (81%) spontaneously delivered one of these features, the use of which was also said to be restricted to only a part (a canton or a canton part) of the *Suisse romande*. Interestingly, according to the *Dictionnaire suisse romand*, all these words are characterized by their dialectal origin. Thus, these results show that the global category name tends to elicit attitudes mostly having for their target dialectalisms (*patois* features), while other Swiss features such as innovations and archaisms are not mobilized by this concept.

5.2   Typicality of specific features

To what extent do specific lexical items (here: the ones from the first set – see Appendix) match the social meaning of the global category name? To explore this, respondents were asked to answer the following question for each item identified as Swiss: "In another research, some informants described the local accent, among other things, as rural and peasant. To what extent would you say the following

---

11.   It should be noted that more than half of these respondents (57%) cited agricultural occupations (especially the peasants), while a third (35%) simply mentioned people with vocational training.

12.   The fact that traditional dialectologists seem to share with lay people the same idea of who speaks "authentic" dialects would demonstrate an ideological approach to regional variation by these dialectologists. Without breaking with the discourse of the respondents, the researchers themselves indeed tend to take a prescriptive stance in describing regional variation, considering the regional dialect as "a set of violations of the norm" (e.g. Voillat 1971: 217). Thus, the term of regional dialect is defined in opposition to that of French, understood as a normative representation of the language (Chambon 1997: 15; Corbeil 1984: 34).

13.   These terms could be translated into English as: *floor cloth* (panosse-serpillière), *puddle* (flaque-gouille), *stumble* (s'encoubler-trébucher), *mess* (désordre-cheni).

word corresponds to this description of the local accent?" For each item (n=17), respondents had to complete a four-point Likert type scale with the following labeled points: not at all, not really, rather well, completely. Figure 1 is a graphic representation of the results (see Appendix for a translation into English).

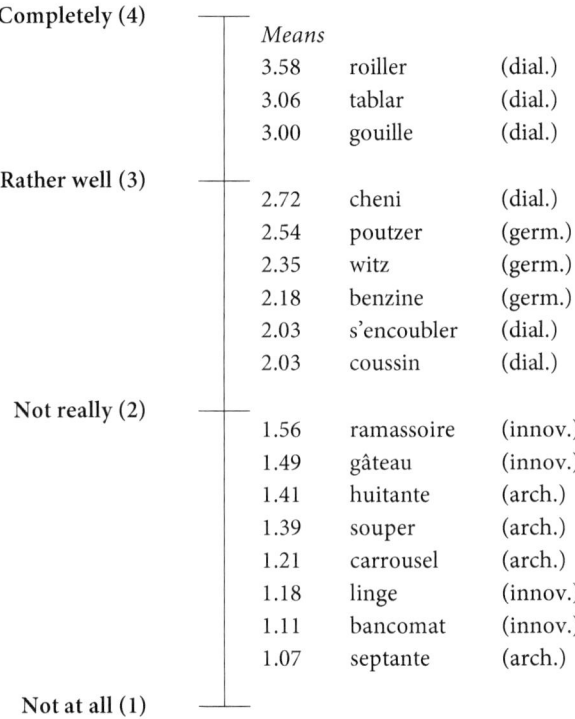

Figure 1. Matching of lexical features with the social meaning of the global category name

The similarity to the social meaning of the global category name tends to depend on the items' origin (see Figure 1). The top of the table (a high degree of similarity) is occupied by dialectal and German variants, which therefore seem to possess a similar connotation in terms of rurality and low level of education. All the archaisms and Swiss innovations occupy the bottom of the table, showing little similarity with the stereotype of the local variety.

Hierarchical cluster analysis (using the Ward method) seems to confirm the observed pattern (see Figure 2).[14] Indeed, as it turns out, all archaisms and

---

14. The capitals A/I/D/G before the items in Figure 2 refer to the category of Swiss variants: archaisms, innovations, dialectalisms, germanisms.

innovations are grouped to form the first cluster. The last two clusters – which eventually aggregate – consist exclusively of dialectalisms and germanisms. A chi-square test supports the assumption that the items' distribution into clusters relates to their origin (X2[6] = 21.250, p =.002, Cramer's V=.791).[15]

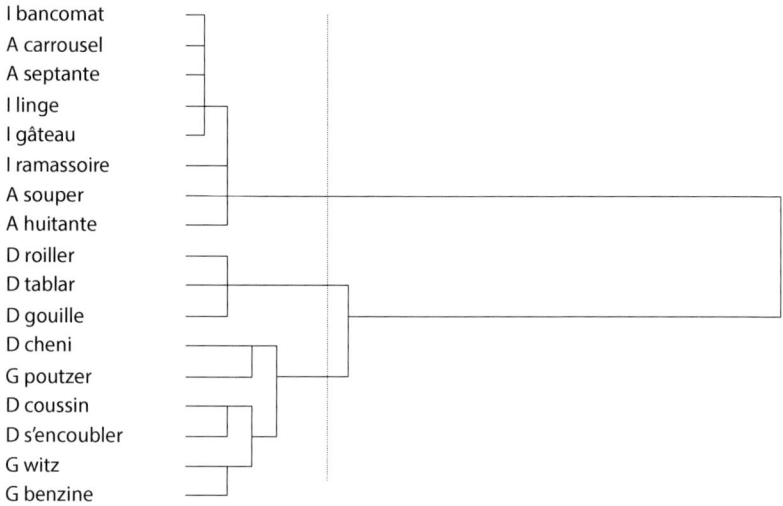

Figure 2. Matching of lexical features with the social meaning of the global category name: Hierarchical cluster analysis (Ward method)

5.3   Elicited use

The use of lexical items was elicited in the first part of the interview (see §4.3). Without being made aware of the purposes of the study, respondents were asked to produce a lexical variant in response to a dictionary definition. It was stated that the informants had only three seconds to answer, and that the investigator was interested in the first word that came to mind. Analysis of the data shows that whereas Swiss variants tend to be preferred in elicited use to French features from France in the case of innovations and archaisms, the opposite seems to hold for dialectal and German items (see Figure 3).[16] Note that this result is similar to that of the reported

---

15.   While chi-square measures whether there is an association between two nominal variables, Cramer's V provides information on the strength of the association between the two variables. The more the value is close to 1, the more the association is strong (David & Sutton 2004: 299–300).

16.   Each lexical variable is presented in this and the following figures by its Swiss variant only.

use (the second part of the interview), when respondents were explicitly asked to indicate what term they used (see Prikhodkine 2011). Finally, the hierarchical cluster analysis output[17] is very similar to the one shown in the previous section (Fig. 2), and a chi-square test again suggests that the items' distribution into clusters is dependent on their origin (X2[3]=10.645, p=.014, Cramer's V=.791).

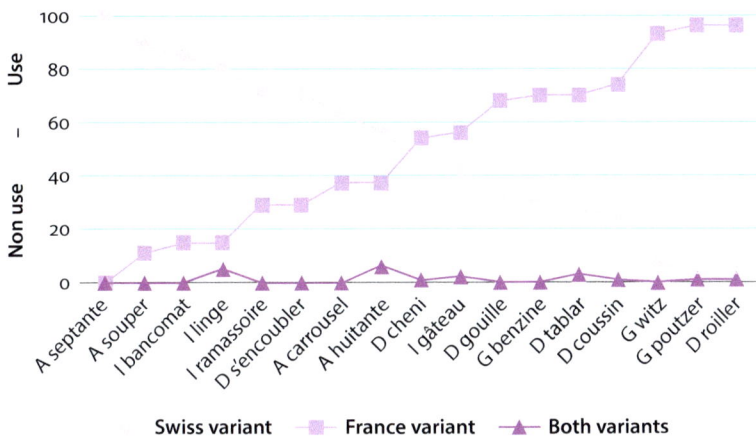

Figure 3. Elicited use of lexical items

5.4   Evaluative dimensions

Respondents were asked to rate each lexical variant from the set presented to them on several four-point semantic differential scales (see §4.3). Both the French and Swiss variants of each variable had to be evaluated next to each other, so as to allow for comparison.[18] On the correctness scale, one can observe that all Swiss variants are not treated the same way (see Figure 4).[19] Indeed, while all dialectalisms and

---

17.   When coding, each term of a lexical variable was assigned the following numbers: 1 when it was elicited; 2 in the opposite case. Hierarchical cluster analysis was performed for each lexical variable from the numbers representing the difference between the score of the Swiss variant and the French one.

18.   As it would be too space-consuming to present the results on all evaluative dimensions in this chapter, I have chosen to look at the results on two scales which provide a good idea of contrasting values of the local lexical features (see Prikhodkine 2011 for a full analysis of these data).

19.   The variants marked with an asterisk in the Figures 4 and 5 show a significant result (p<.05). The means of the two variants of each lexical variable were compared via a paired-samples t-test.

germanisms are clearly perceived as less correct than variants of the French from France, most of the innovations and archaisms are in competition. A chi-square test shows again that the distribution of lexical items into clusters[20] is connected with their origin (X2[9] = 23.092, p =.006, Cramer's V=.673).

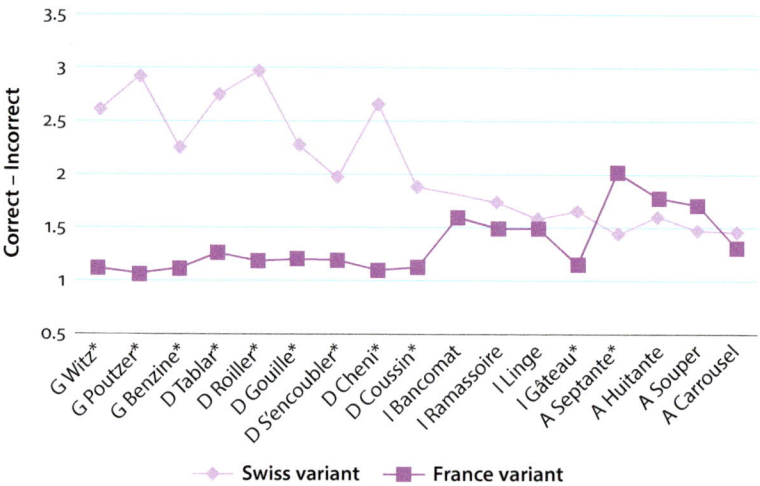

Figure 4. Ratings on the correctness dimension

Although correctness is perhaps the most salient language dimension in folk minds (Preston 1996: 54–59), it is rarely sufficient to describe attitudes to language varieties. There is indeed ample evidence that language attitudes also tend to vary on another major dimension which refers to social characteristics or group solidarity (Ryan et al. 1982: 8–11). To test this dimension, respondents in the present study were asked to indicate to what extent each lexical item could be viewed as warm or cold (labelled "friendliness"), both terms having often been spontaneously used by lay speakers in a pilot study when talking about Swiss lexical variation. Results show some consistency in the evaluation of innovations and archaisms (see Figure 5). Except for the item *bancomat*, these features are regarded as warmer than their equivalents in the French from France. While German variants do not seem to be favored by the respondents, the evaluation is more mixed for dialectal items. As a result, the overall effect of the items' origin on their distribution into clusters is not significant (X2[6] = 8.972, p =.175, Cramer's V=.514).

---

20. On the evaluative dimensions, hierarchical cluster analysis was performed for each lexical variable from the numbers representing the difference between the score of the Swiss variant and that of the France variant.

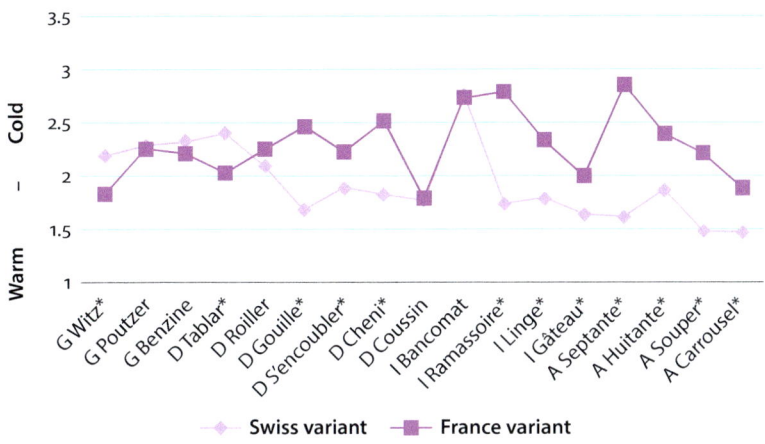

Figure 5. Ratings on the friendliness dimension

The fact that most of the innovations and archaisms show a positive evaluation on both the friendliness and correctness scales is an interesting finding in a broader context of language attitude study of varieties of French. In northern French-speaking countries, the relationship of the solidarity and prescription dimensions of language evaluation was traditionally described with reference to a diglossic model: regional items were described as inferior in prestige, but superior in terms of loyalty, in comparison with the French from France (e.g. Paquot 1988; Lafontaine 1991; Singy 1996). While this scenario seems to be confirmed for several dialectalisms in Swiss French, my results uncover a different kind of interaction of evaluative dimensions for innovations and archaisms. Indeed, they not only fulfill the function of group solidarity, but they also have a certain prestige (a constellation that Ryan et al. 1982 call "pattern C").

5.5 Discourse data

There is extensive evidence in sociolinguistics that Standard Language Ideology (SLI)[21] plays a crucial role in naturalizing language variation and legitimizing standard varieties (e.g. Milroy & Milroy 1987; Milroy 2001; Lippi-Green 2012). I believe ideology is precisely the force that best explains the discrepancy of views on language between professional and non-professional linguists. Ideology

---

21. Lippi-Green (2012:67) defines the Standard Language Ideology as "a bias toward an abstracted, idealized, homogenous spoken language which is imposed and maintained by dominant bloc institutions and which names as its model the written language, but which is drawn primarily from the spoken language of the upper middle class".

is certainly responsible for a certain unfamiliarity with the notions of scientific linguistics: Who believes in the arbitrariness of the sign or in the arbitrariness of the social meaning of the language "facts"? By rejecting the cause and effect relationship between language elements and social groups, lay speakers often tend to believe in the naturalness of this relationship (Preston 1996: 54–56). In fact, the language itself becomes the provider of explanation, and arguments referring to the internal "life" of the language are particularly difficult to challenge for professional linguists. Internal arguments include, for example, appeals to etymology, clarity or logic (Silverstein 1996).

These are precisely the arguments I found in the discourse of the respondents who were explaining their preference for Swiss lexical features. For instance, arguments about etymology and logic concerned particularly the items *septante* (seventy) and *nonante* (ninety). Thus, for the speakers, a long and "noble" history of these features explains the very "reasonable" rejection of their equivalents from the French of France, respectively *soixante-dix* and *quatre-vingt-dix*:

> *Soixante-dix* is banished from my vocabulary. Why say *soixante-dix*, why bother? *Sept* is in *septante*. So I don't understand why it is six plus one. I even managed to convince a French person. This is not reasonable. *Septante* comes from the base of Latin. Portuguese and Italians say *septante*. We speak better than French people.[22]

When it is not etymology, it is frequently referential clarity and precision that are put forward by respondents to explain their preference for a particular lexical variant in their use, as in the case of *bancomat* (ATM), a Swiss innovation that competes with the French feature *distributeur*.

> *Bancomat* is easier to pronounce. *Distributeur* is vague. Distributor of what? Of French fries? I don't know where *bancomat* comes from. But in any case, it is well accepted, well understood by everyone.

In line with the results of the evaluation on the friendliness dimension, there are also many arguments stressing the identity value of archaisms and innovations. However, while the identity value may concern Swiss items of different origins, only innovations and archaisms receive some ideological support and see their prestige being naturalized. Interestingly, we can observe Standard Language Ideology operating in two opposite ways in the case of Swiss features of different origins. For instance, claims for authority are used to both reject the dialectal item *roiller* (to rain) and to legitimize the archaism *septante* (seventy).

---

22. Originally performed in French, this quotation and the following have been translated into English by the author.

Because at school I learned *pleuvoir fort*. *Roiller* was almost a dirty word, it's a word we were trying to avoid.

I've always said *septante*. Because I've always said *septante*. I was taught *septante* at school.

6. Discussion

This article has reported a survey which revealed that language detail does account for language attitude variation. In turn, this can be taken to suggest that the use of global category names (e.g. *accent*, *variety*, etc.) for attitude elicitation in previous studies may have been a determining factor for the outcome of locating Standard French outside the Swiss community. In fact, my study has shown that these global category names tend to elicit attitudes having for their target only a portion of Swiss lexical variants: those of dialectal origin, which are also the most stigmatized ones. At the same time, Swiss prestigious variants – innovations and archaisms – are not triggered by global category names.

Irvine and Gal (2000) commented on the social nature of this kind of cognitive processing:

> Erasure is the process in which ideology, in simplifying the sociolinguistic field, renders some persons or activities (or sociolinguistic phenomena) invisible. Facts that are inconsistent with the ideological scheme either go unnoticed or get explained away.   (Irvine & Gal 2000: 38)

That is, people's beliefs about social groups and associated linguistic features can be holistic in their scope; if certain variables are inconsistent with these beliefs, they can be ignored in order to maintain a coherent vision of the social space. Thus, believing that the global category name referring to the local French has as its target only dialectal features, respondents in my study do not include other features, which still fall within the local French but which are not of dialectal origin.

How could we explain the salience of dialectal features when lay speakers are commenting on global language objects in the context of the French-speaking part of Switzerland? I would invoke socio-historical reasons related to the diffusion of French in the *Suisse romande*. As I have already mentioned (cf. §3), one of the most important aspects of the current linguistic landscape in the *Suisse romande* is a disappearance of indigenous languages (*i.e.* patois). Several arguments have been advanced to explain the extinction of these languages. Among these, one usually mentions the role of the Reformation requiring Bible reading in French and the impact of the French Revolution promoting French as a means of dissemination of new bourgeois values. But it is especially the public education, through the imposition of primary and secondary education at the dawn of industrialization, which played a decisive role in the disappearance of patois (Francard 2001). Indeed, compulsory school was particularly commit-ted to a policy of proscription of patois and penalties for their users. Then, the tendency to focus stigmatization on the items of dialectal (patois) and German origin in local French was reinforced by the purist discourse embodied in col-lections of prescriptive booklets, produced mainly in Switzerland throughout the nineteenth and early twentieth century (see Thibault 1998 for an overview). In the second half of the twentieth century, a great number of dialectological studies emerged, which however continued to share not only a focus on dialec-tal lexical features, but also a prescriptive point of view on them. In fact, these linguistic features were considered as non French and, therefore, as violations of the norm (e.g. Voillat 1971: 217; Tuaillon 1977: 10). These elements have con-tributed, to a large extent, to the prominence of dialectal features within the global concept of the local variety of French. Thus, it is no exaggeration to say that although today patois do not exist anymore (or hardly exist), they are still existent in folk minds.

The data analyzed in this article also show that attitudes elicited by global category names are not always adequate to describe sociolinguistic variation in the sense that they have been unable to capture the emergence of a cer-tain Swiss Standard supported by a number of lexical items such as "innova-tions" – items of French origin which however do not exist in the Standard French of France.[23] Not only do these features elicit group solidarity, but they also have a certain prestige, as my study has shown. How could we explain this trend after years of convergence towards the French of France? It is possible to find an explanation in a process Mattheier (1997) calls the *destandardization* of standard varieties in Europe, beginning in the second half of the twentieth century. Caused by social changes in Western societies after World War II and a certain democratization of European societies (Fairclough 1992), this process is characterized by a growing visibility of non-standard language varieties and an increased tolerance toward sociolinguistic variation. This tolerance may be accompanied by a new creativity and a broadening of the scope of linguistic

23.   See Prikhodkine 2012 for a discussion why the Swiss Standard is supported by the items of French origin, and also how the local identity can be expressed through lexical features structurally related to the forms of the French from France (instead of dialectalisms, i.e. lin-guistic features resulting from contact with indigenous languages and thus presenting more distance from the Standard French from France).

variation (e.g. Androutsopoulos 2000), some of which may become socially acceptable and shared by the whole community (cf. Mattheier 1997; Deumert & Vandenbussche 2003). Results presented in this study precisely show such acceptance for Swiss innovations and archaisms. Indeed, the absence of numerous significant interaction effects in inter-respondent variation indicates a large consensus on the social meaning of prestigious Swiss items. This acceptance, however, does not challenge the Standard Language Ideology (SLI), insofar as ideological support given to innovations and archaisms is still based on the idea of the superiority of one language variety over others (see Coupland & Kristiansen 2011, on the SLI's role within the process of destandardization).

However, despite ideological support, prestigious Swiss items cannot be fully described in terms of a classical standard variety (Haugen 1966; Auer 2005). In fact, contrary to Québec for example (Pöll 1998: 173–175), the absence of dictionaries and prescriptive grammars fixing these features in French-speaking Switzerland reflects their lack of codification. Attempts to codify the Swiss usage exist, however; but in the absence of common intercantonal political structures, language policy is typically carried out at the level of enterprises and cantons. An example is *Dictionnaire féminin-masculin des professions, des titres et des fonctions* (Collectif 1991), which resulted from cooperation between the cantons of Geneva and Jura, and codified female names of occupations, thus marking a clear break with the more conservative France (Thibault 1998: 35–36). The media are another example of the fact that a certain codification of the Swiss prestigious items is indeed taking place. As I have already mentioned (§ 3), the national public radio station explicitly requires their newscasters to use certain homegrown forms and emphasizes the inappropriateness of certain words of French from France. Yet, the fact that the diffusion and acceptance of a number of Swiss lexical items does not go along with a strong codification probably explains why, in folk minds, "Swiss French" remains, to a certain extent, a negative concept associated with dialectal features of low prestige.

7. Conclusion

This chapter has reported a study which investigated the impact of different levels of language detail in the presentation of attitude targets on attitude variation in the outcome. It revealed that, at least in the context of the *Suisse romande*, data elicited via global category names (e.g. *accent, variety*) are not always adequate to describe sociolinguistic variation, that is, in our case, to capture an emergence of a certain Swiss Standard. It seems indeed that the evaluation of a given language variety through a global concept does not equal the sum of average evaluations of each specific feature composing that variety. When reacting to global stimuli with no other details provided, respondents tend to reproduce immediately available ideological schemes, which possibly no longer govern the language variation. In this respect, the validity of language attitude data will be enhanced by taking into account socio-historical and ideological factors involved in the process of sociolinguistic interpretation of global stimuli by lay persons. And secondly, it has become clear that, whenever attitude research is to inform research on sociolinguistic variation, it is necessary to give linguistic features under study the same level of specificity in terms of language regard as well as production.

References

Ajzen, Icek & Fishbein, Martin. 2005.The influence of attitudes on behavior. In *Handbook of Attitudes*, Dolores Albarracin, Blair T. Johnson & Mark P. Zanna (eds), 173–221. Mahwah NJ: Lawrence Erlbaum Associates.

Androutsopoulos, Jannis K. 2000. Non-standard spellings in media texts: The case of German fanzines. *Journal of Sociolinguistics* 4(4): 514–533. DOI: 10.1111/1467-9481.00128

Armstrong, Nigel & Pooley, Tim. 2010. *Social and Linguistic Change in European French*. London: Palgrave Macmillan. DOI: 10.1057/9780230281714

Auer, Peter. 2005. Europe's sociolinguistic unity, or: A typology of European dialect/standard constellations. In *Perspectives on Variation: Sociolinguistic, Historical, Comparative*, Nicole Delbecque, Johan van der Auwera & Dirk Geeraerts (eds), 7–42. Berlin: De Gruyter.

Bishop, Hywel, Coupland, Nik & Garrett, Peter. 2005. Conceptual accent evaluation: Thirty years of accent prejudice in the UK. *Acta Linguistica Hafniensia* 37(1): 131–154. DOI: 10.1080/03740463.2005.10416087

Bouchard, Pierre, Harmegnies, Bernard, Moreau, Marie-Louise Alexei Prikhodkine & Singy, Pascal. 2004. La norme dans la francophonie périphérique: Externe ou interne? Une étude expérimentale en Belgique, au Québec et en Suisse. In *La variation dans la langue standard*, Pierre Bouchard (ed.), 51–71. Québec: Office québécois de la langue française.

Bourdieu, Pierre. 1982. *Ce que parler veut dire*. Paris: Fayard.

Bourhis, Richard & Giles, Howard. 1977. The language of intergroup distinctiveness. In *Language, Ethnicity and Intergroup Relations*, Howard Giles (ed.), 119–136. New York NY: Academic Press.

Chambers, Jack K. & Trudgill, Peter. 1998. *Dialectology*. Cambridge: CUP. DOI: 10.1017/CBO9780511805103

Chambon, Jean-Pierre. 1997. La lexicographie des variétés géographiques du français en France (1983–1993): Éléments pour un bilan méthodologique et desiderata. In *Lalies, Actes des sessions de linguistique et de littérature* 17: 7–31. Paris: Presses de l'Ecole Normale Supérieure.

Collectif. 1991. *Dictionnaire féminin-masculin des professions, des titres et des fonctions*. Genève: Editions Metropolis.

Corbeil, Jean-Claude. 1984. Le 'français régional' en question. *Cahiers de l'Institut de Linguistique de Louvain* 9(3–4): 31–44.

Coupland, Nik & Kristiansen, Tore. 2011. SLICE: Critical perspectives on language (de)standardisation. In *Standard Languages and Language Standards in a Changing Europe*, Tore Kristiansen & Nik Coupland (eds), 11–35. Oslo: Novus.

David, Matthew & Sutton, Carol D. 2004. *Social Research*. London: Sage.

Deumert, Ana &Vandenbussche, Wim (eds) 2003. *Germanic Standardizations, Past to Present* [Impact: Studies in Language and Society 18]. Amsterdam: John Benjamins. DOI: 10.1075/impact.18

Dörnyei, Zoltan. 2007. *Research Methods in Applied Linguistics*. Oxford: OUP.

Fairclough, Norman. 1992. *Discourse and Social Change*. Cambridge: Polity Press.

Francard, Michel. 1998. Entre pratiques et représentations linguistiques: Le lexique des Belges francophones. In *Linguistic Identities and Policies in France and the French-speaking World*, Dawn Marley, Marie-Anne Hintze & Gabrielle Parker (eds), 149–159. London: CILT.

Francard, Michel. 2001. Français de frontière: La Belgique et la Suisse francophones. *Présence Francophone* 56: 27–54.

Garrett, Peter. 2010. *Attitudes to Language*. Cambridge: CUP. DOI: 10.1017/CBO9780511844713

Garrett, Peter, Coupland, Nik & Williams, Angie. 2003. *Investigating Language Attitudes*. Cardiff: University of Wales Press.

Giles, Howard. 1970. Evaluative reactions to accents. *Educational Review* 22: 211–227. DOI: 10.1080/0013191700220301

Haugen, Einar. 1966. Dialect, language, nation. *American Anthropologist* 68(4): 922–935. DOI: 10.1525/aa.1966.68.4.02a00040

Irvine, Judith T. & Gal, Susan. 2000. Language ideology and linguistic differentiation. In *Regimes of Language: Ideologies, Polities, and Identities*, Paul V. Kroskrity (ed.), 35–84. Santa Fe NM: School of American Research Press.

John, Oliver P. & Benet-Martinez, Veronica. 2000. Measurement: Reliability, construct validation, and scale construction. In *Handbook of Research Methods in Social and Personality Psychology*, Harry T. Reis & Charles M. Judd (eds), 339–369. Cambridge: CUP.

Knecht, Pierre. 1996. La Suisse romande: Aspects d'un paysage francophone conservateur. In *Le français dans l'espace francophone*, Vol. 2, Didier de Robillard & Michel Beniamino (eds), 759–770. Paris: Honoré Champion.

Kristiansen, Tore. 1997. Language attitudes in a Danish cinema. In *Sociolinguistics. A Reader and Coursebook*, Nik Coupland & Adam Jaworski (eds), 291–305. New York NY: St. Martin's Press.

Kristiansen, Tore. 2011. Attitude, ideology, and awareness. In *The Sage Handbook of Sociolinguistics*, Ruth Wodak, Barbara Johnstone & Paul Kerswill (eds), 265–278. London: Sage. DOI: 10.4135/9781446200957.n20

Kristiansen, Tore. & Jørgensen, Jens Normann. 2008. Subjective factors in dialect convergence and divergence. In *Dialect Change. Convergence and Divergence in European Languages*, Peter Auer, Frans Hinskens & Paul Kerswill (eds), 287–302. Cambridge: CUP.

Lambert, Wallace E., Hodgson, Richard C., Gardner, Robert C. & Fillenbaum, Samuel. 1960. Evaluational reactions to spoken languages. *Journal of Abnormal and Social Psychology* 60(1): 44–51. DOI: 10.1037/h0044430

Labov, William. 1971. The study of language in its social context. In *Advances in the Sociology of Language*, Vol. 1, Joshua A. Fishman (ed.), 152–216. The Hague: Mouton de Gruyter.

Lafontaine, Dominique. 1991. *Les mots et les Belges*. Bruxelles: Service de la langue française.

L'Eplattenier-Saugy, Caroline. 1999. A perceptual dialect study of French in Switzerland. In *Handbook of Perceptual Dialectology*, Vol. 2, David Long & Dennis R. Preston (eds), 351–365. Amsterdam: John Benjamins. DOI: 10.1075/z.hpd2.24lep

Leyens, Jacques-Philippe & Yzerbyt, Vincent. 1997. *Psychologie sociale*. Sprimont: Mardaga.

Lippi-Green, Rosina. 2012. *English with an Accent. Language, Ideology, and Discrimination in the United States*. London: Routledge.

Lorenzi-Cioldi, Fabio. 1997. *Questions de méthodologie en sciences sociales*. Lausanne & Paris: Delachaux & Niestlé.

Mattheier, Klaus J. 1997. Über Destandardisierung, Umstandardisierung und Standardisierung in modernen europäischen Standardsprachen. In *Standardisierung und Destandardisierung europäischer Nationalsprachen*, Klaus J. Mattheier & Edgar Radtke (eds), 1–9. Frankfurt: Peter Lang.

Milroy, James. 2001. Language ideologies and the consequences of standardization. *Journal of Sociolinguistics* 5(4): 530–555. DOI: 10.1111/1467-9481.00163

Milroy, James & Milroy, Lesley. 1987. *Authority in Language: Investigating Language Prescription and Standardization*. London: Routledge and Kegan Paul.

Moliner, Pascal, Rateau, Patrick & Cohen-Scali, Valérie. 2002. *Les représentations sociales. Pratique des études de terrain*. Rennes: Presses Universitaires de Rennes.

Moreau, Marie-Louise, Bouchard, Pierre, Demartin, Stéphanie, Gadet, Françoise, Guerin, Emmanuelle, Harmegnies, Bernard, Huet, Katy F. Laroussi, Prikhodkine, Alexei, Singy, Pascal, Thiam, Ndiassé & Tyne, Harry. 2007. *Les accents dans la francophonie. Une enquête internationale*. Bruxelles: Service de la langue française.

Niedzielski, Nancy. 1999. The effect of social information on the perception of sociolinguistic variables. *Journal of Language and Social Psychology* 18(1): 62–85. DOI: 10.1177/0261927X99018001005

Niedzielski, Nancy & Preston, Dennis R. 2000. *Folk Linguistics*. Berlin: Mouton de Gruyter. DOI: 10.1515/9783110803389

Office fédéral de la statistique. ⟨www.bfs.admin.ch⟩

Oppenheim, Abraham Naftali. 1986. *Questionnaire Design and Attitude Measurement*. Hampshire: Gower.

Paquot, Annette. 1988. *Les Québécois et leurs mots. Etude sémiologique et sociolinguistique des régionalismes lexicaux au Québec*. Québec: Presses de l'Université de Laval.

Pöll, Bernhard. 1998. *Le français ou les français? La difficile naissance de la pluricentricité. Lengas* 43: 163–182.

Preston, Dennis R. 1996. Whaddayaknow? The modes of folk linguistic awareness. *Language Awareness* 5(1): 40–74. DOI: 10.1080/09658416.1996.9959890

Preston, Dennis R. 2010. Variation in language regard. In *Variatio delectat: Empirische Evidenzen und theoretische Passungen sprachlicher Variation*, Evelyn Zeigler, Peter Gilles & Joachim Scharloth (eds), 7–27. Frankfurt: Peter Lang.

Price, Susan, Fluck, Michael & Giles, Howard. 1983. The effects of language of testing on bilingual pre-adolescents' attitudes towards Welsh and varieties of English. *Journal of Multilingual and Multicultural Development* 4(2–3): 149–161. DOI: 10.1080/01434632.1983.9994108

Prikhodkine, Alexei. 2012. Autonomisation du français en usage en Suisse romande: Quelle évidence? *Journal of French Language Studies* 22(3): 395–417. DOI: 10.1017/S0959269511000500

Prikhodkine, Alexei. 2011. *Dynamique normative du français en usage en Suisse romande. Enquête sociolinguistique dans les cantons de Vaud, Genève et Fribourg.* Paris: L'Harmattan.

Provost, Valérie, Yzerbyt, Vincent, Corneille, Olivier, Désert, Michel & Francard, Michel. 2003. Stigmatisation sociale et comportements linguistiques: Le lexique menacé. *Revue internationale de psychologie sociale* 16(1): 177–200.

Racine, Isabelle & Andreassen, Helene. In press. Swiss French. In *Varieties of Spoken French*, Sylvain Detey, Jacques Durand, Bernard Laks & Chantal Lyche (eds). Oxford: OUP.

Rosch, Eleanor. 1978. Principles of categorization. In *Cognition and Categorization*, Eleanor Rosch & Barbara B. Lloyd (eds), 27–48. Hillsdale NJ: Lawrence Erlbaum Associates.

Rubin, Donald L. 1992. Nonlanguage factors affecting undergraduates' judgments of nonnative English-speaking teaching assistants. *Research in Higher Education* 33(4): 511–531.

Ryan, Ellen Bouchard, Giles, Howard & Sebastian, Richard. 1982. An integrative perspective for the study of attitudes toward language variation. In *Attitudes towards Language Variation*, Ellen Bouchard Ryan & Howard Giles (eds), 1–19. London: Edward Arnold.

Silverstein, Michael. 1996. Monoglot "standard" in America: Standardization and metaphors of linguistic hegemony. In *The Matrix of Language: Contemporary Linguistic Anthropology*, Donald Brenneis & Ronald K.S. Macaulay (eds), 284–306. Boulder CA: Westview Press.

Singy, Pascal. 1996. *L'image du français en Suisse romande.* Paris: L'Harmattan.

Singy, Pascal, Mottaz Baran, Arlette, Amstalden, Martine, Prikhodkine, Alexei & Jufer, Nicole. 2004. *Identités de genre, identités de classe et insécurité linguistique.* Berne: Peter Lang.

Singy, Pascal, Bourquin, Céline, Prikhodkine, Alexei, Schaffter, Manuel & Spencer, Brenda. 2006. *Le sens des messages préventifs du sida: consensus et dissensions au sein de la population générale et chez les intervenants.* UNIL-CHUV: Rapport de recherche.

Soukup, Barbara. 2012. Current issues in the social psychological study of 'language attitudes': Constructionism, context, and the attitude-behavior link. *Language and Linguistics Compass* 6(4): 212–224. DOI: 10.1002/lnc3.332

Speelman, Dirk, Spruyt, Adriaan, Impe, Leen & Geeraerts, Dirk. 2013. Language attitudes revisited: Auditory affective priming. *Journal of Pragmatics* 52: 83–92. DOI: 10.1016/j.pragma.2012.12.016

Thibault, André. 1998. Légitimité linguistique des français nationaux hors de France: le français de Suisse romande. *Revue québécoise de linguistique* 26(2): 25–42. DOI: 10.7202/603150ar

Thibault, André & Knecht, Pierre. (eds). 2004. *Dictionnaire suisse romand,* nouvelle édition. Genève: Zoé.

Tourangeau, Roger & Rasinski, Kenneth A. 1988. Cognitive processes underlying context effects in attitude measurement. *Psychological Bulletin* 103(3): 299–314.

Tuaillon, Gaston. 1977. Réflexions sur le français régional. In *Les français régionaux*, Gerard Taverdet & George Straka (eds), 7–29. Paris: Librairie Klincksieck.

Voillat, François. 1971. Aspects du français régional actuel. In *Actes du colloque de dialectologie francoprovençale*, 216–246. Neuchâtel: Université de Neuchâtel.

Appendix

	First set items		
	Swiss variants	France variants	English translation
Dialectalisms	S'encoubler	Trébucher	Stumble
	Gouille	Flaque	Puddle
	Roiller	Pleuvoir à verse	Rain heavily
	Tablar	Etagère	Shelf
	Cheni	Désordre	Mess
	Coussin	Oreiller	Pillow
Germanisms	Witz	Blague	Joke
	Poutzer	Nettoyer	Clean
	Benzine	Essence	Gasoline
Archaisms	Septante	Soixante-dix	Seventy
	Huitante	Quatre-vingts	Eighty
	Carrousel	Manège	Carousel
	Souper	Dîner	Dinner
Innovations	Bancomat	Distributeur	ATM
	Ramassoire	Pelle à poussière	Dustpan
	Gâteau	Tarte	Pie
	Linge	Serviette	Towel

Topic Index

A

accent XIII, 219, 221–223, 225, 228–229, 235, 237
accent (US) XI, 117–118, 121, 124–132, 140
accent (Danish) 93–94, 96, 101–102, 111
accent (Dutch) XII, 191–192, 194–198, 200–207, 209, 211–214
accent, foreign XI-XIII, 117–118, 121, 124–132, 175, 177–184, 186, 188, 191–192, 194–198, 200–207, 209, 211–214
accent, foreign (Korean in English) XI, 117–118, 121, 124–132
accent, foreign (Asian-East Asian in English) XI-XII, 175, 177–184, 186, 188
accent, foreign (Moroccan in Dutch) XII, 191–192, 194–198, 200–207, 209, 211–214
accent ratings, evaluations – see variety ratings
accent vaudois (Vaud accent) 221–222, 228–229
acceptability 44, 214, 227
action IX, 37–50
activation IX, 9, 31, 37, 40, 45, 47, 49
activation, cognitive – see cognitive activation
activation, phasic – see phasic activation
activation, tonic –see tonic activation
actualization; actualized 37, 42, 45, 48, 50
actuation (problem) 3
APE model – see Associative-Propositional Evaluation Model
Application 42, 44
Associative-Propositional Evaluation Model 121–122, 132

attention – see also selective attention model 6–8, 40, 45, 119–120, 153, 221
attitudes, behavioral 4, 32, 37, 46, 49, 60, 66, 72, 79–80, 88, 119, 121, 132, 137–138, 162, 222
attitudes, evaluative 61–61, 64, 69, 74, 76
attitudes, language – see language attitudes
attitudes, processing (see also implicit and explicit attitudes) 6–12, 43, 118–119, 121, 130, 138, 222, 235
Austria, Austrian dialect 67–70, 72, 74–79
automatic processing 7, 9–12, 113, 119–121, 143

B

Bavarian dialect – see Austrian dialect
beliefs VIII-IX, XIII, 3–5, 8, 21, 32, 37, 48, 121, 138, 235

C

change (language) XIII, 3–4, 6, 23, 28, 30–33, 87–89, 101, 106, 112–114, 171, 192, 196, 219, 222
class – see social class
classification (of varieties) 6, 25, 64, 179, 184, 186–187, 227
cloze-test 105
cognition 39, 41, 141, 144, 152–153, 176
cognitive activation 37, 45, 46
cognitive processing – see language processing
cognitorium (attitudinal) IX, 9–12, 19, 22, 26, 30, 32
compatibility thesis 57
comprehension 6–7, 25–26, 137, 146–147, 153, 177, 201
conscious attitudes – see explicit attitudes

constraint (problem) 3
construction IX, 37, 40, 43, 46–49, 64, 80, 87
constructionism 60–65
constructivism X, 37, 39–40, 45–50, 57, 60–62
contextualization 32, 43, 58, 63, 105–106, 119, 145, 147, 176, 220
Copenhagen, københavnsk X, 31, 90–95, 101–102, 111, 195
correspondence theory 57
covert prestige – see prestige
critical realism 61
culture 26, 39, 46, 121, 159, 164, 171, 198

D

Denmark, Danish X, 31, 88–114, 201
destandardization 192, 236–237
dialect – see accent 69–70, 89, 101, 126, 137–141, 146–147, 149–153, 192, 202, 228
discourse 62
discourse, big-D and little-d 62
discrimination 6–7, 25–26, 28
dynamism XII, 31, 94–95, 111, 191, 196, 206–207, 210–211

E

EEG XI, 144–145, 147, 177
effect size 77
Einstellung vs. Einstellungsäußerung 61
elicitation X-XI, XIII, 9, 65, 70, 160, 219, 235
embedding (problem) 3
emotion 45, 177
English (influence on other languages) 87–88, 96–100, 102–105, 107–113, 192
enregisterment IX
ERP (event-related potential) XI, 141, 144–145, 147, 149–150
erasure IX, 235

ethnicity and race 5, 121–122, 141–143, 179, 186, 188, 198, 200, 202–205, 208–211, 213
evaluation, see accent ratings
evaluation (problem) 3
experiential content 40–43
explicit attitudes (see also implicit attitudes) IX, XI, 3, 8, 10–12, 32, 49, 95–97, 100, 103, 105, 109, 113–114, 117–122, 125, 128–132, 137–139, 143, 160–161, 163–164, 184, 186, 188, 196, 200, 220–221, 227
eye-dialect 5, 67

F
fixation, X, 39
folk linguistics 4, 221
frames of reference 64–66, 70, 76–77, 79

G
gender – see sex and gender

H
hierarchization X, 39, 89–90, 92, 95, 205
high performance 73, 76
human epistemological construct (HEC) 55, 61–66, 69–70, 72, 74–76, 78–80

I
IAT (Implicit Association Test) X–XI, 113, 117–118, 120–125, 129–131, 137, 141–142, 153
iconization IX, 8
identity (sociocultural) X, 3, 48, 90, 95, 109, 159, 161–162, 164, 169, 171, 177, 192, 197, 234, 236
ideology (of language) IX, 5, 88–89, 95–96, 100, 102, 105–111, 113, 194, 219, 233–235
implicit attitudes (see also explicit attitudes) IX, X–XI, 7–8, 10–12, 32, 70, 88, 92, 94–96, 98, 100, 102–103, 105, 107, 111, 113–114, 117–121, 126, 129–132, 137, 141–150, 152–154, 159–161, 164,

169–171, 176, 184, 188, 200, 220
implicit memory model 119–120
implicit social cognition (ISC) 117–118, 121–122, 132
incompatibility thesis 57, 59
indexicality IX, 47
indexical field IX
intentionality 38
interaction (social, conversational) 37, 39–40, 47, 49, 56, 61, 63–66, 76, 80, 194, 196
interaction effect (statistical) 150–151, 167–168, 181–182, 209, 226, 237
intertextuality 63

L
label-ranking task (LRT) 90
LANCHART (Language Change in Real Time) 88, 90–94, 101
language attitudes (see also implicit and explicit attitudes) 4, 37, 50, 55–56, 59, 61–64, 66, 80, 90, 92, 102, 117–118, 120–122, 128–130, 132, 137–139, 159–161, 163, 169–171, 175, 177, 197, 206, 219–220, 222–223, 225, 227, 232
language processing 43, 146, 153
languaging 63
laissez-faire (approach to language) 96, 103
lexicon XII, 224, 226
life-world X, 38–44, 47–50

M
map vs. territory 61–62, 80
matched guise IX, XI, 20, 31–32, 74, 92, 98, 126, 138, 140–142, 161, 163, 214
media 25, 66, 73, 89, 107, 111–113, 170, 196, 202, 237
mental maps 17–19
Michigan (US) 12–26, 30, 32
MIN (Modern import words in the Nordic community) – see English influence on other languages
mixed methods X, 55–57, 64, 80, 167

Moroccan accent – see Moroccan accent in Dutch

N
N400 – see ERP
neural network 10–12
New York City English 4, 13–15, 17, 19, 21–22, 28
nonconscious attitudes – see implicit attitudes
Nordic (attitudes to English influence) 87–88, 96–97, 100, 102–103, 105, 107–110, 112–114
noticing 6–8

O
open guise X, 72, 75
overt attitudes – see explicit attitudes
overt prestige – see prestige

P
paradigm wars 57
perception X, 6, 41–44, 46, 70, 78, 105, 137, 140, 146, 154, 160, 165, 169, 171, 175–177, 179, 186, 193, 195–197, 199, 202–203, 205, 207, 211–213
perceptual dialectology – see mental maps
perspectivation 46
pertinence X, 43–44, 60
phasic activation 45
politics 89, 96, 108, 198–199
positivism 57
prestige XI–XII, 16, 32, 126, 161, 164, 167, 170–171, 193–198, 200, 205–206, 210–214, 223–224, 233–234, 236–237
processing – see attitudes processing, automatic processing, cognitive processing, language processing
purism (approach to language) 96–97, 99–100, 104–105, 107–110, 112

Q
qualitative methods (QUAL) X, 55–60, 64–67, 70, 73, 77, 79–80, 138

quantitative methods
(QUAN) x, 49–50, 55–59,
64–66, 70, 73, 75, 77, 79–80,
117, 120, 132, 194

R
race – see ethnicity and race
rational evaluation
inventory 123
reaction 37, 98, 117–118, 120
reaction time 118, 143, 149, 177
recursivity ix
regard (for language) ix-x,
3–13, 15–19, 21–26, 28, 30–33,
219, 238
register 146–147, 152
relevance ix, 37, 40–45, 47, 49
routinization x, 39, 42, 44–45

S
salience x, 8, 40, 43–44, 235
sedimentation x, 39, 42,
44–45
selective attention model 45,
119–120
semantic differential 50, 75, 77,
227, 231
SES – see social status

sex and gender 28, 73, 78,
141, 148, 177, 199, 202, 207,
222–223, 225
similarity 76, 100, 175, 184–185,
187–188, 227
SLICE (Standard Languages in
Continental Europe) x, xii
social constructionism, see
constructionism
social status xi-xii, 5, 71, 73,
90, 101, 131, 138, 140–141, 148,
159–171, 176, 195–196, 199,
203, 213, 224, 233
southern (US) 8, 13, 15, 19, 26,
28, 137, 139–141, 144, 147,
149–152
speaker design 66–67, 69,
74–76, 79
SPEAKING 65–66, 70–74
speech community xiii, 4, 19,
23, 95, 101, 107, 137, 200
standard (language) 21, 24, 28,
30–32, 50, 67–70, 72, 74–79,
87, 88, 90, 101, 106–107,
138, 159, 161–162, 165–171,
191–198, 201–203, 210–212,
219, 221, 223–226, 233,
235–237

standard language ideology 106,
194, 233–234, 237
status – see social status
stereotype xiii, 3, 28, 75–76,
117, 119, 121–122, 126, 137–138,
141, 143, 146–147, 150–153,
195, 201, 212–213, 221, 229
subconscious attitudes – see
implicit attitudes
symbolic form 46
synchronization x, 39

T
tonic activation 45
tradition x, 15, 39
transition (problem) 3

U
unconscious attitudes – see
implicit attitudes

V
variety ratings xi, xiii, 13–16,
19–20, 73, 77–78, 128, 139,
141, 177–184, 186, 188, 191,
194, 196–197, 207, 209,
211–213, 227, 232–233
verbal guise 77, 92

Name Index

A

Adank, Pati 165
Agha, Asif IX
Ajzen, Icek 60, 222
Albarracín, Dolores 37–38
Allport, Gordon 38
Amodio, David M. 142
Anderson-Hsieh, Janet 178
Androutsopoulos, Jannis K. 237
Arendt, Hannah 61
Armstrong, Nigel 224
Aron, Arthur 77
Auer, Peter 39, 193, 198, 226, 237

B

Baddeley, Alan 153
Bakhtin, Mikhael 61, 63, 80
Banaji, Mahzarin 119–120
Baron, Andrew Scott 131
Barr, Dale J. 181
Bassili, John VIII, 9–12
Baugh, John 138
Baumann, Richard 76
Bayer, Thora Hin 46
Becker, Alton A. 63
Bergman, Manfred M. 55
Bhaskar, Roy 61
Billiet, Jaak 198
Bishop, Hywel 221
Bleich, Erik 199
Blommaert, Jan 62
Botvinick, Matthew M. 131
Bouchard, Pierre 224
Boula de Mareüil, Philippe 178
Bourdieu, Pierre 39, 224
Bourhis, Richard 220
Brennan, Eileen M. 117, 201
Brentano, Franz 38, 49
Bresnahan, Mary Jiang 117, 299
Brink, Lars 101
Brown, Colin 145
Bryman, Alan 56
Buijs, Frank 199

C

Callan, Victor J. 201
Camblin, Christine C. 145
Cameron, Deborah 66
Campbell-Kibler, Kathryn XI, 113, 139–141, 144, 161, 175–190, 220
Cargile, Aaron Castelan 117–118, 121, 126
Cassirer, Ernst 37, 46, 49
Catano, Victor M. 126
Chaiken, Shelly 118
Chambers, J. K. 228
Chambon, Jean-Pierre 228
Cherry, Colin 153
Corbeil, Jean-Claude 228
Coupland, Nik 55–56, 64–65, 73, 76, 87–88, 191, 196, 237
Creswell, John W. 55–57
Crul, Maurice 199
Cunningham, William 39

D

Daan, Jo 16
Dasgupta, Nilanjana 142–143
David, Matthew 230
De Gelder, Beatrice 177
de Jong, Peter J. 131
Denzin, Norman K. 57–59, 80
DeSantis, Andrea 126
Deumert, Ana 191, 237
Devine, Patricia G. 8, 120–121
De Witte, Hans 198
Dodsworth, Robin 161–162
Dörnyei, Zoltan 57–59, 225
Dovidio, John F. 8, 33
Draine, Sean C. 123
Dressler, Wolfgang 67

E

Eadie, Tanya L. 126
Eagly, Alice VIII, 37, 60, 76
Ebner, Jakob 67
Eckert, Penelope IX, 39, 47, 56, 162
Eisenchlas, Susana 200
Erickson, Frederick 63
Eysenck, Michael 45–46

F

Fairclough, Norman 63, 236
Fazio, Russell H. 8, 38, 120
Fishbein, Martin IX, 60
Flege, James Emil 130, 177–178
Fowler, Carol A. 6
Francard, Michel 223–224, 236
Fridland, Valerie 126
Frumkin, Lara 117, 126

G

Gal, Susan 235
Gardner, Richard G. 141
Garfinkel, Harold 61
Garrett, Peter 64, 88, 138, 160, 206, 214, 220
Gass, Susan M. 201
Gawronski, Bertram 118, 121–122, 130
Gee, James Paul 62, 81
Geeraerts, Dirk 192
Geerts, Guido 194
Gergen, Kenneth 60
Giddens, Anthony 39, 45
Giles, Howard 64, 74, 90, 196, 225
Goffman, Erving 61, 63–64, 74–75, 78, 82
Gluszek, Agata 118, 121
Goossens, Jan 192
Graff, David IX
Greenwald, Anthony G. 118–120, 129, 141–143, 149, 160
Grondelaers, Stefan XII, 88, 111, 159–173, 191–218
Grootaers, Willem 16
Gumperz, John J. 39, 61, 63–64, 69–70, 137

H

Haeringen, C. B. van 194
Hagoort, Hagoort 145
Hair, Joseph F. 208
Hall, Stuart 39
Hartmann, Dirk 48, 50
Haugen, Einar 237

Hay, Jennifer 176
Hennerson, Marlene E. 138
Himmelfarb, Samuel 77
Hinskens, Frans 200, 203
Hobsbawm, Eric 39
Hockett, Charles 3
Holcomb, Philip J. 145
Howe, Kenneth R. 57–58
Hymes, Dell XIII, 4, 22, 65–66, 70–73
Hyrkstedt, Irene 56, 60

I
Irvine, Judith IX, 5, 8, 235

J
Jacobi, Irene 165
Jaffe, Alexandra 49
James, William 41
Jarvad, Pia 104–105
Jaspers, Jürgen 192
John, Oliver P. 220
Johnstone, Barbara 56
Jørgensen, Jens Normann 101, 201–202
Jul Nielsen, Bent 101
Jung, Carl 38

K
Kahnemann, Daniel 41
Kaiser, Imtraud 67
Kamachi, Miyuki 176
Kammacher, Louise 102
Kang, Okim 178
Kasper, Simor 48
Katz, Daniel 37–38, 47–49
Kinchla, Ronald A. 153
Knecht, Pierre 224, 226
Knops, Uus 138, 165–166, 169
Koops, Christian 176, 188
Korzybski, Alfred 61
Kristeva, Julia 63
Kristensen, Kjeld 101–102
Kristiansen, Tore IX-XI, 31–32, 87–116, 117, 161, 170–171, 191–192, 195–196, 219–220, 237
Kroeber-Riel, Werner 37, 45
Kruglanski, Arie 4
Kuckartz, Udo 55–58
Kutas, Marta 145
Kvaran, Guðrún 104

L
Labov, William 3–4, 21–22, 23, 29–31, 137–139, 141, 162, 164, 221
Lafontaine, Dominique 233
Lambert, Wallace E. IX, 74, 117–118, 138, 141, 161, 194, 220
Lane, Kristin A. 123, 131
LaPiere, Richard T. 60, 82
Latour, Britt 197
Lavrakas, Paul J. 126
Lee, Richard R. 141
Lenz, Alexandra N. 67
L'Eplattenier-Saugy, Caroline 224
Lev-Ari, Shiri 201
Levon, Erez 176
Leyens, Jacques-Philippe 222
Liberman, Alvin M. 6
Liebscher, Grit 56
Lindemann, Stephanie 126, 201
Lippi-Green, Rosina 194, 201, 233
Long, Daniel 201
Lorenzi-Cioldi, Fabio 222
Loudermilk, Brandon C. IX, XI, 137–156

M
McClelland, James L. 9
McCullough, Elizabeth A. XI, 175–190
McGurk, Harry 176
Maegaard, Marie 102
Mallinson, Christine 160–163
Markard, Morus 39
Masuda, Sayako 177
Mattheier, Klaus 236–237
Meinefeld, Werner 60
Miles, Matthew B. 56, 59
Milroy, James 193–194, 233
Milroy, Lesley 193, 233
Moliner, Pascal 227
Montgomery, Chris 18
Moosmüller, Sylvia 67–69, 74–75
Moreau, Marie-Louise 224
Morgan, David L. 55, 57, 59
Munro, Murray 178
Muysken, Pieter 200
Myers, David 37

N
Newman, Matthew L. 127
Niedzielski, Nancy 7, 25–26, 30, 130, 194, 220–221
Nieuwland, Mante 145
Nortier, Jacomine 202, 213
Nosek, Brian A. 120, 123–124, 129, 131

O
Ó Murchada, Noel P. 195
Omdal, Helge 104
Oostdijk, Nelleke 194
Oppenheim, Abraham Naftali 227
Ortega y Gasset, José 66
Osgood, Charles E. 75, 83
Ottaway, Scott A. 143
Owens, Thompson W. 21

P
Pacini, Rosemary 123
Pantos, Andrew IX-XI, 117–136, 142, 160, 220
Paquot, Annette 233
Park, Hanyong 177
Payne, B. Keith 120
Pedersen, Inge Lise 102
Perkins, Andrew W. 119, 132
Perlman, Gary 207
Perugini, Marco 121
Peterson, Gordon E. 23, 24, 29
Petty, Richard E. 121, 143
Pfaff, Donald 45
Piske, Thorsten 178
Plichta, Bartłomiej 26–29
Potter, Jonathan 39, 60, 83, 113
Pöll, Bernhard 237
Preston, Dennis VII-XIV, 3–36, 40, 113, 130, 220–221, 232, 234
Price, Susan 220
Prikhodkine, Alexei VII-XIV, 219–241
Provost, Valérie 220
Purnell, Thomas 138
Purschke, Christoph X-XI, 8, 37–53

R
Racine, Isabelle 224
Raskin, Jonathan D. 60
Reich, Alan R. 126

Rensink, W. G. 16
Richards, Lyn 57
Rickford, John R. 159
Rohner, Jean Christoph 132
Rosch, Eleanor 222
Rosenberg, Milton 9, 38, 45
Rubin, Donald L. 117, 177, 188, 201, 220
Rudman, Lea A. 143
Ryan, Ellen B. 16, 88, 117–118, 130, 201, 224, 232–233

S
St. George, Marie 145
Sandøy, Helge 88, 103
Saxe, John Godfrey 59
Scheuringer, Hermann 67
Schieffelin, Bambi IX
Schiffrin, Deborah 66, 69
Schiffrin, Richard 119
Schilling-Estes, Natalie 56, 66–67
Schütz, Alfred 37, 39–42, 46, 49
Scollon, Ron x, 58, 61–62
Selback, Bente 104
Sibata, Takesi 8, 16
Silverstein, Michael IX, 8, 39–40, 47, 234
Simmel, Georg 39
Singy, Pascal 221–222, 224, 228, 233
Smakman, Dick 171, 193

Smith, Brewster 38
Soukup, Barbara x, 38–39, 49, 55–84, 220
Spacek, Libor 178
Speelman, Dirk 220
Squires, Lauren 161
Sriram, N. 143
Staum Casasanto, Laura XI, 159–173, 220
Strack, Fritz 160
Steinegger, Guido 67, 69, 75
Stevens, Kenneth N. 6
Strand, Elizabeth A. 176
Stroop, Jan 192
Svavarsdóttir, Ásta 105

T
Tajfel, Henry 138
Tannen, Deborah 63–64, 66
Tashakkori, Abbas 55
Teddlie, Charles 56
Thibault, André 223, 226, 236–237
Thomas, George 104
Tophinke, Doris 56
Torstensson, Niklas 201
Tourangeau, Roger 222
Trudgill, Peter 8, 196
Tuaillon, Gaston 236

V
van Bavel, Jay J. 39
Van Berkum, Jos. J. A. 145

van Bezooijen, Renée 8, 169, 196–197, 201, 206
van den Berg, Rob 165
Vande Kamp, Mark E. 123
Vandenbussche, Wim 192
van der Horst, Joop 192
van de Velde, Hans 165
van Els, Theo 178
van Gent, Paul 191–218
van Hoof, Sarah 194
van Hout, Roeland 159–173, 191–218
van Meel, Linda 202–203
Vervoort, Miranda 199
Voillat, François 228, 236
Vygotsky, Lev S. 63

W
Weijnen, Antonius A. 16
Weinreich, Uriel 3, 5, 23, 30
Wells, Gary L. 126
Wetherell, Margaret 60, 83
Widdowson, Henry 64–65
Wiesinger, Peter 67
Willemyns, Roland 192–193
Williams, John K. 145–146, 152
Wittenbrink, Bernd 119, 130
Wyer, Robert S. Jr. 5

Y
Yarmey, A. Daniel 126